SCHOOL SUPERINTENDENT'S COMPLETE HANDBOOK

Practical Techniques and Materials for the Inservice Administrator

Patricia Cannon Conran

PRENTICE HALL
Englewood Cliffs, New Jersey 07632

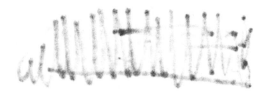

Prentice-Hall International (UK) Limited, *London*
Prentice-Hall of Australia Pty. Limited, *Sydney*
Prentice-Hall Canada, Inc., *Toronto*
Prentice-Hall Hispanoamericana, S.A., *Mexico*
Prentice-Hall of India Private Limited, *New Delhi*
Prentice-Hall of Japan, Inc., *Tokyo*
Simon & Schuster Asia Pte. Ltd., *Singapore*
Editora Prentice-Hall do Brasil, Ltda., *Rio de Janeiro*

© 1989 by
PRENTICE HALL
Englewood Cliffs, NJ

10   9   8   7   6   5   4   3   2   1

Library of Congress Cataloging-in-Publication Data

Conran, Patrician Cannon
    School superintenent's complete handbook : practical techniques
and materials for the inservice administrator / Patricia Cannon
Conran.
        p.   c.m.
    Includes bibliographies and index.
    ISBN 0-13-794462-4
    1. School districts—United States—Administration—Handbooks,
manuals, etc. 2. School management and organization—United States-
-Handbooks, manuals, etc. 3. School superintendents—United States-
-Handbooks, manuals, etc.   I. Title.
LB2817.C69 1989
379.1′535—dc19

                                                                89-30362
                                                                CIP

ISBN 0-13-794462-4

PRENTICE HALL
BUSINESS & PROFESSIONAL DIVISION
A division of Simon & Schuster
Englewood Cliffs, New Jersey 07632

Printed in the United States of America

To
Julia,
My Mother,
and
George,
My Advisor, Colleague, and Friend,
as a loving return for all you have taught me
and for your faith in my accomplishments

About The Author

Patricia Cannon Conran earned her Ph.D. in Curriculum and Administration from Northwestern University. She is presently Superintendent of the Bexley City Schools in suburban Columbus, Ohio. She previously served as a superintendent and held various other teaching and administrative positions in public and private schools and universities in Chicago and its suburban areas.

In 1987, Dr. Conran was appointed Regent of Northwestern University, and has received the University Alumni Merit and Service Awards. She has also been honored by the National School Boards Association as one of North America's Top Executive Educators and by Phi Delta Kappa as a Young Leader in Education. In addition, she is an elected member of the Professors of Curriculum.

Dr. Conran is elected President of Association for Supervision and Curriculum Development (ASCD), the international educational organization with a membership of over 100,000.

Among her publications, Dr. Conran has authored more than two dozen articles for professional journals, monographs, and research papers.

How This Book
Will Help You Do
the Right Things Right

As a superintendent, acting superintendent, or aspiring superintendent, you will find practical suggestions in *School Superintendent's Complete Handbook* to assist you in performing your various roles. The superintendent is sometimes referred to as the Chief Executive Officer of the school district. In reality, you are instructional leader and curriculum director, master teacher of principals, public relations expert and reporter, construction supervisor or rental agent, mediator of disputes and legal clerk, investment counselor, purchasing agent and bookkeeper, strategic planner, guidance counselor, public speaker, lobbyist, negotiator, personnel supervisor, host or hostess, among other roles.

Whether you are a do-it-all superintendent in a small district and perform each of the named duties yourself, or have one to many support personnel to whom you delegate superintendent responsibilities, the ideas contained in this book will help you. The *Handbook* contains specific plans and illustrations for successfully administering a school system. The areas covered include:

- Part One, "Building the Educational System You Want," focuses on developing and improving policy and practices that define the school system. Policy is discussed as a tool to empower individuals to act according to the will of the Board of Education. Factors viewed as important in achieving and maintaining schooling excellence are identified and discussed as parts to a whole. The curriculum and instruction discussion should assist you in modeling instructional leadership behavior for principals.

- In Part Two, "Sharing with Others," various aspects generic to all successful communication are discussed first. Then, specific help is offered for preparation of the agenda and materials for Board of Education meetings. Public relations are discussed from the aspect of working with those who can best assist in your efforts at relating to your various publics — who they are and how to do it. Other areas include facilitating communications and reporting school-district news.

- A researched and planned approach to managing change is presented in Part Three. Various planning models and types of situational changes are discussed.

- In Part Four, "Utilizing Resources," the focus is on conservative and meaningful budgeting and other fiscal practices. Specifics in budgeting, investing, purchasing, and bookkeeping are discussed. Because working with experts can frequently maximize results and minimize costs, some samples of experts you may choose are included. Helpful hints regarding care of your buildings and grounds are also offered.

- Part Five, "Demonstrating Leadership in Employee Relations," gives practical guidance for hiring, dismissing, and relating to employees. Guidelines for successful negotiations are also included.

The sample forms and communications included in the *Handbook* can either be used as is or be adapted to your particular job situation. These forms and suggestions should help you to (1) be effective in all your superintendent roles, and (2) be efficient in carrying out all responsibilities.

School Superintendent's Complete Handbook may be read in its entirety to obtain a bird's-eye view of your various roles and responsibilities, and it can also be kept at hand as a ready reference to use in specific areas or when specific needs arise. In either case, *School Superintendent's Complete Handbook* will help you be an even more effective manager and leader!

Patricia Cannon Conran

CONTENTS

Part II
SHARING WITH OTHERS

Part III
MANAGING CHANGE

Contents / xiii

I

BUILDING
THE EDUCATIONAL SYSTEM
YOU WANT

Developing Policy
That Will Free People to Act

Policy is the principal way a school board, or Board of Education, governs the school or school district. Policy is the most important function of the Board. It is the superintendent, however, who is the catalyst for and leader in policy development.

Power, Authority, and Responsibility

The responsibility for making policy rests with the board. The board derives its power and authority from the state legislature. However, both state and federal constitutions limit the board's authority. In addition, there are a host of other limiting factors.

Chief among constraints to the board's power to make policy are the comprehensive bargaining bills effected in several states in recent years. Most comprehensive bargaining bills mandate bargaining the *impact* of policy with union representatives. Superintendents are learning that there is little the union will not claim impacts working conditions. Some factors that may limit the board's power to make policy are shown in Figure 1-1.

When it adopts policy, the board acts as a lawmaking body. The board's policy *is* the law of the school or district. This point is extremely important to recognize. For example, if curriculum is, as it should be, a matter of board policy, then board-adopted curriculum *must* be taught. Not doing so can be grounds for disciplinary action and, ultimately, dismissal. On a more positive note, knowing board expectations for the teaching of the curriculum facilitates teacher planning and administrator supervision and evaluation.

Written policy will assist board employees to carry out the will of the board. Written policy has other advantages. It gives credence to board actions. Policy establishes a legal record. Well-written policy in sufficient numbers fosters stability and continuity. Without needed policy, employees may be unwilling to act. Alternatively, they may act, but inappropriately.

Whenever possible policymaking should be proactive, rather than reactive. Anticipating the need for policy is preferred to reacting to a problem. Policy that anticipates a need can free the superintendent and all employees to act. An example of policy that may anticipate a need gives guidance for coping with a student or employee afflicted with AIDS and other serious infectious diseases. A sample policy for students is shown in Figure 1-2, and a sample policy for personnel is shown in Figure 1-3. Similar policies can facilitate rational behavior should tragic circumstances occur.

Clear but Not Too Specific

Clarity is important so that policy will have a high reliability in interpretation and implementation. The intent of the policy should not need to be debated in a court of law; nor should it cause debate among those who need to implement policy at the local level.

If the language is clear, the board's intentions will be clear. Further, relations between the board and superintendent will be clear. Consequently both the board and superintendent can operate more efficiently and effectively. An example of policy language that is fuzzy and ways to clarify the language are shown in Figure 1-4.

Policy is intended to guide school district activity, rather than indicate behavior. It is, therefore, important to be precise but not overly specific. Policy should be broad enough to permit the superintendent to act with discretion in administering day-to-day programs. Policy should be specific enough to give clear guidance.

The more specific a policy becomes, the more exclusionary it becomes. At the extreme it becomes a target to justify undesirable behavior. That is offenders will justify actions not specifically identified as being prohibited. On the other hand, being overly specific can prohibit desirable activity not specifically mentioned. Either may become a problem.

Superintendents have lost legal cases because specific lists of behaviors named in policy failed to include the behavior which was the issue in the court matter. Similarly, with overly specific language low risk-takers may use a policy to rationalize an error of omission. Examples of overly specific policy and potential problems are shown in Figure 1-5.

Sound policy will tell what the board wants to happen and it will explain why it should happen. The National School Boards Association offers additional suggestions for writing policy. These are shown in Figure 1-6.

Preliminary to writing policy, one or more individuals or groups may suggest the need for policy. Materials, such as sample policies and legal interpretations, are gathered to assist in the writing. Then, persons charged with policy formation discuss and agree on the substance. *One* person then drafts the policy in written form. When those involved in forming policy agree on the substance, it is taken to the board for readings. Finally all involved with policy implications are informed, and the policy is disseminated, implemented, enforced, evaluated, and revised.

While the process names two readings, the number of required readings is often mandated in state statutes. Beyond that which is required, a board may opt to add an additional reading. If there is a substantive change after a reading, the board may opt to begin again with reading the changed policy.

A word of caution is in order. Most comprehensive bargaining bills require bargaining the *impact* of policy. At least one union has filed an unfair labor practice charge after the first reading of an AIDS policy. The superintendent will want to follow legal developments and seek advice of counsel as courts make decisions relative to impact bargaining as this relates to policy development.

Enough but Not Too Many

There should be a sufficient number of policies to provide a map for directing activity in the school or district. There is no magic number of policies. A guide might be to aim for policy in all categories identified by major institutions and organizations that write policy *when* such categories are directly applicable to school district practice. An example of categories is shown in Figure 1-7.

Various criteria may be used to evaluate the appropriateness of including policies. For example, the effective schools research would suggest that policies as indicated in Figure 1-8 promote effective schools.

If state and national policy services are used, the superintendent will need to use discretion as to the importance of various categories or individual policies. An example of a category that may not be needed is Negotiations. In states that do not have comprehensive bargaining bills, there may be districts that do not practice collective bargaining. Hence, there would be no need for the section.

A second example of unnecessary policy is that which rewrites the law. Statutes may indicate what is important to clarify in policy. However, it is advised that the law itself not be written into policy. Doing so is not necessary and makes the task of writing, interpreting, and implementing policy more cumbersome.

In addition to legislation requirements that may vary from state to state, regional and other differences may require policy differences in one or more categories in some school districts. For example, school closings dictated by ozone levels may be viewed as desirable in California but unnecessary in other states.

When talking numbers of policies, policies that are *explicit* and *written*, are suggested. There are also school or district policies that are *implied*. Implicit policies are those that imply a policy position but may not be covered by explicit, or written policies. For example, actions may be recorded in board minutes and have the full force of policy. Once identified, implicit policy should become part of explicit written policy.

Resources Available to Help

There are numerous resources available to assist in policy development. Some resources include organizations whose principal functions are to research and write policy and to conduct policywriting workshops. Other resources are less formal — the school attorney or a neighboring superintendent, are examples.

When considering a service, it will be useful to know whether an alphabetical or numerical coding system is used. If you are starting from scratch, you will want to consider the pros and cons of each service and system. If you already have a policy manual that does not need to be completely rewritten, you will probably want to use a service whose coding matches that in the existing policy manual.

Educational Policies Service (EPS) of the National School Boards Association (NSBA) provides a comprehensive policymaking service. NSBA uses an alphabetical classification system shown in Figure 1-9. Sample policies from school districts in the United States and Canada are included as idea-starters for policy within each category. To provide the reader with a comparison of coding systems used for classifying policies, Figure 1-10 shows the numeric decimal approach to coding developed by Davies-Brickell.

Other components of the EPS/NSBA program include a variety of handbook publications and periodicals about policymaking and policy trends and issues, an on-call reference service, and other aids.

State organizations, such as the Ohio School Boards Association (OSBA), work with local school districts in compiling policy manuals. One advantage of working with a state organization is the attention given to state mandates. For example, the OSBA includes sample policies in the 19 areas required by the Ohio State Department of Education. Figure 1-11 shows the State of Ohio Department of Education policy requirements. The form is used in state monitoring visits of school districts. In other words, the OSBA assumes superintendents are assisted in meeting Ohio Department of Education mandates. In addition, care has been taken to assure that nothing in the OSBA sample manual conflicts with state law or regulations promulgated by the Ohio State Department of Education.

As with the national service, state services usually have services to supplement the policy reference manual. OSBA issues a supplement entitled, *Policy Development Quarterly*. The quarterly may contain sample new policies. For example, Figure 1-12 illustrates a form proposed for developing policy. Completion of the PIN Form is intended as the first step in the policy-making process. Additional information in the quarterly includes state and federal laws that have implications for school policy and practice.

Other policy services are provided by enterprising individuals. NEOLA, INC. is one such service. NEOLA reviews the district's current policy manual, board meeting minutes for five years, and other district documents. An upgrade of the manual is provided if thought to be needed. Then the district may opt for a continuing policy update service performed quarterly. With the update service, NEOLA reviews board minutes and other district documents that could contain policy or the need for policy. In addition, NEOLA provides a review of state and federal legislation, regulations, and policies which indicate a need for a district policy revision or edition.

Policy services at the national or state level are designed to assist not supplant local efforts. For example, the superintendent may refer to a reference manual to find out how one school board faced and solved a matter of school governance. The superintendent should then consider the needs in the local district. Then, with the assistance of the local policymaking group, the policy might be expanded, modified, and adapted to work locally.

In addition to services that provide individualized assistance or policy reference manuals and aids, policy development workshops are frequently offered locally. Colleagues in other districts can also be of tremendous assistance.

When seeking guidance from colleagues, it may be important to know *who* can be of greatest assistance. For example, if a censorship issue is emerging in your district, it will be helpful to know of other districts who have dealt with this issue *successfully* and then request policy. The successful coping with students and employees with AIDS by three districts in the Chicago area is an example. The *Chicago Tribune Sunday* supplement, December 6, 1987, told the story of how the Chicago suburban Wilmette School District, and Chicago Schools; Pilsen Community Academy; and Nettlehorst Elementary School instituted policies and procedures that allowed schooling to continue without the disruption manifest in some areas where students or employees were discovered to be afflicted with AIDS.

When it becomes evident that areas of policy or individual policies should be added, the superintendent will want to know colleagues or organizations who can help with policy formation. In addition, frequently the superintendent may seek assistance from the school attorney to review or write policy. It will probably not be necessary for the attorney to thoroughly check every policy or to give a written opinion on every policy. But somewhere in between no review and writing every policy, there is opportunity for counsel to assist. The superintendent can create an understanding with the school attorney that policy is to be reviewed, either to avoid its being contrary to law or to avoid wording that will encourage conflicting interpretations and legal suits.

What to Do and Not to Do

There are do's and don'ts to consider when developing policy. What policy is needed? Who should be involved? How should policy be written? Who should be briefed. How will the policy be implemented? What procedures for evaluating and updating are needed? Just as there are things to do in developing policy, so too there are things not to do.

When you become superintendent of a district, you will want to know existing procedures in the district for policymaking. At the extreme you may find that there are no written policies or procedures. As noted above, however, there is always policy and, hence, procedures for creating policy even when there is nothing written on these topics. If there is nothing in writing, begin the process. If policy and procedures exist, determine if updating is needed.

Figure 1-12 illustrated the PIN Form, an instrument designed by the OSBA policy service to initiate the policy development process. The form requests information to demonstrate the Problem, the Issue, and the Need for policy or policy amendment — hence the name, PIN. The PIN Form can be filled out by anyone. A parent, student, teacher, or administrator can, therefore, initiate policy development. The board receives a brief description of the problem, the rationale for the change, and suggested wording. Subsequent steps utilize commonly understood decision-making and problem-solving processes.

Following need identification, there are other crucial steps in policy development. First, alternative policy options and their implications should be generated. This can be accomplished by collecting data and performing a policy analysis relative to the need identified.

Once policy options and their implications have been generated, the board should discuss the advantages, disadvantages, costs, liabilities, and long-term effects of each option. Then a policy can be drafted in accordance with the option selected. When the board has approved or revised the draft, it is scheduled for a public review, or reading. Normally, proposed policies are read at regularly scheduled board meetings open to the public. At least two public readings are recommended. Some boards routinely have three readings before the public prior to adopting policy. Revisions to the policy draft may be made after any of these readings.

Once the policy is adopted, the superintendent is responsible for its dissemination and implementation. Administrative regulations should be developed as deemed necessary for implementation. The superintendent will also be responsible for evaluating the policy's effectiveness. Adding, revising, and recommending rescinding policies are ongoing processes in policy development.

The Process

The National School Boards Association warns that getting the school board to accept the idea of a policy development process can be a challenge. If this is the case, then getting the board to focus on developing new policies or compiling a manual of current policies is the first step.

If the superintendent needs to convince the board of the importance of written policy, reasons are offered by NSBA. First, written policy can alert inexperienced board members to constraints on their own and the board's authority. Second, written policy aids experienced and inexperienced board members to distinguish between governing and administering the school system. Third, written policy helps to give the word "policy" meaning, thereby reducing vagueness. Wherever the board is in its receptivity to policy development, once the process has begun, someone will need to write.

One person should write policy. In a small district, this may be the superintendent or a board member. In a large district, the actual writing task will probably be delegated to a deputy or assistant superintendent. Having a single writer will provide for consistency in the way in which policy is written. A single writer will also be more cognizant of possible overlaps and gaps.

Before the writing phase, any number of persons or groups may have given input. For example, as noted above, a parent, student, teacher, or administrator may make the need for policy known. Or a board member, board committee, P.T.A., or union may track the need for policy updates.

The policy criteria should be reviewed to determine if their purpose is the realization of an educationally valid and desirable goal or objective. Next, the policy criteria should be examined to determine if they will have a substantial relationship to that purpose.

Once the writing begins, guidelines for clarity and specificity should be followed. There should be no jargon or excess words. A positive, direct, and helpful tone should be achieved. The writer will need to decide whether to start from scratch or work with existing language. The writing should be consistent with other board policies. Principles of good writing should be practiced.

The writer should make an outline, starting with key concepts or phrases, and organize these. Choose a format consistent with existing district policy or as shown in policy reference manuals. Reference laws or legal statements, rather than quoting or copying lengthy statements. Write a full first draft. Entering the draft on the word processor facilitates revision. Check details to see that important details from policy discussions have been included.

The superintendent or designee should evaluate the policy draft to assure that it is within the scope of the board's discretionary authority as granted by state statutes, that it is consistent with state and federal laws and within the provisions of state and the United States constitutions, and that it is reasonable and free from arbitrariness and capriciousness.

Who Should Receive

Dissemination is crucial to policy implementation. Every individual who needs to abide by the board's policy needs to have access to a copy of the policy manual and accompanying rules and regulations. Ideally, every employee will have a manual. In addition, parents, students, and the public should have access to board policies.

At a minimum, every board member, administrator, and the school attorney should have a complete and current policy manual. If individual employees are not given a manual for reference, then copies need to be available for their reference.

School and district offices, libraries, workrooms, and lounges are areas where individuals can have easy access to the complete manual. In addition, copies of policies or summaries of those policies which are most apt to affect individuals can be prepared for easy reference by the individuals.

Copies of policy manuals placed in the local public library, city hall, and in other areas where citizens frequent or congregate, can facilitate the public's knowledge about the governance of the school district. Additional copies can be on hand in the district office of individuals to check out and return.

There needs to be an accurate system of accounting for manuals or parts of manuals so that all materials in circulation can be kept current. A master manual or file should be kept in the office of the superintendent. A system that regularly calls in all materials in circulation will assure that necessary updates occur. Sending updates as they occur and calling manuals in yearly can provide a manageable system for keeping materials current.

REFERENCE AND RESOURCES

Brodinsky, Mary S., ed., *Educational Policies Reference Manual* (5th ed.). Alexandria, VA: National School Boards Association, 1984.

——, *Educational Policies Reference Manual* (4th ed.). Washington, D.C.: National School Boards Association, 1979.

Dickinson, William E., ed., *The EPS/NSBA Educational Policies Reference Manual* (3rd ed.). Evanston, IL: The Educational Policies Service of the National School Boards Association, 1975.

Ohio Policy Reference Manual (2nd ed.). Westerville, OH: Ohio School Boards Association.

The Board's policy-making power is limited by several constraints:

1. State Law
2. Federal Law
3. Negotiated Agreements
4. Budget Limitations
5. Court Decisions
6. State Agency Rules and Regulations
7. Federal Agency Rules and Regulations
8. Local Agency Rules and Regulations and Intermediate Agencies (such as Educational Service Regions)
9. Local Traditions and Desires
10. Professional Staff Limitations
11. The Board Itself (Policies, Etc.)
12. Enrollment
13. Other Contracts — Food Service, Transportation

Figure 1-1

STUDENTS

Elementary, Middle, and High Schools

Welfare

Health

Communicable diseases — AIDS

Definition: For the purposes of this regulation, AIDS means Acquired Immune Deficiency Syndrome, AIDS Related Complex, or asymptomatic infection with HIV virus.

The following procedures shall be followed to balance the interests of the student with Acquired Immune Deficiency Syndrome (AIDS) and the interests of the public, including classmates:

1. When district personnel become aware that a student has AIDS:
   a. the superintendent is notified
   b. the school physician is notified
   c. the school physician notifies the Columbus Health Physician or representative
   d. the student is temporarily excluded from school, and home instruction is provided, if necessary, until the conference and review process described in section 4 of these regulations has taken place.

2. The school physician confers with the student's primary care physician to determine whether the student's medical condition would allow the student to attend school.

3. If the student's primary care physician determines that the student should remain at home, the student will be provided home instruction.

Source: Columbus City Schools

Figure 1-2

4. If the student's primary care physician determines that the condition of the student with AIDS is such that attendance at school does not pose a risk to the student, to fellow students, or to school personnel, the primary care physician may recommend to the superintendent that the student be permitted to attend school. The superintendent will be advised of this recommendation. The school physician will then convene a medical team to review the recommendation and make a recommendation to the superintendent. This review will be conducted in a timely manner.

   The medical review team shall consist of:
   a. student's parent and/or legal representative
   b. student's primary care physician
   c. Columbus Health Department's physician representative
   d. school physician, who will act as chairman.

   The medical review team shall consider the student's diagnosis, treatment, and prognosis, which shall be provided by the student's primary physician to the team. The team shall also review, but only as such are medically significant, the student's record of behavior and personal characteristics. Applying current medical information and the guidelines developed by the Ohio Department of Health, the Centers for Disease Control, and the American Academy of Pediatrics, the medical review team shall submit a written recommendation to the superintendent stating whether a student with AIDS shall be:
   a. admitted to school
   b. admitted to school under conditions delineated by the review team
   c. not admitted to school and provided home instruction.

5. All employees of the Board of Education involved in any way in the administration of this regulation, and the members of the medical review team, shall maintain confidentiality of any information received pursuant to this regulation except to the extent otherwise reasonably required to conduct its administration. Information about the condition and identity of a student with AIDS shall not be disclosed by school personnel to nonessential school, or nonschool personnel, except as required by law. However, to properly monitor the student and so that supervisors may exercise appropriate precautions for the student (if monitoring or other precautions are conditions of admission required by the review team), information regarding the medical conditions of a student with AIDS who is admitted to school shall be provided to:
   a. the building administrator where the student attends
   b. the school nurse
   c. the student's teacher.

Figure 1-2 (Cont'd.)

11

the persons given information under this regulation shall be expressly advised of its confidentiality.

6. A student with AIDS who attends school shall be monitored by the school nurse for changes in condition and behavior, and any changes shall be reported to the school physician. In addition, the medical review team shall maintain an active role in monitoring the student's medical condition and may determine that more restrictions and/or exclusion of the student with AIDS is necessary. Reviews of the student's medical condition and behavior will be conducted as described in section 4 of this regulation.

7. If a student with AIDS is determined to be eligible for a special education program because AIDS is considered a handicapping condition, then an appropriate educational program will be developed and provided for that student consistent with all substantive and procedural requirements of applicable law.

Regulation
Approved 12-7-87

Columbus, Ohio City School District

Figure 1-2 (Cont'd.)

PERSONNEL

Certificated and Administrative

Welfare

Health and Safety

Communicable diseases — AIDS

Definition: For the purposes of this regulation, AIDS means Acquired Immune Deficiency Syndrome, AIDS Related Complex, or asymptomatic infection with HIV virus.

The following procedures shall be followed to balance the interests of the employee with Acquired Immune Deficiency Syndrome (AIDS) and the interests of the public, including students and fellow employees:

1. When district personnel become aware that an employee has AIDS:
    a. the superintendent is notified
    b. the Columbus Education Association will be notified by the Superintendent or his designee when a bargaining unit member is so affected, protecting the identity of the individual if requested by the individual
    c. the school physician is notified
    d. the school physician notifies the Columbus Health Physician or representative
    e. If the school physician and the Columbus Health Commissioner concur, the employee may be temporarily reassigned until the conference and review process described in section 5 of these regulations has taken place. Such temporary reassignment shall only be done if there appears to be compelling reason to do so

Source: Columbus City Schools

Figure 1-3

13

2. The school physician shall confer with the employee's primary care physician to determine whether the employee's medical condition would allow the employee to remain at work.

3. If the employee's primary care physician determines that the employee should not continue with employment duties, the employee may utilize whatever leave and/or other benefits that would otherwise be available. In the event the employee does not voluntarily utilize whatever leave that is available, the Board may grant such leave and renewals thereof, but such employee may have a hearing on such unrequested leave or renewals in accordance with section 3319.16 of the Revised Code for certificated employees and division (C) of section 3319.081 of the Revised Code for nonteaching employees.

4. If the employee's primary care physician determines that the condition of the employee with AIDS is such that attendance at work does not pose a risk to the employee, to students, and to fellow employees, the primary care physician shall recommend to the superintendent that the employee be permitted to remain at or return to work. The Superintendent will be advised of this recommendation and shall allow the employee to remain or return to work immediately pending review and concurrence by the school physician. The school physician shall then convene a medical review team to review the employee's physician's recommendation if and when the school physician determines that such a review is warranted.

5. A medical review team consisting of:
   a. the school physician
   b. the employee's primary care physician (any expense to be paid by the Board)
   c. Columbus Health Department's physician or representative

shall meet from time to time at the call of any member to consider the employee's diagnosis, treatment, and prognosis, which shall be provided by the employee's primary physician. Applying current medical information and the guidelines developed by the Center for Disease control, the medical review team shall recommend to the Superintendent, in writing, whether an employee with AIDS shall be:
   a. continued to be admitted to work
   b. not admitted to work

Any subsequent decision will take into account any applicable collective bargaining agreements, established personnel policies, regulation, guidelines, and provisions of law.

Figure 1-3 (Cont'd.)

14

If the employee with AIDS has been temporarily reassigned in accordance with paragraph 1 above, the medical review process will be conducted as quickly as possible.

6. The medical review team may call upon the employee's immediate supervisor to monitor the employee only if monitoring or other precautions are conditions of admission to work and specifically required by the medical review team. Only the employee's immediate supervisor will be used to monitor the employee and the supervisor shall be subject to the confidentiality provisions in paragraph 7. The medical review team may require reports from this supervisor from time to time.

7. All employees of the Board of Education involved in the administration of this regulation, and the members of the medical review team shall at all times maintain the confidentiality of any information received pursuant to this regulation except to the extent otherwise reasonably required to conduct its administration. Information about the condition and identity of an employee with AIDS shall not be disclosed by school personnel to nonessential school, or nonschool personnel, except as required by law. However, the employee with AIDS, the superintendent's designee, and, if elected by the employee, a representative of employee's organization and legal representative, if one is designated, shall be given prior notice of and may attend all meetings of the review team. Such attendance by the employee organization representative shall be for the purpose of safeguarding the employee's legal and contractual rights.

8. An employee with AIDS who works may be monitored as set forth above by their immediate supervisor for changes in condition and behavior, and any changes shall be reported to the school physician who shall report same to the employee's primary physician. In addition, the medical review team shall maintain an active role in monitoring the employee's medical condition and may determine that more restrictions and/or exclusion of the employee with AIDS is necessary. Reviews of the employee's medical condition/behavior will be conducted as outlined in paragraph 5 of this regulation.

Figure 1-3 (Cont'd.)

9. Because AIDS is an illness, any employee with AIDS and disabled by AIDS has available any and all illness leaves and other leaves and benefits available to employees as if afflicted with and disabled by any other diseases. In addition, such employees retain all rights provided under section 3319.13 of the Revised Code and other related or relevant sections of the Revised Code.

Regulation
Approved 12-7-87

Columbus, Ohio City School District

Figure 1-3 (Cont'd.)

POLICY LANGUAGE

Fuzzy

Procedure for Suspension and Expulsion of Students

When the alleged misconduct becomes known, notice will be given to the parent, guardian, or custodian and the student shall be given written notice of the intention of suspension and the reasons for such action by the superintendent or principal. The student will be given an opportunity to appear at an informal hearing before the superintendent, superintendent's designee, principal, or assistant principal and challenge the reasons for the possible suspension or otherwise explain his/her actions.

Clearer

Procedure for Suspension and Expulsion of Students

No student will be suspended unless prior to the suspension the superintendent or principal:

a. gives the student written notice of the intention to suspend him/ her and the reasons for the intended suspension; and

b. provides the student an opportunity to appear at an informal hearing before the principal, assistant principal, superintendent, or superintendent's designee and challenge the reason for the intended suspension or otherwise explain his/her actions.

Comments: The fuzzy language resulted from a Board of Education wanting to alter language in the statutes to have a more humane policy. The clearer language more nearly duplicates Code language.

Figure 1-4

17

POLICY LANGUAGE

Example of Overly Specific Language in Specifying Misconduct

1. Cheating or plagiarizing
2. Possession, Use, Transmitting, Concealing, or Selling Cigarettes or Tobacco
3. Truancy, Tardiness, or Class-Cutting
4. Profane, Vulgar, or Improper Language or Gestures
5. Failure to Comply with Directives
6. Failure to Accept Discipline or Punishment
7. Violation of School Bus Conduct Requirement
8. Hazing
9. Disrespect
10. Disruption of School
11. Damage, Destruction, Theft, or Unauthorized Removal of School Property
12. Assault on or Abusive Language Toward a School Employee
13. Use, Possession, Handling, Transmitting, Selling, Concealing, or Bringing Weapons, Dangerous Instruments, Fireworks, and Explosives on School Grounds
14. Chemical Abuse
15. Trespassing
16. Misconduct Away from School
17. Falsification or Misstatement of Facts or Other Information
18. Gambling
19. Obtaining Property or Things of Value by Use of Coercion and Related Misconduct
20. Public Display of Affection or Sexual Acts

Comments: By being overly specific, looking for a loophole is invited.

Figure 1-5

NATIONAL SCHOOL BOARDS ASSOCIATION
STEPS IN THE POLICY DEVELOPMENT PROCESS

Preliminary: Identifying Need for New Policy

Step 1:   Assembling Material
Step 2:   Study, Discuss, Agree on Basic Substance
Step 3:   Policy Drafting
Step 4:   First Reading
Step 5:   Second Reading, Adoption
Step 6:   Inform, Disseminate
Step 7:   Implement
Step 8:   Enforce, Evaluate, Revise

Source: Mary S. Brodinsky, Editor, *Educational Policies Reference Manual*, Fifth Edition (Alexandria, Virginia: National School Boards Association, 1984).

Figure 1-6

SECTION A: Foundations and Basic Commitments

Section A of the EPS/NSBA policy classification system is a repository for statements related to the district's legal role in providing public education and the underlying principles on which the district operates. The policies in this section provide a setting for all of the school board's other policies.

AA	School District Legal Status
AB	The People and Their School District
ABA	Community Involvement in Decision-making (Also KC)
ABB	Staff Involvement in Decision-making (Also GBB)
ABC	Student Involvement in Decision-making (Also JFB)
AC	Nondiscrimination
AD	Educational Philosophy
AE	School Districts Goals and Objectives
AEA	School District Priority Goals and Objectives
AF	Commitment to Accomplishment
AFA	Evaluation of School Board Operational Procedures (Also BK)
AFB	Evaluation of the Superintendent (Also CBG)
AFC	Evaluation of Professional Staff (Also GCN)
AFD	Evaluation of Support Staff (Also GDN)
AFE	Evaluation of Instructional Programs (Also IM)
AFF	Evaluation of Support Services (Also EJ)
AFG	Use of Independent Evaluators
AFH	Evaluation of Evaluators
AG	Accomplishment Reporting to the Public
AGA	Recognition for Accomplishment

Source: Mary S. Brodinsky, Editor, *Educational Policies Reference Manual*, Fifth Edition (Alexandria Virginia: National School Boards Association, 1984).

Figure 1-7

SECTION B: School Board Governance and Operations

Section B of the EPS/NSBA policy classification system is a repository for statements about the school board — how it is elected, organized; how it conducts its meetings and operates. This section includes bylaws and policies establishing the board's internal operating procedures.

BA	Board Operational Goals
BAA	Priority Objectives of Board Operations
BB	School Board Legal Status
BBA	School Board Powers and Duties
BBAA	Board Member Authority
BBB	School Board Elections
BBBA	Board Member Qualifications
BBBB	Board Member Oath of Office
BBC	Board Member Resignation
BBD	Board Member Removal from Office
BBE	Unexpired Term Fulfillment
BBF	School Board Member Ethics
BBFA	Board Member Conflict of Interest
BC	Organization of the Board
BCA	Board Organizational Meeting
BCB	Board Officers
BCC	Appointed Board Officials
BCD	Board-Superintendent Relationship
BCE	Board Committees
BCF	Advisory Committees
BCG	School Attorney
BCH	Consultants to the Board
BCI	Board Staff Assistants
BD	School Board Meetings
BDA	Regular Board Meetings
BDB	Special Board Meetings
BDC	Executive Sessions

Figure 1-7 (Cont'd.)

BDD	Board Meeting Procedures
BDDA	Notification of Board Meetings
BDDB	Agenda Format
BDDC	Agenda Preparation and Dissemination
BDDD	Quorum
BDDE	Rules of Order
BDDEA	Parliamentarian
BDDEB	Suspension of Rules of Order
BDDF	Voting Method
BDDG	Minutes
BDDH	Public Participation at Board Meetings (Also KD)
BDDI	News Media Services at Board Meetings (Also KBCC)
BDDJ	Broadcasting and Taping of Board Meetings (Also KBCD)
BDDK	Reporting Board Meeting Business
BDE	Board Hearings
BE	School Board Work Sessions and Retreats
BF	Board Policy Development
BFA	Policy Development System
BFB	Preliminary Development of Policies
BFC	Policy Adoption
BFCA	Board Review of Regulations (Also CHB)
BFD	Policy Dissemination
BFE	Administration in Policy Absence (Also CHD)
BFF	Suspension of Policies
BFG	Policy Review and Evaluation
BFGA	Policy Manual Accuracy Check
BG	Board-Staff Communications (Also GBD)
BH	Board Member Services
BHA	New Board Member Orientation
BHB	Board Member Development Opportunities
BHBA	School Board Conferences, Conventions, and Workshops
BHC	Board Office Facilities and Services

Figure 1-7 (Cont'd.)

BHD	Board Member Compensation and Expenses
BHE	Board Member Insurance
BI	School Board Legislative Program
BJ	School Board Memberships
BJA	Liaison with School Boards Associations
BK	Evaluation of School Board Operational Procedures (Also AFA)

SECTION C: General School Administration

Section C of the EPS/NSBA policy classification system provides a repository for statements about the school district management, the administrative structure, and school building and department administration. It also is the location for personnel policies that pertain to one individual — the superintendent.

CA	Administration Goals
CAA	District Administration Priority Objectives
CB	School Superintendent
CBA	Qualifications and Duties of Superintendent
CBB	Recruitment and Appointment of Superintendent
CBC	Superintendent's Contract
CBD	Superintendent's Compensation and Benefits
CBE	Superintendent's Development Opportunities
CBF	Superintendent's Consulting Activities
CBG	Evaluation of the Superintendent (Also AFB)
CBH	Superintendent's Termination of Employment
CBHA	Superintendent's Retirement
CC	Administrative Organization Plan
CCA	Organization Charts
CCB	Line and Staff Relations
CD	Management Team
CE	Administrative Councils, Cabinets, and Committees

Figure 1-7 (Cont'd.)

CF	School Building Administration
CG	Special Programs Administration
CGA	Summer Program Administration
CGB	Adult Education Program Administration
CGC	State and Federal Programs Administration
CH	Policy Implementation
CHA	Development of Regulations
CHB	Board Review of Regulations (Also BFCA)
CHC	Regulations Dissemination
CHCA	Handbooks and Directives
CHD	Administration in Policy Absence (Also BFE)
CI	Temporary Administrative Arrangements
CJ	Administrative Intern Program
CK	Program Consultants
CL	Administrative Reports
CM	School District Annual Report

SECTION D: Fiscal Management

Section D of the EPS/NSBA policy classification system provides a repository for statements concerning district fiscal affairs and the management of district funds. Statements relating to the financing of school construction, however, are filed in the F (Facilities Development) section.

DA	Fiscal Management Goals
DAA	Fiscal Management Priority Objectives
DB	Annual Budget
DBA	Budgeting System
DBB	Fiscal Year
DBC	Budget Deadlines and Schedules

Figure 1-7 (Cont'd.)

DBD	Budget Planning
DBE	Determination of Budget Priorities
DBF	Dissemination of Budget Recommendations
DBG	Budget Hearings and Reviews
DBH	Budget Adoption
DBHA	Budget Referenda
DBI	Budget Appeals
DBJ	Budget Implementation
DBK	Budget Transfers
DC	Taxing and Borrowing
DD	Funding Proposals and Applications
DE	Revenues from Tax Sources
DEA	Revenues from Local Tax Sources
DEB	Revenues from State Tax Sources
DEC	Revenues from Federal Tax Sources
DF	Revenues from Nontax Sources
DFA	Revenues from Investments
DFAA	Use of Surplus Funds
DFB	Revenues from School-Owned Real Estate
DFC	Grants from Private Sources
DFD	Rental and Service Charges
DFE	Gate Receipts and Admissions
DFEA	Free Admissions
DFF	Royalties
DFG	Income from School Shop Sales and Services
DG	Depository of Funds
DGA	Authorized Signatures
DGB	Check-Writing Services
DH	Bonded Employees and Officers
DI	Fiscal Accounting and Reporting
DIA	Accounting System
DIB	Types of Funds
DIC	Financial Reports and Statements

Figure 1-7 (Cont'd.)

25

DID	Inventories
DIE	Audits
DJ	Purchasing
DJA	Purchasing Authority
DJB	Petty Cash Accounts
DJC	Bidding Requirements and Procedures
DJD	Local Purchasing
DJE	Cooperative Purchasing
DJF	Purchasing Procedures
DJG	Vendor Relations
DJGA	Sales Calls and Demonstrations
DK	Payment Procedures
DL	Payroll Procedures
DLA	Payday Schedules
DLB	Salary Deductions
DLC	Expense Reimbursements
DM	Cash in School Buildings
DN	School Properties Disposal

SECTION E: Support Services

Section E of the EPS/NSBA policy classification system provides a repository for statements on noninstructional services and programs, including most of those that fall in the area of business management such as safety, buildings and their management (not construction), transportation, and food services.

EA	Support Services Goals
EAA	Support Services Priority Objectives
EB	Safety Program
EBA	Buildings and Grounds Inspections
EBAA	Reporting Hazards
EBAB	Warning Systems
EBB	Accident Prevention and Safety Procedures

Figure 1-7 (Cont'd.)

EBBA	First Aid
EBBB	Accident Reports
EBC	Emergency Plans
EBCA	Disaster Plans
EBCB	Fire Drills
EBCC	Bomb Threats
EBCD	Emergency Closings
EC	Buildings and Grounds Management
ECA	Buildings and Grounds Security
ECAA	Access to Buildings
ECAB	Vandalism
ECB	Buildings and Grounds Maintenance
ECC	Custodial Services
ECD	Traffic and Parking Controls
ECE	Buildings and Grounds Records and Reports
ED	Material Resources Management
EDA	Receiving and Warehousing
EDB	Maintenance and Control of Materials and Equipment
EDC	Authorized Use of School-Owned Materials and Equipment
EDD	Material Resources Records and Reports
EE	Transportation Services Management
EEA	Student Transportation Services
EEAA	Walkers and Riders
EEAB	School Bus Scheduling and Routing
EEAC	School Bus Safety Program
EEACA	Bus Driver Examination and Training
EEACB	School Bus Maintenance
EEACC	Student Conduct on School Buses (also JFCC)
EEAD	Special Use of School Buses
EEAE	Student Transportation in Private Vehicles
EEAF	Student Transportation Insurance
EEAG	Student Transportation Records and Reports
EEB	Business and Personnel Transportation Services
EEBA	School-Owned Vehicles
EEBB	Use of Private Vehicles on School Business

Figure 1-7 (Cont'd.)

EEBC	Business and Personnel Transportation Insurance
EEBD	Business and Personnel Transportation Records and Reports
EF	Food Services Management
EFA	Food Purchasing
EFAA	Use of Surplus Commodities
EFB	Free and Reduced Price Food Services
EFC	Vending Machines
EFD	Food Sanitation Program
EFE	Food Services Records and Reports
EG	Office Services Management
EGA	Office Communications Services
EGAA	Printing and Duplicating Services
EGAB	Mail and Delivery Services
EGAC	Telephone Services
EGB	Clerical Services
EGC	Office Services Records and Reports
EH	Data Management
EHA	Computerized Data Systems
EHAA	Computer Access and Control
EHB	Data/Records Retention
EI	Insurance Management
EIA	Property Insurance
EIB	Liability Insurance
EJ	Evaluation of Support Services (Also AFF)

SECTION F: Facilities Development

Section F of the EPS/NSBA policy classification system provides a repository for statements on school construction, remodeling and modernizing, temporary facilities, and facilities retirement plans.

FA	Facilities Development Goals
FAA	Facilities Development Priority Objectives

Figure 1-7 (Cont'd.)

FB	Facilities Planning
FBA	Facilities Planning Advisors
FBB	Enrollment Projections
FC	Facilities Capitalization Program
FD	Bond Campaigns (Also KBE)
FE	Facilities Construction
FEA	Educational Specifications
FEB	Architect
FEC	Facilities Development Plans and Specifications
FECA	Site Plans and Specifications
FECB	Construction Plans and Specifications
FECC	Equipment Plans and Specifications
FED	Construction Cost Estimates and Determinations
FEE	Site Acquisition
FEF	Construction Contracts Bidding and Awards
FEFA	Contractor's Fair Employment Clause
FEFB	Contractor's Affidavits and Guarantees
FEG	Supervision of Construction
FEH	Construction Project Insurance Program
FEI	Construction Project Records and Reports
FF	Naming School Facilities
FFA	Memorials
FFB	Names on Building Plaques
FG	Board Inspection and Acceptance of New Facilities
FH	Staff Orientation to New Facilities
FI	Public Dedication of New Facilities
FJ	Temporary School Facilities
FK	Facilities Renovations
FL	Retirement of Facilities

Figure 1-7 (Cont'd.)

SECTION G: Personnel

Section G of the EPS/NSBA policy classification system provides a repository for personnel policies. This section has three main subdivisions: subsection GB presents policy topics that pertain to all employees; subsection GC is for policies that pertain to professional personnel, including administrators, who must hold educational certification by the state to serve in their positions; subsection GD is for policies pertaining to all other personnel.

GA	Personnel Policies Goals
GAA	Personnel Policies Priority Objectives
GB	General Personnel Policies
GBA	Equal Employment Opportunity
GBB	Staff Involvement in Decisionmaking (Also ABB)
GBC	Staff Ethics
GBCA	Staff Conflict of Interest
GBCB	Staff Conduct
GBD	Board-Staff Communications (Also BG)
GBE	Staff Health and Safety
GBEA	Staff Protection
GBF	Staff Participation in Community Activities (Also KE)
GBG	Staff Participation in Political Activities
GBH	Staff-Student Relations (Also JM)
GBI	Staff Gifts and Solicitations
GBJ	Staff Funds Management
GBK	Smoking on School Premises by Staff Members
GBL	Personnel Records
GBM	Staff Complaints and Grievances
GC	Professional Staff
GCA	Professional Staff Positions

Figure 1-7 (Cont'd.)

GCB	Professional Staff Contracts and Compensations Plans
GCBA	Professional Staff Salary Schedules
GCBAA	Professional Staff Merit System
GCBB	Professional Staff Supplementary Pay Plans
GCBC	Professional Staff Fringe Benefits
GCBD	Professional Staff Leaves and Absences
GCBE	Professional Staff Vacations and Holidays
GCC	Professional Staff Recruiting
GCCA	Positioning of Professional Staff Vacancies
GCD	Professional Staff Hiring
GCE	Part-Time and Substitute Professional Staff Employment
GCEA	Arrangements for Professional Staff Substitutes
GCF	Professional Staff Orientation
GCG	Professional Staff Probation and Tenure
GCH	Professional Staff Seniority
GCI	Professional Staff Assignments and Transfers
GCJ	Professional Staff Time Schedules
GCK	Professional Staff Workload
GCKA	Professional Staff Extra Duty
GCKB	Professional Staff Meetings
GCL	Professional Staff Development
GCLA	Professional Staff Visitations and Conferences
GCM	Supervision of Professional Staff
GCN	Evaluation of Professional Staff (Also AFC)
GCO	Professional Staff Promotions
GCP	Professional Staff Termination of Employment
GCPA	Reduction in Professional Staff Work Force
GCPB	Resignation of Professional Staff Members
GCPC	Retirement of Professional Staff Members

Figure 1-7 (Cont'd.)

GCPD	Suspension and Dismissal of Professional Staff Members
GCQ	Miscellaneous Professional Staff Policies
GCQA	Nonschool Employment by Professional Staff Members
GCQAA	Professional Staff Consulting Activities
GCQAB	Tutoring for Pay
GCQB	Professional Research and Publishing
GCQC	Exchange Teaching
GCQD	Professional Organizations
GD	Support Staff
GDA	Support Staff Positions
GDB	Support Staff Contracts and Compensation Plans
GDBA	Support Staff Salary Schedules
GDBAA	Support Staff Merit System
GDBB	Support Staff Supplementary Pay Plans
GDBC	Support Staff Fringe Benefits
GDBD	Support Staff Leaves and Absences
GDBE	Support Staff Vacations and Holidays
GDC	Support Staff Recruiting
GDCA	Posting of Support Staff Vacancies
GDD	Support Staff Hiring
GDE	Part-Time and Substitute Support Staff Employment
GDEA	Arrangements for Support Staff Substitutes
GDF	Support Staff Orientation
GDG	Support Staff Probation and Tenure
GDH	Support Staff Seniority
GDI	Support Staff Assignments and Transfers
GDJ	Support Staff Time Schedules
GDK	Support Staff Workload
GDKA	Support Staff Extra Duty
GDKB	Support Staff Meetings

Figure 1-7 (Cont'd.)

GDL	Support Staff Development
GDLA	Support Staff Visitations and Conferences
GDM	Supervision of Support Staff
GDN	Evaluation of Support Staff (Also AFD)
GDO	Support Staff Promotions
GDP	Support Staff Termination of Employment
GDPA	Reduction in Support Staff Work Force
GDPB	Resignation of Support Staff Members
GDPC	Retirement of Support Staff Members
GDPD	Suspension and Dismissal of Support Staff Members
GDQ	Miscellaneous Support Staff Policies
GDQA	Nonschool Employment by Support Staff Members

SECTION H: Negotiations

Section H of the EPS/NSBA policy classification system provides a repository for statements pretaining to the process of negotiating with staff units recognized by the school board.

HA	Negotiations Goals
HAA	Negotiations Priority Objectives
HB	Negotiations Legal Status
HC	Scope of Negotiations
HD	School Board Negotiating Powers, Duties, and Rights
HE	Board Negotiating Agents
HF	Superintendent's Role in Negotiations
HG	Staff Negotiating Organizations
HH	Privileges/Responsibilities of Staff Negotiating Organizations
HI	Payment of Negotiations Costs

Figure 1-7 (Cont'd.)

HJ	Negotiations Procedures
HK	Release of Negotiations Information
HL	Preliminary Negotiated Agreement Disposition
HM	Announcement of Final Negotiated Agreement
HMA	Negotiated Agreement Implementation
HN	Impasse Procedures
HO	Staff Job Actions
HP	Negotiated Amendments and Renegotiations Procedures

SECTION I: Instruction

Section I of the EPS/NSBA policy classification system provides a repository for statements on the instructional program: basic programs, special programs, activities programs, instructional resources, academic achievement.

IA	Instructional Goals
IAA	Instructional Priority Objectives
IB	Academic Freedom
IC	School Year
ICA	School Calendar
ICB	Extended School Year
ID	School Day
IE	Organization of Instruction
IF	Curriculum Development
IFA	Curriculum Research
IFB	Pilot Projects
IFC	Pilot Project Evaluation
IFD	Curriculum Adoption
IFE	Curriculum Guides and Course Outlines

Figure 1-7 (Cont'd.)

IG	Curriculum Design
IGA	Basic Instructional Program
IGAA	Citzenship Education
IGAB	Human Relations Education
IGAC	Teaching About Religion
IGAD	Occupational Education
IGADA	Work Experience Opportunities
IGAE	Health Education
IGAF	Physical Education
IGAG	Teaching about Drugs, Alcohol, and Tobacco
IGAH	Family Life Education
IGAI	Sex Education
IGAJ	Driver Education
IGB	Special Instructional Programs and Accommodations
IGBA	Programs for Handicapped Students
IGBB	Programs for Gifted Students
IGBC	Programs for Disadvantaged Students
IGBD	Programs for Pregnant Students
IGBE	Remedial Instruction
IGBF	Bilingual Instruction
IGBFA	English as a Second Language
IGBG	Homebound Instruction
IGBH	Alternative School Programs
IGC	Extended Instructional Programs
IGCA	Summer Schools
IGCB	Travel Study
IGCC	Honors Program
IGCD	Advanced College Placement (Also LEB)
IGCE	School Camps
IGD	Cocurricular and Extracurricular Programs
IGDA	Student Organizations
IGDB	Student Publications
IGDC	Student Social Events
IGDD	Student Performances
IGDE	Student Activities Fees
IGDF	Student Fund-Raising Activities
IGDG	Student Activities Funds Management

Figure 1-7 (Cont'd.)

IGDH	Contests for Students
IGDI	Intramural Programs
IGDJ	Interscholastic Athletics
IGE	Adult Education Programs
IGEA	Adult Basic Education
IGEB	Adult High School Programs
IGEC	Adult Occupational Education
IH	Instructional Arrangements
IHA	Grouping for Instruction
IHB	Class Size
IHC	Scheduling for Instruction
IHD	Student Schedules and Course Loads
IHE	Team Teaching
IHF	Differentiated Staffing
IHG	Independent Study
IHH	Individualized Instruction
IHHA	Individual Help
IHI	Contracting for Instruction
IHIA	Performance Contracting
IHJ	Minicourses
IHK	Open Classrooms
IHL	Nongraded Classrooms
II	Instructional Resources
IIA	Instructional Materials
IIAA	Textbook Selection and Adoption
IIAB	Supplementary Materials Selection and Adoption
IIAC	Library Materials Selection and Adoption
IIAD	Special Interest Instructional Materials (Also KFA)
IIB	Instructional Services
IIBA	Teacher Aides
IIBB	Resource Teachers
IIBC	Instructional Materials Centers
IIBD	School Libraries
IIBDA	Professional Libraries
IIBE	Instructional Television
IIBF	Instructional Radio

Figure 1-7 (Cont'd.)

IIBG	Computer-Assisted Instruction
IIC	Community Instructional Resources (Also KF)
IICA	Field Trips and Excursions
IICB	Community Resource Persons
IICC	School Volunteers
IJ	Guidance Program
IK	Academic Achievement
IKA	Grading Systems
IKAA	Final Examinations
IKAB	Student Progress Reports to Parents
IKAC	Student Conferences
IKAD	Parent Conferences
IKB	Homework
IKC	Class Rankings
IKD	Honor Rolls
IKE	Promotion and Retention of Students
IKEA	Makeup Opportunities
IKEB	Acceleration
IKF	Graduation Requirements
IKFA	Early Graduation
IKFB	Graduation Exercises
IL	Testing Programs
ILA	Test Selection and Adoption
ILB	Test Administration
ILC	Use and Dissemination of Test Results
IM	Evaluation of Instructional Programs (Also AFE)
IN	Miscellaneous Instructional Policies
INA	Teaching Methods
INB	Teaching About Controversial Issues
INC	Controversial Speakers
IND	School Ceremonies and Observances
INDA	Patriotic Exercises
INDB	Flag Displays
INE	Assemblies

Figure 1-7 (Cont'd.)

INF	School Fairs
ING	Animals in the School
INH	Class Interruptions

SECTION J: Students

Section J of the EPS/NSBA policy classification system provides a repository for statements concerning students — admissions, attendance, rights and responsibilities, conduct, discipline, health, and welfare services. However, all policies pertaining to the curriculum, instruction of students, and extracurricular programs are filed in the I (Instruction) section.

JA	Student Policies Goals
JAA	Student Policies Priority Objectives
JB	Equal Educational Opportunities
JC	School Attendance Areas
JD	School Census
JE	Student Attendance
JEA	Compulsory Attendance Ages
JEB	Entrance Age
JEC	School Admissions
JECA	Admission of Resident Students
JECB	Admission of Nonresident Students
JECBA	Admission of Exchange Students
JECC	Assignment of Students to Schools
JECD	Assignment of Students to Classes
JECE	Student Withdrawal from School
JED	Student Absences and Excuses
JEDA	Truancy
JEDB	Student Dismissal Precautions
JEE	Student Attendance Accounting
JEF	Released Time for Students
JEFA	Open/Closed Campus
JEFB	Released Time for Religious Instruction

Figure 1-7 (Cont'd.)

JEG	Exclusions and Exemptions from School Attendance
JF	Student Rights and Responsibilities
JFA	Student Due Process Rights
JFB	Student Involvement in Decision-making (Also ABC)
JFBA	Student Government
JFC	Student Conduct
JFCA	Student Dress Code
JFCB	Care of School Property by Students
JFCC	Student Conduct on School Buses (Also EEACC)
JFCD	Underground Student Publications
JFCE	Secret Societies
JFCF	Hazing
JFCG	Smoking by Students
JFCH	Alcohol Use by Students
JFCI	Drug Abuse by Students
JFCJ	Dangerous Weapons in the Schools
JFD	Students of Legal Age
JFE	Pregnant Students
JFF	Married Students
JFG	Interrogations and Searches
JFH	Student Complaints and Grievances
JFI	Student Demonstrations and Strikes
JG	Student Discipline
JGA	Corporal Punishment
JGB	Detention of Students
JGC	Probation of Students
JGD	Student Suspension
JGE	Student Explusion
JH	Student Welfare
JHA	Student Insurance Program
JHB	Student Aid Programs
JHC	Student Health Services and Requirements
JHCA	Physical Examinations of Students
JHCB	Immunization of Students
JHCC	Communicable Diseases

Figure 1-7 (Cont'd.)

JHCD	Administering Medicines to Students
JHD	Student Psychological Services
JHDA	Psychological Testing of Students
JHE	Student Social Services
JHEA	Home Visits
JHF	Student Safety
JHFA	Supervision of Students
JHFB	Student Safety Patrols
JHFC	Student Bicycle Use
JHFD	Student Automobile Use
JI	Student Awards and Scholarships
JJ	Student Volunteers for School and Public Service
JK	Employment of Students
JL	Student Gifts and Solicitations
JM	Staff-Student Relations (Also GBH)
JN	Student Fees, Fines, and Charges
JO	Student Records

SECTION K: School-Community Relations

Section K of the EPS/NSBA policy classification system provides a repository for statements on relations with the general public and with other community and public agencies except other educational agencies and groups.

KA	School-Community Relations Goals
KAA	School-Community Relations Priority Objectives
KB	Public Information Program
KBA	Public's Right to Know
KBB	School-Sponsored Information Media
KBC	News Media Relations
KBCA	News Releases
KBCB	News Conferences and Interviews

Figure 1-7 (Cont'd.)

KBCC	News Media Services at Board Meetings (Also BDDI)
KBCD	Broadcasting and Taping of Board Meetings (Also BDDJ)
KBCE	Sports and Special Events News Coverage
KBD	Speaker Services
KBE	Bond Campaigns (Also FD)
KBF	Use of Students in Public Information Program
KC	Community Involvement in Decision-making (Also ABA)
KD	Public Participation at Board Meetings (Also BDDH)
KE	Staff Participation in Community Activities (Also GBF)
KF	Community Instructional Resources (Also IIC)
KFA	Special Interest Instructional Materials (Also IIAD)
KG	Community Use of School Facilities
KGA	Public Sales on School Property
KGB	Public Conduct on School Property
KGC	Smoking on School Premises at Public Functions
KH	Gifts from the Public
KI	Public Solicitations in the Schools
KJ	Advertising in the Schools
KJA	Distribution/Posting of Promotional Literature
KK	Visitors to the Schools
KL	Public Complaints
KLA	Public Complaints About Policies
KLB	Public Complaints About the Curriculum or Instructional Materials
KLC	Public Complaints About Facilities or Services
KLD	Public Complaints About School Personnel
KM	Relations with Community Organizations
KMA	Relations with Parents Organizations
KMB	Relations with Booster Organizations

Figure 1-7 (Cont'd.)

KMC	Relations with Neighborhood Associations
KMD	Relations with Churches
KME	Relations with Youth Organizations
KMF	Relations with Private Social Service Organizations
KMG	Relations with Business Organizations
KMH	Relations with Labor Organizations
KMI	Relations with Political Organizations
KMJ	Relations with Indian Tribal Councils
KN	Relations with Governmental Authorities
KNA	Relations with Local Governmental Authorities
KNAA	Relations with Fiscal Authorities
KNAB	Relations with Taxation Authorities
KNAC	Relations with Election Authorities
KNAD	Relations with Anti-Poverty Authorities
KNAE	Relations with Housing Authorities
KNAF	Relations with Health Authorities
KNAG	Relations with Welfare Authorities
KNAH	Relations with Parks Authorities
KNAI	Relations with Recreation Authoritites
KNAJ	Relations with Police Authorities
KNAK	Relations with Fire Authorities
KNAL	Relations with Civil Defense Authorities
KNAM	Relations with Environmental Authorities
KNAN	Relations with Planning Authorities
KNAO	Relations with Zoning Authorities
KNB	Relations with County Governmental Authorities
KNC	Relations with State Governmental Authorities
KND	Relations with Federal Governmental Authorities

Figure 1-7 (Cont'd.)

SECTION L: Education Agency Relations

Section L of the EPS/NSBA policy classification system provides a repository for statements which concern the district's relationship with other education agencies — other school districts, regional or service districts, private schools, colleges and universities, educational research organizations, and state and national education agencies.

LA	Education Agency Relations Goals
LAA	Education Agency Relations Priority Objectives
LB	Relations with Other Schools and School Districts
LBA	Shared Services
LBB	Cooperative Educational Programs
LBC	Relations with Nonpublic Schools
LBD	Relations with Home Schools
LC	Relations with Education Research Agencies
LD	Relations with Cultural Institutions
LE	Relations with Colleges and Universities
LEA	Student Teaching and Internships
LEB	Advanced College Placement (Also IGCD)
LF	County Education Agency Relations
LG	State Education Agency Relations
LH	Federal Education Agency Relations
LI	Relations with Educational Accreditation Agencies
LJ	Professional Visitors and Observers

Source: Mary S. Brodinsky, Editor, *Educational Policies Reference Manual*, Fifth Edition (Alexandria, VA: National School Boards Association, 1984).

Figure 1-7 (Cont'd.)

POLICY AREAS PROMOTING EFFECTIVE SCHOOLS

	Does your school system have a policy in this area?	
Board and Community	Yes	No
Community involvement in Decision-making	_____	_____
School District Goals and Objectives	_____	_____
Leadership		
Administrative Organization Plan	_____	_____
School Building Administration	_____	_____
Staff		
Professional Staff Recruiting	_____	_____
Professional Staff Hiring	_____	_____
Professional Staff Evaluation	_____	_____
Professional Staff Development Opportunities	_____	_____
Staff Involvement in Decision-making	_____	_____
Students		
Student Involvement in Decision-making	_____	_____
Student Conduct	_____	_____
Student Discipline	_____	_____
Curriculum and Instruction		
Instructional Goals	_____	_____
Academic Achievement	_____	_____
Curriculum Design	_____	_____
Community Resources	_____	_____
Extracurricular Programs	_____	_____
School Climate		
Recognition for Accomplishment	_____	_____
Board-Staff Communications	_____	_____
Staff-Student Communications	_____	_____
School Building Maintenance	_____	_____
Evaluation and Assessment		
Evaluation of the Superintendent	_____	_____
Evaluation of the Instructional Programs	_____	_____
Assessment of Student Achievements	_____	_____

Figure 1-8

The EPS/NSBA School Board Policy Classification System

(1975 Revised Version)

SECTIONS

A   Foundations and Basic Commitments
B   School Board Governance and Operations
C   General School Administration
D   Fiscal Management
E   Support Services
F   Facilities Development
G   Personnel
H   Negotiations
I   Instruction
J   Students
K   School-Community Relations
L   Education Agency Relations

Source: Mary S. Brodinsky, Editor, *Educational Policies Reference Manual*, Fifth Edition (Alexandria, VA: National School Boards Association, 1984).

Figure 1-9

CURRENT STATUS REPORT

on

SCHOOL BOARD POLICY MANUAL

School District: ___Bexley City Schools___ Date: _____

SUMMARY

POLICY SECTION	POLICY AREA	CURRENT STATUS
0100 - 0999	Government	A
1000 - 1999	Administration	A
2000 - 2999	Program	NIA
3000 - 3999	Certificated Staff	A
4000 - 4999	Classified Staff	A
5000 - 5999	Students	A/NIA
6000 - 6999	Finances	NIA
7000 - 7999	Property	NIA
8000 - 8999	Operations	A/NIA
9000 - 9999	Community Relations	A

Current Status Code:

E = Excellent

A = Adequate

NIA = Needs Immediate Action

ANC = Action Not Critical

Figure 1-10

FRANKLIN B. WALTER
SUPERINTENDENT OF
PUBLIC INSTRUCTION

MARY J. POSTON
DIRECTOR
DIVISION OF ELEMENTARY
AND SECONDARY EDUCATION

TO: Superintendents and Central Office Personnel

RE: POLICIES ADOPTED BY THE BOARD OF EDUCATION

DISTRICT: Bexley City Schools   SUPERINTENDENT: Patricia C. Conran

Complete columns A and B. If possible copy the following policies. If policies are not copied, please have policy book(s) available with specified policies identified.

Educational Program The kindergarten through twelfth grade educational program shall be implemented in accordance with the Revised Code and board of education policies governing the following:	A Where Policy Can Be Found	B Page & Section Number	Evaluator Use Only
(A) philosophy of education and educational goals	AD-AE-AF		o,k.
(B) curriculum and instruction	IF/IFD/IFA		ok.
participation of handicapped pupils in competency based education program	IB/ACB		o k,
(C) educational options (if applicable)	IGBH		ok
(D) experimental programs (if applicable)	Not Applicable		—
(E) educational program evaluation	AFC-3		ok
Educational Resources Resources for implementation of the educational program shall be allocated in accordance with the Revised Code and board of education policies governing the following:			
(A) certificated and classified staff	GCA/GDA		ok
(B) instructional materials and equipment	IIAA--Pg.1		ok
selection of materials, textbooks, and equipment	Pp.1-2 IIAA-IIAB-IIAC		ok
selection of library collection	IIAA-Pg.2		rk.
(C) facilities	FA/FBB		oh
(D) health and safety	JHC/JHCB/JHCC		ok.
(E) cumulative records	JO		Ok
(F) pupil admission	JEC		ok
(G) pupil attendance and conduct	JFC/JG/JF		Ok.
(H) school guidance and conduct	JHCD		Ok
(I) pupil activity programs	IGDA		ak
(J) planned community relations	KA/KG		Ok
(K) educational resources evaluation	AFC-4		Ok.

"AN EQUAL OPPORTUNITY EMPLOYER"

Source: Ohio Department of Education.

Figure 1-11

PIN FORM

(Problem-Issue-Need for Policy Development)

CODE: _____

(Office Use Only)

PROBLEM-ISSUE-NEED (Brief Description) _____

_____

_____

_____

SUPPORTIVE DATA AS TO WHY A CHANGE IS NEEDED _____

_____

_____

_____

SUGGESTED LANGUAGE CHANGE _____

_____

_____

_____

Submitted By   Name: _____

                              Address: _____

                              Phone: _____

Date Submitted: _____

Figure 1-12

2

Achieving and Maintaining Educational Excellence

Educators have researched and discussed effective schools, how to recognize them, and what to do to make schools effective. Perhaps this interest came as a reaction to the original Coleman Report which found our nation's schools did not make a difference. Perhaps the interest was a natural outgrowth of the accountability movement in education. Whatever the exact origin, what makes effective schools has been identified. Superintendents aspiring to effectiveness have been putting the findings to work.

Schooling Effectiveness Factors

Various definitions of effective schools have been offered by educators researching them. Dr. Ron Edmonds defined effective schools as those where certain relations *don't* exist. In a conversation in 1983, Dr. Edmonds said the belief that how well children do is *caused* by where they come from, who their parents are, their color, etc., is *wrong*. By Edmonds' definition effective schools are those where the relations just described *don't* prevail, even under the most potentially disabling factors.

Dr. Larry Lezotte defines an effective school as one where the *proportional increase in student achievement is the same among the group one would not normally expect to achieve as in the high achieving group*. Lezotte disaggregates data on standardized achievement tests to determine the proportional increases between or among groups. For example, Lezotte says that the level of the mother's education has been found to be the factor most associated with student performance. For the purpose of determining if the school is effective, then, test results could be sorted by those students whose mothers attained a college degree or beyond and those students whose mothers attained a high school education or less. A second way, among numerous other ways to sort the data, is by level of family income.

With many researchers studying and discussing effective schools, there were many characteristics identified. One of the more prominent figures until his untimely death in 1983, Dr. Edmonds identified five characteristics that correlate with effective schools. The characteristics are shown in Figure 2-1.

Style of Leadership of the Principal

In effective schools, all are preoccupied with instructional issues. Instructional issues are the principal's number-one concern, where the most time is spent and what is given most thought. A superintendent who desires effective schools will set the tone by making thinking about and discussing instructional issues a priority.

Instructional Focus

When asked what the school cares most about, all adults in an effective school have a very similar understanding of the major themes on which the school fixed its attention. By contrast, adults in ineffective schools had enormous variability in responses to the question. A superintendent can be the catalyst for providing this focus at the district level.

Climate

Effective schools were found to be safe, clean, serious, organized, systematic places in which resources were appropriately distributed, physical space was properly used, and the setting was cared for and maintained. The superintendent, having ultimate responsibility for resources and facilities, can monitor their availability and use these to facilitate a climate conducive to effectiveness.

High Expectations

In effective schools, staff uniformly manifest high expectations in observable behavior. High expectations are exhibited both for the proportion of students expected to do well in their acquisition of basic school skills and for the significant number who go beyond minimum mastery. The superintendent sets the tone for high expectations, starting with his or her own performance.

Use of Pupil Performance on Standardized Measures of Achievement

Pupil performance on standardized measures of achievement is used in effective schools as an important way to evaluate the efficiency or effectiveness of school programs, instructional materials, and instructional strategies.

What is significant about all the identified characteristics of effective schools is that they derive from *inside* the school. As Dr. Edmonds noted, schools can be effective regardless of the existence of the most potentially disabling factors external to the school. A *single* school is effective, but the superintendent can influence effectiveness in *all* schools for which he or she is responsible.

We believe that present personnel in schools are educable. Present personnel are capable of acquiring the observable professional behaviors associated with effective schools. The superintendent must make available human resources that can introduce behaviors associated with characteristics of effective schools.

Since the original focus of effective schools on school effects, researchers have learned that many other aspects of schooling are important and related to effectiveness. The Northwest Regional Educational Laboratory identified six aspects of effective schooling research. These are shown in Figure 2-2.

School Effects

The whole school is studied to identify what facilitates student learning in the school as a whole.

Teacher Effects

Classroom teaching is studied to determine what practices are effective in helping students learn.

Instructional Leadership

Principal behaviors that support teaching and learning are studied.

Curriculum Alignment

Effective means of organizing and managing the curriculum are studied.

Program Coupling

The interrelationships among school district, school building, and classroom practices are studied.

Educational Change

The process of creating and sustaining desirable educational change is studied.

The Northwest Regional Educational Laboratory found that a synthesis of all six parts of the effective schools research provided a broad and integrated picture of effective schooling.

We have been discussing effective schools. Having the characteristics of effective schools in place can bring us to the threshold of excellence. It is important to strive for effectiveness first, but then we must do more to achieve excellence.

Going Beyond Effectiveness

Certainly it is reasonable to expect that effectiveness is necessary to achieve excellence. But excellence is a level above. Excellence is greatness. For an individual to achieve excellence, one must be achieving at the highest levels of productivity, athletic performance, or moral and ethical behavior, among other possible achievements.

Defined

Excellence at an individual level was defined in *A Nation at Risk* as "performing on the boundary of individual ability in ways that test and push back personal limits." Applying this to schools, to achieve instructional excellence, teachers set high expectations and goals for all learners, then try in every way possible to help students reach them. Achieving the ideals expressed in the definition would probably translate into excellent student performance and achievement scores.

For a teacher to achieve excellence in the classroom, each student would be working to his or her fullest potential most or all of the time. That is, within the time allocated for learning, the student would be working at maximum challenge, interest, and success levels 100% of the time. Extending this to a school level, we can conceive of every student producing maximum learning all of the time. Similarly, for an excellent district, all students in the district would be excellent performers at all times. Of course 100% excellence at all times is ideal, but working toward excellence can be real.

Use of Resources

Doing the most with resources at hand is the first step toward achieving effectiveness or excellence. While it is easy to decry the lack of adequate resources or to wish one had more or better, most of us can do much better with resources at hand. This was one of the strong messages in *In Search of Excellence* as well as its sequel, *Passion for Excellence*.

Excellent companies do not have the option of selecting in or out; they work to improve what they have. Similarly, schools must develop and utilize human and other resources to the fullest to achieve excellence.

When you read *In Search of Excellence* by Peters and Waterman or *Passion for Excellence* by Peters and Austin, you realize that the behaviors described are what every effective school superintendent practices. The authors organized the behaviors and gave them labels.

In their model shown in Figure 2-3, Peters and Austin focus on care of customers, constant innovation, and turned-on people. To complete the model, the authors add leadership. Because the guide for achieving excellence, as explained especially by Peters and Austin, is so simple, I have chosen to use their five categories to discuss excellence.

Common Sense

The obvious is the way Peters and Austin refer to common sense. MBWA, or Management by Wandering Around, is so simple. Being there — everywhere — takes time and commitment, but there is really nothing difficult about it. Excellence demands that the superintendent be out and about paying attention.

Watching the customer and product, for the superintendent, means that the superintendent must be in the school and in the classroom, gaining knowledge about students and their performance. Get in touch. Keep in touch. Hold meetings in your schools. Randomly pop in. Knowing students' capabilities, imagining oneself in the learning situation, and knowing teachers' expectations and their capabilities are a few reasons for being in schools and classrooms. Moreover, both students and teachers will be delighted that you have come.

Another obvious task is listening. Listen because we want to hear. Listen without planning an answer in return. Listen with no hidden motive or agenda. Listen merely because it is important to our customer — the student and his or her parent or guardian — to tell. Listen because it is vital to our survival that we listen. Meet people face-to-face. Watch their eyes. Common sense and common courtesy?

"Naive listening" is a term coined by one company. It simply means listening to those who use the product. By being present in settings where the superintendent can observe and listen to students, naive listening can be practiced. By extension, we can apply the need for and the importance of listening to school district residents: parents and the 75-80% of residents who are nonparents of students in our schools. Call residents on a regular basis, setting some minimum number per week. Call your schools and ask how the day or week has gone. Bring residents in to show off all aspects of the school. Ask them how you are doing. Fix the things that are not going right. Follow up with a "How did we do?" In this way the entire school program can be based directly on the needs of our customers.

We are told that when IBM sells a lemon, they make darned sure that the customer knows they are very, very sorry. Common sense! What happens when we "sell a lemon?" Do we make it tough or awkward to complain? What do we do with the information once received?

Figure 2-4 is a copy of a letter I received from Chairman of the Board and President of the Marriott Corporation, Bill Marriott. I registered a complaint following a stay in a Marriott. Will I return? You betcha! Today I have the Marriott letter posted next to my computer terminal as a model for apologies when needed.

Figure 2-5 is a copy of a letter I wrote when I felt it was needed in the Bexley community. I am including it to affirm that it is okay to need to be sorry and to tell people that you are. Listening and common sense will serve as guides to the appropriate response at the appropriate time.

The flip side of being there to listen is being there to teach the values or mission of the school district to every member of the organization. Beyond listening there is the teaching and reinforcing of values or mission. This is leadership.

Customers

Students and parents are the school district customers. Think of them as your guests and you will know how to treat them. Brag about them. Thank them. Coddle them. Welcome guests to the family and have your house in company order. Constantly considering our customers as our guests will guard against the forces of entropy in our relationships; that is, the erosion of sensitivity and attentiveness.

By MBWA we listen directly to customers and act on what we hear. By naive listening we consider customer perceptions more important than our superior technical knowledge of our service (teaching and administering) or its product (learning). We also listen to our salespeople (teachers, secretaries, custodians, and others important to the learning process). In these ways we can be responsive to our customers. We can get the winning edge, that measurable difference that earns a reputation for excellence.

No one thing will clinch winning. But countless things done a little bit better add up to making or not making a winning difference. Similarly, our customers' satisfaction, or lack of it, is comprised of their cumulative memory of a long string of experiences with our schools.

We must believe in unlimited quality. Anything can be made better. Quality must become the mind set of the district and all its people must live it. Quality comes from people who care and are committed. This means *all* our people. Quality is an obsession. It is about passion and pride. Love what you do — or leave it. Superintendents must believe that *everybody* in the district can contribute creatively to the quality of our product — learning.

One of the findings in the effective schools research revealed the involvement of all in the schools. When all support personnel as well as teachers are involved with the customer, morale will be positive. Recognizing these personnel as heroes will enable them to take ownership. How do your bus drivers, food service personnel, custodial, and maintenance personnel talk about your schools and their teachers and students? About you? One of the first impressions I had of the Bexley City Schools was the pride detected when the Director of Buildings and Grounds, Mr. Davy, toured the facilities with me. Since then Mr. Davy has been responsible for constructing bridges and other structures to provide a 3-mile nature trail for use by students and the community. This is only one of the ways Mr. Davy manifests pride in the schools and community. There are numerous other examples. What a positive salesperson for our school system!

Last year I had the opportunity to participate in a civic leaders tour of Shaw and Langley Air Force Bases. General Bill Creech is given credit for turning these bases around from inefficient, neglected, centralized units to highly efficient, well-maintained, decentralized units where the men and women on the base exuded competence and pride. For them the airplane was the customer; by turning over management to the support personnel, they provided and maintained immaculately clean and inviting work environments for themselves. Men and women in the units compete against the clock to reduce down time of an airplane from hours to a matter of minutes. At the bases we saw pictures of the bases before and after. We saw supply and repair records.

Seeing at Shaw and Langley was believing. Seeing in this case was perceiving. It is important for us to remember that our customers also gain perceptions of our school districts. And the customers' perceptions are the only reality. Their perceptions will earn us our reputation. By putting them first always, developing a mutual trust, and acting with conviction, the customers' perceptions will be what we intend as our mission — the most productive teaching and learning possible.

Innovation

The superintendent needs to set a tone for change. Change is okay. Change is expected. Companies that are successful innovators regularly send the message that "something had better be going on." Employees should aggressively be seeking improvement. In a sense this is what the university professor does in research efforts — and he or she had better be working on something! Similarly, school district employees need to be constantly trying new ideas, sharing these with peers, and inviting their judgment.

Innovation doesn't need to mean some major change where students are guinea pigs for anyone's new idea. Innovation can be a mnemonic device that will help students learn faster and remember longer. Innovation can be an intervention designed to reteach or reinforce previously taught material. Innovation can be the day-to-day attempts we make to assure that we can say to students, "This is all work you can do." Innovation comes from listening to the needs of our customers and adapting our product to their needs. It is what gives us the winning edge.

Peters and Austin tell us that innovation is passion-filled and serendipitous. It is also messy and unpredictable. We encourage it by celebrating it and the resulting sucesses and failures. I remember hearing Warren Bennis tell the story of an IBM executive who made a major blunder and, as a result, expected to get fired. When called in for a reckoning, he was given a raise instead. In shock, the executive said he thought he would be fired. The retort from management was, "What? After we have invested over a million dollars in you?"

Innovation takes time and is highly uncertain. Innovation is affected by champions, mavericks who create or sell the innovation. Recently I heard a neighboring superintendent tell colleagues that two of his principals were relentless in getting him to agree to training staff in the elements of effective instruction. It is this kind of determined, and frequently irrational, championing of an idea that leads to innovation and change.

Constant experimentation is the order of the day. A climate for innovation is created where the experimenters and champions of ideas are heroes. The climate, sometimes referred to as the corporate culture that encourages innovation, is one that rewards risk-taking, supports (rather than punishes) those who have a bad year or two, and one which allows ideas to percolate upward. The climate is informal. All are involved in the new idea and are having fun.

By now, most have heard the expression, "Don't just stand there; do something." Management sets the tone or invites a climate that induces trying things. Champions create or sell the innovation and get others to carry the idea further.

What is required for innovation to occur? Learn to live with uncertainty and ambiguity within a strategic plan. Experiment and move fast. Recognize champions. Get usually distinct functions to interface. (A North Central Association, or some similar self-study process, can be instrumental to this interface.) Create small units within big. (It has been demonstrated that quality as well as innovation is generated in small units.) Recognize that a good plan now may be better than the perfect plan later. Strive for what is timely, fills a practical need, and works. This plan will serve the real world of schooling better than a formula-driven optimal plan. Listen to users, lead users who are way ahead of their peers. The latter idea is illustrated in Figure 2-6. There are innovators and users who are always leaders or laggers. Innovation occurs where the leaders among innovators and users intersect.

People

Schooling is a people business. For this reason, superintendents are less likely than corporations not to recognize the importance of people. However, we can be equally remiss in not recognizing that the productivity of the school system comes from the power of ownership our people have in their jobs. It is somewhat like the well-known Theory Y. Given a chance, the average employee will be his or her best.

Each superintendent needs to examine his or her beliefs about people. Some management lives the Golden Rule. This is the minimum behavior expected.

For some time I have been talking with staff in terms of our being servants of the community. Actually, I first heard this idea voiced by professors at the Gymnasium in Vienna. Professors in Austria are reminded regularly that they are servants of the people. As superintendent, we must model the servant role; we must live leader as servant.

Superintendents must act confidently, consistently, and with integrity. When we make a mistake, we must be ready to admit it. Ask your people;

let them talk back to you. These are two ways to avoid mistakes or to be able to correct them. Ownership and some control over one's destiny leads to awesome results. This is what the term empowerment means. And it builds pride.

The most recent people-oriented movement to sweep the corporate world and find spin-offs in education is the concept of the quality circles. The concept originated in the United States, but gained prominence in Japan and found its way back here to become popularized. Quality circles are comprised of small numbers (10-20) of people who have a great deal of control over the ownership in their production. In a small school, an entire staff can be comprised of one or two teams. In larger schools, there may need to be several quality circles for the concept to work effectively.

Basic to the functioning of the quality circle is the agreement among members to adhere to a code of conduct. Figure 2-7 shows a typical code of conduct. Once the ground rules are established, steps similar to those shown in Figure 2-8 are followed. Brainstorming is shown as the first step. Figure 2-9 lists the results of brainstorming issues facing administrators in one city school district. There are 28 issues identified. The next step for the administrators is to order priorities; in the process, related issues can be clustered. In the example given, each administrator rated the issues three separate times. Then issues rated most often as priorities by all administrators were clustered and selected for problem-solving. Once the problem has been identified for each priority, problem-solving can proceed according to the identified steps. In the illustration, the administrators chose to begin problem-solving with the Levy issue and to limit the initial problem-solving to the one issue. If the quality circles process is used, the superintendent is advised to limit the scope of problem-solving initially to *one* issue for which the group can reach a successful solution or resolution of the problem.

I mentioned earlier that I had visited two Air Force bases and observed for myself the difference General Creech brought about in his units. Organizational principals shown in Figure 2-10 demonstrate how Creech accomplished his results through people on the bases. If we look back on our own experiences, we will see that professional organizations (Association for Supervision and Curriculum Development and Phi Delta Kappa, for example), athletic teams, phone-a-thon teams, and others apply Creech's laws if they are on top year after year.

Another aspect that you find in teams that get unparalleled results is a sense of celebration. Members enjoy each other and enjoy getting and giving recognition. Leslie Wexner, among the wealthiest persons in the world, was recently pictured in a Columbus, Ohio newspaper blowing a kazoo at a stockholders' meeting. This was his way of leading management to celebrate. Taking Wexner's example, administrators in Bexley City Schools blow their horns and toot their whistles after sharing good news about their school or an employee's performance.

A not-too-common thought in this regard is to celebrate failure. Like IBM, we should expect that our million-dollar investments will not always be perfect or run without glitch or error. When a bond referendum fails, when a levy is defeated, at other times when we experience failure, let us celebrate the effort and its purpose, learn from the failure and proceed to a new and higher level or more successful level of functioning. We have only to think of the scientists and their slavish pursuit of what works until they achieve the "aha" insight to temper our expectations for success and to accept the possibility of failure.

Leadership

The superintendent as leader needs to be eternally optimistic, the bearer of glad tidings, enthusiastic. More is said about this aspect of leadership in the section on Cheerleading.

Paying attention to what is important is what Peter Drucker and Warren Bennis call "doing the right things." Leaders do the right things right. Leaders advance those who speak a consistent message about the leader's values. Leaders need to pay attention to advancement of employees at all levels. I remember eating lunch with two school building custodians who had been promoted from night to day custodians. They seemed genuinely pleased and surprised when I congratulated them on their promotions and asked how everyone was treating them.

Another aspect of attention is that it gets things done or facilitates change. If we want administrators to become better as coaches of teachers, we will pay attention to this. If we want teachers to use test results to design interventions in their teaching, we will pay attention to this. Analyzing time spent — how and with whom — tells a message about our priorities. And all of our employees pay attention to our priorities!

Paying attention consistently assumes that there is a vision that the leader has. This vision needs to be communicated symbolically and with drama. It needs to be communicated clearly and passionately. The superintendent, as leader, may want to seek input from others to develop a vision, or mission statement. But once developed, the vision should be repeated over and over again and become the basis for all activity in the system.

Finally, the leader needs to care passionately. Caring passionately about the job will translate into enthusiasm and joy. Caring passionately about people will translate into love and empathy for them.

It has been and remains the trend to identify characteristics of effective leaders. Analyzing leader characteristics is an alternate way to think about effective leadership. Eugene Jennings identified 14 leadership skills and traits. In brief, the successful leader:

1. Gives clear work instructions—keeps others informed;
2. Praises others when they deserve it—understands the importance of recognition—gives positive feedback;
3. Is willing to take time to listen to others—understands the powerful

effect of good leadership listening for building a cooperative relationship and avoiding tension and grievances;

4. Is cool and calm most of the time—maintains emotional control—manages anger well;

5. Has confidence and self-assurance;

6. Has appropriate technical knowledge of the work being supervised—uses this knowledge to coach, teach, and evaluate rather than for getting involved in the "doing" of the work;

7. Has empathy for the group's problems—demonstrates this by careful and attentive listening;

8. Maintains the group's respect—this is accomplished through personal honesty with the group;

9. Is fair and consistent with everyone—this is demonstrated through patterns of work assignments—consistent enforcement of rules, policies, and procedures—avoidance of favoritism;

10. Demands good work from everyone—maintains consistent standards of performance—will not expect the work group to "take up the slack" for a "lazy" worker—enforces discipline;

11. Gains the people's trust—this is demonstrated by the leader's willingness to represent the group to "higher management," regardless of his agreement or disagreement with them—but he must "carry their message."

12. Goes to bat for the group—will work for the best and fair interest of the work group—will not shrink from approaching higher management when necessary—has loyalties to both higher management *and* the work group;

13. Is not aloof—maintains a relationship of friendliness while remembering he is *not* "one of the boys."

14. Is easy to talk to—wants and seeks input from the work group.

The superintendent may want to use the above traits for self-awareness or to develop self-improvement targets.

Schooling as a Ball of Wax

Thinking of schooling as a ball of wax helps to emphasize the connectedness and interrelatedness of everything in the system. Human and tangible resources, how these are secured and improved, distributed and utilized, how these work together to bring desired results are components of the ball of wax. We can't take out any one component and study it under a microscope; we must study the components in context and as they function together with other components. For the ball of wax to hang together, all its components must interact in mutually supportive and consistent ways. (Figure 2-12).

Using the effective schooling research, the Northwest Regional Laboratory has helped us to see just how complex schooling is and how each of the components shown in Figure 2-11 contributes to excellence.

1. **Classroom Characteristics and Practices.**

   1.1 Instruction is guided by a course of study or preplanned curriculum. Teachers and other district personnel have identified learning goals objectives and sequence these for desired learning outcomes. Instructional resources and activities enable teachers to choose from alternative paths to help students accomplish what they are expected to know and be able to do as a result of schooling. Adaptations of the planned curriculum and interventions based on evidence of student learning need to be designed and utilized for maximum effectiveness in helping students learn.

   1.2 There are high expectations for student learning. Within the overall goal of teachers being able to say to students, "This is all work you can do," teachers set high standards and expect students to meet them. Standards and instruction should be at students' challenge and interest levels. Teachers expect students to earn good grades and to do well on tests.

   1.3 Students are carefully oriented to lessons. Teachers explain the objective of a lesson and its purpose in clear language that students can understand. Posting or distributing objectives helps students maintain a sense of direction. Transitions between and among learnings are carefully planned so students can see the relationships among learnings. Students know what is expected and are challenged to learn. Their concern level is raised sufficiently to motivate a desire to learn, but not so high as to create anxiety that inhibits learning or effort.

   1.4 Instruction is clear and focused. Teaching is to the objective. Input is varied and modeling or demonstration is used to clarify. Means are designed to continuously check for students' understanding as monitoring the learning and adapting the curriculum are practiced interchangeably. Guided practice to assure students' success with the learning precedes independent practice in the form of homework or research or other means. Parents are partners in the learning and can provide assistance both in school and at home.

   1.5 Learning progress is monitored closely. Teachers measure learning against objectives being taught. A variety of testing techniques are applied to assure that students have the ability to reveal knowledge and that tests are valid and reliable. Student learning becomes the means for teachers to monitor and adjust their teaching. We should be aiming for a high percentage of students to get high grades; the normal curve distribution must cease to be the measure of satisfaction with teaching.

1.6 When students don't understand, they are retaught. Critical objectives, those necessary to learning at more difficult or complex levels in a subject or area, must be retaught until they are learned. A course of study or curriculum that has been constructed sequentially will allow for identification and review of key prerequisite concepts and skills necessary to further learning.

1.7 Class time is used for learning. Ideally, every moment of allocated time will be used with every student involved in learning tasks at the appropriate level of difficulty. Using class time as efficiently as possible means minimizing time spent on nonlearning activities. Teaching and learning are kept at a brisk pace. Students are held accountable for keeping pace or catching up.

1.8 There are smooth, efficient classroom routines. An anticipatory set, or an activity to focus on the learning task, helps students get a mind-set for the desired learning as they enter the classroom. A well-organized and well-managed instructional setting helps maintain this focus. Classes and activities have smooth and swift transitions between them. And nonlearning routines are kept to a minimum and disposed of quickly.

1.9 Instructional groups formed in the classroom fit instructional needs. Direct, whole-group instruction has been shown to be an effective means of introducing new material. Smaller groups, sometimes differentiated by achievement level may then be used to accomplish a variety of purposes. If achievement levels are used for grouping students, these groups should be monitored and adjusted frequently to reflect changes in student achievement.

1.10 Standards for classroom behavior are explicit. Classroom behavior standards may be developed with the assistance of students. With or without student help, standards are clear, posted, reviewed periodically, and strictly enforced. Consequences for undesirable behavior are administered swiftly and connected to the inappropriate behavior, and they are proportional to the offense. Administration of consequences is consistent and fair.

1.11 Personal interactions between teachers and students are positive. Teachers let students know they care. They know student interests, problems, and successes in and out of school. Students are helped to develop responsibility and independence.

1.12 Incentives and rewards for students are used to promote excellence. A variety of forms of recognition are used to reward achievement, behavior, effort, and other manifestations of excellence. Recognition is appealing to the person or persons receiving it; types of rewards and how to earn them are known by all eligible to receive them. Rewards may be both immediate and delayed according to their meaningfulness to students. Parents are notified of student success; their help in continuing to motivate students to achieve excellence is solicited.

2. **School Characteristics and Practices.**

2.1 Everyone emphasizes the importance of learning. All have high expectations for all students. All know that in this school the focus is on learning. Student learning is the focus of all decision-making when educational issues arise.

2.2 Strong leadership guides the instructional program. Leaders focus on high achievement as the reason for schooling. Speeches and writings emphasize its importance. The leader is the cheerleader for the school's mission; this and the focus on instruction unify staff. There is a belief that all students can learn and that schooling can make a difference. The leader knows pertinent research and can apply and model effective teaching practices. Leaders guide high quality curriculum development and its implementation. Superintendents, as leaders, have high expectations that curriculum and its implementation are at high levels and improve over time. Time on task is encouraged by protecting learning time and minimizing disruptions. This may be as simple as forbidding the use of the public address system during classroom learning time. Leaders see to it that learning environments are safe and orderly. Leaders check student achievement regularly, communicate results, and set standards for comparison and progress. Leaders recognize excellence of teachers and students by setting up reward systems and delivering awards. Leaders secure and allocate resources to accomplish priorities. Superintendents have open communication with parents and systems to encourage their involvement in the learning process.

2.3 The curriculum is based on clear goals and objectives. The course of study, or curriculum goals and objectives, are known and displayed. The course of study is used to plan lessons and to design interventions. There is a clear relationship among the school's philosophy, curriculum, instruction, testing, and interventions. Critical objectives within the curriculum are clearly identified.

2.4 Students are grouped to promote effective instruction. The subject of student grouping is controversial. Whenever possible, mixed or heterogeneous groups are recommended with tracks being avoided. Within the classroom, grouping can be used for a variety of purposes to keep the teacher-or adult-to-student ratio low.

2.5 School time is used for learning. The school schedule and school events are planned to maximize learning time and to avoid disruption. New programs and procedures are analyzed prior to adoption or implementation for their potential impact on learning time. Time use guidelines are developed for individual subjects. Pullouts are minimized and the amount of pullout activity is continuously monitored so that corrective action as deemed necessary may be taken. Extra learning time is provided for students who need or want it; students can get extra help outside of regular school hours. For example, instead of a study hall, students may go to a math or writing lab and benefit from teacher or peer tutoring.

2.6 Learning progress is monitored closely. Test results, grade reports, attendance records, and other sources are used to judge successes and hallmarks of excellence as well as to indicate the need for interventions or changes in instruction and school procedures. All in the system need to be working together and avoiding duplication of effort. Information-gathering about student performance is related to expected learning outcomes. The existence of learning outcomes, however, does not limit flexibility in curriculum and instruction. Results of testing are shared with those who can use them to intervene in learning. Results are also reported to the community.

2.7 Discipline is firm and consistent. The school code of conduct specifies student behavior expectations in writing. Both the code and consequences for violations are known to staff, students, and parents. Initial training and periodic review are required to keep all knowledgeable. Consequences of inappropriate behavior follow quickly and are consistent with the code; these are easy and quick to administer. The focus for disciplinary action is on growth and change in behavior. Out-of-school suspensions or expulsions are to be minimal; suspensions may be reduced if the student seeks appropriate professional help for a problem such as chemical or substance abuse.

2.8 There are high expectations for quality instruction. All staff believe all students can learn. Staff frequently discuss instructional issues when they get together. Supervision and evaluation procedures are written and designed to help individuals attain personal goals as well as to focus on school and district goals. Classroom observations are in accord with understood guidelines and feedback follows quickly. The focus for classroom observation should be increasing student learning and the instruction necessary to do this. Inservice should be designed to have continuity and to facilitate growth. Superintendents may want to consider the benefits of having the entire staff knowledgeable about a particular instructional model — Madeline Hunter as one example. A principal value of using a model is the development of a common vocabulary. Having all using the same language to discuss instruction facilitates communication about instruction.

2.9 Incentives and rewards are used to build strong motivation. Rewards for excellence and achievement are encouraged for both students and staff. We recognize the difficulty in getting teachers to accept the concept of recognition, but when rewards come often and are varied and within reach of all, there is less resistance among teachers. All rewards are given for accomplishing or surpassing commonly understood standards, not for comparison with peers. Student performance is a key element in recognizing teachers. Incentives and rewards foster effort and intrinsic motivation and are meaningful to those who receive them. Rewards can be both formal and informal, public or private.

2.10 Parents are invited to become involved. There are many and varied opportunities for parents and the nonparent community to become involved, especially in ways that support the instructional program. Procedures for involvement are clearly communicated and consistently practiced. Staff provide the necessary information and resources to parents to help students learn.

2.11 Teachers and administrators continually strive to improve instructional effectiveness. There is an overall focus on improvement by all in the school. Goals for improvement are set at all levels and are based on the need to improve or grow or learn something new or different. Efforts at and progress toward improvement are publicized and celebrated. Figure 2-9 shows an article from a District Newsletter which serves to encourage a united improvement effort.

2.12 There are pleasant conditions for learning. Physical facilities are clean and attractive. Damage is repaired immediately. Vandalism, if any, is tended to immediately and all traces removed. Grounds are clear and neat. All are responsible to assure that the environment is litter-free. Bright colors chosen with input from teachers and students will enhance pride in and care of the environment.

3. District Characteristics and Practices.

3.1 High expectations pervade the organization. District leaders and staff believe that all students can learn, and that what happens in district schools can make a difference in whether students learn or not. All are focused on learning and helping students grow as being most important. The superintendent and others set high goals and establish priorities for improvement, and publicize these. Improving instructional effectiveness is a theme that permeates all district plans and activities.

3.2 There are policies and procedures that support excellence in student performance. Policies and procedures are established and reviewed to promote maximum student achievement. Policies and procedures should require ongoing improvement effort at all levels. Building principals are expected to be instructional leaders and to generate action plans for improvement and to carry them out. All involved in decisions participate in the planning efforts.

3.3 Student learning is checked regularly. At the district level, as well as at school and classroom levels, student performance data are collected and interpreted. Strengths and weaknesses are analyzed. Results are shared with the community. Progress is related to district goals and priorities. Duplication of effort is prevented. Alignment between tests and the course of study, or curriculum, is checked and adjusted routinely. District assessments are planned with input from staff and carried out with support as needed with a minimum of disruption.

3.4 Improvement efforts are monitored and supported. The implementation of policies and procedures is monitored in each school. Depending on the size of the school system, the superintendent may directly supervise this effort or may delegate it to a district supervisor. Staff need to have a support mechanism that they can rely on for consultation, training assistance, and other services. Budgets are developed to reflect improvement priorities.

3.5 Excellence is recognized and rewarded. Award programs are established by district leaders for schools, administrators, teachers, students and parents, and others who support the schools' efforts. Awards to staff are based on contributions made to improving student performance. As with other awards, the criteria are known and recognition is to be based on meeting or surpassing standards rather than comparison with peers.

3.6 Curriculum planning ensures continuity. Many states are now mandating a course of study or learning outcomes, if not prescribing a statewide curriculum. Objectives clarify what students are expected to know and be able to do in various subject areas and at various grade levels. The objectives are sequenced so as to eliminate gaps or overlaps. The objectives should be teachable within an established time-frame. Appropriateness of the objectives should be regularly reviewed. District support for building and classroom curriculum efforts is provided.

Tension That Facilitates or Impedes

Organizational development experts use terms like a healthy climate or a corporate culture to describe a work environment where all appear to have a match between personal and organizational goals. For many years, reseachers debated the merits of a task orientation versus a people orientation. Other theorists identified satisfiers and dissatisfiers. Work environments that were overly social were found to be as unproductive as those where a high level of anxiety prevented workers from doing their best or from making a personal commitment to the work effort.

Madeline Hunter tells us that a certain level of concern needs to exist for learning to occur. If concern, or anxiety, is too low, students will not be motivated to learn. If concern is too high, students will be prevented from learning. This principle applies in the workplace for teachers and administrators, as well as in the classroom for students. It is important to note that both raising and lowering tension, or concern level, are important. Too much tension, or tension at inappropriate times, can impede the work effort. Too little tension can also impede the work effort. Both raising and lowering tension, or concern level, must be used for the desired effect as the occasion demands.

Coaching and Cheerleading

The importance of coaching and cheerleading to achieve and maintain educational excellence cannot be stressed enough. Each of these activities has common reference points in our experience, most commonly in sports or athletics.

Imagine a young student of horseback riding, for example. The trainer will remind the rider to keep heels down and toes pointed, to keep the "tush" tucked into the saddle, to hold the reins in a certain position and how and when to move the reins to get desired results, and so on. As the trainer observes the rider's performance, specific feedback is given on these and other expected behaviors. The rider has learned the behaviors and understands the feedback so corrective measures can be taken. Similarly in other sports or athletics.

The leader as coach molds and shapes behavior and brings out the best. The leader as coach nurtures champions, clarifies and dramatizes goals, builds skills and teams. The leader as coach encourages, teaches, listens, facilitates, and supports. The leader as coach excels and is consistent and, therefore, believable.

Saying it over and over again and patiently helping others develop the skills that will help them make quality and sustained contributions to the organization are what the leader as coach does. Every winning coach knows that it is the players' efforts that win. Surely a game plan and commonly understood techniques help the win, but there is no win without all-out player effort.

To motivate, the coach gives exposure and provides latitude to the players. The leader as coach pays attention to people and builds a personal relationship with them. The leader as coach is able to pull people with diverse backgrounds, talents, experiences, and interests together and to encourage them to take responsibility and to continuously achieve and improve. The coach finds ways to get the whole team together to emphasize: "We're all in this together so we better do what we can to help each other out." The leader as coach makes clear that there is no room for prima-donnas or individualists on the team. The "I" must give way to the "we." Similarly the leader as coach makes clear what each member can contribute to the team and, thus, encourages aggressive cooperation.

Factors that facilitate the work effort were identified above. The leader as coach is a facilitator, one who makes the work effort easier, though not less demanding, one who encourages trying. The leader as coach finds ways to remove restrictions on performance.

Remember MBWA? Well management by walking around is what a coach does. The coach has to be there when the game is played. Wandering around, being there where "the action is" is demanded of the leader as coach. In this way, one of the most vital aspects of coaching, value-shaping, can be realized. The leader as coach pays extraordinary attention to communicate the philosophy or mission of the work effort and to help newcomers understand how shared values affect individual performance.

The team will see values of the coach reflected in actions. It is, therefore, important for the leader as coach to examine his or her actions; these reflect what is really important. Value-shaping is doing the right thing. The leader as coach also gives others a chance to do the right thing. The better the coach has communicated shared values, acted consistently to develop trust and reflect integrity, and provided training and coaching, the less often will be the need to intervene and "fix" things.

We do not mean to make coaching sound easy. It is demanding work. To give an indication of how demanding, the characteristics of good coaches, as identified in seminars given by Peters, are shown in Figure 2-13. The coach needs to know what approach to take, what to emphasize, what to leave alone, and where to start. The coach must be flexible. What works with one will not work with another.

Robert Dyer has identified four roles, in addition to coaching, that coaches must perform. When not coaching, the coach is counseling, sponsoring, confronting, or educating. It is time to educate when goals, roles, or conditions change; when there is a newcomer; and when new skills are needed. It is time to sponsor, or mentor, when an individual can make a special contribution and to let an outstanding skill speak for itself. It is time to counsel when problems damage performance and a turnaround, enhanced sense of ownership and accountability and renewed commitment, are expected. It is time to confront when persistent performance problems are not resolved, when an individual seems unable to meet expectations or is failing. The consequences of the latter are reassignment, a chance to succeed in another position, restructuring of the current job, curtailing of responsibilities or dismissal.

As important to excellence as coaching is cheerleading. The cheerleader spreads irresistible enthusiasm and pride. The cheerleader is a catalyst for excitement. The leader will find every opportunity to get people tuned in and turned on. Whether in speeches, written communication, small-group conversation, or one-on-one, the cheerleader will be encouraging support for the team.

The kind of cheerleading a superintendent does should present factual information in a positive manner. Brag about the system, and about parents, students, and staff. Tell about the parent and community support. Tell about close and positive relations between the city or village and the schools. Tell about staff and student achievements. Tell about plans to improve the schools and student performance. Tell about the achievements of staff and students. Cheer about everything and anything that will promote the school district's mission and motivate those in the school district to fulfill the mission with purpose and pride.

REFERENCES AND RESOURCES

Bennis, Warren, and Burt Nanus, *Leaders: The Strategies for Taking Charge.* New York, NY: Harper and Row, Publishers, 1985.

Onward to Excellence: Making Schools More Effective. Portland, OR: Northwest Regional Educational Laboratory, 1984.

Peters, Thomas J., and Robert H. Waterman, Jr., *In Search of Excellence: Lessons from America's Best Run Companies.* New York, NY: Harper and Row, Publishers, 1982.

Peters, Tom, and Nancy Austin, *A Passion for Excellence: The Leadership Difference.* New York, NY: Warner Books, 1985.

Sheive, Linda T., and Marian B. Schoenheit, eds., *Leadership: Examining the Elusive.* Alexandria, VA: The Association for Supervision and Curriculum Development, 1987.

FIVE CHARACTERISTICS THAT
CORRELATE WITH EFFECTIVE SCHOOLS

1. Style of Leadership of the Principal

2. Instructional Focus

3. Climate

4. High Expectations

5. Use of Pupil Performance on Standardized Measures of Achievement

Figure 2-1

SIX ASPECTS OF EFFECTIVE SCHOOLING RESEARCH

1. School Effects
2. Teacher Effects
3. Instructional Leadership
4. Curriculum Alignment
5. Program Coupling
6. Educational Change

Figure 2-2

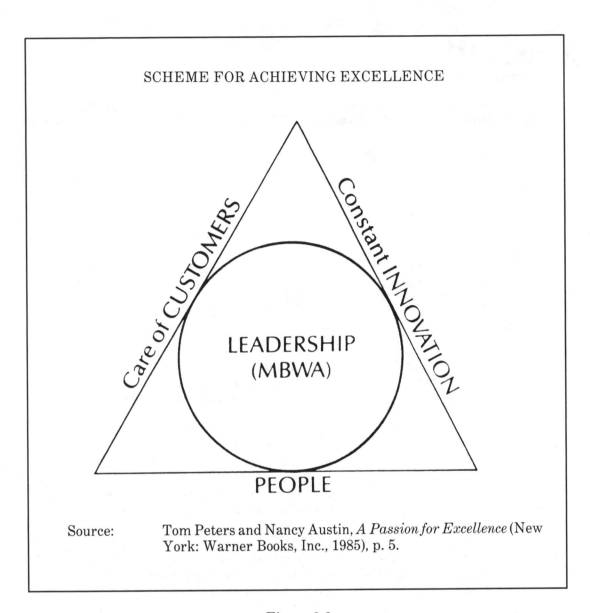

SCHEME FOR ACHIEVING EXCELLENCE

Care of CUSTOMERS

Constant INNOVATION

LEADERSHIP
(MBWA)

PEOPLE

Source: Tom Peters and Nancy Austin, *A Passion for Excellence* (New York: Warner Books, Inc., 1985), p. 5.

Figure 2-3

Marriott
corporation

INTERNATIONAL
HEADQUARTERS

Marriott Drive
Washington, D.C. 20058

J. Willard Marriott, Jr.
Chairman of the Board
and President

April 17, 1987

Dr. Patricia C. Conran
2551 East Broad Street
Bexley, Ohio 43209

Dear Dr. Conran:

Thank you for your comments about our New Orleans Marriott. I always appreciate hearing from our guests. It helps me keep in touch with how well we are measuring up to your expectations.

While you indicated you were pleased with your visit, I will forward your evaluation to our General Manager concerning the problems you had with incorrect information from our staff and the other problems you mentioned. Your comments are helpful to us in our efforts to provide a comfortable and enjoyable visit for our guests.

Thank you for giving us the opportunity to serve you and for sharing your dissatisfaction with us. We look forward to your continuing to select Marriott Hotels as you travel.

Sincerely,

Bill Marriott

J. W. Marriott, Jr.
   Courtesy of the Marriott Corporation

Figure 2-4

Bexley City Schools

348 South Cassingham Road • Bexley, Ohio 43209 • Phone (614) 231-7611

Date

Dear Bexley Resident:

Over the past several weeks, I have been listening to the expressions of concern from community members. Knowing how the community feels on educational issues is very important to me and of great value in executing my charge as superintendent.

Unfortunately, communication on important educational issues has not been what it should be. To improve communications, I want to take an important step: the appointment of an informal input group. This group's charge will be to listen and facilitate interaction among the various groups that can help us make informed decisions. By working with a committee of community, Board and staff representatives, we can establish a dialogue that will benefit the educational process in Bexley.

My primary goal is to promote quality, cost effective education in the Bexley Schools. It is important that we demonstrate to our community that we are using their monies efficiently, always keeping in mind the concerns and traditions that have made Bexley one of the best school systems in this nation. Certainly, this broad-based committee can address financial and educational challenges and make sound recommendations for solutions by the Board.

Together, we have done so much to improve our schools:

   *We have worked to lower class sizes in the high school, sometimes as large as 28 to 30 students, to a maximum size of 25 students.

   *We have completed the preliminary work needed to gain North Central Association accreditation for all our schools. Membership in this prestigious organization will insure ongoing efforts to sustain quality.

   *We are acting now to devise a plan to integrate the appropriate use of computers into our schools--thanks to the generosity and work of so many in our community.

Everyone regrets the turmoil caused by the failure to communicate adequately. Having worked closely with many in our community on fundraising and other efforts, I have come to understand and appreciate the depth of involvement and concern that exists in this community. I want that involvement to be positive and productive.

As my next step in working closely with you, I am withdrawing my recommendation to the Board for the nonrenewal of John Doe's contract. My recommendation was made using the best information available to me. However, I have listened to the expressions of parents and students, and I am recommending that the Board give John Doe an opportunity to have a successful teaching experience in Bexley.

Despite the recent challenges, I hold Bexley and our community members and schools in the highest regard. I pledge to you and our community my best efforts to make a positive and significant contribution to the quality of education in Bexley.

   Closing and Signature

Courtesy of Bexley City Schools.

Figure 2-5

LEAD USERS

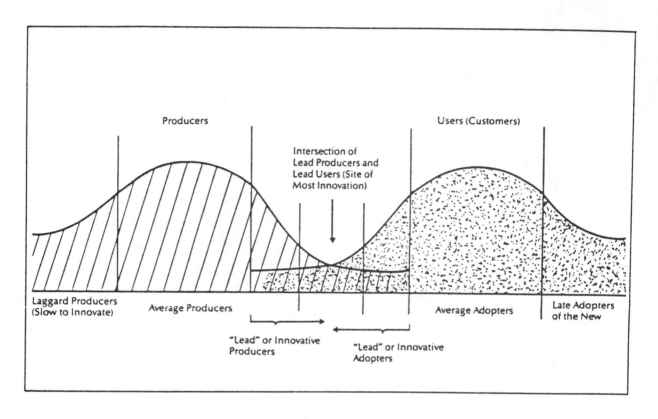

Source: Tom Peters and Nancy Austin, *A Passion for Excellence* (New York: Warner Books, Inc., 1985), p. 186.

Figure 2-6

QUALITY CIRCLE
CODE OF CONDUCT

1. Everyone is equal during meeting/one person, one vote.

2. Don't speak when someone else is speaking.

3. Make comments constructive/be positive/maintain a friendly atmosphere/no sarcasm.

4. Don't discuss individuals by name.

5. Outside of the group, discuss topics but not individual opinions.

6. Strive to attend every meeting.

7. Carry out assignments on schedule.

8. Be an active listener/encourage total participation.

9. Strive for win/win situation.

10. Avoid actions which delay progress/stay on task.

Figure 2-7

QUALITY CIRCLES

STEPS:

1. Brainstorm
2. Order Priorities
3. Define Problem for Each Priority
4. Collect Data on Each Problem
5. Brainstorm Solution to Each Problem
6. Plan to Implement Solution
7. Implement Solution

Figure 2-8

February 29, 1988
Administrative Workshop — Quality Circles
Results of Brainstorming — Issues Facing Administrators
All Administrators Present — David Hilliard, Facilitator

1. Space
2. Coordinate Curriculum
   (i.e., articulate curriculum)
3. Board/Administrator Relationships/Responsibilities
4. Levy
5. Lack of Administrative Support
   (i.e., teachers' perceptions of lack of support for their teaching: staying out of the way versus overt support of teaching)
6. Organization of Educational Council
   (i.e., need to look at all paid to see if there is a better way to organize and to manage and communicate what is being done)
7. Facilities/Heating
8. Administrator Solidarity
9. Additional Dollars/Resources in Labs
   (i.e., personnel and equipment)
10. Standardized Testing/Competency Testing
    (i.e., CAT does not measure curriculum)
11. Community Anger
    (i.e., comment by Sue Gross that community is angry with all in the system)
12. Specific Curriculum for Computer
13. Greater Staff Involvement in Computer Planning
    (i.e., equity in implementation of computer education plan)
14. Cooperative Work Environment
    (i.e., solidarity issue)
15. Unequal Application of Rules/Contract/Guidelines
    (i.e., granting of personal days)
16. Elementary Schools Schedule for Integrated Planning
17. Strategic Planning/Enrollment Figures
18. Plan for Improvement (North Central)
19. Parent Expectations
    (i.e., individual expectations and what an individual can do and has authority to do)
20. Trust
21. Too Much Board Involvement in Decision-Making
22. Use of Teacher Aides
23. Community Involvement/Stake in Schools
24. Administrator Communication
    (i.e., what is communicated, how, where, and to whom)
25. Administrative Style
    (i.e., fine line in participation: teacher wishes and Board decisions)
26. Athletics
    (i.e., what we want and what we provide)
27. Alternative Funding
28. Legal Fees

Figure 2-9

Creech's Laws

General Creech, as he prepared to turn over his command in the fall of 1984, published a set of fifteen "organizational principles." Here they are:

1. *Have a set of overarching principles and philosophies. Have an overall theme and purpose.*

2. *Use goals throughout*—goals at *all* levels, from crews to senior command. There should be darned few of them—in general, paperwork should be kept to a minimum—and they should be clearly achievable—i.e., most people should end up as winners.

3. *Measure productivity at several levels*. But "don't strangle in paperwork." Also: "Micro-information should not be used to micromanage [that is, it should be used primarily to spur peer-versus-peer competition]." All information should be "oriented to the product"—i.e., the aircraft sortie.

4. *Create leaders at many levels.* With this goes a plea to "get leaders [e.g., dedicated crew chiefs] where the action is. Staff supports the line. Not vice versa."

5. *Match authority and responsibility and instill a sense of responsibility.* "Ninety-nine percent will accept responsibility if authority goes with it," and authority should always be product (i.e., aircraft)-oriented, not function-oriented. "I'm not wild about accepting responsibility without authority," says the general. "Why should my people be?"

6. *Set up internal competition and comparison where feasible.* "Reward success" is the key corollary. The resultant pressure is high: "Nobody wants to report that his unit is last, month after month."

7. *Create a climate of pride.* "Instill individual dignity. Provide challenge and opportunity to each. Intangibles matter."

8. *Create a climate of professionalism.* "Esprit is the critical measure."

9. *Educate, educate, educate.* By means, first and foremost, of *regular* feedback.

10. *Communicate, communicate, communicate.* Do *not* depend on the formal hierarchy; skip down several levels—regularly.

11. *Create organizational discipline and loyalty.* This is vital, but will inevitably "stifle initiative." Hence, specific devices must be in place to lead people to disregard the system and reward initiative.

12. *Provide everyone with a stake in the outcome.* Make each job meaningful. Reward good performance (lavishly) in all areas.

13. *Make it better.* Create a sense of individual and organizational worth. Create an "optimistic organization." Provide a climate for continuous change. Above all: "The leader is not just a scorekeeper and steward. He is responsible for creating something new and better."

14. *Make it happen:* "Vigorous leadership at all levels is the key." The leader is at once responsible for creating "the dynamic spark" and simultaneously "working the details" that make it happen.

15. *Make it last.*

Source: Tom Peters and Nancy Austin, *A Passion for Excellence* (New York: Warner Books, Inc., 1985), pp. 281-282.

Figure 2-10

COMPONENTS OF EFFECTIVE SCHOOLS

1. *Classroom Characteristics and Practices*
   1.1 Instruction is guided by a course of study or preplanned curriculum.
   1.2 There are high expectations for student learning.
   1.3 Students are carefully oriented to lessons.
   1.4 Instruction is clear and focused.
   1.5 Learning progress is monitored closely.
   1.6 When students don't understand, they are retaught.
   1.7 Class time is used for learning.
   1.8 There are smooth, efficient classroom routines.
   1.9 Instruction groups formed in the classroom fit Instructional needs.
   1.10 Standards for classroom behavior are explicit.
   1.11 Personal interactions between teachers and students are positive.
   1.12 Incentives and rewards for students are used to promote excellence.

2. *School Characteristics and Practices*
   2.1 Everyone emphasizes the importance of learning.
   2.2 Strong leadership guides the instructional program.
   2.3 The curriculum is based on clear goals and objectives.
   2.4 Students are grouped to promote effective instruction.
   2.5 School time is used for learning.
   2.6 Learning progress is monitored closely.
   2.7 Discipline is firm and consistent.
   2.8 There are high expectations for quality instruction.
   2.9 Incentives and rewards are used to build strong motivation.
   2.10 Parents are invited to become involved.
   2.11 Teachers and administrators continually strive to improve instructional effectiveness.
   2.12 There are pleasant conditions for learning.

3. *District Characteristics and Practices*
   3.1 High expectations pervade the organization.
   3.2 There are policies and procedures that support excellence in student performance.
   3.3 Student learning is checked regularly.
   3.4 Improvement efforts are monitored and supported.
   3.5 Excellence is recognized and rewarded.
   3.6 Curriculum planning ensures continuity.

Source: *Onward to Excellence: Making Schools More Effective* (Portland, Oregon: Northwest Regional Educational Laboratory, 1984).

Figure 2-11

79

Bexley City Schools

348 South Cassingham Road • Bexley, Ohio 43209 • Phone (614) 231-7611

VOLUME ONE NUMBER TWO | DISTRICT NEWSLETTER | FALL 1986

A BETTER BEXLEY

Helping a superb school system accomplish its potential is the goal of new superintendent, Dr. Patricia Conran. She views working with others as the key to making Bexley schools better.

Efforts are underway to bring about improvements in the quality of education and more productive learning. There are many key players in this effort:

*The Board of Education provides direction to the staff, asks critical questions about plans for change and supports leadership efforts toward making Bexley schools better.

*The Administration work with staff in the change effort, assist staff in school improvement, promote scientific decision-making and problem-solving efforts and provide service and support for instruction. Primary objectives call for using test results to design interventions for more, better and faster learning; and for providing challenging learning activities while being able to say to students, "This is all work you can do."

*Teachers and Support Staff who cause learning to happen. Teachers are there, not merely to teach, but to assure that students learn. An experienced and well-educated staff continue to learn and to grow in the effort of serving students' learning needs better.

*Maintenance, Custodial and Secretarial Staff provide a pleasant environment and serve student and staff needs in the interest of learning.

*Parents and Students are respectively partners in the educational process and the benefactors of teaching efforts. You are what has made Bexley a superb system and what will make it better.

As you can see, there are many key players in the improvement effort. With all working together, we can keep our schools strong and make them stronger!

Courtesy of Bexley City Schools.

HERITAGE

LECTURES

CONTINUE

Arts in Education is the topic for the third annual Heritage Lectures, funded initially by the Bexley Education Fund. Art as the window of culture is the unifying theme for the series of four lectures. The final lecture in the series will be held on December 3 at 7:30 p.m. in the high school auditorium. Superintendent Conran will present, "The Dynamics of Changing Space Time."

Social Studies Department Chairperson Ben Trotter assisted in the planning of this and previous series and provides the transition among lectures.

Figure 2-12

Challenges me to do my best.
Sets a good example.
Never divulges a confidence.
Explains the reasons for instructions and procedures.
Helps me polish my thoughts before I present them to others.
Is objective about things.
Lets me make my own decisions.
Cares about me and how I'm doing.
Does not seek the limelight.
Won't let me give up.
Gives personal guidance and direction, especially when I'm learning
    something new.
Is empathetic and understanding.
Is firm but fair.
Keeps a results orientation.
Makes me work out most of my own problems or tough situations,
    but supports me.
Lets me know where I stand.
Listens exceptionally well.
Doesn't put words in my mouth.
Is easy to talk to.
Keeps the promises he or she makes.
Keeps me focused on the goals ahead.
Works as hard or harder than anyone else.
Is humble.
Is proud of those managers he or she has developed.
Gives credit where credit is due.
Practices MBWA.
Never says "I told you so."
Corrects my performance in private.
Never flaunts authority.
Is always straightforward.
Gives at least a second chance.
Maintains an Open Door Policy.
Uses language that is easy to understand.
Lets bygones be bygones.
Inspires loyalty.
Really wants to hear my ideas, and acts on them.
Lets me set my own deadlines.
Celebrates successes.
Is open and honest.
Doesn't hide bad news.

Figure 2-13

Gives me enough time to prepare for discussion.
Is enthusiastic.
Follows through.
Is patient.
Wants me to "stretch" my skills.
Gives me his or her full attention during discussions, won't be distracted.
Has a sense of humor.
Handles disagreements privately.
Reassures me.
Makes me feel confident.
Tells me the "whole story."
Says "we" instead of "I."
Makes hard work worth it.
Can communicate annoyance without running wild.
Is courageous.
Insists on training.
Is a stabilizing influence in a crisis.
Gets everyone involved.
Wants me to be successful.
Is optimistic.
Operates well under pressure, or in a rapidly changing environment.
Has a reputation for competence with his or her peers.
Has a good understanding of the job.
Is tough and tender.
Believes we can do it.
Sets attainable milestones.
Communicates philosophy and values.
Is perceptive—doesn't require that everything be spelled out.
Has a strong sense of urgency.
Preserves the individuality of his or her team members.
Thinks and operates at a level above that expected.
Wants to make the organization the best in the industry.
Is willing to act on intuition; believes feelings are facts.
Empowers us.
Is there when we need him or her.
Enjoys his or her job.
Likes to spend time with us.

Source: Tom Peters and Nancy Austin, *A Passion for Excellence* (New York: Warner Books, Inc., 1985), pp. 422-424.

Figure 2-13 (Cont'd.)

3

Improving
Curriculum and Instruction

This section is artificially divided into curriculum and instruction issues. It is important for the reader to understand, however, that decisions about what to teach, how teach it, and when to teach it are inextricably linked together. The commonality between curriculum and instruction is what we want students to know, to be able to do, and to be capable of experiencing.

Improving Curriculum

What the Reports Have Said and Reforms Are Expecting

Since the inception of this work, the American Association of School Administrators in cooperation with the Far West Laboratory for Education Research and Development has prepared the publication, *Excellence in Our Schools: Making It Happen.* This report written by Spady and Marx focuses on nine of the reform reports from literally hundreds written since 1983. The nine, as shown in Figure 3-1 are *The Paideia Proposal, A Nation at Risk, Making the Grade, Academic Preparation for College, Action for Excellence, A Study of High Schools, A Place Called School, Educating Americans for the 21st Century,* and *High School.* The reports generally concern themselves with both curriculum and instruction matters. For example, *The Paideia Proposal* advocates a liberal education for all students and identifies three teaching methods: didactic instruction, demonstration, and Socratic dialogue. *A Nation at Risk* advocates Five New Basics and advocates raising teaching standards. Both *A Study of High Schools* and *A Place Called School* make recommendations based on time-bound problems with curriculum and instruction. *Educating Americans for the 21st Century* calls for reforms in both curriculum organization and teacher qualifications. The reports have been criticized for their absence of a comprehensive analysis of the body of research and thinking available on effective instruction.

The definition of excellence from *A Nation at Risk* required that the curriculum be organized around clear and visible goals and that instruction be continually targeted toward them.

Goals and Curriculum Priorities

Decisions about goals or learning outcomes are based on what we want students to know and be able to do and be like at the end of a particular phase of schooling; for example, the sixth or eighth or twelfth grade. Curriculum goals are targets toward which instruction is directed. Goals also reflect the values and purposes of the particular instructor, school, or district. There are several key curriculum issues in the reform reports. A "core curriculum" is advocated to provide focus and coherence to the curriculum. But important questions need to be answered to determine this core and, thereby, to identify curriculum priorities. These questions have to do with determining and explicitly stating competencies, capacities, and qualities we want *all* students to demonstrate as schooling outcomes; identifying the experiences necessary for students to have to attain the stated goals; determining if the stated goals and experiences should form the basis of the curriculum; determining the impact of a curriculum designed around these goals and experiences on present curriculum; and finding ways to promote individual excellence within a core curriculum structure. Goals for today and tomorrow should focus on "enabling" knowledge and skills — those which assist students in accessing and using rather than merely acquiring information.

Standards, Expectations, and Requirements

Standards, expectations, and requirements and other aspects of schooling are sometimes referred to as the "hidden" curriculum. These are the rites of passage, those conditions which determine eligibility for academic credit for achievements. Testing and grading are major aspects of standards, expectations, and requirements. In turn, testing and grading to a large extent reflect the "hidden" values of the system since they control student credit, eligibility, opportunity, placement, promotion, graduation, and, frequently, what happens after graduation or dropping out. Once again, there are several key issues that emerge from the reform reports. Performance standards, high achievement expectations, and rigor in course requirements are assumed to be keys to increasing learning. Each of these is different although they are not always differentiated in the reports. Raising performance standards requires improvement in student learning opportunities to reach them if failures and dropouts are not to occur. Standards define the actual performance levels that signify success or failure, that qualify or disqualify, and that make students eligible or ineligible. For example, that students must pass all courses and attain a 1.5 grade-point average can be a standard for eligibility to participate in athletics and other extracurricular activity. High achievement expectations refer to the level of performance hoped for or expected.

The operational components identified by Spady and Marx provide a framework below for discussing curriculum issues:

Course requirements determine what must be taken and passed in order to fulfill graduation requirements. Important questions to be answered deal with the match between expected outcomes and performance standards, the basis of eligibility for progressing through the curriculum, whether tests and standards should qualify and disqualify students from progressing through the curriculum, whether credit and promotion or diplomas should be awarded when clearly defined performance standards are reached, and how standards can be raised without increasing failure and dropout rates.

The Need for Explicit Outcome Goals

Some reform reports put the responsibility on the states to identify those goals of schooling on which there is agreement. Others put this responsibility on the high school — to articulate purposes widely shared by teachers, students, administrators, and parents. Still others advocate a shorter and better defined list of goals in lieu of the present subject area claims.

The Essential Outcome Goals

Adler advocates a one-track system of public education that would aim for mental, moral, and spiritual personal growth or self-improvement; the individual's role as an enfranchised citizen in this republic; and the adult's need to earn a living in one or another occupation by acquiring information and organized knowledge, by developing intellectual skills, and by enlarging understanding. Other report writers identify higher-order thinking skills for reasoning, imagining, analyzing, and synthesizing as the core of high school work and the central goal of schooling to have students wish to be able to teach themselves these skills. Literacy in the English language is listed as the most important objective of elementary and secondary education by another. The report from the Education Commission of the States upgraded the definition of the basics to include nine: reading, writing, speaking and listening, mathematics, science, reasoning, basic employment competencies, economic competencies, and computer literacy competencies. Finally, Boyer stressed that school goals should focus on language mastery, a common learning core, preparation for work and further education, and community and civic service. To accomplish these goals, Boyer advocated a core curriculum consisting of literature, United States history, western civilization, nonwestern civilization, science and the natural world, mathematics, foreign language, the arts, civics, technology, health, and work. Ravitch and Finn, in a controversial study, found students to be lacking in knowledge of literature and history content. Ravitch and Finn suggested focusing curriculum goals in the latter areas. Similarly Hirsch, in another controversial study, advocates cultural literacy. Hirsch has prepared lists of literature titles and advocates knowledge of literature content.

Translating Goals into Curriculum Priorities

Dialogue on the meaning of and relative emphases to be placed on goals identified in the reform reports needs to be extensive at the district and building levels. The core academic structure of high school is said to maintain a "ferocious hold on our thinking" while the inadequacies of the present subject area studies are revealed. Topics newly found to be important may require shifting curriculum emphases. Chief among such shifts will be movement away from acquiring information to movement toward accessing and using information.

Deciding Whose Theory to Follow

Curriculum is grounded in philosophy. Depending on what one determines after reflecting on life experience, a theory will emerge or be acceptable if it has a fit with that experience. We believe professional curriculum activity must be grounded in theory that has emerged from practice. Whose theory to follow is quite another question. Generally practitioners are atheoretical or eclectic in theories applied. Geneva Gay recommends theory either to guide practice or to use as a "perceptual screen through which practice is interpreted and ordered." Geneva Gay referred to four models in curriculum: the academic, the experiential, the technical, and the pragmatic. Exemplars and explanations follow.

The first organized work in the field of curriculum was done by Franklin Bobbitt; his work is identifed as an activity analysis. Bobbitt scientifically analyzed human life to determine specific activities performed. He believed that the curriculum should prepare children for the kind of adult life identified through his activity analysis. Werrett Charters followed in a similar vein with a scientific analysis of adult occupations to be used as a basis in curriculum decisions. These exemplars are sometimes referred to as technical models.

Dewey provided a philosophical framework for curriculum following that which emerged during the scientific or society-centered movement in education. The progressives led the child-centered movement — a shift away from preparation for adult life. Kilpatrick was a leader in this type of curriculum which fits the experiential model. Children's interests and needs, or life in the present, became the focus. With the shift, movement was away from a preplanned curriculum to one that demanded the involvement of children in the planning. By the end of the 1950s, reversals again occurred as debates took place about the value of instruction in the traditional disciplines and practical knowledge.

Also by mid-twentieth century, the central issues in curriculum theory had been identified. At this time in 1950, Ralph Tyler published a course syllabus. Tyler's theorizing can be characterized as an academic model. Tyler, an octogenarian, is still active in the field and his rationale serves as a foundation for much curriculum practice. Practical considerations in Tyler's rationale are: 1) educational purposes, 2) educational experiences to attain purposes, 3) organization of educational experiences, and 4) determining whether purposes are attained. Hilda Taba's work also fits the academic model. For both Tyler and Taba, identifying objectives is central to the curriculum task.

Underlying the prescriptions of various authors in the field is the scientific or philosophical view of curriculum. George Beauchamp preferred the scientific notion which stressed technical terminology, analysis and classification of knowledge, and predictive research to increase generalizations, or laws. Consistent with this notion is the systems approach to thinking about curriculum. Terms such as input, output, and feedback are common in systems approaches. Because Beauchamp stressed the subject-centered curriculum, he fits the academic model. On the other hand, B. Othanel Smith stressed the role of philosophy in curriculum theory: formulating and justifying educational purposes, selecting and organizing knowledge, and dealing with language used.

Persons like McDonald, Walker, and Kirst acknowledged the political nature of curriculum decisions and fit a pragmatic model. This curriculum is localized for a particular school context and recognizes the influence of individuals, groups, and agencies and the interplay of values, interests, demands, and power of special interest groups.

Models generated by curriculum writers can be useful in helping us see components and relationships among components. Figure 3-2 shows a model for thinking about schooling by Broudy, Smith, and Burnett. A very different model was developed by George Beauchamp. Beauchamp's diagram is shown in Figure 3-3. The schema developed by Broudy, Smith, and Burnett shows curriculum as a part of a total system of schooling and modes of teaching are individual as part of the components. Though the authors say modes of teaching are not strictly speaking part of the curriculum, they cannot be ignored. The schema of schooling developed by Beauchamp includes "all activities essential to the purposeful maintenance and operation of schools." Categories are curriculum, instruction, and evaluation. Beauchamp intended that the interaction of the systems portray the continuity among curriculum, instruction, and evaluation.

Definitions of curriculum reveal the orientation of the particular theorist. For example, for Mauritz Johnson curriculum is a structured series of intended learning outcomes (i.e., intentions rather than occurrences). For those who use the term "hidden" curriculum, the focus is on the occurrence.

The degree of structure or allowance for flexibility reveals basic philosophical underpinings. For example, for Beauchamp the curriculum is a document. The document should prescribe what is taught for groups for whom it has been written.

Researching Recommendations

Today we are fortunate to have a body of research on effective practices. Unfortunately, there are still too many debates that detract from the credibility of what we do in education.

There are many sources for researching recommendations. When reading a theory or thinking in the field of curriculum, one can apply criteria to judge whether the research itself is sound. Beyond that, one can look to applications in practice, being careful to judge the conditions under which the research was put into practice.

In some cases, projects are funded and then nationally validated after implementation occurs. In other cases, such as effective schools research, the interventions can be designed and judged for their effectiveness. Different schools which attempt the same effective school practice can compare notes on implementation strategies and outcomes. Professional journals regularly research various recommendations in the field. And, of course, ERIC and other clearinghouses keep current data on a broad range of recommendations.

Deciding the Organization for Curriculum

We have already noted early curriculum content arrangements according to activities and objectives. The focus of activities changed from the 1920s to the 1950s, from society-centered to child-centered, from more to less structured.

Following the publication of Bruner's, *The Process of Education*, in the late 1950s, the spiral curriculum and the structure of the discipline regained prominence.

Another swing occurred as the romantics took hold in the 1960s and 1970s and stressed the importance of relevance. Authors such as Kozol, Holt, and Postman thought the curriculum should be less structured. Simultaneously the accountability movement was developing and continues with fervor into the 1980s.

Curriculum writers in the 1980s have received much guidance in organizing curriculum as a result of reform reports. One set of recommendations is found in the College Board's, *Academic Preparation for College: What Students Need to Know and Be Able to Do*. The "Green Book," as it is called, recommends specific competencies and spells out objectives of the academic subjects. Following from this lead, states began generating competencies in the form of statements. Such statements generally took the form of what students should know and be able to do when leaving school at some level.

Glatthorn simplifies the mystery in curriculum writing with his model of the four curriculums shown in Figure 3-4. First the discipline or subject is divided into basic and enrichment objectives. Basic are those objectives that all, or all except the bottom 10%, should learn. The enrichment objectives are left, nice but not essential. Next the curriculum is divided as either structured or nonstructured. Structured objectives are thought to be best learned when they are carefully planned, specifically taught, and carefully measured. Nonstructured require less specificity. Within the four-part division, there are four types of curriculum: Mastery, Organic, Team-planned, and Student-determined. Mastery curriculum is essential for all and carefully structural. Mastery curriculum objections are critical objectives, carefully sequenced and articulated — those that permit learning at the next higher level. They require explicit teaching, probably require a text, and can be qualified and measured. The Organic curriculum, on the other, hand, does not require highly structured organization, focused teaching, and careful measuring. Affective outcomes are Organic and are nurtured by a classroom culture. Other Organic outcomes may be nurtured through instuctional reinforcement. For example, curiosity in science teaching might be consciously nurtured by higher level thought questions. The Team-planned curriculum includes enrichment as opposed to basic content, and it requires careful structuring. The Student-determined curriculum is unstructured enrichment — the emerging interests of students.

There are alternative ways to look at organization:

1. *Bottom-up or top-down.* The bottom-up approach is illustrated by the manner in which Hilda Taba organized individuals to develop units in social studies. The basic unit in the bottom-up approach is the individual class. Gradually a framework is built to include all levels and subjects. At the extreme is the top-down approach. Beauchamp offers an example where all proceeds from a framework at the top. In the latter, goals and objectives are decided first and then allocated to the various subject fields.

2. *Fusion to separate subjects.* We have focused much on separate subjects as a way to organize the curriculum. This organization is popular because it is efficient and requires less planning than less-defined areas. At the extreme is fusion. Stratemeyer's curriculum around problems of living is an example of fusion where subjects completely lose their identity. Various terms along the continuum of choices from separate subjects to fusion include: coordinated, correlated, interdisciplinary, and core curriculums. In a coordinated curriculum, activities of two or more subjects are orchestrated so that common learnings occur across the subjects. In a correlated curriculum, activities in one subject may be used to teach concepts or expand content in another subject, so that relationships between or among the subjects are understood. In an interdisciplinary curriculum, a team of two or more teachers may plan together and merge the content of two or more subjects, such as in the humanities where social studies, literature, and fine arts may be taught as a unit. In the core curriculum (unlike the manner in which the reform writers of today use the term to refer to a common curriculum), a theme or a subject area forms the basis for all other curriculum. Communications, social studies, or other content could be selected. For example, the author worked in schools

where MACOS, *Man a Course of Study*, served as the basis of a core curriculum for high school students.

Curriculum Mapping

Curriculum mapping is a term popularized as a process to identify gaps and overlaps in the curriculum. It assumes that for each of the subject areas, goals and subgoals have been identified and organized in a chart similar to that shown in Figure 3-5. Subject areas are identified as primarily responsible for or contributing to each of the goals and subgoals. If there are gaps when the above process is completed, additional mapping is recommended. Glatthorn names four alternative choices to accomplish the goal: through the Organic curriculum (day-to-day teacher-student interactions), guidance program, activity program, or other elements of the organization that are specifically named. The determinations are mapped in a form similar to Figure 3-6. Such a document is intended as a road map for school improvement and for improving a field of study.

Eliminating the Gaps and Overlaps

It is important to structure and sequence (and teach!) the curriculum in a way that will allow for productive movement through it. The elementary curriculum should provide an adequate stepping-stone to high school and high school must be more than a repetition of elementary work. Nonessential and peripheral courses must be given less emphasis than core academic subjects. The curriculum mapping process described above is ideal for identifying gaps and overlaps. It is only one process that can be used. It is a bottom-up approach. A top-down approach can be equally useful.

Articulating Within and Across Grade Levels

Curriculum mapping is a useful way to do the articulation task. Figure 3-7 illustrates a scope and sequence for mathematics in a separate subjects curriculum. For the curriculum shown, goals are then identified. The last step in the process is to articulate the scope and sequence in mathematics by strand or concept for all grade levels. Figure 3-8 illustrates the scope and sequence for sets, logical reasoning, and patterns in, K-8. There are many alternative forms of presenting a scope and sequence. One popular format is a grid showing objectives down and grade levels across the page with Introduce (I), Develop (D), Master (M), or Reinforce (R) being specified at particular grade levels. Figure 3-9 illustrates the use of such a grid format.

The illustrations above are an example of vertical articulation in one subject area. For complete articulation, a similar process would occur in each subject area. While vertical articulation in each area is being achieved, horizontal articulation also requires attention. Horizontal articulation is of two types: across subjects and across grade levels.

Working with Committees

Leading a group to reach consensus is probably the goal of most curriculum efforts. Success in the process assumes a clear charge, an identified product and time lines, adequate resources to accomplish the task, and a skillful facilitator. The reward of doing curriculum in a manner that generates broad-based involvement and support is that it will be more likely implemented or implemented as intended.

Before a committee is formed, basic information is needed:

1. Who will comprise the committee and what are strengths and weaknesses of the committee as a whole? A basic determination is the level of expertise to get the job done.

2. What resources in terms of time, materials, access to experts, and money are available for the committee work?

3. How will the curriculum provide for all in the school or district?

4. What is expected as a product; what will this look like; and how detailed will it be?

5. What teaching and testing materials will be used?

6. How will the curriculum be evaluated?

Committees may be formed on various subject areas according to a regular cycle, — e.g. five years — or they may be formed to respond to the results of a needs assessment process or plan for improvement. Results of standardized achievement tests may also signal the need to form a curriculum committee.

In writing curriculum, the focus is on what should be taught. Committee members may broaden their horizons before attempting to determine what should be taught. There are several ways to do this: review the existing curriculum, survey strengths and weaknesses of existing curricula, read the research, talk with experts by going out or having them in, visit other schools, and find out what professional organizations are recommending.

Drafting the document is the next step. Figure 3-10 illustrates partial contents common to curriculum guides. Once the committee drafts a document, it can be reviewed by a subject matter specialist, circulated to staff, and changed based on feedback. Those analyzing the document will see that objectives accomplish the scope and sequence, that all writing is clear, that objectives are comprehensive, and that they are at the appropriate level of difficulty.

Selecting Materials

The importance of matching materials, or the tools of instruction to what is to be learned has generally been overlooked. Materials that will bring about more active participation by students in the learning process are in demand.

More than likely, districts will need to take a look at their textbook selection process and procedures and supplement textbooks with identified supplemental, or resource, materials.

The report, *A Nation at Risk,* urged that "New instructional materials should reflect the most current applications of technology in appropriate curriculum areas, the best scholarship in each discipline, and research in learning and teaching." While not wanting to advocate one set of materials over another, the new Addison-Wesley mathematics materials can be cited as an example of newly published materials where effective instruction techniques are incorporated. Publishers should be expected to demonstrate the effectiveness of their materials. Selection should be demanding with texts being evaluated for their ability to present material with rigor, challenge, and clarity. Science materials should incorporate scientific and technical knowledge and be oriented toward practical issues. Boyer recommends that key questions in selecting materials and computer hardware should be asked and answered satisfactorily. "Why is this purchase being made? What educational objectives will be served? Is available software as good as the equipment? Which students will use the new equipment, when, and why?"

Evaluating the Curriculum

There are any number of ways to evaluate curriculum. Basic to deciding on an evaluation process is knowing what uses are to be made of the results. For example, Popham advocates knowing in advance if decision-makers intend to take action based on the results of evaluation. By way of contrast, Popham advocates avoiding evaluation as ritual, doing it because it is essentially praiseworthy, and evaluation for interest, merely to see if one or more of the elements were thought-provoking.

The evaluator needs to know who influences curriculum decisions and what values and perspectives will be used in evaluating the program. The evaluator will also need to know what is germane to the evaluation. For example, if the evaluation is formative, information on implementation is crucial. Instructional materials, lesson plans, interviews, and classroom observations can be used to analyze implementation. If the evaluation is summative, to be used to determine continuance or termination, information on program effects is crucial. The latter might include cognitive and affective pupil behaviors. Cognitive gains can be measured by criterion-referenced and norm-referenced tests. The skills to be tested then need to be determined; for example, if the goal of a program was to improve communication skills, knowledge and skills and various ways to measure growth in these should be identified. Unanticipated results can also be secured from students in the form of surveys. It is important to note that it is sufficient to use measures that yield group data for program evaluation; individual data are not needed. What is important is seeking reliable information and distinguishing what is relevant information. One way to obtain information is to wander around

— look and listen. If interviews are to be used, it is important to know when individuals or groups will be included. Finally, the nitty-gritty of determining access, protection of confidentiality, and other factors need to be thought and worked through before beginning.

Once data collection samples, instrumentation, and procedures have been identified, the next steps are data collection and analysis. The evaluator will collect data that address the values. Finally, findings are presented in a way that addresses the charge. For example, the cost and opportunity cost of the program can be presented. What benefits are derived from the program and what benefits are given up by continuing the program? An evaluation plan can be presented to the board in advance to determine reactions and modify where appropriate. Interim feedback can also be given to assist in shaping the evaluation.

Much of the above information is summarized in Figure 3-11, showing Bonnet's five phases in evaluation, or purposeful inquiry. A more elaborate system is shown in Figure 3-12. The latter figure illustrates the use of Stufflebeam's CIPP model. CIPP (Context, Input, Process, Product) is a comprehensive process to delineate, obtain, and provide useful information for judging decision alternatives. Stufflebeam identified four major types of evaluation: 1) context evaluation to feed planning decisions, 2) input evaluation to feed programming decisions, 3) process evaluation to feed implementing decisions, and 4) product evaluation to feed recycling decisions. Context evaluation attempts to determine a rationale for objectives by assessing the environments, needs, and problems that prevent the needs from being met. Input evaluation assesses the capabilities for implementation and identifies strategies for achieving the objectives and designs for implementing the strategies. Process evaluation provides feedback to the implementers, helps detect faults, and makes corrections. Finally, as discussed above, product evaluation assesses effects of educational programs. In the context of Stufflebeam's model, Webster has defined necessary steps in program evaluation as shown in Figure 3-13.

Most evaluation models are written to be comprehensive. They can be designed to be accomplished in six months or less to ten years or more.

Improving Instruction

The Superintendent as the Teacher of Principals

First and foremost, the superintendent can be a model for effective use of time. In this indirect way, and then in more direct ways, the superintendent teaches the importance of time. Whether the superintendent advocates a longer school year or a longer school day or simply more effective use of the time already allocated are key issues. The latter should certainly be the first to be addressed. Careful use of time available for learning has been shown to have important benefits. The superintendent, as teacher of principals, can be instrumental in helping principals develop skills that will enable them to obtain more productive use of instructional time. The superintendent needs to know the research and to encourage administrators and teachers to operate from a research base. For example, in determining time standards, the recommendations of Goodlad can provide a basis for determining allocations. In *A Place Called School*, Goodlad recommends the following allocations: 18% in each of the areas of literature and language and of math and science; 15% each in the areas of social studies and society, the arts and vocational education, and career preparation; 10% individual choice. Beyond the time allocated for learning, time on task is an important variable in instruction and productive learning. Here again, the superintendent must know the research and encourage learning and application by principals and teachers. For example, the superintendent will stress the importance of having a clearly stated objective or performance expectation in the instructional model; the importance of having the instruction and assessment aligned to the stated objective; the importance of assuring that the student has the necessary prerequisite knowledge and skills and that the student is motivated; the importance of assuring that the student doesn't already know what is to be taught. This takes us back to the importance of organizing and managing the instruction tasks, areas where the superintendent can be a teacher of principals, to maximize what is commonly referred to as "academic learning time." In other ways, by school organization and the structuring of instructional time, the superintendent communicates values to principals and others on the staff. Permitting tracking or advocating a common curriculum, using age grading or skills groups, and determining how long and how often particular groups of students will work with particular teachers on particular learning goals or curriculum components foster or hinder instructional effectiveness.

Does the superintendent model team management as a way of encouraging team concepts at the building level? The management team can reduce isolation, enhance professional communication and advancement, and utilize time and resources more effectively, and promote peer teaching. The superintendent can be a teacher of principals so that they can help teachers derive these same benefits in teaming for instruction.

Knowing Individual Strengths and Weaknesses

There are various ways to judge individual strengths and weaknesses. The most direct means is to ask people. Responses may be more or less structured. For example, Figure 3-14 shows an appraisal instrument for administrators and supervisors. The instrument is comprehensive and assumes that the individual does a self-assessment to determine strengths and weaknesses. A more personalized format uses the Redfern model as a basis. Working from a comprehensive set of criteria, the evaluatee selects a limited number of areas of focus and develops Action Plans to give specific attention to the identified areas. The goal areas and Action Plans are finalized in conference with the evaluator. Then the evaluatee sets to work detailing and implementing Action Plans. A set of sample Action Plans is shown in Figure 3-15. An alternative model for teacher assessment is shown in Figure 3-16. Input into the evaluation by the evaluatee is assumed. For this evaluation there is a separate conferencing form for each objective to show criteria for judging the objective. See Figure 3-17 for criteria for objective I.A. regarding instructional management.

All of the above examples are district-developed means to assess individual strengths and weaknesses. In addition, there are many commercial systems. For example, the Teacher and Administrator Perceiver Interviews have been developed by SRI, Selection Research Institute. SRI trains interviewers to develop inter-rater reliability in the interview process. The Perceiver Interviews identify strengths and limitations of management personnel and teachers. The follow-up Professional Development Interview and Management Action Profile facilitate understanding and use of the Perceiver Interview information and a personalized development plan. Figure 3-18 shows the areas judged by responses to questions asked in SRI Perceiver and Professional Development Interviews.

Still other means are useful for judging the strengths and weaknesses of the group. For example, the Illinois Department of Education required that a seniority listing of teachers be prepared on an annual basis. The author, in preparing the first listing, reviewed the transcripts of each teacher and listed credit hours by subject area. The result was a visual picture of strengths and weaknesses by subject matter preparation for each teacher and the teaching staff as a whole. Similar compilations can be done for areas of expertise, personalities, and management styles or other categories to determine strengths and weaknesses.

Observing Accurately and Giving Helpful Feedback on Performance

Once again, the superintendent has the opportunity to be a teacher of principals. Accurate observation assumes that there are criteria for observing. Certainly the items in an evaluation instrument and job description can be useful in providing criteria by which to observe and judge performance. As a basis for observing and giving feedback, developing a common language is important. Once the language is shared, it can be applied to the criteria for observing.

Guided practice in observing and giving feedback is the best way to improve skills. The use of script taping, or taking anecdotal notes, audio, and video taping are all means to record the observation. Criteria are then applied in analyzing the observation and labeling and categorizing for feedback. Details on these steps are given below.

Once there is a trained cadre who have observation and feedback skills, individuals can practice peer coaching to help others and to improve their own skills.

Feedback should be close to the observation. It should be specific.

Depending on the model being used, there may be a variety of conferences which may be selected. These may range from giving only positive feedback to delineating the steps for termination. The latter process is not detailed here since states have their own requirements. The most important aspect of the remediation and termination processes is to give specific feedback on performance and to indicate specific improvements required.

Working with an Instructional Model

The importance of working with an instructional model cannot be overemphasized. While the focus here is on strengthening the teacher's instructional skills, the importance of enhancing teacher subject matter knowledge is not intended to be overlooked. For purposes of illustration, we shall be using the Madeline Hunter Instructional Model. The first benefit to be derived is that a common language is learned across schools. This, in itself, is a boon to talking about instruction and the principles of learning. The reform reports focus on the improvement of instruction so that conceptual/ thinking abilities can be taught in combination with skills and facts. Therefore, having a common vocabulary is important. Active participation by students in the learning process can be stimulated if all concerned with the process can share common understandings in the discussion.

Purposeful variety in teaching is urged. The effort should be to engage students actively in learning by applying methods appropriate to each part of the curriculum. For example, Adler advocates didactic instruction, or lectures and responses, textbooks, and other instructional aids to enhance student acquisition of organized knowledge; coaching, exercises, and supervised practice to enhance intellectual skills; and Socratic questioning and active participation to enlarge student understanding of ideas and values.

Similarly, Goodlad calls for teachers to be better able to teach in different ways to accomplish different purposes. Goodlad advocates applying Mastery Learning principles to the tasks of varying the medium of instruction used, student groups, diagnosing student problems, giving clear instructions, giving positive and helpful feedback, using time efficiently, providing personal attention to students, getting and keeping students engaged in the learning, and teaching higher-order thinking skills.

Important in all of this is that, while students are being met at their challenge level, every minute of every day teachers ideally will be able to say, "This is all work you can do." That is, instruction must be keyed to students' present performance levels as well as to the stages of their intellectual development.

Knowing and Applying Principles of Learning

The Madeline Hunter Instructional Model has been selected for purposes of illustration of learning principles. Figure 3-19 lists the principles of motivation, reinforcement, retention, and transfer, as well as other important aspects of effective educational instruction that motivate students to learn.

Six key variables in motivation are:

1. *Feeling tone.* Pleasant feeling tone increases motivation and may be created by showing respect and liking for students. Unpleasant feeling tone demotivates and may be created by intimidating or otherwise showing lack of respect for students.

2. *Rewards: intrinsic-extrinsic.* The goal should be toward internal, or intrinsic, motivation and away from extrinsic, or external, motivation. Learning or doing can be its own reward.

3. *Interest.* Interest is related to self or novelty. Using students' names or having students be the teacher or find teachers' errors adds interest.

4. *Level of concern — raising and lowering the level of anxiety to create sufficient tension for learning.* Activities and verbal or nonverbal signals can be used to increase or reduce tension. Some tension is required to facilitate learning. Too much tension will impede learning. Announcement of a test can raise concern; news that it is open book may lower concern.

5. *Knowledge of results.* Students need to know what they are doing specifically that is good and correct.

6. *Success.* Providing students with work at the correct level of difficulty and providing reinforcement for correct work ensures success.

The six variables above can be controlled in teaching and they affect learning. Important variables in reinforcement are:

1. *Positive — anything desired or needed by the learner.* It will strengthen the response it follows and make the response more likely to occur. The reinforcer must follow the action immediately. It is more effective if the desired behavior is praised.

2. *Negative — anything unpleasant or not desired by the learner.* A negative reinforcer weakens the response it immediately follows. Taking away a recess may be a negative reinforcer. A teacher's unexpected silence or stare can be a negative reinforcer.

3. *Extinction.* Witholding reinforcement can result in extinction — nothing happens.

4. *Schedule of reinforcement.* A regular schedule reinforces a response every time it occurs. An intermittent schedule develops resistance to forgetting.

Five generalizations about retention include:

1. *Meaning.* We remember what is meaningful better than if it isn't. For example, a sentence will be easier to remember than a group of nonsense words.

2. *Feeling tone.* Feeling tone is related to memory. We tend to remember what is pleasant or unpleasant. Pleasant feeling tone motivates learning.

3. *Transfer — positive and negative.* When past learnings facilitate present learning, transfer is positive. When past learning inhibits present learning, transfer is negative.

4. *Practice — massed and distributed.* Concentrated practice is massed. Massed practice may be used in learning something new or reviewing particularly troublesome spots in the learning. Distributed practice is revisiting the learning on occasion.

5. *Adequate level — degree of original learning.* Learning something well the first time influences retention.

Four variables in transfer are:

1. *Similarities.* Transfer is generated by the similarity of the situation in which something is learned and the situation to which that learning may transfer.

2. *Association.* Transfer of learning is generated by an association of two learnings.

3. *Degree of original learning.* Degree of transfer is related to the degree of effectiveness of the original learning.

4. *Critical attributes — essential elements.* Transfer is generated by the identification of essential and unvarying elements which signal that a past learning has relevance and is applicable to a present situation.

Figure 3-19 was presented to show all the elements in effective instruction. The focus here has been limited to the principles of learning.

Finding Ways That Work Best for Each Student

Many automatically assume that finding ways that work best requires groupings, either homogeneously, according to similarities, or heterogeneously, without regard to similarities, except perhaps age and grade levels.

Originally students were taught without being grouped in particular classes. This began to change in the 1800s with the introduction of the graded McGuffy readers. Since then educators have become increasingly aware of individual differences in learning rates. The race was on to meet individual needs.

Several ways to group students have been tried in an effort to find what works best. Twelve such grouping practices are shown in Figure 3-20. In nongraded grouping the focus is generally on having students continually progress through a sequence of objectives. Multigrade or multiage grouping generally occurs in special education classes or in schools with shifting enrollment patterns. When a conscious choice, multigrade or multiage groupings offer the students opportunities for peer assistance. Team learning is known more popularly today as cooperative, where groups of students pursue tasks and share responsibility for team learning. Interest grouping is based on options geared to increasing relevance. The Trump plan is popular as the large group, small group, and independent study classroom clusters. Self-contained classroom implies that students are assigned to one classroom with a teacher. In departmentalization, students or teachers move for each subject. The dual-progress plan allows for splitting the time in the school day to pursue academic subjects and interests; many vocational educational programs are organized on this basis. In contract grouping, students have agreed to pursue certain learnings. Minicourses are short courses in the curriculum. In student-formulated curriculum, students devise their own curriculum. Grouping among schools creates alternative schools and choice.

A second way to approach finding ways that work best is to look at the arguments for and against structure. The so-called Bloom's taxonomies launched the objectives' movements. Teaching for behavioral objectives was popularized when departments of education and grant institutions increased their demands to have applications written in such terms. The underlying assumption is an empiricist argument; that is, the primary purpose of schooling is to change the behavior of students in specific predetermined ways. One can think of any number of worthwhile curriculum-related activities that do not meet pre-determined objectives: taking field trips, acting out dramas, preparing a school newspaper, and others. It is assumed, for purposes of discussion, that teaching without objectives is according to criteria and activities are worthwhile.

Teaching for Independence

Special note is made of teaching for independence. During effective instruction training, it was pointed out to the author that we give students choices and assume they will manifest appropriate independent behaviors. The point to be made is that we must move from more structure to less structure and from fewer to more choices gradually. Benchmarks need to be established along the way. What are the rules? The expectations? What knowledge and skills are required for the desired behaviors to occur? Do students have these learnings to facilitate appropriate choices? Successful independent functioning? Analyzing the situation and the particular strengths and weaknesses of individuals in a class — backing up and teaching or waiting — can assure successful independent functioning.

Teaching for Thinking

In recent years, the teaching of thinking has received much lip service. More recently individuals like Arthur Costa and Robert Marzano have done serious work in the area that enables teachers to integrate thinking skills into their teaching.

We are recognizing that helping students become more effective thinkers is critical to becoming effective citizens. In this information age, more and more citizens will be working in jobs that move information. Because we live in a high tech information age, knowledge increases rapidly. Thinking skills are important for acquiring, accessing, and using information that is ever-expanding.

There are a variety of skills that have been identified by Costa, et al., in *Developing Minds* (Association for Supervision and Curriculum Development) as effective for various purposes:

1. *Directive strategies to help students master discrete cognitive skills.* With the use of directive strategies, students are expected to accurately imitate skills taught.

2. *Mediative strategies to teach students problem solving, decision making, and inductive reasoning.* These strategies are intended to enable different points of view in controversial issues, respect opinions and beliefs of others, and use alternative problem-solving processes. The strategies help students act on and transform information, skills, and concepts into new meanings and practice.

3. *Generative strategies to teach students creative thinking.* Generative strategies help students create new knowledge and develop new and insightful ways to approach and solve problems.

4. *Collaborative strategies for teaching students to share, listen, and cooperate.* Collaborative strategies provide ways to structure student groups to help them cooperatively think, solve problems, accomplish tasks, and to practice and process social skills needed for success.

ASCD has assumed leadership in the area of thinking. Among its many publications, *Dimensions of Thinking: A Framework for Curriculum and Instruction* assists the practitioner to focus in thinking categories and processes. In *Dimensions*, Marzano, et al., separate critical and creative thinking from thinking processes. Marzano considers use of the terms "critical," or rational thinking, and "creative," or inventive thinking, to imply judgments are in relationship to an ideal — thinking more or less critically, more or less creatively. Rather than a difference in kind, the difference is in degree and emphasis. "Critical thinkers generate ways to test assertions; creative thinkers examine newly generated thoughts to assess their validity and utility." (*Dimensions*, p. 17.)

Another dimension of thinking is the set of thinking processes, or mental operations. Figure 3-21 shows eight overlapping thinking processes; concept formation, principle formation, comprehension, problem-solving, decision-making, and research. Concept formation is the foundation of knowledge acquisition. Principle formation and comprehension are also directed toward knowledge acquisition and serve as a basis for other processes. Problem-solving, decision-making, research, and composition build on the first three processes to produce and apply knowledge. Oral discourse is used both in knowledge acquisition and production.

Recent research and publication in the area of thinking has facilitated the teaching of thinking. Core thinking skills, as they frequently occur in the thinking processes, have been identified. Core thinking skills are shown in Figure 3-22. Rankin and Hughes have provided explanations for the thinking skills (*Dimensions*). Focusing skills help the learner attend to selected pieces of information and ignore others. Information-gathering skills are the skills used to bring to consciousness the substance or content to be used for cognitive processing. Remembering skills involve information storage and retrieval in and out of long-term memory. Organizing skills are used to impose structure on information, arrange information to be understood or presented more effectively. Analyzing skills assist the learner in taking information apart to examine parts and relationships of existing information. Generating skills require using prior knowledge to go beyond what is given; a scheme is built to hold new and old information together. Integrating skills assists the learner in putting together the parts of a solution, understanding, principle, or composition. Evaluating skills help the learner make judgments about the quality or reasonableness of ideas.

An alternative framework is offered by Art Costa. Drawing on the research of others, Dr. Costa listed a dozen characteristics of intelligent behavior that can be observed. The list is not intended to be complete. The behaviors are believed to indicate thinking abilities.

1. Persistence — persevering when the solution to a problem is not immediately apparent to develop a repertoire of problem-solving skills and the ability to draw on it;
2. Increasing impulsivity — deliberateness;
3. Listening to others — with understanding and empathy;
4. Flexibility in thinking;
5. Metacognition — awareness of our own thinking;
6. Checking for accuracy and precision;
7. Questioning and problem-posing;
8. Drawing on past knowledge and applying it to new situations;
9. Precision of language and thought;
10. Using all the senses;
11. Ingenuity, originality, insightfulness — creativity;
12. Wonderment, inquisitiveness, curiosity, and the enjoyment of problem-solving — a sense of efficacy as a thinker.

Others can be added: a sense of humor and special intelligence (cooperating, reaching consensus, and working as a team). The importance of learning what human beings do when they behave intelligently is that we can help them behave more intelligently. The superintendent can facilitate having students acquire, access, and use information, and behave more intelligently by supporting curriculum and instruction to strengthen thinking processes and teach thinking skills.

Focus on Mastery of Language

Language has emerged as the reform priority. As used by Boyer in the Carnegie report, language covers every form of communication: speaking, reading, writing, listening, analyzing, thinking, the language of mathematics, and the language of the computer. Today and tomorrow language and communication are the central skills students need to be productive citizens.

"Writing to Read" and other programs have been developed to help children focus on the learning of language. In John Martin's "Writing to Read" program, developed for IBM, students move naturally from writing letters to words to sentences. As they write, they learn to read. Technology facilitates the learning process. As students form letters, words, and sentences on the computer, or word processor screen, they are entering the process of writing to read. The latter is only one example of programs developed to assist in the effective teaching of communication skills.

Evaluating Learning

A host of means to evaluate learning exist. These form both scientific and aesthetic evaluation. Scientific are more quantitative measures, whereas aesthetic are more qualitative.

Standardized tests and criterion-referenced tests are instruments used in scientific measurement. What Elliott Eisner refers to as connoisseurship and criticism are acts used in aesthetic evaluation.

Standardized tests, or norm-referenced tests are intended either for group or individual or diagnostic use. CAT and IOWA Tests of Basic Skills are two examples of norm-referenced group tests. Tests designed for group use differ from diagnostic tests primarily in the number of items to test a particular learning.

Aesthetic evaluation can also be adapted for group or individual use. We referred above to the terms of connoisseurship and criticism. Connoisseurship, as used by Eisner, refers to the art of *appreciation*. Take as examples, connoisseurs of wine and food. Connoisseurship is *private* in nature. Eisner used criticism to refer to the art of *disclosure*. By contrast with connoisseurship, criticism is *public* in nature.

Connoisseurship requires expertise in an area of human endeavor. Connoisseurship implies an awareness of qualities, relationships among qualities, and an understanding of the "other states and values against which the present state can be compared and contrasted (Eisner, 1975)." Conclusions of the connoisseur are judgments grounded in reason. The judgments imply a degree of inter-rater (inter-connoisseur, if you will) reliability.

Criticism is aimed at revealing the characteristics and qualities that constitute a human product. The critic provides a "rendering in linguistic terms of what it is he or she has encountered in such a way that others not possessing his level of connoisseurship can also enter the work (Eisner, 1975)." The measure of adequacy of the criticism is its brightness of illumination; that is, the extent to which there are adequate referents in the subject or event subject to criticism. The brightness of illumination, or referential adequacy, determines the validity of the criticism.

The value of aesthetic evaluation is that it permits a rendering of educational phenomena which cannot be measured. Eisner charged: ". . . scientific studies in education are more often defined by the form of research one has learned to use than by the substantive problems one believes to be significant. Becoming familiar with correlation procedures too often leads simply to questions about what one can correlate; the existence of statistically reliable achievement tests too often leads to a conception of achievement that is educationally eviscerated. Our tools, as useful as they might be initially, often become our masters (Eisner, 1975)."

Over time we will most likely become less reliant on quantitative measures to evaluate learning and other human endeavors and human products.

REFERENCES AND RESOURCES

Academic Preparation for College: What Students Need to Know and Be Able to Do. New York, NY: The College Board, 1983.

Adler, Mortimer, *The Paideia Proposal.* New York, NY: McMillan Publishing Co., Inc., 1982.

Beauchamp, George A., *Curriculum Theory* (4th ed.). Itasca, IL: F. E. Peacock Publishers, Inc., 1981.

Bloom, Benjamin S., ed., *Taxonomy of Educational Objectives, Book 1: Cognitive Domain.* New York, NY: Longman, Inc., 1956.

Boyer, Ernest L., *High School.* New York, NY: Harper and Row, Publishers, 1983.

Brandt, Ronald S., ed., *Applied Strategies for Curriculum Evaluation.* Alexandria, VA: Association for Supervision and Curriculum Development, 1981.

——————, *Content of the Curriculum.* Alexandria, VA: Association for Supervision and Curriculum Development, 1988.

Broudy, Harry S., B. Othanel Smith, and Joe R. Burnett, *Democracy and Excellence in American Secondary Education.* Chicago, IL: Rand McNally and Co., 1964.

Costa, Arthur L., *Developing Minds: A Resource Book for Teaching Thinking.* Alexandria, VA: Association for Supervision and Curriculum Development, 1985.

Educational Leadership, December, 1982.

——————, September, 1984.

——————, March, 1985.

——————, May, 1985.

Eisner, Elliot W., "The Perceptive Eye: Toward the Reformation of Educational Evaluation." (Mimeographed.) An unpublished paper presented at the

Annual Meeting of Division B of the American Educational Research Association, Washington, D.C., March, 1975.

English, Fenwick W., ed., *Fundamental Curriculum Decisions*. Alexandria, VA: Association for Supervision and Curriculum Development, 1983.

Foshay, Arthur W., ed., *Considered Action for Curriculum Improvement*. Alexandria, VA: Association for Supervision and Curriculum Development, 1980.

Gardner, John W., *Excellence: Can We Be Equal and Excellent Too?*. New York, NY: Harper and Brothers, Publishers, 1961.

Glatthorn, Allan A., *Curriculum Renewal*. Alexandria, VA: Association for Supervision and Curriculum Development, 1987.

Goodlad, John I., *A Place Called School*. New York, NY: McGraw-Hill Book Company, 1983.

Hirsch, E. D., *Cultural Literacy: What Every American Needs to Know*. Boston, MA: Houghton Mifflin, 1987.

Hunter, Madeline., *Mastery Teaching*. El Segundo, CA: TIP Publications, 1983.

Jones, Beau Fly, *Strategic Teaching and Learning: Cognitive Instruction in the Content Areas*. Alexandria, VA: Association for Supervision and Curriculum Development, 1987.

Marzano, Robert J., et al., *Dimensions of Thinking: A Framework for Curriculum and Instruction*. Alexandria, VA: Association for Supervision and Curriculum Development, 1988.

A Nation at Risk: The Imperative for Educational Reform. Washington, D.C.: The National Commission of Excellence in Education, 1983.

Phi Delta Kappan, June, 1983.

Ravitch, Diane, and Chester E. Finn, Jr., *What Do Our 17-Year-Olds Know? A Report on the First National Assessment of History and Literature*. New York, NY: Harper and Row, Publishers, 1987.

Roberts, Arthur D., and Gordon Cawelti, *Redefining General Education in the American High School*. Alexandria, VA: Association for Supervision and Curriculum Development, 1984.

Rubin, Louis, *Curriculum Handbook*. Boston, MA: Allyn and Bacon, Inc., 1977.

Rutter, M., et al., *Fifteen Thousand Hours: Secondary Schools and Their Effects on Children*. Cambridge, MA: Harvard University Press, 1979.

Sizer, Theodore R., *Horace's Compromise: The Dilemma of the American High School*. Boston, MA: Houghton Mifflin, 1984.

Squires, David A., William G. Huitt, and John K. Segars, *Effective Schools and Classrooms: A Research-Based Perspective*. Alexandria, VA: Association for Supervision and Curriculum Development.

The Nine Reports

• **The Paideia Proposal.** Mortimer Adler's 1982 treatise advocates strengthening America's democratic institutions through a one-track, 12 year system of public schooling dedicated to a thorough general/liberal education for **all** students. Its three primary goals are (1) mental, moral and spiritual growth and improvement; (2) effective enfranchised citizens in a healthy democracy; and (3) the capacity for every adult to earn a living in our advanced industrial economy. These goals would be accomplished by giving every student stimulating opportunities for (1) acquiring information and organized knowledge through didactic instruction and lecturing, (2) developing intellectual skills through demonstration and coaching, and (3) enlarging his/her understanding and appreciation of values and human culture through Socratic dialogue and discussion.

• **A Nation at Risk.** The product of many months of collecting testimony and reviewing documents addressing the quality of education in the United States, this report focuses primarily on the high school years. Its main concerns are adding rigor and raising standards in both teaching and learning. Many consider its emphasis on traditional academic curricula, teacher roles and school structures as a strength. Others view it as a fundamental weakness. The report's recommendations fall into five categories: content, standards and expectations, time, teaching and leadership and fiscal support. Its curriculum recommendations, "The Five New Basics," are identical to those advocated by the Committee of Ten in 1893, but its concerns about textbook evaluation and quality are considered by many to be long overdue.

• **Making the Grade.** This report, produced by the Twentieth Century Fund, focuses on the legitimate and essential role of the federal government in supporting elementary and secondary education. Its task force members included a cross section of distinguished educators. The report also emphasizes the need for English language skills as the key to educational success and full participation in adult society and points out a number of areas in which enlightened federal support is vital.

• **Academic Preparation for College.** This College Board publication is the outgrowth of a multi-year program called "Project EQuality." The purpose of the project was to identify the essential competencies and knowledge required of college entrants. This report reflects consensus views of hundreds of academic specialists, teachers, guidance counselors and admissions officers from all parts of the country. It documents in some detail seven major competencies needed for academic success in college and describes factual knowledge and understanding needed in six major areas of academic study. A significant message included in the report is that high school diplomas are inadequate indicators of preparation for college work: Only documentation of skills and knowledge will suffice.

• **Action for Excellence.** This dynamic report came from a distinguished task force of state governors and major corporation officers who addressed the relationship between a strong national economy and the educational support needed to foster and sustain it. Organized by the Education Commission of the States (ECS), the task force stressed improvements in math, science and technology, and effective school-business cooperation. The report borrows directly from *Academic Preparation for College* in defining an expanded version of "basic skills."

Although its recommendations are often general and directed at state agencies and business leaders, the report does have implications for major changes in typical school operations.

• **A Study of High Schools.** This major study was headed by Theodore R. Sizer, former Dean of Harvard University Graduate School of Education and cosponsored by the National Association of Secondary School Principals (NASSP). Sizer's perspective on needed change in high schools is more "radical" than that found in other reports. He draws attention to the limiting character of the schools' time-bound structure and procedures and the damaging effect on curriculum, teaching and learning that can result. Sizer's book, *Horace's Compromise: The Dilemma of the American High School,* was published by Houghton Mifflin in 1984. Many of the quotes in this publication came from a June, 1983 article by Sizer in *Phi Delta Kappan,* in which he discussed his recommendations.

• **A Place Called School.** Published by McGraw-Hill in 1983, this report culminates John I. Goodlad's multi-year "Study of Schooling," begun in the mid 1970s and published in a long series of technical reports over the past several years. Its many recommendations are based on Goodlad's research in more than 1,000 classrooms and his long experience in working with schools to bring about change. Similar to Sizer's recommendations, Goodlad's reflect deep concern with negative consequences of age-graded, time-structured instructional systems. The Goodlad comments used in this publication have been drawn from both the book and from his article in the April, 1983 issue of *Phi Delta Kappan.*

• **Educating Americans for the 21st Century.** This thorough, well-documented "plan of action for improving mathematics, science, and technology education for all American elementary and secondary students," was produced for the National Science Foundation by the National Science Board Commission on Precollege Education in Mathematics, Science and Technology. Its recommendations naturally reflect curriculum, teaching and improvement strategies in those particular areas. The report's reasoning about curriculum organization and teacher qualifications is sound and can be applied across the board to other instructional policies and procedures.

• **High School.** This Harper and Row publication was released by the Carnegie Foundation for the Advancement of Teaching in September, 1983, following 30 months of work in 15 states. Its author, Ernest L. Boyer, the Foundation's president and former U.S. Commissioner of Education, stressed change that would strengthen teachers and teaching in high schools. Like Sizer and Goodlad, Boyer believes that to operate more effectively, high schools require clearly defined goals. He feels those goals should shape curriculum priorities (i.e., a "core curriculum"), essential student outcomes, and opportunities for teachers to grow professionally. Boyer makes extensive recommendations concerning the recruitment, training and working conditions of teachers. He also emphasizes the crucial need to effectively teach thinking skills through language arts and writing.

NOTE: Quotes from each of these reports are included among operational components from pages 11 through 21 of this publication.

★ ★ ★ ★ ★ ★ ★ ★ ★ ★ ★ ★

Source: William G. Spady and Gary Marx, *Excellence in Our Schools: Making It Happen* (Arlington, VA, American Association of School Administrators and San Francisco: Far West Laboratory for Educational Research and Development, 1984), p. 7.

Figure 3-1

Design for common curriculum in general education (grades 7–12)

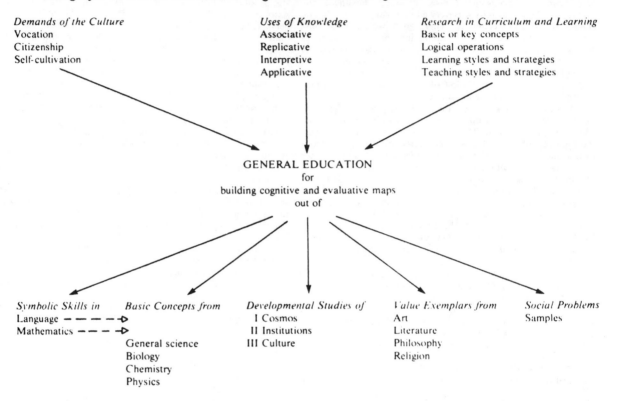

Source: Harry S. Broudy, *The Uses of Schooling* (Reprinted from *The Uses of Schooling* with the permission of the publisher, Routledge, Chapman & Hall, New York, 1988), p. 80.

Figure 3-2 (Cont'd.)

A diagram representing the systems of schooling

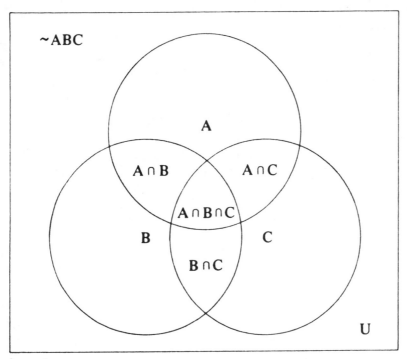

Legend:

U	=	The universe of discourse(the systems of schooling)
~ABC	=	All systems of schooling except systems A,B, & C.
A	=	The curriculum system.
B	=	The instructional system
C	=	The evaluation system.
A ∩ B	=	The intersection of system A and system B.
B ∩ C	=	The intersection of system B and system C.
A ∩ C	=	The intersection of system A and system C.
A ∩ B ∩ C	=	The intersection of system A, system B, and system C.

Source: George A. Beauchamp, *Curriculum Theory*, Fourth Edition (Itasca, IL: F.E. Peacock Publishers, Inc., 1981) p. 144.

Figure 3-3

The Four Curriculums		
	Basic	Enrichment
Structured	MASTERY	TEAM PLANNED
Nonstructured	ORGANIC	STUDENT DETERMINED

Source: Allan A. Glatthorn, *Curriculum Renewal* (Alexandria, Virginia, Association for Supervision and Curriculum Development, 1987), p. 5. Reprinted with permission of the Association for Supervision and Curriculum Development. Copyright (c) by ASCD. All rights reserved.

Figure 3-4

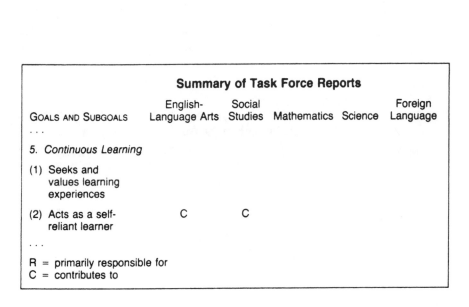

Summary of Task Force Reports

GOALS AND SUBGOALS	English-Language Arts	Social Studies	Mathematics	Science	Foreign Language
. . .					
5. Continuous Learning					
(1) Seeks and values learning experiences					
(2) Acts as a self-reliant learner	C	C			
. . .					

R = primarily responsible for
C = contributes to

Source: Allan A. Glatthorn, *Curriculum Renewal* (Alexandria, Virginia, Association for Supervision and Curriculum Development, 1987), p. 14. Reprinted with permission of the Association for Supervision and Curriculum Development. Copyright (c) by ASCD. All rights reserved.

Figure 3-5

Final Mapping of All Goals and Subgoals				
GOALS AND SUBGOALS	English-Language Arts	Social Studies . . .	Activity Program	Guidance Program
10. Participates in satisfying leisure-time activities	C	C	R	C

Source: Allan A. Glatthorn, *Curriculum Renewal* (Alexandria, Virginia, Association for Supervision and Curriculum Development, 1987), p. 15. Reprinted with permission of the Association for Supervision and Curriculum Development. Copyright (c) by ASCD. All rights reserved.

Figure 3-6

SCOPE AND SEQUENCE FOR MATHEMATICS

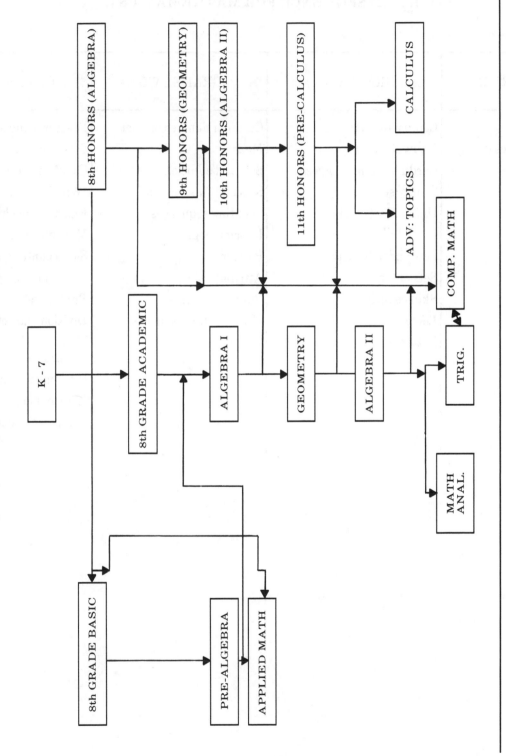

Figure 3-7
111

SCOPE AND SEQUENCE FOR MATHEMATICS (K - 8)

KINDERGARTEN	GRADE ONE	GRADE TWO	GRADE THREE
Concept of sets	Comparing sets	Cardinal number of a set	Fractions and sets
Comparisons of sizes	Equivalent sets	Maze	Sets, numbers, and numerals
Similarities and differences	Cardinal number of a set	Sets and addition	Counting sequences
Patterns	Empty set	Sets and subtraction	"What's My Rule?"
Maze	Union of sets and addition	Counting sequences	Function machine
	Sets and subtraction	Informal logic	Multiplication and sets
	Sets of ten	Patterns	Skip counting sequences
	Skip counting	Attribute pieces	Multiplication patterns
	Logic	Puzzle problems	Product sets
	Patterns	Multiplication and sets	Division and sets
			Union and intersection of sets
			Odd and even numbers
			Informal logic
			Comparing sets

Figure 3-8

112

SCOPE AND SEQUENCE FOR MATHEMATICS (CONT'D.)

GRADE FOUR	GRADE FIVE	GRADE SIX	GRADE SEVEN	GRADE EIGHT
Addition and sets	Sets	Naming sets	Recognizing equal sets	Intersection and union of sets
Muliplication and sets	Logic and sets	Classifying attribute	Recognizing equivalent sets	
Sequences and patterns	Patterns	Logical reasoning	Intersection and union of sets	Concept of replacement set
Divisions and sets	Number line sequences	Patterns	Mathematical symbols	Mathematical symbols
Product sets	Union and intersection of sets	Union and intersection of sets		
Sets of equivalent fractions	Sets of equivalent fractions	Fractions and sets		
Informal reasoning	Rational number sequences	Sets of equivalent fractions		
	Sets of ordered pairs	Repeating decimal sequences		
		Sets of ordered pairs		

Figure 3-8 (Cont'd.)
113

READING   OVERVIEW

	K	1	2	3	4	5	6	7	8
I. Visual Perceptual Development									
The student will be able to									
A. distinguish size, shape, and color	I								
B. label size, shape, and color	I								
C. identify likenesses and differences in letters	I								
D. recognize left/right and top/bottom of a page	I								
E. track without head movement	I								
F. visualize part to whole	I								
G. name capital letters	I								
H. name small letters	I								
I. match capital and small letter pairs	I								
II. Word Attack									
A. Phonetic Analysis									
1. Letters of Alphabet									
The student will be able to									
a. identify capital and small	I	R	R						
b. match capital and small	I	R	R						
c. name vowels	I	R	R						
d. write capital and small letters	I	D							
2. Sounds of Letters									
a. Consonants									
The student will be able to									
1. associate consonant sounds with letters		I	D	R					
2. discriminate consonant sounds in initial position		I	D	R					
3. discriminate consonant sounds in final position		I	D	R					
4. discriminate consonant sounds in medial position		I	D	R					
5. associate consonant cluster sounds with letters		I	D	R					
6. discriminate consonant cluster sounds in initial position		I	D	R					
7. discriminate consonant cluster sounds in final position		I	D	R					
8. discriminate hard and soft c sounds		I	D	R					
9. discriminate hard and soft g sounds		I	D	R					
b. Vowels									
The student will be able to									
1. associate short vowel sounds with letters		I	D	R					
2. associate long vowel sounds with letters		I	D	R					
3. associate "r" controlled vowels with their sounds		I	D	R					
4. associate diphthong sounds with their letters		I	D	M	R				
5. associate digraph sounds with their letters		I	D	R					
6. associate vowel patterns with long vowel sounds		I	D	R					
7. associate schwa sound with letters		I	D	M					

Figure 3-9

R-O-2 READING

	K	1	2	3	4	5	6	7	8
II. Word Attack — Continued									
c. Phonograms									
The student will be able to									
1. read phonograms at grade level	I	D	M	R					
2. recite phonograms at grade level	I	D	M	R					
B. Structural Analysis									
1. Singular and Plural Forms of Words									
The student will be able to									
a. label word forms in which "s" to "es" rules apply	I	D	R						
b. reproduce word forms in which "s" and "es" rules apply	I	D	R	R					
c. label word forms in which "y" to "i" rules apply	I	D	R						
d. reproduce word forms in which "y" to "i" rules apply	I	D	R	R					
e. label word form in which "f" to "v" rules apply	I	D							
f. reproduce word form in which "f" to "v" rules apply	I	D	R						
g. label irregular plural forms	I	D	M						
h. reproduce irregular plural forms	I	D	M						
2. Compound Words									
The student will be able to									
a. identify	I	M	R						
b. reproduce	I	D	M	R					
3. Base Words and Affixes									
a. Endings -ing, -er, -ed									
The student will be able to									
1. identify base words in which no change has been made	I	D	R						
2. identify base words in which final consonant-doubled	I	D	R						
3. identify base words in which final "e" has been dropped	I	D	R						
4. identify base words in which "y" has been changed to "i"	I	D	R						
b. Common Syllables									
The student will be able to									
1. decode words	I	D	M	R					
2. reproduce words	I	D	M	R					
c. Prefixes									
The student will be able to									
1. identify the prefix and the base words	I	I	I	M	R				
2. define the prefix and the base words	I	D	D	D	D	D	D	D	D
d. Suffixes									
The student will be able to									
1. identify the suffix and the base words	I	I	I	M	R				
2. define the suffix and the base words	I	D	D	D	D	D	D	D	D

Figure 3-9 (Cont'd.)

115

R-O-3

READING — OVERVIEW

	K	1	2	3	4	5	6	7	8
II. Word Attack — Continued									
4. Comparative and Superlative Forms									
The student will be able to									
a. name the comparative/superlative form of the base word-regular form		I	D	M					
b. use the appropriate form in a given context-regular form		I	D	M	R				
c. name the comparative/superlative form of the base word-irregular form			I	M	R				
d. use the appropriate form in a given context-irregular form		I	D	M					
5. Contractions									
The student will be able to									
a. identify contractions	I	D							
b. define contractions		I	D	M	R				
c. reproduce contractions			I	D	M	R			
6. Possessives									
The student will be able to									
a. identify and differentiate from contractions			I	D	M	R	R		
b. distinguish between owner and object of ownership			I	D	M	R	R	R	
7. Syllables									
The student will be able to									
a. identify the number of vowel sounds in a word			I	D	M	R	R		
b. divide words into syllables using given rules									
1. v/c/v rule			I	D	M	R	R		
2. v/c/c/v rule			I	D	M	R	R		
3. c/c rule			I	D	M	R	R		
4. c/le rule			I	D	M	R	R		
5. prefix/baseword/suffix rule			I	D	M	R	R		
8. Accents									
The student will be able to									
a. auditorily identify accented syllable in words			I	D	M	R			
b. mark an accented syllable in a given word			I	D	M	R			
c. differentiate between primary and secondary accents in a given word			I	D	M				
III. Comprehension									
A. Literal									
1. Sequence									
The student will be able to									
a. arrange pictures in logical order	I	D							
b. arrange isolated words to form sentences	I	D	D						
c. arrange the events in a story in logical order		I	D	D	M	R	R		
d. arrange the paragraphs in a selection in logical order			I	D	M	R	R		
e. arrange the events in a paragraph in logical order		I	D	D	M	R	R		

Figure 3-9 (Cont'd.)

READING

OVERVIEW

III. Comprehension — Continued

	K	1	2	3	4	5	6	7	8
2. Directions — The student will be able to									
a. follow oral 4-step commands using prepositions	I	D							
b. give simple directions to others	I	D							
c. follow written directions		I	D	D	M	R	R	R	
d. follow stage directions		I	D	M	R				
3. Main Idea — The student will be able to									
a. state the main idea of a story/selection read to the student	I	D	M						
b. state the main idea of a story/selection read by the student			I	D	D	M	R	R	R
c. state the main idea of paragraphs in a story/selection				I	D	D	M	R	R
d. summarize and restate the main idea of material					I	D	D	M	R
4. Details — The student will be able to									
a. answer specific questions about a story with regard to plot, main character, and setting	I	D	D	D	R				
b. categorize details as to their relevancy				I	D	D	M	R	R
c. verify statements by selecting relevant details					I	D	D	M	R
d. correlate specific details to appropriate paragraphs					I	D	D	M	R
5. Context Clues — The student will be able to									
a. Use pictures as context clues	I	D	M						
b. supply a relevant word or phrase to complete a sentence read to the student	I	D	M						
c. supply a relevant word or phrase to complete written sentences		I	D	D	M	R	R	R	R
B. Interpretive — The student will be able to									
1. intepret pictures	I	D	M						
2. choose a title		I	D	M					
3. associate pronoun with its referent		I	D	D	M				
4. identify speaker		I	D	D	M				
5. predict outcomes		I	D	D	M	R	R	R	R
6. draw conclusions		I	D	D	M	R	R	R	R
7. make generalizations				I	D	M	R	R	R
8. interpret figurative language									
a. idioms					I	D	M	R	R
b. similies					I	D	M	R	R
b. metaphors					I	D	M	R	R
d. personification						I	D	M	R
e. euphemism							I	D	M
f. hyperbole								I	M

Figure 3-9 (Cont'd.)

	K	1	2	3	4	5	6	7	8
III. Comprehension — Continued									
9. recognize writer's technique									
a. sensory image					I	D	D	M	R
b. dialect					I	D	M	R	R
c. onomatopoeia							I	D	D
d. sarcasm								I	D
e. irony								I	D
f. alliteration								I	D
g. foreshadowing								I	D
h. satire								I	D
i. symbolism									I
10. make inferences									I
11. distinguish fact from opinion			I	D	D	M	R	R	R
12. perceive relationships					I	D	M	R	
a. time and place									
b. cause and effect		I	D	M	R	R	R	R	R
13. compare and contrast material			I	D	D	M	R	R	R
14. make analogies				I	D	M	D	D	D
15. recognize									
a. narrative						I	D	D	D
b. expository						I	D	D	D
C. Evaluative									
The student will be able to									
1. relate story to own experience at grade level		I	D	D	D	D	D	D	D
2. discriminate between fact and fantasy		I	D						
3. predict what would happen if circumstances changed				I	D	D	D	D	D
4. evaluate character's action				I	D	D	D	D	D
5. identify author's purpose				I	D	D	D	D	D
6. identify author's point of view						I	D	D	D
7. explain moral of story						I	D	D	D
8. judge validity						I	D	D	D
9. identify mood						I	D	D	D
10. identify tone							I	D	D
11. recognize bias							I	D	D
IV. Literary									
A. Literary Types									
1. Poetry									
The student will be able to									
a. identify haiku					I	D	M		
b. identify limerick						I	M	R	

Figure 3-9 (Cont'd.)

118

OVERVIEW

READING

IV. Literary — Continued

	K	1	2	3	4	5	6	7	8
2. Play									
The student will be able to									
a. identify comedy								I	D
b. identify drama								I	D
3. Fiction									
The student will be able to									
a. identify historical fiction					I	D	M	R	R
b. identify myths					I	D	M		
c. identify tall tales					I	M			
d. identify biographical fiction							I	M	R
e. identify science fiction							I	D	R
f. identify fable							I	M	
g. identify mystery								I	D
h. identify legend								I	D
i. identify novel								I	D
j. identify short story								I	D
4. Non-fiction									
The student will be able to									
a. identify biography					I	M			
b. identify auto-biography					I	M			
B. Literary Techniques									
The student will be able to									
1. identify setting					I	D	M		
2. identify plot					I	D	M		
3. identify characterization					I	D	M	R	
4. identify climax							I	D	
5. identify theme							I	D	
6. identify resolution of conflict							I	D	
V. Vocabulary									
The student will be able to									
A. demonstrate Boehm concepts	I								
B. read specified high frequency words at grade level		I	I	I					
C. differentiate between word relationships									
1. identify antonyms			I	D	M	R			
2. identify synonyms			I	D	M	R			
3. identify homonyms			I	D	D	M	R		
4. identify homographs			I	D	D	M	R		

Figure 3-9 (Cont'd.)

READING

OVERVIEW

VI. Oral Reading
The student will be able to

	K	1	2	3	4	5	6	7	8
A. employ punctuation clues when reading		I	D	M					
B. employ phrasing techniques		I	D	M					
C. use proper voice intonation to express meaning		I	D	M					
D. accurately pronounce grade-level words		I	D	D	D	D	D		D
E. avoid substitutions, omissions, and repetitions of words		I	D	M					
F. adjust rate according to material read						I	D	M	R

VII. Silent Reading
The student will be able to

	K	1	2	3	4	5	6	7	8
A. read without subvocalization, lip movement, head movement		I	D	M					
B. adjust rate to purpose					I	D	D	M	R

NOTE: In some cases more than a single skill development level is called for at a grade level (eg., I/D, D/M). In such cases this overview shows only the lowest level of development; however, individual grade-level sheets will show all developmental level expectations (e.g., I and D or D and M, etc.).

Figure 3-9 (Cont'd.)

```
┌─────────────────────────────────────────────────┐
│        Sample Objectives Developed from         │
│          Scope-and-Sequence Chart               │
│                                                 │
│  SUBJECT: Earth and Space Science               │
│                                                 │
│  MASTERY SKILL OR CONCEPT: Earthquakes          │
│                                                 │
│  MASTERY OBJECTIVES:                            │
│                                                 │
│     1. Explain causes of earthquakes.           │
│     2. Explain how seismograph works.           │
│     3. Identify major effects of earthquakes.   │
│     4. Explain what to do when earthquake       │
│        warning is received.                     │
│                                                 │
│  NUMBER OF INSTRUCTIONAL PERIODS: 2             │
└─────────────────────────────────────────────────┘
```

Source: Allan A. Glatthorn, *Curriculum Renewal* (Alexandria, Virginia,
            Association for Supervision and Curriculum Development, 1987), p.
            33. Reprinted with permission of the Association for Supervision and
            Curriculum Development. Copyright (c) by ASCD. All rights reserved.

Figure 3-10

1. Obligation

The products of this phase are the agreement to conduct an evaluation and the ground rules for doing so. The tasks are to:

a. Verify that the climate is amenable to the ethical conduct of an evaluation with a reasonable likelihood of effecting a desirable impact.

b. Set the evaluation's overall goal and boundaries.

c. Establish the roles of evaluation specialists and other participants in the study.

d. Reach agreements with the evaluation's commissioners on the handling of potential threats to the study's feasibility, accuracy, propriety, and utility.

In the humanities program's case, this phase would consist of an examination of the study committee report, my initial discussions with the principal, and contract negotiations.

2. Exploration

The main product of this phase is an understanding of the evaluation's context and potential accomplishments.

a. Collect basic facts about the program and its setting: history, official goals, administrative structure, and so on.

b. Develop a tentative sense of the character of the program and environment: distinctive features, human interactions, operational goals, possible side-effects, and so forth.

c. Probe the perspectives of other observers and participants.

d. Analyze the program as a system and as a part of other systems.

e. List salient features, issues, discrepancies.

f. List all the purposes, audiences, and questions the evaluation might address.

g. Identify factors affecting the feasibility of various data collection and reporting options.

In the humanities program, the tasks labeled "learn more about the program and the setting," "identify decision makers and their perspectives," and "list all possible purposes, audiences, and questions," fall into this phase. However, exploration would continue through the aftermath of the final report even though more visible activities were underway.

3. Design

The products of the design phase are plans for data collection, analyses, and reporting. This and the next phase are often repeated several

Figure 3-11

times during the course of an evaluation. In fact, "exploration" is essentially the first cycle of phases 3 and 4.

    a. Set priorities for potential purposes and audiences.
    b. Outline possible methods for each proposed question.
    c. Estimate the cost and feasibility of each method.
    d. Predict the validity of the findings from each method.
    e. Decide which questions to pursue and which methods to use.
    f. Integrate the selected methods into a cohesive plan.
    g. Develop the plan into specific tools and procedures—develop or choose instruments, select samples and software packages, and so on.
    h. Develop specifications for the audiences, contents, and formats of evaluation reports.

"Outline methods," "decide which questions to answer," and "complete the evaluation plan" discuss these tasks for the humanities program.

4. Execution

The products of this phase are written evaluation reports. The tasks are to:

    a. Collect data
    b. Analyze data
    c. Write evaluation reports

These activities vary from the mechanical to the artistic, depending on what information is collected, how liberally it is interpreted, and how creatively it is presented. "Collect and analyze data" and the first part of "report findings" are in this phase.

5. Application

The product here is the evaluation's impact. If all goes well, this includes new insights, rational decisions, program improvements, and freshly motivated staff. The evaluation specialist's part is to:

    a. Produce sound information in response to real information needs.
    b. Report the findings in ways that are understandable, credible, and palatable to the evaluation's audiences.
    c. Ensure that the audiences have access to the findings and aggressively encourage them to use them.
    d. Venture beyond the findings themselves to what should be done about them, or lead the evaluation audiences in doing this for themselves.

That's the evaluator's part. The rest of the job of making evaluations effective is up to the people who run the schools.

Figure 3-11 (Cont'd.)

Source: Deborah G. Bonnet, "Five Phases of Purposeful Inquiry," in Ronald S. Brandt, Editor, *Applied Strategies for Curriculum Evaluation* (Alexandria, VA, Association for Supervision and Curriculum Development, 1981), p. 23. Reprinted with permission of the Association for Supervision and Curriculum Development. Copyright (c) by ASCD. All rights reserved.

Figure 3-11 (Cont'd.)

Schematic for an Integrated Research and Evaluation System

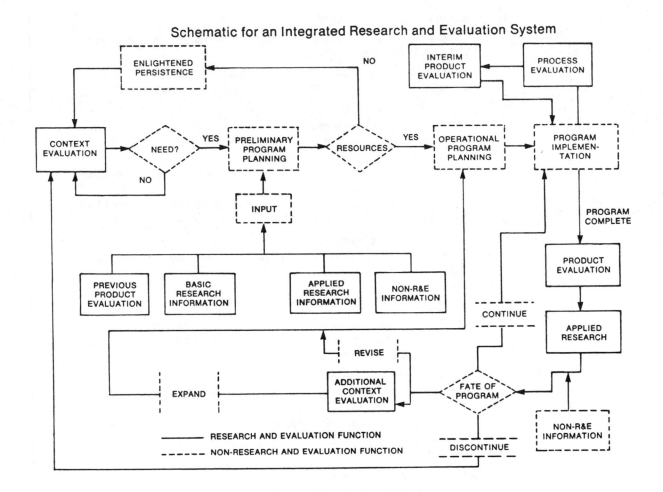

Source: William J. Webster, "CIPP in Local Evaluation," in Ronald S. Brandt, Editor, *Applied Strategies for Curriculum Evaluation* (Alexandria, VA, Association for Supervision and Curriculum Development, 1981), p. 50. Reprinted with permission of the Association for Supervision and Curriculum Development. Copyright (c) by ASCD. All rights reserved.

Figure 3-12

Necessary Steps in Program Evaluation

1. Determine program objectives
   a. Meet with decision makers and program managers to determine program objectives.
   b. Refine objectives through thorough analysis, reviewing literature, questioning decision makers, analyzing input data, and so on.

2. Identify decisions and sources of information
   a. Using the objectives, meet with decision makers to generate a list of the critical decisions to be made concerning the objectives and the program.
   b. Determine the types of information necessary to make the various decisions.
   c. Estimate the critical decisions and plan the information sources so those decisions receive the most information.

3. Define measurable objectives and related decisions
   a. Work with project personnel to mold objectives so they may be measured.
   b. Operationalize the basis for decision making to relate to measured achievement of objectives.

4. Plan evaluation dissemination
   a. Identify the various audiences of the evaluation and estimate the level of sophistication of each intended audience.

5. Identify measuring instruments
   a. Review objectives and decisions and evaluate existing instruments to determine which can be used in the evaluation.
   b. Determine areas where no satisfactory instruments are available and develop complete specifications of instruments to be constructed.

6. Develop and test instruments.
   a. Develop needed instruments.
   b. Test new instruments, if necessary, on a sample of subjects.
   c. Refine new instruments on the basis of these tests.
   d. Test administration of any unconventional instruments or observation procedures.

7. Schedule information collection
   a. Specify sampling procedures to be used.
   b. Determine the schedule of observations and the instruments to be administered at each observation point.
   c. Schedule the personnel needed to administer instruments.

8. Organize data analysis
   a. Determine various formats of data including card and tape format

Figure 3-13

specifications at various stages of collection and analysis. Specify processing necessary to put data into correct format at each stage of analysis.
  b. Plan nonstatistical analysis of data and resources necessary to perform analysis.
  c. Plan statistical analysis of data and programs necessary to analyze data.
  d. Determine which programs are already written and ready to use, which are written but need modifications to handle data in their intended formats, and which programs need to be written with specifications of these programs.

9. Design formal evaluation/research
  a. Prepare design including specifications of:
    • objectives
    • instrumentation
    • analysis methodology
    • data collection and reporting schedules
    • sampling procedures
    • data analysis schedules
    • final reporting schedules
  b. Type, print, and collate design.
  c. Disseminate formal design.

10. Develop computer program
  a. Develop necessary programs for analysis
  b. Modify existing programs
  c. Run all programs to be used on sample data in the proper medium and format. Construct sample data to simulate problems in actual data (mispunching, missing data, and so on).

11. Context evaluation
  a. Collect or supervise and coordinate collection of context evaluation information.
  b. Prepare context evaluation information for analysis.

13. Product evaluation
  a. Collect or supervise and coordinate the collection of product evaluation information.
  b. Prepare product evaluation information for analysis.

14. Analyze interim data
  a. Organize interim data.
  b. Perform analyses of interim data.

15. Report on formative evaluation
  a. Prepare formative evaluation reports.
  b. Type, print, and collate formative evaluation reports.
  c. Disseminate formative evaluation reports to project management and staff.

Figure 3-13 (Cont'd.)

16. Analyze summative data
    a. Organize summative data.
    b. Perform analyses of summative data.

17. Report on summative evaluation/research
    a. Prepare the various summative evaluation/research reports for each audience; include objectives, findings, and recommendations expressed in an appropriate manner for each intended audience. This preparation includes the abstract of the report.
    b. Have report carefully proofread and corrected.
    c. Type, print, and collate the summative evaluation reports.
    d. Disseminate the summative evaluation/research reports to project personnel, district management, and the board of education.

18. Interpret reports
    a. Meet with project personnel to interpret reports.
    b. Meet with district management and the board of education to aid in report interpretation.

19. Disseminate reports further
    a. Disseminate summative evaluation/research reports to district administrators and interested professional staff.
    b. Prepare and disseminate a book of evaluation and research abstracts to professional staff.

20. Report feedback
    a. Meet with decision makers to obtain feedback regarding the report to improve reporting activities.

Source: William J. Webster, "CIPP in Local Evaluation," in Ronald S. Brandt, Editor, *Applied Strategies for Curriculum Evaluation* (Alexandria, VA, Association for Supervision and Curriculum Development, 1981), p. 50. Reprinted with permission of the Association for Supervision and Curriculum Development. Copyright (c) by ASCD. All rights reserved.

Figure 3-13 (Cont'd.)

EVALUATION OF
ADMINISTRATIVE/SUPERVISORY PERFORMANCE

SYMBOLS — To be used by Appraisee and Appraiser (s)

O = Outstanding — This rating will only be used to identify areas of special strength or to recognize exceptional performance.

S = Successful Performance.

I = Improvement Recommended.*

U = Unsatisfactory Performance.*

NC = No Chance to Demonstrate or Perform.

* The appraiser must provide written recommendations for any items marked I or U.

	Initial Appraisal Conference		Summary Appraisal Conference	
	Appraisee	Appraiser	Appraisee	Appraiser

A. *Administration*

1. Sees that each person's responsibilities are clearly defined

2. Effectively delegates authority

3. Coordinates work of staff members

4. Meets deadlines

5. Makes prompt and workable decisions

6. Recognizes situations which require attention and takes appropriate action

7. Fairly and accurately administers budget

Comments _____

_____

_____

B. *Planning*

1. Establishes realistic goals

2. Plans and utilizes time to best advantage

3. Plans and develops budget effectively

Comments _____

_____

_____

Figure 3-14

129

C. *Communications*

　　1. Encourages staff members to express ideas

　　2. Keeps staff members well-informed

　　3. Keeps parents well-informed

　　4. Expresses self clearly

Comments _____

_____

_____

D. *Relationship with Staff*

　　1. Shows concern for each staff member's welfare

　　2. Is cooperative

　　3. Has respect of staff

　　4. Shows appreciation for a job well done

　　5. Offers constructive criticism when appropriate

　　6. Is accessible and responsive

Comments _____

_____

_____

E. *Relationship with Community*

　　1. Supports community activities

　　2. Is accessible and responsive

　　3. Utilizes community resources

　　4. Interprets school program to community

Comments _____

_____

_____

Figure 3-14 (Cont'd.)

F. *Professional Growth and Ethics*
   1. Assumes responsibility for one's own professional growth
   2. Is receptive to new approaches
   3. Is professionally ethical

Comments _____

_____

_____

G. *Instructional Leadership*
   1. Helps develop and maintain an effective instructional program
   2. Supervises implementation of graded course of study
   3. Supervises instructional program
   4. Encourages effective use of materials
   5. Facilitates innovation and creativity in instruction
   6. Provides opportunities for group planning and discussion
   7. Encourages and supports an on-going program of staff development

Comments _____

_____

_____

H. *Personal Characteristics*
   1. Is physically healthy
   2. Maintains control in stressful situations
   3. Presents favorable appearance
   4. Is tactful and courteous

Comments _____

_____

_____

Figure 3-14 (Cont'd.)

131

I. *Relationship with Pupils*

1. Maintains positive school climate

2. Encourages self-discipline

3. Demonstrates concern for student's individual welfare

4. Supervises assigned program of pupil services

5. Is available and responsive to pupils

Comments _____

_____

_____

Figure 3-14 (Cont'd.)

132

AREAS FOR PROFESSIONAL GROWTH

Instructions: Prior to the initial appraisal conference, the appraisee should decide on at least one (1) but not more than three (3) "Areas for Professional Growth." These should be areas which will add to your overall effectiveness with at least one related to either a building or district goal. At the initial appraisal conference, you and your appraiser(s) will agree upon a combination of growth areas offered by both you and the appraiser(s). The *total* list is not to exceed five (5) growth areas. A cooperatively developed written plan of action must be attached to this form within five (5) working days after the initial appraisal conference. Items decided upon will be appraised in January by both you and your appraiser(s).

— DO NOT WRITE BELOW THIS LINE PRIOR TO FIRST CONFERENCE —

(Attach additional sheets as needed)

Areas for Growth   Appraisal

1.

Signatures: _____

Appraisee   Date of Appraisal

_____

Appraiser(s)   Date of Appraisal

Figure 3-14 (Cont'd.)

SUMMARY

Preliminary Conference — Comments and/or recommendations

_____

_____

_____

_____

_____

_____

_____

_____

Date: _____   _____
                             * Signature of Appraisee/Signature of Appraiser

Summary Conference — Comments and/or recommendations

_____

_____

_____

_____

_____

_____

_____

Date: _____   _____
                             * Signature of Appraisee/Signature of Appraiser

* Signature does not indicate either approval or rejection but simply means that
the information has been reviewed and discussed by the involved parties.

Original to Superintendent's Office
Copy to Appraisee
Copy to Appraiser

4/87

Figure 3-14 (Cont'd.)

134

ACTION PLAN

Name of Evaluatee _____ Patricia Conran _____

Name of Evaluator _____ Board of Education _____

School Year _____ 1987-88 _____

Category #100 Statement of Need Areas of Curriculum and Instruction Effectiveness — Improvement (400 Staff Development) — Curriculum Comment: This area was a focus in 1986-87 and continues. Articulation efforts begun last spring indicate the need to work toward continuity across grade levels in all subject areas. Continuing work is also needed in follow-through from curriculum and instruction to testing and intervention.

Action Steps (List the steps or action that will be taken to meet the need indicated above.)
Provide leadership and direction in using test results and adopting curriculum and instruction for effectiveness. Continue to focus on guidance, special education, library, and computers.

SEPT - DEC
— Meet with Director of Curriculum.
— Monitor Curriculum Committee work for appropriateness and articulation across grade levels.
— Conference with all first- and second-year employees

SEPT - JUN
— Meet with Electronic Communications Coordinator to monitor implementation of computer plan.
— Continue Effective Instruction training with goal of developing trainers. Continue to visit classes and provide feedback to teachers; re: behaviors believed to be productive of student learning.
— Provide leadership and direction to E.C.C. and Cassingham principal as well as to other administrators. Provide leadership and direction in Danforth-O.S.U. Mentor program as well as in development of district mentoring program

OCT - JUN
DEC
— Direct planning for Summer School.
— Do status check on all program development including recommendations for 1988-89 changes.
— Secure Summer School director.

JAN - APR.
— Direct accomplishment of North Central Association Self-Study.
— Monitor planning for Summer School, and survey needs and interests.

APR
— Do status check on all staff development for Summer, 1988 and 1988-89.
— Seek Board approval for all recommendations for curriculum adoptions/changes.

Complete a separate action plan for each need. Prepare in *duplicate*. Evaluatee keeps one copy, the other copy is given to the evaluator.

Note: Follow-up with appropriate personnel will be ongoing for implementation of others' Action Plans assumed to be needed to accomplish above.

Figure 3-15
135

ACTION PLAN

Name of Evaluatee _____Patricia Conran_____

Name of Evaluator _____Board of Education_____

School Year _____1987-88_____

Category #500 Statement of Need Budget - Levy _____

Action Steps (List the steps or action that will be taken to meet the need indicated above.)

Revise five-year plan based on administrator and architect input into needs and priorities for repairing, replacing, and adding to building contents and buildings and grounds. Monitor staffing needs. Project long-range levy needs for anticipated short-term and long-term budget needs.

SEPT	— Seek Board approval of appropriations and discuss long-term financial projections. — Discuss short-term and long-term financial projections with C.B.S. — Monitor budget process throughout year with administrators.
OCT & NOV - MAY	— Seek Board determination of levy need and, if Board determines levy is needed in 1988, provide leadership in preparing for and carrying out levy campaign.
JAN	— Assess financial projections with Board based on outcome of negotiations.
FEB	— Determine summer work; update 5-yr. plan for capital outlay.
MAR	— Make recommendations to Board relative to staffing needs.
APR	— Make recommendations to Board for textbook adoptions and costs.
MAY	— Assess financial projections with Board based on outcome of levy, if held..

Note: Provide ongoing leadership and direction for processes affecting budget.

Complete a separate action plan for each need. Prepare in *duplicate*. Evaluatee keeps one copy, the other copy is given to the evaluator.

Figure 3-15 (Cont'd.)

ACTION PLAN

Name of Evaluatee _____Pat Conran_____

Name of Evaluator _____Board of Education_____

School Year _____1986-'87 and 1987-'88_____

Category #600 Statement of Need Area of Leadership and Management _____

_____

_____

Action Steps (List the steps or action that will be taken to meet the need indicated above.)

Provide leadership and direction to each locus of administrator responsibility.

SEPT	—	Begin goal-setting process with administrators. Schedule regular meetings to continue throughout the school year with COS, Treasurer, Business Manager, Director of Curriculum, JHS and SHS Principals, Elementary Principals, All Administrators, and BEA President.
OCT	—	Work with Administrators to complete Action Planning process.
JAN	—	Review Action Plan with Administrators.
Note:		Schedule of all regular meetings that will continue throughout the school year will be distributed to the Board of Education (completed).
		Goals of administrators will be shared with Board of Education. Monitoring of administrator goals; action plans will be ongoing.

Complete a separate action plan for each need. Prepare in *duplicate*. Evaluatee keeps one copy, the other copy is given to the evaluator.

Figure 3-15 (Cont'd.)

Addendum to 1987-1988 Action Plans
Category 600
Area Leadership and Management
Patricia C. Conran

In response to the Board's request to include the subject of coaching in my action plans, I have worked out some measures with principals.

- At a meeting of all coaches on November 11, seeds for performing evaluations in the future were to have been planted. Recommendations for employment and, hence, criteria for evaluation, are and should be:

  - Knowledge of the activity
  - Ideas on the development of a program and utilization of coaches
  - Statement of philosophy to determine if the coach has an understanding of what he or she is doing
  - Ability to handle situations with parents in a manner that indicates openness
  - Ability to handle situations with students in a manner that students know consequences in advance
  - Motivation for coaching that indicates the coach is watching for students' growth, enjoys helping students grow, and is able to assist in this growth
  - Knows how and is willing to work with individual students on weaknesses without excessive focus of negative attention on a student
  - Knows and accepts that the focus should not be on the coach
  - Knows and accepts that the coach sets the tone for the activity
  - Knows and accepts that fair treatment of all is expected

- Plan will be developed for administrator to evaluate head coach and for head coaches to evaluate assistants. Planning will include recommendation for personnel responsible for this function.

- In an ongoing manner, principals will continue to meet with coaches who have demonstrated what principals believe to be unacceptable behavior or performance.

Figure 3-15 (Cont'd.)

ACTION PLAN

Name of Evaluatee _____Patricia Conran_____

Name of Evaluator _____Board of Education_____

School Year _____1987-88_____

_____
_____

Category #700 Statement of Need ____Negotiations/Contract Administration_____

_____
_____
_____

Action Steps (List the steps or action that will be taken to meet the need indicated above.)

Provide leadership and direction in formulating Board-BEA contract proposals, in negotiations process and in understanding and implementing new contract.

ONGOING   —   Meet regularly with negotiators to formulate contract proposals and language.

—   Provide for updating Board and administrators on negotiations progress and recommended actions.

—   Monitor preparation and distribution of new contract.

Note: This process was begun in Spring, 1987 and will continue through the negotiations process through review of new contract with administrators.

Complete a separate action plan for each need. Prepare in *duplicate.* **Evaluatee keeps one copy, the other copy is given to the evaluator.**

Figure 3-15 (Cont'd.)

ACTION PLAN

Name of Evaluatee _____ Patricia Conran _____

Name of Evaluator _____ Board of Education _____

School Year _____ 1987-88 _____

Category #1100 Statement of Need ____ Public Relations _____

Action Steps (List the steps or action that will be taken to meet the need indicated above.)

— Provide leadership and direction in assessing and improving school climate.
— Provide information for levy campaign re: *quality* education, *efficiency* of use of tax dollars, and promises kept since last levy.
— Prepare and conduct survey of residents regarding satisfaction with schools and suggestions for improvements.
— Provide leadership and direction to C.B.S. Committee.
— Continue quarterly publication of district newsletter and "This is Bexley."
— Continue poolside chats in June when pool reopens.
— Continue telephone calls to residents.
— Prepare press releases and other communications with media and speeches as required.
— Continue to attend meetings of school organizations and functions, athletic games, City Council, and other community groups.
— Hold regular meetings with staff to apprise of mission and report on activity relative to mission.
— Report regularly to Board on activities.
— Ongoing input requests from staff.

Note: All activities are considered ongoing.

Complete a separate action plan for each need. Prepare in *duplicate*. Evaluatee keeps one copy, the other copy is given to the evaluator.

Figure 3-15 (Cont'd.)

TEACHER EVALUATION INSTRUMENT

Name _____ Assignment _____ Bldg. _____ Yr. _____

LEVEL OF PERFORMANCE

CRITERIA	Outstanding	Successful	Unsuccessful
I. Classroom Management			
A. The teacher utilizes effective instructional management practices in the classroom.	☐	☐	☐
B. The teacher utilizes effective student management practices in the classroom.	☐	☐	☐
II. The Teaching Act			
A. The teacher employs effective teaching techniques.	☐	☐	☐
B. The teacher promotes an atmosphere and utilizes techniques conducive to intellectual stimulation.	☐	☐	☐
III. Interpersonal Relations			
A. The teacher maintains positive relationships with students.	☐	☐	☐
B. The teacher maintains positive working relationships with colleagues.	☐	☐	☐
C. The teacher maintains a positive relationship with parents and community.	☐	☐	☐
IV. Professional Self			
A. The teacher participates in activities for professional commitment and growth.	☐	☐	☐
B. The teacher demonstrates a commitment to personal growth.	☐	☐	☐

Teacher _____ Supervisor _____ Date _____

Due: **April 1 for** Group I Teachers
May 15 for Group II Teachers

White Copy: Personnel File ☐   Yellow Copy: Supervisor ☐   Pink Copy: Teacher ☐

Courtesy of Bexley City Schools

Figure 3-16

CONFERENCING FORM

Name —————— Assignment —————— Bldg. —————— Yr. ——

I.	CLASSROOM MANAGEMENT	A.	TEACHER		
	CRITERIA		LEVELS OF PERFORMANCE		
			Outstanding	Successful	Unsuccessful
I.A.	The teacher utilizes effective instructional management practices in the classroom. Documentation: • direct observation • lesson planning • IMS records • teacher interview • class records • communication with subject area specialists ☐ Not Observed		☐ Consistently and creatively extends instructional management standards that maximize student time on appropriate learning tasks. (Comments required.)	☐ Demonstrates a thorough knowledge of subject matter. Establishes goals based on district curriculum plans. Utilizes diagnostic/prescriptive methods and procedures. Sets realistic instructional goals for students. Plans daily and long-term activities to meet established goals and objectives. Shows evidence of preparation that maximizes time on tasks. Performs record-keeping duties effectively.	☐ Lacks mastery of standard instructional management techniques and/or does not consistently apply such techniques. (Comments required.)

Comments:

Copy to: Teacher ☐   Supervisor ☐

Figure 3-17
142

SELECTION RESEARCH INCORPORATED
(SRI)
INTERVIEW THEMES AND AREAS OF INFORMATION

Teacher Perceiver Interview

Themes:

Mission	Rapport Drive
Empathy	Activation
Gestalt	Objectivity
Innovation	Input Drive
Focus	Investment
Listening	Individualized Perception

Administrator Perceiver Interview

Themes:

Mission	Ambiguity Tolerance
Relator	Group Enhancer
Arranger	Audience Sensitivity
Leader	Discriminator
Catalyzer	Human Resources Developer
Gestalt	Work Orientation
Delegator	Performance Orientation

Professional Development Interview

Areas of Information:

Focusing
Motivating
Learning
Supervising
Relating

Source: SRI Perceiver Academies, Inc.

Figure 3-18

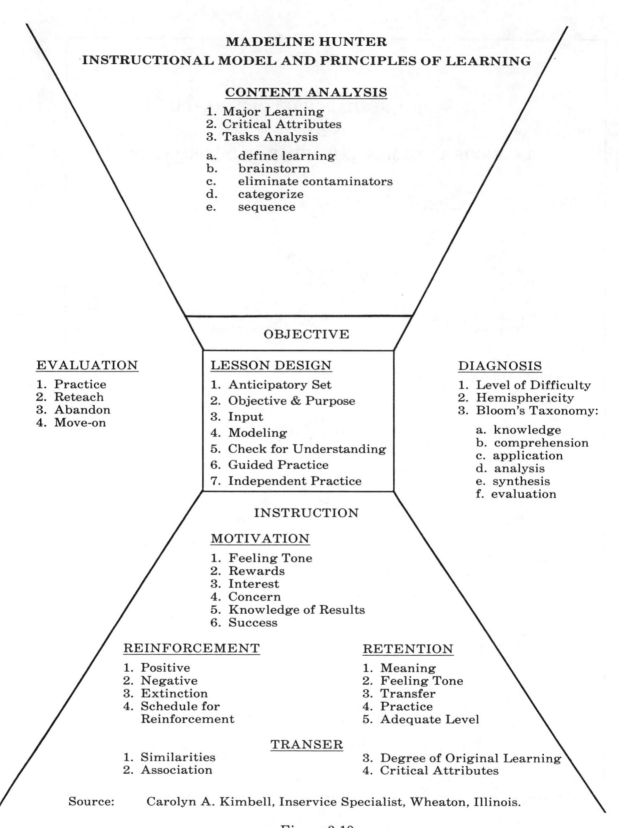

MADELINE HUNTER
INSTRUCTIONAL MODEL AND PRINCIPLES OF LEARNING

CONTENT ANALYSIS

1. Major Learning
2. Critical Attributes
3. Tasks Analysis

a. define learning
b. brainstorm
c. eliminate contaminators
d. categorize
e. sequence

OBJECTIVE

EVALUATION	LESSON DESIGN	DIAGNOSIS
1. Practice	1. Anticipatory Set	1. Level of Difficulty
2. Reteach	2. Objective & Purpose	2. Hemisphericity
3. Abandon	3. Input	3. Bloom's Taxonomy:
4. Move-on	4. Modeling	
	5. Check for Understanding	a. knowledge
	6. Guided Practice	b. comprehension
	7. Independent Practice	c. application
		d. analysis
		e. synthesis
		f. evaluation

INSTRUCTION

MOTIVATION

1. Feeling Tone
2. Rewards
3. Interest
4. Concern
5. Knowledge of Results
6. Success

REINFORCEMENT

1. Positive
2. Negative
3. Extinction
4. Schedule for
   Reinforcement

RETENTION

1. Meaning
2. Feeling Tone
3. Transfer
4. Practice
5. Adequate Level

TRANSER

1. Similarities
2. Association
3. Degree of Original Learning
4. Critical Attributes

Source: Carolyn A. Kimbell, Inservice Specialist, Wheaton, Illinois.

Figure 3-19

GROUPING PRACTICE

1. *Nongraded grouping:* Students who fall within a certain broad age range are helped to progress through prescribed curriculum to the extent that capacity allows. Usually a large number of hierarchies are established for teaching children who have progressed to various levels.

2. *Multigrade or multiage grouping:* Children of three or more grade levels or age levels are grouped together (sometimes in a self-contained classroom, sometimes in other settings). The intent is to provide students with the benefits of a family-type atmosphere, which holds potential for peers providing assistance to one another.

3. *Team learning:* Students of the same or different grade levels are encouraged to pursue tasks as a team, emphasizing cooperation, mutual assistance, and the achieving of consensus.

4. *Interest grouping:* Grouping is based on student interest either by providing options among content for student selection or options among teachers who offer different topics at the same time, or allowing student groups to evolve around different interest areas. The rationale is that students who are interested will find relevance in their learning, and that such relevance might then be geared into other channels that enhance further learning.

5. *Trump plan:* This plan establishes a program whereby students are involved in a scheduled large group activity, small group activity, and independent study. Opportunity is thereby provided for several types of learning styles(*23*).

6. *Self-contained classroom:* Students are homogeneously or heterogeneously assigned to a room with one teacher. Teachers are felt to have the advantage of knowing and providing for student needs and interests more fully.

7. *Departmentalization:* Students move to different teachers for each subject. This approach is believed to provide for greater expertise in the several subject fields.

8. *Dual-progress plan:* This is an attempt to provide a combination of subject- and interest-oriented approaches. Academic subjects are pursued during one-half of the day; interest areas are developed during the second half(*12*, pp. 127–128).

9. *Contract grouping:* Students are grouped according to the manner in which they choose or accomplish learning tasks that they have agreed to pursue. (This is not to be confused with "performance contracting," i.e., agreements made by business and industry to accomplish certain learning tasks in specified periods of time.)

Figure 3-20

10. *Minicourses:* Part or all of the curriculum is composed of a number of short courses to be pursued. In some cases students are able to select courses from a range of options. The intent is to expose students to a wide range of areas without allowing a topic to go beyond the student's attention span.

11. *Student-formulated curricula:* Students of an entire school, or a smaller group within a school, are allowed to devise their own curriculum. The rationale is that considerable learning will accrue from the decision-making processes, as well as from pursuit of the actual studies selected.

12. *Grouping among schools:* Several school systems have begun to offer alternative schools within their own district, which would provide for choice on the part of parents and students relative to particular beliefs, persuasions, and orientations. The possible advent of the voucher system (granting a certificate to parents that represents tax dollars to be spent for the education of their children in any of the alternative educational systems available) could provide for educational diversity of unrealized magnitude.

Source: William H. Schubert, "Grouping: Practices, Controversies, and Beyond," in Louis Rubin, *Curriculum Handbook* (Boston: Allyn and Bacon, Inc., 1977) pp. 217-218.

Figure 3-20 (Cont'd.)

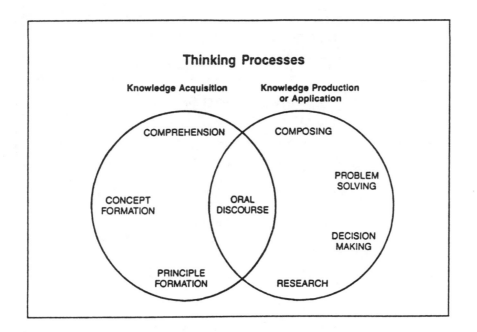

Thinking Processes

Knowledge Acquisition

Knowledge Production
or Application

COMPREHENSION

COMPOSING

PROBLEM
SOLVING

CONCEPT
FORMATION

ORAL
DISCOURSE

DECISION
MAKING

PRINCIPLE
FORMATION

RESEARCH

Source: Robert J. Marzano, et. al., *Dimensions of Thinking: A Framework for Curriculum and Instruction* (Alexandria, VA, Association for Supervision and Curriculum Development, 1988), p. 33. Reprinted with permission of the Association for Supervision and Curriculum Development. Copyright (c) by ASCD. All rights reserved.

Figure 3-21

Core Thinking Skills As They Frequently Occur in Thinking Processes

FOCUSING SKILLS

Defining Problems   Setting Goals

INFORMATION GATHERING SKILLS

Observing   Formulating Questions

REMEMBERING SKILLS

Encoding   Recalling

ORGANIZING SKILLS

Comparing   Classifying   Ordering   Representing

ANALYZING SKILLS

Identifying Attributes   Identifying Relationships
and Components   and Patterns

Identifying Main Ideas   Identifying Errors

GENERATING SKILLS

Inferring   Predicting   Elaborating

INTEGRATING SKILLS

Summarizing   Restructuring

EVALUATING SKILLS

Establishing Criteria   Verifying

Source: Robert J. Marzano, et. al., *Dimensions of Thinking: A Framework for Curriculum and Instruction* (Alexandria, VA, Association for Supervision and Curriculum Development, 1988), p. 66. Reprinted with permission of the Association for Supervision and Curriculum Development. Copyright (c) by ASCD. All rights reserved.

Figure 3-22

II

SHARING WITH OTHERS

4

Communicating
for Desired Results

Communication is central to all superintendent roles. Communication is also frequently responsible for success or failure on the job. That is communication, not technical know-how, may determine whether the superintendent makes it or not. Selecting the target of communication and deciding among several variables that comprise a communication are critical to success.

Knowing the Who, What, When, Where, Why, and How of Communicating

With Whom Will the Superintendent Communicate?

Various individuals, groups, and institutions within and outside the district will be the target of communications at one time or another.

Within the school district the superintendent will communicate with board of education members, administrators, staff, students, parents, residents who do not have children enrolled in district schools, and representatives of business, government, and religious faiths. Outside the school district the superintendent will communicate with professional colleagues, other schools, professional organizations, experts, partnerships and consortia, networks, and legislators. Media and their representatives, both within and outside the district, will be regular communicators with the superintendent. With each the superintendent will need to choose among several variables in the communication. These include the what, where, when, why, and how of communicating.

What Will the Superintendent Communicate?

Determining who should receive what information when creates a continuing balancing act for the superintendent. One is reminded of the chicken and egg story. Some suggestions of what to communicate to various audiences follow:

Board. At a minimum, board of education members should receive timely information on everything for which they will need to discuss and take action. The superintendent may periodically share important events such as a court opinion in a district legal suit, noteworthy investments, or significant student or staff accomplishments. In addition, board of education members may need to be polled periodically for advice. A memo similar to that in Figure 4-1 will assist a board of education member absent from a meeting to keep current with actions taken or information shared by members. Memos to board members may be used to keep all members of the board fully informed, to supply information necessary to make responsible decisions, and to convey the expectation that members will seek, in advance of meetings, information required to facilitate board actions. The quality of communication with board members will largely determine the quality of board and superintendent relations. More will be said about board and superintendent relations as the other variables of communication are discussed below.

Administrators. Administrators will communicate regularly with the superintendent on matters of importance in serving children's learning and running the schools. The superintendent may also communicate on matters of personal and professional growth. In Figure 4-2 the superintendent communicates expectations relative to student health and welfare. The situation calls for quick action and implementation of uniform procedures. Memos may be used in similar situations where it is important to impart or to request information or to direct action.

Staff. Staff members as individuals, as a whole and as some subgroup, such as by building or position or committee, will communicate periodically with the superintendent. The communication may share a superintendent or board plan, position, policy, or procedure. The communication may also be an open dialogue or question/answer and listening sessions. If there is a union (or unions), the superintendent may schedule regular meetings with the union president or other leadership about contract matters and employee concerns. The information in Figure 4-3 enables all to celebrate one teacher's recognition. It also invites other faculty members to strive for excellence and future recognition. Such memos sent to all staff may prevent negative interpretations derived from information received piecemeal.

Students. In communicating with students, the superintendent may demonstrate support for the building principal and other staff. The superintendent may also cheerlead for school and district events and programs. Communication with student council and other groups and individuals may also include open dialogue, question/answer, and listening sessions. Figure 4-4 responds to concerns that students have related. It serves to inform students of possible needs and action and it indirectly encourages risk-taking.

Parents. Parents will communicate with the superintendent as individuals or as members of a group, such as a Parent Teacher Association. The superintendent may communicate student performance results, budget statistics, board plans, and actions and information about school programs and events. As noted with other individuals and groups, communication may include open dialogue and question/answer and listening sessions. The greetings to parents or guardians contained in Figure 4-5 convey appreciation for cooperation received in educating the recent graduate and invite pride rather than resentment for planned improvements that are to follow graduation. Letters to parents can be used to keep them enthused about school events and improvements, to allay fears, to communicate common expectations, and to impart information.

Nonparent Residents. The superintendent will find many occasions to communicate with residents who are not parents of school children. This is of growing importance since this group makes up the majority in most school districts. Budget reports, events, and plans that affect tax levies, benefits to be derived from supporting schools, student and staff accomplishments, interests and concerns of residents are among items to be communicated. The mailer shown in Figure 4-6 is intended to accompany a survey to provide board and administration with perceptions of residents about district schools. Included with directions is information intended to create a positive mental set and to motivate a response. In general, communications with nonparent residents will require informational background material as well as information designed to win support.

Business, Government, and Religious Faiths. Representatives of business, government, including the State Department of Education, and religious faiths will be regular communicators. In addition to being informed about the district, business can provide a partnership with a school or district. The business can communicate needs that have importance for curriculum, concerns that may impact upon discipline or inspire service, expertise in one or more areas, and others. Representatives in the categories named will share matters for cooperation and concern, items that may require board action or district planning. For example, inclusion of district input into long-range village planning is reflected in Figure 4-7. Similar communication may be indicating a willingness to cooperate or requesting the cooperation or assistance of representatives of business, government, or religious faiths.

Professional Colleagues. In addition to the above receivers and senders of communications within the district, there are audiences for and participants in communication outside the district. The superintendent will communicate with any number of professional colleagues about items of mutual concern and interest. The latest in legal mandates, practical applications of research, demographic and other significant trends, effective speakers and consultants, and numerous other items will be of mutual interest and concern. Colleagues may also extend or need help.

Other Schools. Other schools will be regulars in communicating with the superintendent. Communications may pertain to articulation of the instructional program, policies and procedures, student performance, shared personnel, cooperative board of education meetings, legislative breakfasts or other meetings related to legislation, cooperative inservice or parent meetings, and others. Communications may also be with area vocational schools and junior colleges, colleges, or universities. Such communications may be about programs, teacher preparation and placement, expertise and resources available to schools, and research, to name a few. While the memo, Figure 4-8, conveys information about a meeting, it indicates existing efforts at articulation among elementary schools and their high school and the willingness of the high school to consider enrolling elementary school children in high school courses.

Professional Organizations. The superintendent will communicate with professional organizations as a member contributing to or receiving service from the organization. Communication may also survey or otherwise seek opinions and solicit membership and support. Responsibilities for organizing meetings of colleagues may prompt the writing of a memo such as Figure 4-9.

Experts. Experts advise the superintendent regularly upon request. Such experts may be the district attorney, architect, and investment banker. While many other experts may be in regular communication with the superintendent, the three named have been selected for illustration.

The attorney will respond to questions asked by the superintendent or board and may initiate communication regarding pending litigation, legislation of concern, and other matters. The district architect will respond to the superintendent's requests to perform safety surveys that may be required by law and other requested inspections. The architect will prepare plans and specifications for building and grounds constructive work. The architect may also initiate communications about work-in-progress and other matters. The investment banker may respond to the superintendent's request to compare types of investments permitted by law and to advise the superintendent regarding investing at specific times or on a regular basis. The investment banker may also be requested to issue bonds and to advise the superintendent regarding needs or advantages of advance refunding of bonds and other matters.

Partnerships and Consortia. Partnerships, such as school-business partnerships, and consortia, such as special education consortia, may be important in the chain of superintendent communications. Communications may promote opportunities for attaining common goals or combining or sharing scarce resources. The communication for Corridor Partnership for Excellence in Education in Figure 4-10 represents one of many kinds of organizations who join with education to accomplish mutually beneficial goals.

Networks. Networks may also be included in the superintendent's communications. Such communications may seek to promote cohesiveness or esprit among groups or individuals or to accomplish some special purpose of the network. Communications in networks may be informative or may urge action or poll opinions.

Legislators and lobbyists. The superintendent will communicate regularly with legislators and lobbyists or lobby groups. Communications may urge "Yes" or "No" votes, question, or respond to questions. Communication should also thank legislators for actions favorable to schools. The communication in Figure 4-11 reflects the interest of a professional education association. Communications with legislators may propose, support, or oppose legislation and thank legislators for their efforts.

Media. Newspapers, TV, and other media and their representatives will receive regular and timely communications concerning all aspects of the district operation or performance and news about individual schools, staff, and students. Newspapers will also receive notices for publications as mandated by law. In addition, reports will seek information at board meetings, from files or other public records, and by interview. The superintendent should look upon the media as vehicles and their representatives as agents in getting out the district message to a broad audience. Newspaper editors, reporters, and other representatives of media should receive thanks for their interest in the schools and for accurate news coverage. In addition to requesting coverage of events or submitting press releases, communication with the media, such as that in Figure 4-12, conveys appreciation for coverage and supplies support-building information.

When to Communicate

Once the superintendent knows with whom he or she will communicate and what is being communicated, there are still several variables that need attention. When will the communication take place? The superintendent may choose to communicate when this is not necessary either to invite or thank, to extend a welcome or otherwise build relationships, to solicit help in the form of human or material resources, and so on. In addition, much communication will be viewed as necessary or important.

Board. As one aspect of developing positive relations with the board, the superintendent will communicate when members express a need for information or the superintendent feels it is important to seek advice or to share information, at the time of a board meeting or in preparation for a meeting, and upon other occasions that may be of a social or professional nature. Anticipating a board's need to know is an important challenge for the superintendent to meet. The more the superintendent can anticipate the need to know and supply information to board members before they ask for it, the more favorably the board views the superintendent and the more positive the relationship.

Administrators. Communication with administrators will occur on a regular basis as a team and as individuals. The quality of the communication will influence the cohesiveness among members. A weekly meeting of the administrative team may serve as a guideline and may vary according to district size, conditions, and the superintendent's leadership style. Ad hoc meetings will also take place as the superintendent feels the need to call such meetings for special purposes. And the superintendent will communicate with various administrators upon request, when visiting schools, for supervisory and evaluation conferences, and on other social and professional occasions.

Staff. Communication with staff as a whole may occur monthly or more or less frequently. Communication with staff in groups or with individuals may be scheduled as needed or at regular intervals to accomplish specific purposes. The superintendent may participate in the interview process when new staff are employed and so communicate with them from their employment onward. The particular leadership style of the superintendent or size of district may warrant the superintendent's participation inservice, committee, and other teacher or staff activity. After visiting classrooms and upon other observations of teachers' performance, the superintendent will want to give feedback on performance. There will also be occasions appropriate for giving commendations and reprimands or for participating in the negotiations and grievance processes.

Students. The superintendent will find may occasions to communicate with students upon their request or his or her own initiative. The superintendent may choose to attend a variety of student activities and communicate with students as individuals or in groups at those times. Communications with students may also be scheduled in response to expressed needs or concerns by either party. Communication may be initiated to recognize commendable behavior and scholarship, to visit the sick, to observe student performance in curricular and extra-curricular activity, to seek opinions, and so on.

Parents. Parent communications may be scheduled at specific times throughout the school year when the Parent Teacher Association or its leadership meets. The superintendent may have a plan for contacting parents new to the district and on special occasions. Other parent communication may occur spontaneously or as scheduled.

Nonparent Residents. The superintendent will communicate with residents who do not have children enrolled in district schools enough to let them know all they want and need to know but not too much. As with any communication, if there is information overload, the receiver will turn off and become confused or otherwise disturbed. This group needs to receive information at regular intervals so the schools are kept foremost in their minds. They also need to receive communication at times when board plans or district events will have significant impact on them, such as in school reorganization or when referenda are planned. At other times the superintendent may initiate communication with individuals or groups to build relationships and to respond to concerns.

Business, Government and Religious Faiths. Representatives of business and government may communicate with the superintendent either on a regularly scheduled or ad hoc basis. In general such communication will be less frequent than with other parties, unless the district is in the planning stages of some cooperative project. Communication may be initiated by either representatives or the district when there are opportunities for service or cooperation and when some program will impact on the functioning of another organization.

Professional Colleagues. The superintendent will communicate with professional colleagues frequently enough to keep the pulse of what is happening or about to happen, to do environmental scanning, to be helpful to either party, and to maintain positive working relationships.

Schools. Communications with schools should be frequent enough to permit both parties to have sufficient knowledge to service students most effectively. In addition, communications should be frequent enough to allow for maximum benefits to be derived from shared resources and cooperative planning. Obtaining knowledge to prevent misunderstanding and building positive and supportive relationships take time. Since time is scarce, it should be put to best use. If meetings are planned for the communication, an agenda may assure that meetings take place only as needed and that they are purposeful and efficient.

Professional Organizations. Communications with professional organizations will take place as needed to satisfy the member's role within the organization. In addition, the superintendent should be seeking ways in which various professional organizations may be of service to the district.

Experts. Experts generally communicate with the superintendent when either party feels it is important to share information. Depending on how much activity involves the use of experts, communication will vary from very infrequently to very frequently (sometimes taking up large blocks of time within a day or several days or weeks).

Partnerships, Consortia, and Networks. As with communications with experts, those among partnerships, consortia, and networks will vary depending how much activity the district may be involved in with the particular group. Communications will also vary depending on whether the superintendent has a leadership role in the governance of the group.

Legislators and Media. More effective communications with legislators and the media will be on a regular basis, monthly or weekly, so that understanding and trust relationships can be formed. In addition, special purpose communication may occur any time as either party to the communication feels the need.

Most of the emphasis in discussing when communications take place has been on the frequency of the communication. Length and duration and the time at which communications take place are also important. Much of the latter will be determined by the annual cycle of events, demand, and availability. Enough but not too much should provide a general guideline for length and duration. The time at which communications take place may be determined by office hours, by need, and by the personal preference or work schedule of either party to the communication.

Where?

Where the communication takes place is an additional important decision. The attempt here is not to be all-inclusive in naming locations, but to offer examples that may stimulate creative thought upon the part of the reader.

Face-to-face. Face-to-face communication with individuals or groups will take place virtually everywhere. The superintendent will be communicating verbally and nonverbally wherever he or she may be, and whether acting to receive or send a communication. An office, hallway, meeting hall, ball field, gym, shopping center, board room, and auto are only a few locations where face-to-face communications can take place.

Other Spoken or Written Communication. Communications that are not face-to-face, either spoken or written (both terms being used broadly here), may take place in numerous locations. A spoken communication may occur on radio, cable or commercial TV, a mobile or standard telephone, a recording played anywhere, and the school public address system, to name a few. A written communication may be sent or received from an electronic conferencing device or computer; a telegram, letter, memo, newsletter, or press release; bulletin boards; directional or instruction signs and symbols in important locations; and others.

Why?

The why of communication, or the purpose of the superintendent imparting information to any individual or group, is to update the person or group on district events and matters of concern and to "sell" the district. The superintendent will also want to receive information as a way of helping others or to obtain counsel and news.

Board. The superintendent's communication at board meetings will be to clarify, recommend, and at times to facilitate. At meetings, if the superintendent can help the board look good by the quality of preparation of board packets, board and superintendent relations can be strengthened. Between board meetings the superintendent may communicate to build and maintain relationships, to impart noteworthy news, and to determine consensus for approving actions or expenditures between board meetings.

Administrators. Communication among administrators will serve several purposes. Communication may assist in team building, planning, keeping updated, and giving or receiving counsel and clarification. The communication may be to supervise and evaluate. The superintendent will want to be sharing a vision and goals and building enthusiasm for district events when communicating with admninistrators.

Staff. Group meetings with staff may be for the purposes of developing esprit or assuring that the same communication is received by all. The superintendent may communicate with individuals to discuss employment and other matters of interest or concern to either party. Special-purpose communication may be to respond to a grievance, to give a commendation or reprimand, to relate referendum or other plans in progress, to name some examples.

Students. Student communication may allow for expression of needs, interests, and concerns by either party. The superintendent may also communicate with students to obtain input into decisions and to praise or reprimand.

Parents. Parent communication is for the purpose of hearing and responding to concerns, explaining and clarifying board and staff plans and actions, promoting and persuading, brainstorming ideas and urging action, among other purposes. In districts with several schools, the superintendent may meet regularly with presidents of all P.T.A.s to assure coordination of activity, to promote cooperative planning, and to accomplish other purposes.

Nonparent Residents. Residents who are nonparents include the business community. Purposes to be accomplished in communications with these groups include soliciting support for education in general and for district schools in particular. The superintendent will also communicate to inform, to "sell" the schools, to obtain input for recommendations and decisions, and to secure goods and services for the district.

Professional Colleagues. Communication with professional colleagues, as in the case with other communications, may be initiated by either party. The purpose may be to share information, to help and to plan, to name a few.

Schools. The superintendent will want to have close, continuing cooperation with nearby schools (e.g., those who feed into the same high school in dual districts, those whose boundaries are contiguous, and those who are similar in size, grade level, and racial or ethnic composition). Purposes of such communications will be many and varied and will include: to share successes and struggles in developing and improving curriculum and instruction, personnel or various aspects of working with personnel, union contracts or progress in negotiations, information concerning the impact of proposed or recently passed legislation, consultants and speakers, cooperative bidding and purchasing practices, and numerous others. Additional communication with area vocational schools and institutions of higher education will again have many and varied purposes. The latter include to share information about district students attending such institutions, information about student teachers and expectations, experts and other resources available to assist the district, and educational options, to name a few.

Professional Organizations. The superintendent will become a member of professional organizations and in other ways initiate or be the recipient of communication with professional organizations. Purposes of such communication will be to read or contribute to professional journals and other media whose production is sponsored by the organization. Also, the superintendent will seek confirmation or redirection of efforts, information for school improvement, and to lend or benefit from expertise, as well as other purposes.

Experts. Experts serve specific purposes in communicating. The attorney will provide counsel to assist the superintendent in fulfilling legal mandates, to provide assistance in collective bargaining matters, and to prevent or defend the board in law suits. The architect will provide expertise in building or maintaining facilities and grounds that are safe, efficient, accessible, and aesthetic. The investment banker will counsel the superintendent to invest funds to meet board purposes of safety and maximum return. The investment banker will assure the district complies with legal restrictions and will keep the district informed about proposed and recently passed legislation that may require board action (e.g., prohibitions on the advance refunding of bonds that will impact on a district's future tax levies). The investment banker may also assist the district to determine cash flow for the purpose of maximizing investments.

Partnerships, Consortia, and Networks. Communications among partnerships, consortia, and networks will have specific purposes. These may include promotion of business-school partnerships, sponsorship of special student programs or inservice, providing research sites, seeking strength in numbers or support for common interests, etc.

Legislators and Media. The purposes of communication with legislators and the media are to inform and persuade. The superintendent may respond to questionnaires, testify at hearings, and partake in other special-purpose communication. Purposes for communicating with these groups should include giving thanks for their interest, support, and otherwise helpful actions towards the schools.

How?

The final variable to be discussed here is the how of communicating. In general communications with those close at hand and those with whom we communicate most frequently will receive the least consideration as to how the communication occurs and its impact. This represents reality, not necessarily what should be. More time spent to plan professional communication with those we see often would conserve time and prevent errors and misunderstanding. Forethought would, therefore, free the superintendent for additional communications. In particularly difficult communications, for example when calling up behavior or denying a request, making notes and rehearsing communications may make these easier, more satisfying, and more effective.

The how of communications of less frequency or with persons at a greater distance should usually receive more careful planning. Will the message be open or closed? Should the tone be pleasant or firm? Is equipment needed? Does the occasion require excitement and enthusiasm or somberness? Is it the time to sell the district or assuage hurt feelings or anger? Is the contact likely to be made on this day or at this time? Should there be an agenda, list of questions, or items to be discussed? How much time has been allocated for the communication? Should closure and followup be planned? Without getting overly structured, planning many of the hows in advance will result in more productive communication.

In addition to thinking about communication in terms of the above variables, the mode of communication is important. Is listening, speaking, reading, writing, or some combination of these appropriate?

Listening, Speaking, Reading, and Writing

Listening

As superintendent you will spend a large portion of your time listening. The test of listening is frequently considered as the ability to give back what has been said. But listening implies much more.

First, we listen with our entire body. Many books have been written on this topic. The attempt here is not to duplicate all that has been written about body language and its role in communication. Rather some aspects are named here to stress its importance.

We listen with all of our senses. Our eyes take in the environment and conditions. Eyes tell us many things about the person or persons with whom we are communicating, the building we are visiting, the ball game we are attending, and so on. We can sense truth and dishonesty, approach and avoidance or withdrawal, contentment or worry, interest or boredom, pleasantness or hostility, confidence or anxiety when we listen with our eyes.

Our ears and hearing are what others usually associate with listening. Did we *hear* what was communicated? Our ears pick up voice quality: volume, pitch, and tone. Each of these communicate. Our ears also pick up the sounds or lack of them in the environment. In these ways our ears, like our eyes, listen and communicate.

Other senses — smell, taste, and touch — figure less into listening, but we should be aware of all signals we are receiving in communications. While listening we should simultaneously be sending messages — acceptance, glad to hear, friendly, likeable, warm, empathetic. Writers in the area offer several listening habits that can be developed:

1. Defer judgment — listen for the other person to say something new and useful. Do not "tune out" the other person, prejudge, or guess what the speaker is going to say.
2. Pay most attention to content — do not allow grammar or speaking skill to supercede the substance of the message.
3. Listen completely first — then plan the response.
4. Listen for the main idea — the principle(s) being presented and the

feeling dimensions. Do not listen for facts or miss emotional content.

5. Concentrate on remembering general ideas. Do not worry about committing all information to memory.
6. Work at keeping attentive — give oneself internal cues. Do not fake attention.
7. Do one thing at a time — realize listening is a full-time job.
8. Be confident of understanding — listen carefully and ask questions.
9. Feel anger but control it. Do not get distracted by negative emotional trigger words.
10. Keep mental energies on the subject.

Some suggestions for improved listening are offered:

1. Maintain eye contact with the speaker or at least look at the speaker frequently.
2. Reinforce yourself and the speaker as you go along; give yourself verbal reminders.
3. Listen for meaning; ask yourself, "Do I know for sure what he or she means?"
4. Listen for new ideas.
5. Do not discount the entire message because of disagreement with one point.

Among techniques good listeners use are the following:

1. Identify the elements of the speaker's message — try to establish the pattern of the message.
2. Make frequent mental summaries employing the memory technique of repetition.
3. Periodically feed back one's understanding — by paraphrasing content and reflecting feelings — to insure progressive listening effectiveness.

Speaking

Speaking is the second mode by which the superintendent communicates. As the educational representative to a number of publics, the superintendent will be called upon to give many speeches. But in addition to what we normally consider to be speaking, there are numerous other ways the superintendent speaks.

As in listening, the senses will also be speaking. Eyes convey our emotions and our understanding or lack of it. They are indicators of our physical condition and general well being. Touch or lack of it conveys a closeness and warmth or detachment, a sense of urgency, praise or reprimand, happiness or anger, and other messages. Other senses, too, may be important. In addition, our facial movements and expressions will speak, as will our body position and shifting positions, location during the communication, distance from the speaker in face-to-face communication, and so on. When empathy is called for, we should be responding first to the other's feelings and then to the content of what we heard. A guideline in speaking is to be clear, concise, and coherent.

Reading

Reading is an alternative way to receive information. The superintendent will be literally swamped with materials to be read. It will be important to skim and speed-read. In addition, it will be important to focus on key issues in reading and on who and what are priority in reading.

Writing

Writing is frozen thought. As such the superintendent will want to be sure that the written record is what was intended. Writing, like other modes of communication, has many variables. To whom will the superintendent respond? Should the response be a formal letter or informal memo? Should others receive copies? Like the spoken word, written communication should be clear, concise, and coherent.

A Workable Model of Communication

The superintendent will be engaged in communication for various effect. Richard Foster uses a model of communication with four categories: interactive, proactive, relinquishing, and defensive. The four types cover the spectrum of communication.

Interactive Communication

Interactive communication is described as exploring and informing. The sender asserts in an open communication such that he or she is open to change or correction. For example, the superintendent may suggest that the best time for a weekly meeting with administrators is Friday morning. In interactive communication, the superintendent will be allowing for a suggested alternative for reasons that may not have been known previously. Both the sender and receiver in interactive communication are okay. Both maintain their self-worth throughout the communication. The goal is to keep in the interactive mode to the greatest extent possible.

Proactive Communication

Proactive is the second type of communication in this model. It needs some preliminary explanation since proactive is frequently used in contrast to reactive and is viewed as desirable, particularly in terms of influencing legislative efforts. In Foster's model, proactive communication orders or directs and is intended as a closed communication. It is viewed as appropriate when someone's life is in danger or in other threatening situations. For example, if you see someone about to back off a height that would result in a fall, you might warn, "Stop!" If a severe weather or other life-threatening situation arises, you might order, "Take cover!" As a final resort in correcting behavior, you might demand, "Sit!" The superintendent will not entertain a response. Clearly the sender in this type message is assumed to be okay. But the receiver is not okay. The self-worth of the receiver is diminished. Proactive communication should be used rarely. Of most importance is that the superintendent is conscious of the type of communication being used. The sender decides if other than interactive communication is called for in the situation.

Relinquishing Communication

A third type of communication is relinquishing. This is a voiced giving up. As in proactive, this communication is assumed to be rarely necessary. A situation where it might be appropriate may be in a job-threatening situation between superior and subordinate. For example, the superintendent may feel that some action is against his or her better judgment but that it does not involve a value position and is required. In such a case the superintendent may vocalize, "If you are directing me to do it, I will." Other examples would include judicial orders and other government mandates when obedience is assumed to be required. The sender in this case, the person giving up, is not okay. The receiver, assumed to be in a power position, is okay. Hence the sender's self-worth is diminished.

Defensive Communication

Defensive communication is a type that is never desirable. Like other types, however, it may be viewed as necessary at times by the sender. Defensive communication is described as either fight or flight. It is undesirable because neither party in the communication is okay. Both lose self-worth.

Fighting may be physical, verbal, or nonverbal. Withdrawal may be physical or emotional. When fighting is physical, we are attacking with our body or being attacked. In verbal fighting, we are using some form of abusive language or it is being used on us. In nonverbal fighting we may be using icy stares, daring glares, and so on. Physical withdrawal may involve leaving a room or moving away from a table. Emotional withdrawal may be focusing on someone or something other than what should be receiving our attention, suffering silently, etc.

One can practice, alone or with another, converting less desirable to more desirable communication. For example, assume that one desires and thinks it appropriate to use interactive communication but orders and directs: "The Parent Teacher Association must have all communications that are to be taken home by children approved by the superintendent." The superintendent can convert this to: "It is important that children bring home messages that convey our goal of achieving excellence. How can we assure this happens in Parent Teacher Association communications?"

A helpful guide is to rely on "I messages." For example, rather than labeling (many "is" messages), the sender of a communication can assert, "I believe. . ." or "I feel . . ." Such messages will frequently prevent or diffuse emotional situations. In addition, the communication will be satisfying to the greatest extent and effective. It will produce the desired results.

In addition to aspects of communication considered above, it is important to take responsibility for our communication and action. We should avoid victim language (e.g., "I can't. . .") that indicates we are not in control and practice using "I can. . ." and "I will. . ." messages. One of the regular needs in avoiding being a victim is in handling the in-basket, a task that frequently covers the spectrum of communicating.

Handling the In-Basket

Dealing efficiently and effectively with the in-basket is critical. The goal is to spend the minimum time needed to get maximum results.

Delegating to Reduce In-Basket Contents

To some extent the superintendent can control contents of the in-basket. The superintendent can delegate disbursement of mail so that only those communications which require his or her personal attention and those known to be of particular interest reach the superintendent. This will require that the superintendent create clear expectations for the contents. In some cases determination can be made for handling of in-basket contents by the superintendent personally or by a secretary or administrative assistant.

Sorting In-Basket Contents

Now assume that the contents are necessary or desirable. A commonly espoused view is that contents of the in-basket should be handled only once. This is not always desirable and is frequently not possible.

A first time through may be to pull out information required for a special purpose while quickly sorting the remainder. For example, the superintendent may be waiting to receive a message about some matter before a board meeting, telephone call, or other imminent communication need. If time permits, a pass-through may include scanning such that a determination can be made to file contents or dispose of them in some other manner. Items can further be classified as requiring a spoken or written response or additional reading and so on. Depending on the time available and the personal preference of the superintendent, a secretary or tape recorder may be utilized during the handling of the in-basket for directing disbursement of its contents and for drafting responses. At other times a preference may be for written notes or the use of some other medium.

In-Basket Followup

Whatever remains after handling the in-basket should receive prompt attention by the superintendent and all charged with disposing of its contents. One sure method is to make a "To Do" list that will include whatever action is required for in-basket items. One caution that applies for such lists is to keep realistic. A guide is to list only those items which can be accomplished in one day. Priorities should be taken care of first. Then, if any item on the list did not receive attention, it can be reassessed and, if necessary, moved to the list for the following day.

The in-basket is a special case of communications. In addition to special ways in which communications may be received, many will also be special-purpose communications.

Special-Purpose Communications

There are any number of occasions which will require special-purpose communications. These will make use of a variety of media and will call for the use of all modes of communication.

Vita

Frequently the superintendent will be asked to submit a vita for purposes of introduction and other matters. The vita may need to be written specially for the occasion to highlight particular training, skills, or experiences. One commonly accepted format is illustrated in Figure 4-13.

Letters of Reference

Letters of reference are frequently requested for employment, schooling, awards, and other purposes. The superintendent will want to know if any particular qualities or experiences should be highlighted. If the superintendent is not able to give an unqualified, positive recommendation, he or she may want to be up front and suggest that another person may be more helpful to the individual making the request. Figure 4-14 is illustrative of a supportive letter of reference.

Summary Information

Summaries of important information can be helpful on a variety of occasions. If the district is involved in one or more law suits, transcripts of depositions and briefs will be received regularly. Whether these are a few or a few hundred pages, the board of education may appreciate having a concise summary highlighting the central testimony and issues in the case. Not only will this enable the board to keep current on such matters, but the summary will save unnecessary costs for copying. Similarly, if the superintendent regularly forwards reading material to the board, members will appreciate concise summaries of important points in the reading.

Evaluations and Performance Reports

Sending evaluations or reports of performance that accurately reflect performance and give direction to activity is crucial. The superintendent will want to have these skills carefully honed for his or her own use. In addition, the superintendent will want to serve as a model and coach in assisting subordinates to improve their own skills. Figure 4-15 illustrates the kind of information that can be shared with the employee and board of education. It implies that the superintendent provides a program for professional growth and advancement.

Praise

Praise should be offered generously in a variety of ways. Though pleasant and easy to do, giving praise is frequently overlooked. In addition, the worry that someone who receives praise may later need to be reprimanded or possibly dismissed frequently inhibits the superintendent from praising when it is warranted. A guideline is to praise behavior in clear, specific, and noninferential terms. Future behavior and communication will then be independent of prior action and praise. Figure 4-16 illustrates well-deserved praise.

Reprimand

Reprimand, too, is frequently overlooked. This is so because it is not pleasant. Calling up behavior and confronting a person or group is often avoided. It is not unusual for a person to be recommended for dismissal without having received open and accurate feedback on performance. This is unfair to the individual. Such seemingly unexplainable action also threatens other employees and lowers staff morale. Reprimands given in an objective and caring way, and allowing for explanation and correction or adjustment of perceptions are a must. Figure 4-17 illustrates the kind of occasional reprimand that the superintendent may deem necessary.

Additional information on performance feedback, praise, and evaluation can be found in more detail in Chapter 16.

Beyond a reprimand, occasionally the legal Notice to Remedy must be used. Legal advice before and during such a process is recommended. But regardless of the quality of advice, the task of documentation falls to the superintendent. The Notice to Remedy is not illustrated here since it will need to contain language specific to fulfilling state mandates.

Media Presentations

Illustrating other than the printed word is difficult here, but the superintendent may be preparing a slide show or video presentation for a parent or student orientation. Or the special-purpose communication may be a spot commercial or public service message for radio or TV. Cable TV, specifically, is available for use by superintendents in many areas. Regular use should be made of the press release. An unusual kind of press release (alternatively published as a display ad) is illustrated in Figure 4-18. Other press releases can inform and promote support for school and district events.

Other Special-Purpose Communication

Messages of welcome, thanks, congratulations, sorrow, get well, bon voyage, invitation, and requests are additional special-purpose communications that the superintendent will use frequently.

The superintendent will want to involve many individuals and the Parent Teacher Association in assisting with special-purpose communications. This will give many individuals and groups a sense of caring, pride, and responsibility for the district. These goals can also be accomplished by involving many individuals and groups in decision-making.

Involving Others in Decision-Making

A guideline for involvement is frequently heard as, "All those to be affected by the decision should be involved in it." While lip service is paid to the guideline it is too often ignored in practice. There are numerous ways to involve others in decisions.

Two district-wide committees operative in Benjamin School District No. 25, West Chicago, Illinois are the Curriculum Committee and the Community-Board-Staff (CBS) Committee. The Curriculum Committee deals with matters related to curriculum and instruction, including staff development, textbook selection, progress reports, and other matters. The CBS Committee deals with all items not directly related to curriculum and instruction: such as policy, evaluation, benefits, needs assessments, facilities planning, and public relations, among other matters. Both committees are described in more detail below.

Curriculum Committee

The Curriculum Committee operates as a committee-of-the-whole and monitors activity of various subcommittees such as Computer Education, Gifted Education, Inservice, Time Standards, Progress Reports, and a number of subject-area and other committees. Several subcommittees may be operating at any given time and cease to function when their tasks have been accomplished. Agenda items for the Curriculum Committee are either initiated by subcommittees or in the committee-of-the-whole. See Figure 4-19 for guidelines for the curriculum committee operation.

Community-Board-Staff Committee

The Community-Board-Staff (CBS) Committee also operates as a committee-of-the-whole and monitors the activity of various subcommittees: such as Facilities Planning, Insurance, Before- and After-School Child Care, Playground, and Teacher Evaluation, to name a few. As in the Curriculum Committee, anyone may initiate agenda items. Guidelines for CBS operation are shown in Figure 4-20.

Needs Assessment Committee

Other district-wide committees may be considered of value. A needs assessment committee may perform periodic assessments. Two instruments and planning processes devised by the Illinois State Board of Education are the *Illinois Problems Index* (IPI) and the *Illinois Quality Schools Index* (IQSI). Both processes recommend facilitation of a 24- to 30-member committee. Open discussion is encouraged. Both processes are geared toward consensus about needs. In turn, needs become the input into determining district priorities, goal-setting, budgeting, and action. Assuming a needs assessment committee is representative of all strata in the educational community, the value of the involvement is the contribution to justifying and lending credibility to district plans and action. Additional information on needs assessments can be found in more detail in Chapter 9.

Considerations When Involving Groups

Any number of ad hoc and standing committees and task forces may be used by the superintendent for involving others in decisions. Groups who are frequently overlooked are taxpayers who are nonparents, parents, and students. Consideration needs to be given for each of these groups to determine helpful and appropriate involvement.

Several considerations become important in seeking input into decisions from individuals and groups. Is the input advisory only? Should the structure be formal or informal? What is the proper setting? What medium of communication is appropriate? Is an outside facilitator or observer of group activity needed? Should there be an agenda and minutes? Who initiates agenda items? What are the objectives? What will be done with the product? If a group, what size and what composition? If the committee is ongoing, how should the superintendent provide for continuity as well as turnover? Who will chair and how will this and other matters be decided? How will others outside the group be kept apprised along the way?

With proper attention given to considerations in involving others in decisions, faith in the group product, and skillful facilitation of group processes, such involvement will lead to investment in and support for decisions as well as an increased self-confidence and positive morale. With all this going for the superintendent, it will be easier for the superintendent to become a cheerleader in communicating.

Serving as Cheerleader in Communicating

The superintendent will be the cheerleader of cheerleaders in district communications. W. Clement Stone is famous for having his staff exude daily: "I feel healthy! I feel happy! I feel terrific!" For Stone there seems to be almost no obstacle that cannot be overcome: "Whatever my mind can conceive and believe, I can achieve!" What Stone is doing with such expressions is affirming a positive mental attitude. He is serving as a cheerleader.

The first requirement in cheerleading is that the superintendent have something worth cheering about. The assumption here is that every district has many things worth shouting about. Regardless of how much work may need to be done, good news will be happening daily.

Beacons, or opinion-setters in the district, as well as staff and students, should be regularly identifying items worth cheering about. The superintendent should serve as a role model in this process as well as a supporter. As a model, the superintendent will be actively seeking forums and taking advantage of those that arise unexpectedly to show and win support for the district. The superintendent will praise the board, administrators, staff, students, parents, and others in the district. In turn, the superintendent will convey expectations of mutual support.

As in other cheerleading efforts, the superintendent will find that being positive is catching. The stronger the cheering the better the performance. The better the performance the more to cheer about.

Caution needs to be advised. While it is assumed that cheerleading will be warranted and will occur at every opportunity, the intent is not to conceal needed improvement. The superintendent should always be open and honest with the board of education, media, and others. As a guideline, concerns should be aired with those who are directly involved in the problem's creation and/ or solution. When this is necessary, every effort should be exercised to avoid sensationalizing. In addition, corrective action should be taken, with every care given to preserving dignity and in a problem-solving, rather than a blaming, manner. When this is done, even those who need corrective action can become cheerleaders.

The attempt in this chapter has been to emphasize the importance of communications, to examine several aspects of superintendent communications, and to offer illustrations of communications. Like any skill, the more effectively communications are practiced, the easier and more natural they will become. Since communications impact greatly on the superintendent's performance, they deserve continual effort toward improvement. In addition, superintendent communications will impact greatly upon the health of the schools and the district — another reason to assure that these are positive, productive, and satisfying.

REFERENCES AND RESOURCES

Bagin, Don, Donald Ferguson, and Gary Marx, *Public Relations for Administrators*. Arlington, VA: American Association of School Administrators, 1985.

Bennis, Warren, and Burt Nanus, *Leaders: The Strategies for Taking Charge*. New York, NY: Harper and Row, Publishers, 1985.

Blanchard, Kenneth, and Spencer Johnson, *The One Minute Manager*. New York, NY: William Morrow and Company, Inc., 1982.

D'Aprix, Robert, *Communicating for Productivity*. New York, NY: Harper & Row, Publishers, 1982.

Deal, Terrence E., and Allan A. Kennedy, *Corporate Cultures: The Rites and Rituals of Corporate Life*. Reading, MA: Addison-Wesley Publishing Company, 1982.

Hoyle, John, Fenwick English, and Betty Steffy, *Skills for Successful School Leaders*. Arlington, VA: American Association of School Administrators, 1985.

Peters, Thomas J., and Robert H. Waterman, Jr., *In Search of Excellence: Lessons from America's Best-Run Companies*. New York, NY: Harper and Row, Publishers, 1982.

Peters, Tom and Nancy Austin, *A Passion for Excellence: The Leadership Difference*. New York, NY: Warner Books, 1985.

Sheive, Linda T., and Marian B. Schoenheit, *Leadership: Examining the Elusive*. Alexandria, VA: Association for Supervision and Curriculum Development, 1987.

Other Resources

Communications Briefings. 140 S. Broadway, Pitman, NJ 08071.

Journal of Educational Communication. Publication of the Education Communications Center, Camp Hill, PA 17011.

MEMO

To: _____ , Member of the Board of Education

Fr: _____ , Superintendent

Re: INFORMATION FROM APRIL 4 BOARD OF EDUCATION MEETING

We missed you! I hope you are enjoying the holiday.

Enclosed is information distributed at the April 4 meeting. I would like to call your attention to a few items.

1. Budget Projections for the Education and Operations, Building, and Maintainance Funds are enclosed. Although expenses are very close to estimates, I believe these are still overestimated and revenue underestimated. Parts that appear shaded on your copies were line items I highlighted for various reasons. I shall be happy to discuss any of the figures with you at your convenience.

2. Policy enclosed will have a first reading at the April 18 meeting.

3. Please complete the Statement of Economic Interest at your earliest convenience and return it in the enclosed, self-addressed, stamped envelope.

Figure 4-1

MEMO

To: Principals and Staff

Fr: _____, Superintendent

Re: Health Hazard

Due to the continuing Salmonella threat, I request that you notify parents to send only wrapped snacks for distribution in school. Please have children return home with any treats that are not wrapped and provide an appropriate explanation for your actions.

In addition, if you are not already doing so, please have children wash their hands with soap before handling food: lunch, snacks, etc. Thank you.

Figure 4-2

MEMO

To: All Staff

Fr: _____, Superintendent

Re: TEACHER AWARD

We are delighted to inform you that our teacher, Pat Gebauer, will receive the "Those Who Excel" Certificate on October 28. We know that you will want to share in Pat's happiness and that of the Board and me.

Last year, for the first time in our district, administrators selected a nominee for the prestigious excellence award given by the Illinois State Board of Education. I submitted the required documentation in June and awaited results. It is my intention to submit a nomination for the award each year. We certainly have a sufficient number of truly outstanding teachers to monopolize awards for some time.

Congratulations, Pat! May you continue the award-winning performance for many years to come.

Figure 4-3

MEMO

To: Mrs. Chris Hlinak and Fifth Period Class

Fr: _____, Superintendent

Re: OUR MARCH 30 DISCUSSION

I was pleased to be able to meet with you on March 30. Thanks for being so open in suggesting desirable changes for Benjamin. Many of the things you suggested are those which we have been planning. Others will need to wait for additional revenues.

Those changes which are possible for next year or the near future are

- adding a foreign language
- rescheduling art and music to allow for a variety of courses in these subjects
- creating locker rooms and finding more suitable lockers for students
- improved landscaping around Benjamin and resurfacing the Benjamin blacktop.

One area for which you can begin planning right now is the color of classrooms. Please do this with your teachers.

Other topics you mentioned will need to be considered by the new Benjamin principal. Some of these include playground area and equipment and benches for sitting.

I was proud of your ability to communicate. Thank you for your interest in Benjamin.

Figure 4-4

LETTERHEAD

Dear Partner in Education of a Jefferson School Graduate:

Thank you for the care and responsible parenting you have provided your child to enable him or her to graduate from elementary school. I appreciate the energy you have expended in the school district during your child's school years.

The remarks made by Mr. Pagels and me reflected what we truly believe: we are at our best when we are positive, set goals, and work hard to achieve goals and take risks. Hopefully, your child will want to do well in high school and beyond. Our task as educators and parents is to help children visualize worthwhile goals and to encourage them to risk pursuing those goals with all of their energies. As you look forward to your child's future growth and success, I would like to share briefly some of the plans we are looking forward to and that we trust will be accomplished.

Our district motto has been, "Maintaining a tradition of excellence in education." We continue to implement many plans toward this end. A few changes are mentioned briefly here: the completion of plans for an addition to the Jefferson School facility, a computer course for all eighth graders, computer testing in language arts, expansion of the Learning Center Program, a homework hotline, and more.

As desirable changes occur, we hope that you will look on these developments with pride. We want our graduates to be proud they are from and enjoy returning to Jefferson.

We shall pray for your continued success as parents and for the success of your child as a high school student. We shall look forward to your continued support, and we pledge our continued support to you and our students.

Sincerely yours,

_____ ,
Superintendent

Figure 4-5

SURVEY INSTRUCTIONS
IMPORTANT

Please help us

. . . Help our children,

FACT: The value of your property largely depends upon the quality of your schools.

FACT: The quality of life for your child *now* and for the *future* largely depends upon the quality of school experiences.

FACT: Benjamin School District has established and is dedicated to maintaining a tradition of excellence.

BELIEF: To sustain excellence we must continuously improve.

REQUEST: Help us evaluate our present effort to help us know where we can strive to do better.

Complete the enclosed questionnaire and return.

DIRECTIONS FOR RETURN:
— Complete the questionnaire.
— Use the reverse side of this page as a mailer — no postage is necessary.
— Fold this sheet over the questionnaire and staple or tape ends together.
— Drop in mailbox.

We appreciate your cooperation!

PLEASE CHECK (✓) <u>ONE:</u>

_____ I/we have children attending Benjamin School District schools <u>now.</u>

_____ I/we had children attend Benjamin School District schools in the past.

_____ I/we have <u>never</u> had children attend Benjamin School District schools.

Figure 4-6

MEMO

To: President and Members of the Board of Education

Fr: _____, Superintendent

Re: MEETING WITH CAROL STREAM VILLAGE PRESIDENT

After talking with President Courtin and Village President Jan Gerzevske, I have set up a meeting to enable Jan to meet with us and the Wayne Homeowners Association to do a fiscal analysis of the Carol Stream Comprehensive Land Use Plan. Specifically, President Gerzevske wants to discuss tax rates and their effect on the homeowners of the Benjamin District and on Benjamin. Jan reported that there would be a $.40 to $.60 increase in the Benjamin area if all land remained residential. She would like to present options for a better tax base. Jan mentioned she would send information in advance for copying and distribution to Board members. The meeting has been set as follows:

> ADMINISTRATION CENTER — COMMUNITY CENTER
> TUESDAY, JANUARY 5
> 7:30 p.m.

Jan will appreciate having all Board members present, if possible.

Figure 4-7

MEMO

To: Robert Cobb, Superintendent, District 34

       John Hennig, Superintendent, District 33

       Mary Korrision, Principal, St. Mary School

       Faye Stone, Superintendent, District 27

       Pat Conran, Superintendent, District 25

Fr: Richard Kamm, Superintendent, District 94

This memorandum will confirm arrangements made by telephone today
to meet at <u>West Chicago High School</u>
       <u>Monday, July 2 at 9:00 a.m.</u>
to discuss Early Admissions to High School English.

You may wish to invite your junior high principals to participate.

Figure 4-8

MEMO

To: WEST SUBURBAN SUPERINTENDENTS' ASSOCIATION —
Members and Friends

Fr: Ron Barnes — Host for December 9 Meeting

We planned a December 9 meeting of the West Suburban Superintendents' Association that promises to be enjoyable and informative.

The meeting will be held at PHEASANT RUN in the EL POCO ROOM on Bourbon Street. The meeting will begin at 11:30 a.m. with an adjustment period; lunch will be served at 12:00 noon.

The menu for the lunch includes Roast Sirloin of Beef, Tossed Salad with choice of dressings, Baked Potato with sour cream, Green Beans Almondine, and Chocolate Sundae. Rolls and beverage will be served.

The speakers for the luncheon meeting will be James D. Lynch and Anthony G. Scariano, from the firm of Scariano, Kula & Associates, P.C. The topic is COLLECTIVE BARGAINING. A description of the program follows:

> Messrs. Lynch and Scariano will be discussing the current state of Illinois public sector collective bargaining law, especially as it affects education. They will provide an analysis of current legislative proposals under consideration, including the forthcoming legislative initiative from the Illinos State Board of Education. Finally, they will discuss the use of interest arbitration (binding arbitration used to resolve the negotiation impasses in which the arbitrator's award establishes the actual terms of the collective bargaining agreement) and its impact on local Board of Education in light of the Wisconsin experience with interest arbitration.

Textual materials will be distributed the day of the luncheon to each registrant. The cost is $10.50 per person. Please complete the registration sheet and mail to Dr. Ron Barnes, _____. I need to have reservations in my office no later than Thursday, December 2. Make all checks payable to the West Suburban Superintendents' Association.

Figure 4-9

LETTERHEAD

Dear _____ :

On behalf of the Corridor Partnership for Excellence in Education and its Board of Directors, we wish to acknowledge your membership contribution of $100.00 and present to you our Certificate of Appreciation. Your sincere commitment to the Partnership's goals of enhancing education is a key factor in determining its success. The benefits to students, teachers, business/industry, and the community will be realized through your leadership role and your supports.

We welcome your membership into this unique consortium and pledge our efforts to work closely with you so that it may be a true "Partnership."

Sincerely,

John J. Swalec   John H. Johansen
Chairman of the Board   Executive Director

Figure 4-10

LETTERHEAD

Senator Alan J. Dixon
United States Senate
Washington, D.C.   20510

Dear Senator Dixon:

I am asking you to support Senate Joint Resolution 346. That resolution asks that 1985 be proclaimed as the "Year of the Teacher."

We recognize that at the very center of the total educational process stands the individual teacher. Schools are only as good as the teachers that teach in them. A meaningful way to give credit to the teaching profession and education in general would be to recognize 1985 as the "Year of the Teacher."

If you are already supporting that legislation, then allow me to thank you for that effort. If there are ways individual members or a group can assist you in dealing with education issues, we would work toward that end.

Sincerely yours,

_____
Superintendent

Figure 4-11

LETTERHEAD

Randall Petrik, Editor and Publisher
Carol Stream Examiner
120 Church Street
Winfield, IL 60190

Dear Mr. Petrik:

Thank you for the coverage given the February 18 Scholastic Chess Tournament held at Evergreen School. Your photographer, Tom Sistak, deserves praise for the appealing pictures you published which really capture the mood of the young participants. Please express our appreciation for his work.

I appreciate the favorable press you have been giving Evergreen School. You may have guessed that we are proud of our schools and we are being critical of our efforts and working hard to keep improving our efforts to benefit students.

Sincerely yours,

Superintendent

Figure 4-12

VITA

PERSONAL

Name _____   Marital Status _____

Address _____   Age _____

Telephone _____ Home   Children _____

_____ Office

PROFESSIONAL PREPARATION (List most recent first.)

Institution   Degree   Date

CERTIFICATION (List all you have.)

PROFESSIONAL EXPERIENCE (List most recent first. Make certain all time is accounted for.)

Location   Position   Period

PROFESSIONAL ORGANIZATIONS

Name   Offices Held   Date

COMMUNITY ACTIVITIES

Name   Offices Held   Date

PARTICIPATION IN PROFESSIONAL MEETINGS (Speeches, Moderator, Panelist, Etc.)

PUBLICATIONS

Figure 4-13

LETTER OF RECOMMENDATION

This recommendation is being written on behalf of Jane Doe at her request. I have known Jane for a period of two years as her employer. She has been serving as the Director of Pupil Personnel Services for the Community School District from August, 1983 to the present.

Jane Doe is a friendly and likeable person who also performs in a professional manner. She has technical competency that she uses in a flexible and appropriate manner. In the two years we have benefited from her services, she has worked to bring about many changes and improvements in our special education services.

Jane works in a quiet and forceful manner in effecting change. By developing a team approach to work with special education staff, many procedures have been effected to organize and strengthen special education services. Building teams of nonspecial education personnel have also been developed for the purposes of assuring that referrals are appropriate and of assuring that classroom teachers get quick help with their problems and that they learn a repertoire of teaching behaviors and curriculum/instruction adaptions.

Jane has worked with parents in a sensitive manner in attempts to gain their cooperation and support for special education recommendations. All parent communication has been satisfactory.

I believe that Jane has the drive and the leadership and management skills to succeed in a building principalship or in a Central Office special education position. Further, I believe that any institution would benefit from having Jane as an employee. I can give Jane Doe my highest recommendation without any hesitation or qualification.

Respectfully submitted,

_____
Superintendent

Figure 4-14

SUMMARY EVALUATION AND RECOMMENDATION
FOR CONTRACT EXTENSION — JOHN DOE

John continues to demonstrate performance that has made a positive difference at the Community School. In addition to carrying forward projects started in his first two years, John has made new initiatives this year.

John has worked with the Learning Center Director to initiate a computer course for eighth graders. The course is now in a draft and pilot stage and we expect to bring a proposal to the Board shortly so that it will become a regular part of the curriculum for eighth graders.

John has continued to show interest in improving his skills relating to evaluation of teachers and helping them improve instruction. To this end, he has been an active participant in the clinical supervision training sessions for adminstrators.

John has revised his student discipline plan, developed a student handbook, and initiated a homeroom program. He continues to foster respect and responsibility among students for each other and adults. His activities have improved esprit at the homeroom and school levels. Reinforcement and reward systems show the exercise of professional judgment and work to motivate students.

John has taken an active part in fulfilling his role as Administrative Assistant. He has proposed areas where he might make a contribution and has shown real interest in knowing all aspects of Central Office operations.

John participated in inservice to gain more knowledge of the teacher contract provisions. He also sat in as an observer during some of the contract negotiations sessions. It would appear that teachers feel that provisions of the contract are being carried out fairly.

There is no question that John is respected by staff and parents as the educational leader and manager of the Community School.

Next year will be a challenge for John. He will need to maintain a positive attitude during the period of construction and reorganization; of course, the Superintendent and Board will need to support his efforts toward making this period of construction, and curriculum and organization changes, go smoothly. I believe John can meet this challenge in a successful manner.

I recommend that John's contract be extended for an additional school year. I further recommend that he continue in the position of Administrative Assistant and that he be awarded the title Assistant Superintendent when he has completed all requirements and has been approved for certification for Superintendent and Chief School Business Official.

Respectfully,

_____
Superintendent

Figure 4-15

186

MEMO

To: COACHES JOHN SHALANKO AND JIM ROACH AND
       SOCCER TEAM PLAYERS

Fr: _____, Superintendent

Congratulations to each of you on your performance and behavior at the conference soccer finals. I want to add my own recognition to that of the Board.

We noted especially the quality of your athletic performance, your display of spirit when down, and your attitude of sportsmanship regardless of results.

You certainly have been noticed this year for the manner in which players support other members of the team and play as a team. Keep up the fine effort.

Figure 4-16

MEMO

To: _____

Fr: _____, Superintendent

This note is being written to direct you to maintain professional relationships supportive of teacher morale and the educational process during your employment. It is understandable that persons may occasionally have disagreements arising from interpersonal contact or other sources. It is not the duty or business of the school district to monitor personal behaviors not related to performance or their impact on the educational process. On the other hand, the district, represented by the Board of Education and me, must insist that behavior that affects any stratum of the educational community or process be professional.

I am aware that you feel you are the offended. Nevertheless, the problems arising from your interpersonal relationship have, at a minimum, disturbed the morale of the staff. We cannot permit this kind of situation to continue or to reoccur.

Figure 4-17

PRESS RELEASE

A THANK YOU TO OUR COMMUNITY
FROM THE BENJAMIN SCHOOL DISTRICT NO. 25
BOARD OF EDUCATION

The Board of Education and Administration of Benjamin School District No. 25 are deeply grateful to our community members for your support of the recent building bond referendum. After the recent election, Board members expressed feeling proud to live in District 25 and to share their efforts in providing quality education for children with other community members.

The referendum to build additional classroom space at both Benjamin and Evergreen Schools received voter approval by approximately a two-to-one margin. Board members feel these results are a clear indication that the vast majority share similar feelings with them about the quality of the District and proposed solutions to providing additional space.

There are too many individuals to thank as individuals; however, the Board acknowledges that the success of the referendum was due to the efforts of many. Community members were generous in opening their homes to receive Board members, the Superintendent, and other community members to discuss the space crunch and alternative solutions. Other community members attended public presentations about the referendum and in other ways gave of their time and effort to contribute to a positive vote. Administration and staff worked diligently to research conditions and solutions and to present these data to the community. Each, in his or her own way, did what was possible to contribute to voter approval. The Board wishes to sincerely and generously thank each person who helped.

Figure 4-18

CURRICULUM COMMITTEE

PURPOSE

The purpose of the Curriculum Committee shall be as follows:
- To provide direction for establishing District 25 needs, goals, and priorities in curriculum and instruction;
- To provide for periodic review of existing curriculum;
- To initiate or endorse recommendations for changes in curriculum;
- To provide a sounding board for discussing curriculum concerns;
- To plan and recommend inservice activities for the staff, including: institute and half-day inservice days and summer curriculum planning;
- To encourage and participate in articulation activity between the District and the high school;
- To provide articulation among and between grade levels within the District;
- To provide opportunities for community input into curriculum endeavors.

PROCEDURES

Procedures for the Curriculum Committee shall include:
- The Superintendent to serve as Chairperson;
- The meetings to be open to the public to observe with the opportunity to request in advance to be placed on the agenda;
- All intended recommendations shall be brought to the principals and the teaching staff for their review;
- The function to be a recommending body to the Superintendent.

COMPOSITIONS

The Curriculum Committee shall be composed of:
- One Board of Education Representative and one BOE alternate;
- Four teacher representatives and four teacher alternates;
- One principal;
- Three community representatives and three community alternates;
- Superintendent;
- One liaison to the Community-Board-Staff Committee.

RENEWAL

To provide for annual review and updating of the Purpose, Procedures, and Composition of the Curriculum Committee as stated.

Figure 4-19

COMMUNITY-BOARD-STAFF COMMITTEE

1. PURPOSE

   The Community-Board-Staff (CBS) Committee has as its purpose, the use of rational inquiry, open discussion, and peaceful persuasion in an effort to reach consensus on policy and other issues of broad concern to Community, Board, and Staff. Concerns that properly belong to Curriculum and Instruction shall be excluded. The CBS Committee shall be a recommending body to the Superintendent.

2. COMPOSITION

   a. The CBS Committee shall be constituted as follows:

      1) One teacher representative for grades K-2, elected by the Evergreen School teaching staff;

      2) One teacher representative for grades 3-5, elected by the Evergreen School teaching staff;

      3) One teacher representative for grades 6-8, elected by the Benjamin School teaching staff;

      4) One building principal, selected by mutual agreement between principals;

      5) One Board of Education member, elected by the Board;

      6) One representative for all special areas elected at large;

      7) Whenever possible, one parent representative from each school, and one taxpayer who is not a parent of district students, appointed by the Board of Education.

         An alternate shall be elected/appointed for each of the elected/appointed members to assure representation at each meeting. In the event the representative is unable to complete his/her term, the alternate shall serve to complete the unexpired term.

   b. Members shall be elected/appointed for two-year terms from the time of their appointment, except that after the first election, a lottery shall be held to provide each teacher with either a one-, two-, or three-year term; this will allow for change as well as continuity among the teaching staff; and the organizational year shall constitute a full year.

      No member shall serve more than two consecutive terms in any single capacity on the CBS. This applies to representatives and/or alternates.

Figure 4-20

An appointee, who is appointed mid-term, shall finish out the term for the representative he/she is replacing and shall serve two full-year terms.

3. PROCEDURES

   a. CBS meeting activity shall be a collaborative process based on mutual respect, mutual trust, and open communication;

   b. A problem-solving process shall be used in an effort to reach consensus. Steps similar to the following shall be followed:

      1) Identifying the problem statement; i.e., precisely what will be the focus of discussion;

      2) Creative thinking to identify alternative solutions;

      3) Identifying criteria to judge alternatives;

      4) Identifying implications of selecting each alternative;

      5) Selecting an alternative.

   c. Members shall appoint a chairperson for each school term. No member shall serve more than two consecutive one-year terms as chairperson.

   d. Any committee member may initiate an agenda item, and the agenda shall be mutually agreed upon by committee members. The following criteria must be met for topics to be considered by the CBS Committee.

      1) Reflect general interest and have implications for involvement by each of the participating groups;

      2) Reflect a need for participatory integration of opinions by all groups involved;

      3) Have the potential for mutual benefit by all (i.e., children, parents, teachers, administrators, Board of Education).

      4) Be evaluated relative to the legal implications of the topic prior to deliberation.

      Items introduced to the CBS Committee are evaluated by the above-stated criteria and screened relative to these guidelines prior to establishing the item on the agenda. Items introduced must be defined as to specific intent and meaning by the party submitting the topic for CBS Committee consideration. In the event an item does not meet these criteria, it is the responsibility of the CBS Committee to suggest alternative avenues of communication for resolution of the given question, topic, or issue.

   e. Before discussion is initiated, guidelines shall be established and agreed upon by all participants. The chairperson shall be responsible for the establishment of guidelines.

Figure 4-20 (Cont'd.)

f. Meetings shall be open to the public and audience input is encouraged. Notice of such meetings shall be posted. The chairperson shall moderate audience participation.

g. Agreement is reached by consensus, with a single topic sometimes being carried over for a number of meetings to insure feedback and input from each group represented. Parents and other members of the audience have an opportunity to participate in the discussions.

h. Minutes of each meeting shall be kept, and shall be distributed to teachers, Board members, principals, and the PTC president. Summary of minutes shall be published in the District Newsletter.

i. Meetings shall be held quarterly or as deemed necessary by the CBS Committee.

j. In order that a meeting be called to order, the following members must be present:

    2 teachers, 1 each from Benjamin and Evergreen;

    1 Board member;

    1 Administrator, who must at a minimum be the Superintendent;

    2 Parents/Taxpayers.

k. Roberts Rules of Order shall be followed in spirit.

l. Community-Board-Staff guidelines and procedures shall be evaluated annually.

Adopted by the Board of Education

November 9, 1981

Revised and adopted by the Board of Education

Figure 4-20 (Cont'd.)

5

Preparing
the Board of Education
Agenda and Packet

Maintaining a Board Box

Whatever frequency of meetings schedule the board of education has adopted, the superintendent will find it helpful to keep a "board box" organized for the year's meetings. Such a file box will have a file folder identifying the meeting date for each meeting in the present fiscal year. Writing dates in pencil facilitates changing dates for meetings that are rescheduled. Items that can be kept in each folder include: the agenda, confidential notes on the agenda, and support data. In addition to a file folder for each meeting in a particular year, this superintendent finds it useful to further break down the file for each scheduled meeting. The individual meeting file folder contains a worksheet that corresponds to each category on the agenda outline. The worksheets and outline are progressively filled in as the time to prepare the agenda approaches. Advance preparation cuts final board packet preparation to a minimum. At the end of the fiscal year, the agendas and corresponding confidential notes can be removed from the file folders and placed in a looseleaf ring binder for easy reference.

Helpful additions to the board box or board meeting folders include: a folder containing materials for board president and other signatures; a folder containing the year's treasurer's reports and statements of financial position and other budget reports; a folder containing employment recommendations; a folder for information that may be placed on a future agenda; a folder for future policy considerations; and a copy of the tentative outline for placement of agenda items throughout the year.

Scheduling Items for the Year

If you are new to the superintendency, reviewing past minutes of board meetings will be helpful in planning a tentative outline for the year's meeting. Asking to be placed on the mailing list to receive neighboring superintendents' agendas will also help to assure that items are scheduled for discussion and action in a timely manner. For the experienced superintendent, this tentative outline can be adjusted annually to assure that items are placed and spaced appropriately. To the extent possible, the superintendent will want to eliminate overloading a particular agenda. While a particularly short or lengthy agenda cannot always be avoided, planning ahead for the year will facilitate meetings of average length. An example of such a tentative outline for a medium-sized district is shown in Figure 5-1.

Making It Easy for the President

A "no surprises" approach to board meeting activity is generally advocated by school board associations and appreciated by board members and superintendents alike. Making it easy for the president to be president will facilitate the "no surprises" approach.

Regular communication on recurring issues as well as spontaneous communication around unpredictable issues will make it easy for the board president. Of course, it is assumed that all communication is timely, open, and not self-serving. Ideally, the superintendent will be able to meet with the board president and, perhaps, vice-president, on a weekly basis.

At a minimum, the superintendent needs to secure a commitment from the board president to meet to plan the agenda. It is assumed that the superintendent will have this well thought out prior to the meeting and will invite changes, additions, and deletions to the suggested agenda items. In addition, if a Consent Agenda format is used (as described below), the board president can assist in determining which of the action items is presumed to be routine and not requiring discussion. Alternatively, an item may have been sufficiently discussed at previous meetings to warrant board action without discussion.

Once the agenda is set or if there is difficulty in deciding agenda placement, the superintendent can offer to poll the board on matters where the board president is undecided. Similarly the board president can offer to communicate with board members when this will facilitate movement through the agenda at the meeting itself. Confidential notes on the agenda can be further helpful to the board president. A sample agenda and accompanying confidential notes are found in Figures 5-2 and 5-3. For example, notes will give background information on each agenda item with the superintendent's recommendation clearly identified. In addition, the superintendent may, especially for a newly elected president, specify when a roll call vote is needed, etc.

In addition to keeping the board president involved in planning board agendas, the superintendent will want to inform the board president in advance about matters that may come to the attention of board members.

The Consent Agenda

The Consent Agenda is a particularly useful format for moving efficiently through an agenda. There may be some resistance to adopting the Consent Agenda format in communities where participation at board meetings is strongly encouraged; however, the Consent Agenda need not limit this involvement.

Managing Community Input

It is important to digress briefly here to discuss the board meeting as a meeting in public as opposed to a public meeting. Different boards and administrators hold various views as to what the nature and extent of community participation should be at meetings. Most would agree that the board should not become engaged in dialogue with other than those sitting at the board table for purposes of deciding action on agenda items. There is less agreement on just how community input will be managed. For example, some will favor allowing those in attendance to speak on an item — any item — prior to board discussion. Others would disagree and would place such participation in the context of a public meeting, rather than a meeting held in public. If the public is not to be permitted to comment on agenda items anytime during the meeting, one possibility is to hold an open forum exchange at an established time prior to the meeting; for example, all board members could be expected to be in attendance at some specified time prior to the start of the meeting to give those in attendance an opportunity to speak on any item.

Personally, I favor allowing the public the opportunity to address the board prior to the start of their discussion of a particular item. By permitting this opportunity, participants are more likely to feel that they have been heard. Further, the times when community members request such an opportunity is rare and generally comes when a highly emotional issue is raised. It is precisely at these times that the board will want to give the appearance of being open to hear the community input. Policy and procedures should guide participation at board meetings so that this does not prevent business from getting done in a timely and orderly manner.

Placement of Agenda Items

Since there is presumed to be no discussion on the Consent Agenda items, the board will want to feel comfortable with the placement of items on this portion of the agenda. Careful planning of the agenda with the board president, as noted above, with communication with other board members as deemed necessary will facilitate a comfort level. In addition, clear and concise information about each item can be included in the confidential notes that accompany the agenda in packets sent to board members. Finally, board members need to know that they can ask to have items pulled from the Consent Agenda and placed among items for discussion and action.

Deciding the Agenda

How and when items are placed on the agenda and subsequently discussed and acted upon are major decision points. Two factors should guide decisions about agenda construction: timeliness and spacing of items throughout the year.

It is important to advocate being up front in planning agendas. For example, placement of items should not be deliberately planned to make difficult or to preclude community participation or expression of community concern. Items such as the certificate of tax levy, employment and dismissal of personnel, school reorganization issues, consideration of controversial curriculum issues, budget hearings, and other high-interest items should be well-publicized so that the public has every opportunity to provide their input prior to board consideration of the items. Similarly, the wording of agendas should not be such as to conceal the intent of action. By fostering and maintaining open, interactive communication, the public is less likely to feel that the board has ignored their wishes, that the board has used the back-door approach in acting or has railroaded through actions, or that the board is a rubber stamp for administration.

Contents of the Board Packet

The contents of the board packet should be enough to fully inform the board so they can take deliberate and responsible action and have meaningful discussion. On the other hand, the contents should not be so weighty that board members will be intimidated by the sheer volume. Similarly, items should not be included merely for fill. Duplications of communications that may be received for other sources (such as the school board association) should be avoided. Confidential notes should accompany the board information and support data. As noted above, these confidential notes should — item-for-item on the agenda — explain the item, give alternative positions and pros and cons of positions on the items, make a clear recommendation for action, and suggest the appropriate vote by the board. Highlighting, in **bold** print or *italics*, parts to call to the attention of the board is helpful. See Figure 5-3 as an example where **bold** type is used to highlight.

A few remarks are added here to discuss supplements to the board packet. Particularly in districts where the board meetings are held only once each month, the superintendent will want to consider more frequent packets, perhaps a weekly memo with support data that is distributed as a packet to board members and administrators who participate in board meetings. The weekly memo, as illustrated in Figure 5-4, will serve to keep board members informed of important and not-so-important events that take place during the week. It can be used as a way of informing the board of an intended hiring or other personnel situations, as an example.

7/9/87

BEXLEY CITY SCHOOLS
BOARD OF EDUCATION
TENTATIVE AGENDA SCHEDULE 1987-1988

MONTHLY

— Minutes
— Treasurer's Report
— Establish Date and Time of Next Meeting

ONGOING

— Employment
  — Hire/Dismiss < Regular
  —   < Subs
  — Resignations
  — Leaves
  — Salary Adjustments

— Policy/Handbook/Codes
  — Job Descriptions

— Executive Sessions
  — Employment/Dismissal Personnel
  — Pending Litigation
  — Collective Bargaining

PERIODIC

— Approve Capital Expenditures (> $5,000)
— Establish Funds
— Fund Transfers
— Appropriations/Adjustments/Additions
— Advance of Funds
— Approve Special Funds Projects (Title II, Etc.)
— Audit Report
— Superindentent/Treasurer Professional Travel
— Legal Matters
  — Suits
  — Suspensions
  — Grievances
  — Negotiations < OAPSE
  —   < BEA

Courtesy of Bexley City Schools

Figure 5-1

- Accept Gifts
- Approve/Accept Fundraisers
- Tuition Agreement with Other Schools
- Insurance Renewal
- Curriculum Changes

YEARLY

- Establish Date and Time of Budget Hearing
- Set Organizational Meeting

JULY

- Approve Budget Appropriations

- Approve F.C.-D.O.E. Contract for Handicapped Classroom Use

- Establish Administrators' Salaries (Eff. 8/1)

- Approve Superintendent's Professional Dues

- Appoint B.E.F. Board Members
  - Board President
  - Other Member(s)

AUGUST

- Approve Substitute Lists < Certified
    < Noncertified

- Approve Out-of-District Special Education Placements

EXECUTIVE SESSION

- Review Superintendent's Action Plans

SEPTEMBER

- Approve Superintendent's Action Plans
- Approve Student Insurance

OCTOBER

- Approve Superintendent's Conference Attendance and Expenses (ASCD)

EXECUTIVE SESSION

- Evaluate Treasurer and Notify of Intent to Reemploy

NOVEMBER

- Approve Renewal of Membership in F.C.E.C.
- Approve Summer School and Summer School Director Position

Figure 5-1 (Cont'd.)

— Approve Co-Sponsors of Education Appreciation Banquet and Education Appreciation Banquet Awards

DECEMBER

— Establish F.Y. — Budget Hearing

— Set Organizational Meeting

JANUARY

SPECIAL ORGANIZATIONAL MEETING

— Adjourn Sine Die

— Appoint President Pro Tempore

— Nominate and Elect President

— Organize (Cal.Yr.) B.O.E.
   — Nominate and Elect Vice-President
   — Swear in Vice-President
   — Establish Time and Place of Regular Meetings
   — Appoint Committee Representatives
      — Athletic Board
      — Recreation Board
      — P.T.O. Council
      — M.E.C. Council
      — Community Liaison
      — Legislative Liaison to OSBA
      — B.E.F.
      — C.B.S.
   — Renew Faithful Performace Bonds (several)
   — Renew Standing Authorizations (several)
   — Approve F.Y. — Budget
   — Approve Establishment of (Cal. Yr.) Service Fund
   — Set Compensation ($, # meetings)
   — Approve Membership
   — OSBA
   — MEC
   — Gov. Finance Office Assn. (Treasurer)

SPECIAL BUDGET HEARING

REGULAR MEETING

— Renew Administrators' Contracts

EXECUTIVE SESSION

— Evaluate Superintendent/Other Administrators

Figure 5-1 (Cont'd.)

FEBRUARY

— Approve School Calendar

MARCH

— Accept Rates for Tax Duplicate

APRIL

— Nonrenew Certified Personnel $<$ Regular
$<$ Supplemental

— Reemploy $<$ Regular $<$ Limited
$<$ Supplemental $<$ Continuing Contracts
$<$ Subs (Nonrenewed Certified Employees)

— Adopt Textbooks

— Approve Summer School + Fees

MAY

— Approve Temporary Budget Appropriations (next F.Y.)

— Authorize P.I. Transfer — $300,000

JUNE

SPECIAL MEETING

— Approve End-of-Year Appropriations/Transfers

— Approve End-of-Year Fund Transfers

REGULAR MEETING

— Approve Summer School Director (if not employed earlier)/
Teachers

— Approve Teachers for Summer Staff Developement

— Renew Memberships
— SSCO
— OHSAA
— MECC

— Renew Agreements
— Student Teaching — Capital
— Student Teaching — Ohio Dominican
— Student Agreement — Otterbein

— Establish Salaries Effective 7/1
(Classified/Nonunion)

Figure 5-1 (Cont'd.)

203

BEXLEY BOARD OF EDUCATION
Bexley, Ohio

ORGANIZATIONAL MEETING OF THE BOARD OF EDUCATION

January 4, 1988
4:30 p.m.
Bexley High School Conference Room

Agenda

I. Call to Order

II. Call Roll

III. Adjourn the 1987 Board of Education, Sine Die

IV. Administer Oath of Office and Seat Newly Elected Board Members

V. Appoint President Pro Tempore

VI. Nominate and Elect President

VII. Administer Oath of Office and Seat President

VIII. Organize the 1988 Board of Education

    A. Nominate and Elect Vice-President

    B. Administer Oath of Office and Seat the Vice-President

    C. Establish Time and Place of Regular Meetings of the Board of Education for 1988

    D. Appoint Committee Representatives

        1. Athletic Board
        2. Recreation Board
        3. P. T. 0. Council
        4. Metropolitan Education Council
        5. Community Liaison
        6. Legislative Liaison to O.S.B.A.
        7. Community-Board-Staff Committee

IX. Approve Agenda

X. Action Items

    A. Consent Agenda

        1. Renew Faithful Performance Bond, $20,000 per Person
           a. Treasurer — $432 Premium per Year (1 Year Remaining)

Courtesy of Bexley City Schools

Figure 5-2

  b. All Board Members — $102 Premium Prepaid for 3 Years

  c. Superintendent — $102 Premium Prepaid for 3 Years

  d. Business Manager — $102 Premium Prepaid for 3 Years

 2. Renew Standing Authorizations

  a. Treasurer Is Authorized to Invest All Interim Funds at the Most Productive Interest Rate

  b. Treasurer Is Authorized to Pay All Bills Within the Limits of the Appropriations Resolution

  c. Business Manager Is Designated to Serve as Purchasing Agent for the School District

  d. School Principals Are Designated to Serve as Purchasing Agents for Activity Funds

  e. Treasurer Is Authorized to Request Advances from the County Auditor of All Property Tax Money

  f. Treasurer Is Authorized to Sign All Warrants with His Signature

  g. Superintendent Is Designated to Serve as Hearing Officer for All Suspension and Expulsion Hearings

  h. Superintendent Is Authorized to Apply for the Appropriate Federal and State Funds as Follows:

   (1) Chapter I
   (2) Chapter II
   (3) Chapter VI-B
   (4) Auxiliary Funds
   (5) Teacher Development
   (6) Other, as Needed and as Funds Become Available

B. Approve the 1988-1989 Budget

C. Approve the Establishment of the 1988 Service Fund

D. Set Compensation for Board Members

 1. Board Members Whose Terms Expire December 31, 1991, $60 per Meeting for a Maximum of 12 Meetings per Year

 2. Board Members Whose Terms Expire December 31, 1989, $40 per Meeting for a Maximum of 12 Meetings per Year

Figure 5-2 (Cont'd.)

E. Approve Membership in the Following Organizations
1. Ohio School Boards Association Membership and Subscriptions

Membership Dues	$1,138.00
Briefcase	80.00
Negotiator	125.00
Total	$1,343.00

2. Metropolitan Education Council

F. Approve Direct Deposit of Payroll

XI. Discussion Items

A. Discuss Resident Request for Admission of Foreign Student

B. Discuss Cooperation with Yassenoff Jewish Center to Develop Site

C. Discuss Job Descriptions
1. Student Council Advisor
2. Lamplight Advisor

D. Discuss Proposals for Future Program Development

XII. Executive Session

XIII. Adjourn

Figure 5-2 (Cont'd.)

CONFIDENTIAL NOTES

January 4, 1988 Meeting of the Board of Education

    I.   Call to Order

        Brian Freeman will call the meeting to order.

    II.   Call Roll

        Chris Essman will call the roll.

   III. Adjourn the 1987 Board of Education, Sine Die

        A motion will be in order to adjourn the existing Board.

   IV. Administer Oath of Office and Seat Newly Elected Board Members

        The Treasurer will administer the following oath to Judie Hise and Fred Meister:

Oath of Office
Member

Do you, _____, solemnly swear that you will support the Constitution of the United States and the Constitution of the State of Ohio, and that you will perform faithfully the duties as a member of the Board of Education of the Bexley City School District, Franklin County, Ohio, to the best of your ability, and in accordance with the laws now in effect and hereinafter to be enacted, during your continuance in said office, and until your successor is elected and qualified.

Judie and Fred will, hopefully, *respond, "I do."*

    V.   Appoint President Pro Tempore

        The Board appoints a President Pro Tempore. The immediate *Past President* has assumed this function.

   VI. Nominate and Elect President

        The President Pro Tempore will call for nominations and conduct the election of the President.

  VII. Administer Oath of Office and Seat President

        The Treasurer will administer the following oath to the President:

Oath of Office
President

Do you, _____ , hereby solemnly swear that you will support the Constitution of the United States, and the Constitution

Figure 5-3

207

of the State of Ohio, that you will perform faithfully to the best of your ability the duties of President of the Board of Education of the Bexley City School District, Franklin County, Ohio, so help you God?

The President will *respond, "I do."*

VIII.   Organize the 1988 Board of Education

    A.   Nominate and Elect Vice-President

        The President will call for nominations and conduct the election for Vice-President.

    B.   Administer Oath of Office and Seat the Vice-President. The President will administer the following oath to the Vice-President:

        Do you, _____ , solemnly swear that you will support the Constitution of the United States, and the Constitution of the State of Ohio, that you will perform faithfully to the best of your ability the duties of Vice-President of the Board of Education of the Bexley City School District, Franklin County, Ohio, so help you God?

        The Vice-President will *respond, "I do."*

    C.   Establish Time and Place of Regular Meetings of the Board of Education for 1988

        Meetings have traditionally been held on the *third Monday* of each month in the *high school conference room.*

    D.   Appoint Committee Representatives

        1.   Athletic Board
            Currently Gene Weiss serves this role.

        2.   Recreation Board
            Currently Judie Hise serves this role.

        3.   P. T. O. Council
            Currently Melinda Blakie serves this role.

        4.   Metropolitan Education Council
            Currently Judie Hise serves this role.

        5.   Community Liaison
            Currently Tom Williard serves this role.

        6.   Legislative Liaison to O.S.B.A.
            Currently Brian Freeman serves this role.

        7.   Community-Board-Staff Committee

            Currently Tom Williard serves as CBS Representative and Melinda Blakie serves as CBS Alternate.

Figure 5-3 (Cont'd.)

IX. Approve Agenda

I don't anticipate additions. *I recommend approval*

X. Action Items

A. Consent Agenda

1. Renew Faithful Performance Bond, $20,000 per Person
    a. Treasurer — $432 Premium per Year (1 Year Remaining)
    b. All Board Members — $102 Premium Prepaid for 3 Years
    c. Superintendent — $102 Premium Prepaid for 3 Years
    d. Business Manager — $102 Premium Prepaid for 3 Years

2. Renew Standing Authorizations
    a. Treasurer Is Authorized to Invest All Interim Funds at the Most Productive Interest Rate
    b. Treasurer Is Authorized to Pay All Bills Within the Limits of the Appropriations Resolution
    c. Business Manager Is Designated to Serve as Purchasing Agent for the School District
    d. School Principals Are Designated to Serve as Purchasing Agents for Activity Funds
    e. Treasurer Is Authorized to Request Advances from the County Auditor of All Property Tax Money
    f. Treasurer Is Authorized to Sign All Warrants with His Signature
    g. Superintendent Is Designated to Serve as Hearing Officer for All Suspension and Expulsion Hearings
    h. Superintendent Is Authorized to Apply for the Appropriate Federal and State Funds as Follows:
        (1) Chapter I
        (2) Chapter II
        (3) Chapter VI-B
        (4) Auxiliary Funds
        (5) Teacher Development
        (6) Other, as Needed and as Funds Become Available

All the above are routine items to meet State requirements and/or to facilitate carrying on district business. *I recommend renewals as indicated.*

Figure 5-3 (Cont'd.)

B. Approve the 1988-1989 Budget
Chris distributed copies of budget earlier. If all appears in order, *I recommend approval*.

C. Approve the Establishment of the 1988 Service Fund

In the past $2,000 has been set aside for Board travel. *I recommend continuation of this Fund.*

D. Set Compensation for Board Members

1. Board Members Whose Terms Expire December 31, 1991, $60 per Meeting for a Maximum of 12 Meetings per Year

2. Board Members Whose Terms Expire December 31, 1989, $40 per Meeting for a Maximum of 12 Meetings per Year

The amounts as shown are in accordance with Board discussion earlier. *I recommend compensation as shown.*

E. Approve Continuation of Membership in the Following Organizations

1. Ohio School Boards Association Membership and Subscriptions

Membership Dues	$1,138.00
Briefcase	80.00
Negotiator	125.00
Total	$1,343.00

2. Metropolitan Education Council

Amount has been increased for OSBA dues, up from $900 last year. I shall have amount for MEC membership for Monday's meeting. We receive library materials and services from MEC. *I recommend continuation of both memberships.*

F. Approve Direct Deposit of Payroll

Chris has prepared an enclosed explanation for this item. There is a one-time setup charge. Benefits include lower per item charge than the present per check charge and avoidance of stop payment charges on lost checks.

Figure 5-3 (Cont'd.)

XI. Discussion Items

A. Discuss Resident Request for Admission of Foreign Student

Enclosed is policy dealing with request to admit a foreign student as you were requested. There appears to be no reason to deny the request.

B. Discuss Cooperation with Yassenoff Jewish Center to Develop Site

I am meeting with Greg Scott Monday a.m. and I shall ask him about the legal implications of using Board monies to develop a non-Board site.

C. Discuss Job Descriptions

1. Student Council Advisor
2. Lamplight Advisor

Copies of the job descriptions as developed by staff and administrators are enclosed.
(For Board information, I discovered that the wrong numbers were put on job descriptions as approved at the last meeting. I shall have these corrected and corrected copies distributed.)

D. Discuss Proposals for Future Program Development
Enclosed are the proposals we are considering for further development and funding. I shall appreciate knowing Board priorities for development should external funding be secured or not.

XII. Executive Session

XIII. Adjourn

Figure 5-3 (Cont'd.)

Bexley City Schools

348 South Cassingham Road • Bexley, Ohio 43209 • Phone (614) 231-7•

MEMO

February 25, 1988

To: President Gene Weiss and Members of the Board of Education, Central Office Administrators and Principals

From: Pat Conran

Re: Weekly Memo — Confidential

PERSONAL

- We have received information that John Doe was hospitalized after collapsing last night with an apparent heart attack. John is in Mercy Medical Center in Springfield in intensive care. He will be moved to Columbus as soon as this seems advisable.

BOARD FOLLOWUP

- Correspondence has been received from Greg on various matters mentioned earlier by Board, including the Residency Policy and the Student Discipline Code. I have enclosed copies and will include information in appropriate places for future activity.

- Information regarding summer school has been reviewed with the principals and Karen Haylor. Revised information is enclosed.

- Thanks to Judie, Melinda, and Fred for meetings held to date with principals. I shall be preparing a summary of points raised.

BOARD AGENDA

- Results of ESL testing have been secured and show a need for some of our students to have tutoring. Appropriations can be moved to fund this. I have discussed my recommendation for this with Gene and Judie and will include this item in a poll of the Board early next week.

- After the Board meeting, Chris and I discussed the placement of administrator salaries on the Board agenda. Our preference

Courtesy of Bexley City Schools.

Figure 5-4

is that this be done in June. I have discussed this alternative with Gene and Judie. Please give the suggestion some thought and I will include this item in next week's poll.

- Separate packet contains personnel information. I shall be including recommended process re: Jane Doe when I poll the Board next week.

ACADEMY FIELD — CONTINUED

- Meeting was held at City Hall today with the Mayor, Joanne Ranft, Gene Weiss, Jim Gordon, Gene Millard, John Barr, and me. The City is proceeding with negotiations to sign a ten-year lease for use of the field owned by Columbus.

  All appear committed to cooperating and working out problems that will occur. The Mayor and I will meet with President Blackmore March 9 to discuss this matter and express our optimism about the arrangement.

LEGAL

- Greg informed me that Squire, Sanders, and Dempsey will be merging with Murphey, Young, and Smith. Interesting.

- Greg is still pushing for closure on the contract. OEA knows there will be no contract without the Grievance language as discussed. He is holding the position that it would not be in our best interest to push for the April 1 clause. I have discussed these items with Gene and Judie.

FOR YOUR INFORMATION

- A message was received during the lunch period today at Montrose that the "School is going to blow." We followed through with the police.

- I have been asked to speak to the BAC in April on the education program with regard to the levy. Mr. Perrin was present at the leaders meeting and asked me to give a similar address to the senior citizens.

COMMUNICATIONS

- Checkpoints.

- Summary of February 22, 1988 Board meeting activity.

- Copy of letter to Jack Lucks, thanking him for computer lab furniture.

Figure 5-4 (Cont'd.)

- Copy of letter to Jim and Sue Gross, thanking them for agreeing to serve as levy co-chairpersons.

- Phi Delta Kappa mailing regarding the Supreme Court ruling on censorship.

- I have been elected ASCD President. ASCD publicity is enclosed. When I learn about duties, I shall be discussing these with the Board. My intent is to use my vacation time for fulfilling responsibilities of this position.

- Board members and administrators are urged to write to our legislators regarding the "Instant Tenure" bill. See enclosure.

- Financial information received from the Ohio Department of Education.

- Montrose Newsletter.

- Bexley Junior High School Newsletter.

THE WEEK THAT WAS

Carolyn Kimbell worked with Level I people on Effective Instruction training. This appeared to go well, as usual.

In addition to regular group meetings the following were some activities:

- Met with Anne and Karen Monday (and later on Wednesday) to finalize summer school plans. Monday I visited Torah Academy; it was a get-acquainted tour and meeting and I learned that they plan a $1 million dollar expansion that will include a high school. Other meetings included Board Banquet meeting at the home of Beth Grimes and fruitless meeting with Patt and Chuck DeRousie re: levy.

- Tuesday I attended meeting of North Central chairs at Maryland. Linda Lucks exercised leadership in scheduling meeting.

- Among other items Wednesday, I set CBS agenda with Bob Madaffer. Greg Scott came to discuss a variety of pending items. The Danforth program had a dinner meeting in the p.m.

- Today, Thursday, I started off at OSU with a Critical Thinking Conference, for which I served on the planning committee. I returned to meet with Sue Gross re: levy. Next I attended the City Hall meeting re: the field. Then I met with ODE persons regarding differentiated timing and North Central. When I returned, I met with a host of persons regarding the Kindergarten screening. Conclusion was that main concern was

Figure 5-4 (Cont'd.)

around scheduling. We are going to be sending a survey with opportunity for all affected to specify priorities for scheduling; in addition, persons responding will be asked to specify pros and cons of specified priorities and impact of choice(s) on other scheduling and school activity. End result should satisfy most all. Ended the day's meetings with Gene and Judie. In between, we investigated the "blow up" scare at Montrose.

NEXT WEEK

- All administrators will be in a two-day workshop on Monday and Tuesday. We have a full agenda of items.

- Tuesday I'm meeting with Pam Workman to work out some alternatives for levy organization.

- Danforth mentors and mentees will be meeting on Thursday.

- Kevin Freeman has asked to meet to discuss "Just Say No" activity.

FUTURE

- CAT activity begins week of March 7.

- Anne and I will be leaving for ASCD Wednesday p.m.

- I have scheduled three optional-attendance meetings with staff regarding levy; the first of these is March 8.
  Happy weekend!
  I have taken Friday as a vacation day and am skiing in Michigan. Ruth Ann will have a number in case of emergency.

Figure 5-4 (Cont'd.)

6

Maintaining
Positive Public Relations

If you are the superintendent of a large district, you will probably hire a public relations administrator or an expert consultant. However, the task of maintaining positive public relations falls to most superintendents directly. This section is intended to be helpful to both the public relations administrator as well as to the superintendent who does his or her own public relations. At the same time, we recognize the importance of the students and school employees in creating a public image. The message here should help the superintendent to utilize staff and students as public relations ambassadors. The task of the public relations ambassador is to earn public understanding and acceptance.

The National School Public Relations Association refers to school public relations as:

> a planned and systematic, two-way process of communications between an educational organization and its internal and external publics. Its program serves to stimulate a better understanding of the role, objectives, accomplishments, and needs of the organization. Educational public relations is a management function that interprets public attitudes, identifies the policies and procedures of an individual organization with the public interest, and executes a program of action to encourage public involvement and to earn public understanding and acceptance. (*Armistead*)

To emphasize, public relations are planned, systematic, and two-way.

Planning a Program

An effective public relations plan requires an understanding of the community. A convenient way to achieve this understanding is through a comprehensive analysis, such as that done by the School and Community Committee in a North Central Association self-study. In addition to overall district characteristics, each school in the district probably has its own character. Therefore, the school personnel need to know expectations of the particular school community. What is the history of the community? How has the community changed? What is the community like? What is the stability of the pupil population? Why do students withdraw? What portion of students come from homes with non-English-speaking backgrounds? What is the education level of parents or guardians? What is the occupational status? What is the stability of the family? What resources are available and how are these allocated? What community resources and services are available and what is the type and extent of usage? What is the climate of the school and community?

Figures 6-1 to 6-3 show possible questions on student, parent, and teacher opinion inventories. Figure 6-1 is a student opinion inventory. Questions focus on quality of student involvement, quality of teacher and counselor performance, and satisfaction with the school and the students' various other involvements and interactions. Figure 6-2 is a parent opinion inventory. Questions focus on the quality of student relationships; the amount and quality of information received from the school; parent and student involvement in the school; affective and cognitive learnings; the quality of instruction and support services; and various health, welfare, and safety issues. Figure 6-3 is a teacher opinion inventory. Questions focus on satisfaction with the profession and situation, on the amount and quality of teacher involvement in school policies and procedures, the amount and quality of interaction with parents and administrators, and the quality of instruction and services offered students. A Likert-type rating scale using a four-point rating system was used in constructing the inventories used as examples. Various manuals or examples can be studied in choosing a format for questions and responses when constructing questionnaires, surveys, or inventories. When analyzing results of the surveys, significant differences among groups, if any, should receive attention toward resolution.

In addition to information about the community, the public relations planner needs to know where community people gather and who meets with whom regularly. Planners also need to know who gets what information from whom. How is information exchanged? Is this mostly face-to-face, by mail, through the media, by telephone, or by some other medium?

Identifying Your Publics

There may be common publics for schools, but the extent to which the superintendent or the public relations administrator needs to develop an ongoing plan to communicate with various publics will depend on several variables inside and outside the school system. Size, education, and socioeconomic level of the community; geographic location; organization of the district; and other factors will need to be considered in identifying publics.

Parents and students, the clients whom we serve, are probably tops on the list of those with whom we must maintain positive public relations and who, in turn, help create the public image of our schools.

Today, more than ever in the past, it is necessary to work with government officials. States are increasingly mandating action in schools; at the least it is necessary for educators to assure that legislators are informed on key issues for which they will vote. Beyond this, it is imperative for educators to attempt to influence voting of legislators toward mandates that will be in the service of students' learning.

Parallelling importance of government relations are news media relations. Whether via television, radio, or print, media sources are powerful opinion-shapers.

Citizens who are nonparents have a powerful and usually a majority voice in school matters. Members of the business community are also powerful shapers of public opinion. The latter groups must have targeted communications to create and sustain a positive image.

Each of the groups identified in the chapter on communications, Chapter 4, is an important player on the public relations team. Within the school district, groups include the board, administration, staff, students, parents, and resident nonparents. Outside the district, groups include colleagues, schools, professional organizations, experts, partnerships and consortia, networks, and legislators. Groups both in and out of the district include the media, government, and clergy.

The grid illustrated in Figure 6-4 can serve as a helpful starting point for identifying your publics and selecting appropriate communications channels. Beginning with internal communications and extending, in some cases, to international relations, it describes the possible scope of public relations.

Identifying and Using Beacons

Beacons are key communicators who will serve to assure that the school district understands the community and that the community, in turn, understands the school district. Beacons will be both internal and external to the school system. Working together, beacons can develop a public relations plan for a particular district program and school building as well as for the district as a whole.

Using beacons is an ongoing process. While the beacons may change for various reasons — relocation out of the district or changing demographics that require changing beacons, as examples — continuing and systematic communication with them is required. In discussing excellence and ways in which excellence is achieved (Chapter 2), we advocated keeping close to the customer. Using beacons is one way to keep close to the people we serve and close to those on whom we depend for success.

It is important to recognize that our beacons, or key communicators, are frequently very busy people. Therefore, it may be advisable to get them to attend one meeting of defined length. At that meeting they can be requested to contact you when they hear rumors or need information about the schools. Similarly they can be relied on to disseminate information. This process can be repeated so that there are many beacons, or groups of key communicators.

Having Something Worth Bragging About

Good public relations is not merely telling others what you want them to know. Similarly, the AASA tells us it is not doing a snow job; nor is it a panacea or substitute for doing a good job. One aspect of public relations is identifying those aspects of the school district worth bragging about and then doing it. The other aspect is structuring situations to get meaningful input into decisions and feedback on performance.

Being Upfront

How we say and do things is as important as what we say and do. Planning a strategy that will permit the superintendent to be up front in relating to the public is important. Interactive communication has been advocated in Chapter 4. Interactive communication implies being open and honest.

Some guidelines for being up front are suggested. First, the person who is the subject of a particular discussion or decision should be privy to the communication first. This is common courtesy and allows for any possible misperception to be corrected. Next, the same thing that is communicated to the person or group directly involved should be what is communicated to others. Consistency in communication makes this easier and facilitates building trust. Finally, it is not necessary that you tell people more about penguins than they need or want to know; that is, being up front is not necessarily telling all to everyone, or letting it all hang out.

Building Pride and Other Elements of Esprit

Caring about our students, staff, and community is essential to achieve excellence. It is also essential to build the pride and esprit necessary to positive public relations.

Caring implies listening. This means we must make the environment safe for our students, staff, and community to be willing to communicate anything — about themselves or the school system. Similarly, caring means listening with empathy — putting yourself in another person's shoes — and listening because it will help them, not listening with hidden messages.

To assure that you have listened, paraphrase the remarks of another and allow for correction. Or vice versa, have another listener paraphrase the point you are trying to communicate. Similarly, perceptions of feelings can be communicated with "I messages" and checked for accuracy. Pride and esprit are also more likely when those involved in the problem and its solution assume ownership.

Building pride and esprit are part of building public confidence in our schools. Much has been written on this topic in the last decade. Of course, the best way to build confidence is to have something worth bragging about. In addition, there are definite steps recommended by the AASA. The 12 steps are listed below and described in Figure 6-5.

1. Strive for quality.
2. Create a spirit of caring.
3. Share the good news about schools.
4. Show connections.
5. Work with each other, not against each other.
6. Get the community on the school team.
7. Help people more, hassle people less.
8. Demonstrate a sense of direction.
9. Be an educational leader in the community.
10. Create substantive themes.
11. Be an effective communicator.
12. Have confidence in yourself.

The steps are put forward as a way to build confidence and as a model for a public relations plan.

Putting on a Class Act

How many times have you heard, "If it's worth doing at all, it's worth doing well." We believe this to be true and so we speak of putting on a class act all the time, every time. The ever-existent class act is necessary for excellence to be achieved and for positive public relations.

The superintendent or public relations administrator or ambassador needs to be ever conscious of the effect of communicating information. Some helpful tips in making a public presentation are offered. First, be prepared or don't attempt to communicate. The message should be adapted to the group but should have some thought-out structure. For example, I recently delivered remarks to a group of about 50 Realtors during American Education Week. I had prepared packets and was about to expand on the virtues of the Bexley City Schools. Immediately prior to starting, I was informed that some members of the group were strong supporters of our neighboring Columbus City Schools and would not take kindly to hearing the virtues of Bexley extolled. Knowing this, but having an outline in mind, I was able to adapt my remarks to stress the importance of keeping all schools strong and the resulting effect on the business environment. This incident emphasizes the point of preparation and flexibility in communication; at the same time, it reinforces the importance of having and relying on beacons. Second, listen to a question or argument, and seek clarification if necessary, before responding. Third, respond only if you have accurate information and be honest and accurate in providing this. However, don't withhold comment; defer to someone who knows. Fourth, be concise and clear. Fifth, be enthusiastic, friendly, and likeable; look at those with whom you are communicating in a direct and pleasant manner; avoid a monotone. Finally, try to satisfy your own needs to communicate information while satisfying the specific needs of others to know.

Because publications are considered to be among the most effective channels for conveying information about the schools to internal and external publics, they are given special treatment here. Once again, each publication should be a class act. In this effort, the National School Public Relations Association can be of great assistance in providing tips on and samples of award-winning publications.

Award-winning publications reflect planning: identification of the purpose and the audience, and determination of format. The actual content of the publication should be interesting and should accomplish the purpose for which it was intended. Getting information from the grass roots is one way to assure that the publication is communicating accurately. The actual writing should be brief (to be read in 30 seconds to 3 minutes) and should contain short sentences. The style should be warm and conversational — folksy. It goes without saying that correct grammar, spelling, and punctuation should characterize each publication. Donald Hymes of the Montgomery, Maryland schools offers "20 Rules for Good Writing." These are:

1. Prefer the plain word to the fancy.
2. Prefer the familiar word to the unfamiliar.
3. Prefer the Saxon word to the Romance.
4. Prefer nouns and verbs to adjectives and adverbs.
5. Prefer picture nouns and action verbs.
6. Never use a long word when a short one will do.
7. Master the simple, declarative sentence.
8. Prefer the simple sentence to the complicated.
9. Vary your sentence length.
10. Put the words you want to emphasize at the beginning or end of your sentence.
11. Use the active voice.
12. Put statements in a positive form.

13. Use short paragraphs.
14. Cut needless words, sentences, and paragraphs.
15. Use plain, conversational language. Write the way you talk.
16. Avoid imitation. Write in your natural style.
17. Write clearly.
18. Avoid gobbledygook and jargon.
19. Write to be understood, not to impress.
20. Revise and rewrite. It can always be improved.

Other factors that will make your publication look classy are the use of white space, an easy-to-read typeface, and headlines — professional-looking headlines and photography that's *good*. Whether or not the communication is a publication or uses technology, the same principles apply for producing the class act. Using cable, teleconferencing, instructional television, and videotape or disc require even more preplanning and care in delivery to assure that limited and expensive time is used to maximum benefit.

Communicating Fully and in a Timely Manner

Communicating fully and in a timely manner requires that the strategies and channels for sending and receiving information are varied. In thinking through the means for listening and responding, serving the educational needs of the community should guide decisions. Surveys of the staff and community, advisory groups, parent groups, and others can help schools identify needs, values, and expectations. Being responsive to information received will foster positive and effective school-community relations.

As careful as we need to be in planning for receiving information, it is equally important to be aware of how our verbal and nonverbal communication can be instrumental in building positive public relations or vice versa. Everything about us influences how our communication is received: how we listen, speak, dress, treat others, function in a meeting, handle the news media, and other characteristics and behaviors.

To communicate fully implies identifying the methods of communication that will serve as efficient and effective channels. Among those to be considered are home-school coffees, district and school newsletters and brochures, advisory councils, surveys, phone calls, notes, media releases and reports, person-to-person communication with individuals and groups, open houses, luncheons and other forums, recognition programs, lobbying efforts, and others. Bagin, Ferguson, and Marx advocate spelling out the following information for each communications activity:

- A description of the activity,
- A list of objectives for the activities,
- A list of procedures that includes who will do what by when,

- A list of resources needed,
- A means of measuring success.

These activities are illustrated in Figure 6-6 in an outline for a public relations project. The project — forming principals' advisory groups — is described. Five objectives of the advisory groups are listed. Six activities (what) are listed with those responsible (who) and timelines (when) identified. A list of six resources needed has been prepared. Finally, success is to be measured by an evaluation of participant opinions and activity accomplishments.

REFERENCES AND RESOURCES

Bagin, Don, Donald Ferguson, and Gary Marx, *Public Relations for Administrators*. Arlington, VA: American Association of School Administrators, 1985.

Bagin, Don, Don Gallagher, and Leslie W. Kindred, *The School and Community Relations*. Englewood Cliffs, NJ: Prentice Hall, 1984.

Business and Industry . . . Partners in Education. Arlington, VA: American Association of School Administrators, 1985.

Center, Allen, and Scott M. Cutlip, *Effective Public Relations*. Englewood Cliffs, NJ: Prentice Hall, 1982.

Citizens and the Schools . . . Partners in Education. Arlington, VA: American Association of School Administrators, 1985.

Evaluating Your School PR Investment. Arlington, VA: National School Public Relations Association, 1984.

Grunig, James E., and Todd Hunt, *Managing Public Relations*. New York, NY: Holt, Rinehart and Winston, 1984.

Lesly, Philip, *Lesly's Public Relations Handbook*. Englewood Cliffs, NJ: Prentice Hall, 1983.

Parents . . . Partners in Education. Arlington, VA: American Association of School Administrators, 1982.

Other Resources

National School Public Relations Association, 1501 Lee Highway, Arlington, VA 22209. (Publishes NSPRA *Impact, It Starts in the Classroom*.)

National Study of School Evaluation, 5201 Leesburg Pike, Falls Church, VA 22041.

PR Reporter, Dudley House, P. O. Box 600, Exeter, NH 03833. Weekly newsletter.

Public Relations News, 127 E. 80th St., New York, NY 10021. Weekly newsletter.

Public Relations Quarterly, College Park, PA. Quarterly journal.

Public Relations Society of America, 845 Third Ave., New York, NY 10022.

STUDENT OPINION INVENTORY

Directions: Circle the number that is the nearest indicator of how you
                feel about the question being asked. Circle only *one* number
                for each item.

1. I help plan student activities in which I participate:

    Always   1. . . . .2. . . . .3. 4   Never

2. I feel accepted in school activities:

    Always   1. . . . .2. . . . .3. 4   Never

3. I feel I can participate in those student activities (athletics,
   newspaper, plays, etc.) in which I would like to participate:

    Always   1. . . . .2. . . . .3. 4   Never

4. I feel that I belong in my school:

    Always   1. . . . .2. . . . .3. 4   Never

5. Sponsors and coaches of activities in which I participate seem
   qualified:

    Always   1. . . . .2. . . . .3. 4   Never

6. Teachers seem to care if I learn the subject they teach:

    Always   1. . . . .2. . . . .3. 4   Never

7. Teachers clearly explain what to do on assignments:

    Always   1. . . . .2. . . . .3. 4   Never

8. Teachers give me the help I need with my schoolwork:

    Always   1. . . . .2. . . . .3. 4   Never

9. Teachers make sure I understand what they teach in class:

    Always   1. . . . .2. . . . .3. 4   Never

10. Teachers clearly explain how assignments are to be done:

    Always   1. . . . .2. . . . .3. 4   Never

11. Teachers give students individual help outside of class time:

    Always   1. . . . .2. . . . .3. 4   Never

12. Teachers give me the encouragement I need in my schoolwork:

    Always   1. . . . .2. . . . .3. 4   Never

Figure 6-1

13. The methods teachers use in classes are satisfying:

       Always   1. . . . .2. . . . .3. 4   Never

14. I can say I am learning a lot in my subjects this year:

       Always   1. . . . .2. . . . .3. 4   Never

15. I feel my studies will be useful in everyday living:

       Always   1. . . . .2. . . . .3. 4   Never

16. I feel I am learning as much as I can in my schoolwork:

       Always   1. . . . .2. . . . .3. 4   Never

17. I am satisfied with the way I am treated by my counselor:

       Always   1. . . . .2. . . . .3. 4   Never

18. My counselor gives me the help I need to select courses:

       Always   1. . . . .2. . . . .3. 4   Never

19. My counselor gives me the help I need to select a vocation or career:

       Always   1. . . . .2. . . . .3. 4   Never

20. My counselor gives me the help I need to select a college, vocational, or trade school:

       Always   1. . . . .2. . . . .3. 4   Never

21. My counselor gives me the help I need to solve personal problems:

       Always   1. . . . .2. . . . .3. 4   Never

22. In general, I am satisfied with the way I am treated by the administration:

       Always   1. . . . .2. . . . .3. 4   Never

23. I feel I can talk with the administration when I have a suggestion or problem:

       Always   1. . . . .2. . . . .3. 4   Never

24. The administration seems to really care about me as an individual:

       Always   1. . . . .2. . . . .3. 4   Never

25. The administration includes the students in making decisions about matters which directly affect students (dress code, assemblies, etc.)

       Always   1. . . . .2. . . . .3. 4   Never

Figure 6-1 (Cont'd.)

26. The administration encourages me concerning school:

       Always   1. . . . .2. . . . .3. 4   Never

27. When I talk with the administration, I feel I am treated as an individual:

       Always   1. . . . .2. . . . 3. 4   Never

28. In general, I am satisfied with my school:

       Always   1. . . . .2. . . . .3. 4   Never

29. The things I should be learning right now are being taught in my school:

       Always   1. . . . .2. . . . .3. 4   Never

30. I am satisfied with the variety of subjects that my school offers:

       Always   1. . . . .2. . . . .3. 4   Never

31. I am satisfied with the variety of student activities that my school offers:

       Always   1. . . . .2. . . . .3. 4   Never

32. I am satisfied with the quality of student activities that my school offers:

       Always   1. . . . .2. . . . .3. 4   Never

33. School spirit is evident in my school (Consider student support of athletic teams, fundraisers, attendance at plays and concerts, etc.):

       Always   1. . . . .2. . . . .3. 4   Never

34. I am proud of my school:

       Always   1. . . . .2. . . . .3. 4   Never

Figure 6-1 (Cont'd.)

PARENT OPINION INVENTORY

Directions: Circle the number that is the nearest indicator of how you feel about the question being asked. Circle only *one* number for each item.

1. My child's progress reports from school are adequate:

    Always   1. . . . .2. . . . .3. 4   Never

2. I am informed about the school's educational practices:

    Always   1. . . . .2. . . . .3. 4   Never

3. My concerns are reflected in school decisions:

    Always   1. . . . .2. . . . .3. 4   Never

4. The community has a say in school activity:

    Always   1. . . . .2. . . . .3. 4   Never

5. I am satisfied with my involvement in the school:

    Always   1. . . . .2. . . . .3. 4   Never

6. Satisfactory emphasis is placed on school grades:

    Always   1. . . . .2. . . . .3. 4   Never

7. Class periods are a proper length for the courses taught:

    Always   1. . . . .2. . . . .3. 4   Never

8. Students help plan student activities:

    Always   1. . . . .2. . . . .3. 4   Never

9. Student participation in school activities is an important aspect of education at our school:

    Always   1. . . . .2. . . . .3. 4   Never

10. I can get an appointment with an administrator when I need to talk:

    Always   1. . . . .2. . . . .3. 4   Never

11. School rules and regulations for students are reasonable:

    Always   1. . . . .2. . . . .3. 4   Never

12. Students in our school are helped to cope with a rapidly changing society:

    Always   1. . . . .2. . . . .3. 4   Never

Figure 6-2

13. Students in our school are helped to become responsible citizens:

       Always   1. . . . .2. . . . .3. 4   Never

14. Students in our school are helped to understand world problems:

       Always   1. . . . .2. . . . .3. 4   Never

15. Our school does an effective job in teaching basic skills (such as math, science, reading):

       Always   1. . . . .2. . . . .3. 4   Never

16. Our school does an effective job in helping students understand their moral and ethical responsibilities:

       Always   1. . . . .2. . . . .3. 4   Never

17. Our school's program helps students understand and get along with other people:

       Always   1. . . . .2. . . . .3. 4   Never

18. Our school helps students understand and appreciate the diversity in our community:

       Always   1. . . . .2. . . . .3. 4   Never

19. Physical education offers a wide variety of appropriate activities:

       Always   1. . . . .2. . . . .3. 4   Never

20. Health classes include appropriate attention to physical and mental health:

       Always   1. . . . .2. . . . .3. 4   Never

21. Our school places the appropriate emphasis on teaching history:

       Always   1. . . . .2. . . . .3. 4   Never

22. The school's program is adequate for students planning to continue their education beyond high school:

       Always   1. . . . .2. . . . .3. 4   Never

23. The educational program in our school is of high quality:

       Always   1. . . . .2. . . . .3. 4   Never

24. Course offerings in our school are adequate:

       Always   1. . . . .2. . . . .3. 4   Never

25. The amount of innovation and change in the school program is adequate:

       Always   1. . . . .2. . . . .3. 4   Never

Figure 6-2 (Cont'd.)

26. Discipline in the school is adequate:

       Always   1. . . . .2. . . . .3. 4   Never

27. The health, welfare, and safety of all in the school are assured:

       Always   1. . . . .2. . . . .3. 4   Never

28. Students are respectful of each other:

       Always   1. . . . .2. . . . .3. 4   Never

29. Teachers and students have positive working relationships:

       Always   1. . . . .2. . . . .3. 4   Never

30. Teachers are competent:

       Always   1. . . . .2. . . . .3. 4   Never

31. Teachers emphasize thinking skills (problem-solving, analyzing, etc.):

       Always   1. . . . .2. . . . .3. 4   Never

32. I can get an appointment with a teacher when I need to talk:

       Always   1. . . . .2. . . . .3. 4   Never

33. Teachers are concerned about my child as an individual:

       Always   1. . . . .2. . . . .3. 4   Never

34. The emphasis on students' social development is adequate:

       Always   1. . . . .2. . . . .3. 4   Never

35. The school guidance program is adequate for students' needs:

       Always   1. . . . .2. . . . .3. 4   Never

36. My child receives help in class and guidance in selecting courses to the extent needed:

       Always   1. . . . .2. . . . .3. 4   Never

37. Support services are adequate (nurse, library, food):

       Always   1. . . . .2. . . . .3. 4   Never

38. The school building and grounds are well-maintained:

       Always   1. . . . .2. . . . .3. 4   Never

39. The morale of students in our school is positive:

       Always   1. . . . .2. . . . .3. 4   Never

40. My child looks forward to going to school each day:

       Always   1. . . . .2. . . . .3. 4   Never

Figure 6-2 (Cont'd.)

TEACHER OPINION INVENTORY

Directions: Circle the number that is the nearest indicator of how you feel about the question being asked. Circle only *one* number for each item.

1. Students learn all they can from their school experiences:

    Always   1. . . . .2. . . . .3. 4   Never

2. Teachers help students with their schoolwork:

    Always   1. . . . .2. . . . .3. 4   Never

3. Teachers are willing to give individual help outside of class time:

    Always   1. . . . .2. . . . .3. 4   Never

4. Teachers give enough personal encouragement to students in their schoolwork:

    Always   1. . . . .2. . . . .3. 4   Never

5. I am satisfied with the consistency of teachers in handling discipline:

    Always   1. . . . .2. . . . .3. 4   Never

6. I am satisfied with the way students are treated by teachers:

    Always   1. . . . .2. . . . .3. 4   Never

7. I welcome parent contacts:

    Always   1. . . . .2. . . . .3. 4   Never

8. I am well-acquainted with parents of my students:

    Always   1. . . . .2. . . . .3. 4   Never

9. Teachers have a high status in our community:

    Always   1. . . . .2. . . . .3. 4   Never

10. I am satisfied with our school:

    Always   1. . . . .2. . . . .3. 4   Never

11. I am satisfied with being a teacher:

    Always   1. . . . .2. . . . .3. 4   Never

12. Teachers in our school help develop policies which affect their work:

    Always   1. . . . .2. . . . .3. 4   Never

Figure 6-3

13. When I need to talk with an administrator, I can do so:

      Always   1. . . . .2. . . . .3. 4   Never

14. Faculty workloads in our school are equitable:

      Always   1. . . . .2. . . . .3. 4   Never

15. Class interruptions are appropriate:

      Always   1. . . . .2. . . . .3. 4   Never

16. I am satisfied with the way I am treated by administration:

      Always   1. . . . .2. . . . .3. 4   Never

17. Class visitations by my principal are supportive of my efforts to improve instruction:

      Always   1. . . . .2. . . . .3. 4   Never

18. Teachers have sufficient freedom in selecting teaching materials:

      Always   1. . . . .2. . . . .3. 4   Never

19. Teachers have sufficient freedom in selecting effective teaching methods:

      Always   1. . . . .2. . . . .3. 4   Never

20. Teachers have sufficient freedom in presenting different points of view on controversial issues:

      Always   1. . . . .2. . . . .3. 4   Never

21. The number of class periods I teach is appropriate:

      Always   1. . . . .2. . . . .3. 4   Never

22. Teachers have sufficient time to prepare adequately for teaching:

      Always   1. . . . .2. . . . .3. 4   Never

23. Students avoid student activities because they are too expensive:

      Always   1. . . . .2. . . . .3. 4   Never

24. I am satisfied with student involvement in decision-making about matters which directly affect discipline (school rules, etc.):

      Always   1. . . . .2. . . . .3. 4   Never

25. I can get help from administration when I have a discipline problem:

      Always   1. . . . .2. . . . .3. 4   Never

26. I am satisfied with the way students are treated by administrators:

      Always   1. . . . .2. . . . .3. 4   Never

Figure 6-3 (Cont'd.)

27. Teachers are involved in planning building inservice programs:

       Always   1. . . . .2. . . . .3. 4   Never

28. Building inservice programs are helpful:

       Always   1. . . . .2. . . . .3. 4   Never

29. District conferences/inservice/workshops are helpful:

       Always   1. . . . .2. . . . .3. 4   Never

30. Faculty meetings are helpful:

       Always   1. . . . .2. . . . .3. 4   Never

31. Committee work contributes to the school's effectiveness:

       Always   1. . . . .2. . . . .3. 4   Never

32. Students are studying what will be useful in everyday life:

       Always   1. . . . .2. . . . .3. 4   Never

33. The things students should be learning are taught in our school:

       Always   1. . . . .2. . . . .3. 4   Never

34. Students do enough individual work to learn what I teach:

       Always   1. . . . .2. . . . .3. 4   Never

35. Students participate in as many school activities as they should:

       Always   1. . . . .2. . . . .3. 4   Never

36. Students feel that they belong in this school:

       Always   1. . . . .2. . . . .3. 4   Never

37. I am satisfied with the way students are treated by counselors:

       Always   1. . . . .2. . . . .3. 4   Never

38. Students get the help they need to solve personal problems:

       Always   1. . . . .2. . . . .3. 4   Never

39. Students get the help they need to select courses:

       Always   1. . . . .2. . . . .3. 4   Never

40. Students get the help they need to select a college, vocational, or trade school:

       Always   1. . . . .2. . . . .3. 4   Never

41. Students get the help they need to select a vocation or career:

       Always   1. . . . .2. . . . .3. 4   Never

Figure 6-3 (Cont'd.)

42. Parents have adequate knowledge about the schools' programs:

      Always   1. . . . .2. . . . .3. 4   Never

43. I am satisfied with the emphasis being placed on learning how to learn:

      Always   1. . . . .2. . . . .3. 4   Never

44. I am satisfied with the amount of individualization:

      Always   1. . . . .2. . . . .3. 4   Never

Figure 6-3 (Cont'd.)

Sample of a Communications Grid, Representing Some of the Publics and Channels

Some school systems use a grid or matrix to check up on which communication channels reach certain key publics. You may want to try this technique in your schools. A √ means that channel or activity reaches a specific public. A (√) indicates a possible benefit as a by-product.

Channels	Publics	Parents	Students	Teachers	Custodians	Secretaries	Nonparent taxpayers	Board of Education	News Media
Parent-Teacher Conference		√	√	√					
Surveys		√							
School Brochures		√							
News Releases—TV, Radio, Newspapers		√	√	√	√	√	√	√	√
Activity Calendar		√	√	√	√	√	√	√	√
Fact Card		√		√	√	√	√	√	√
Phone Calls to Parents		√							
Supt. Advisory Council		√	(√)					√	(√)
School Newsletters		√	√	√	√	√	√	(√)	
Open Houses		√	√	√	√	√	(√)		
Board of Education Meeting		√	(√)	√	√	√	√	√	√
Student Advisory Board			√						√

Source: Don Bagin, Donald Ferguson, and Gary Marx, *Public Relations for Administrators* (Arlington, VA: American Association of School Administrators, 1985), p. 30.

Figure 6-4

235

Building Public Confidence In Our Schools

The AASA publication *Building Public Confidence In Our Schools* suggests 12 steps schools might consider in undertaking confidence-building efforts. Each step is accompanied by a number of suggested activities. The premise is that schools must first be committed to providing a high quality product, then effectively communicating through interpersonal and mass communications techniques. The 12 steps are:

■ *Strive for quality.* No matter how good the schools are, strive to make them better tomorrow.

■ *Create a spirit of caring.* We must demonstrate that we care about students, staff, and community so that they will care about us.

■ *Share the good news about schools.* Be honest. Let staff and community know what is working well. Also let them know what needs improvement and what is being done about it.

■ *Show connections.* Help staff and community see the connection between high quality education and the quality of life in the community.

■ *Work with each other, not against each other.* All staff groups in the schools should communicate with each other and work in common purpose for high quality education.

■ *Get the community on the school team.* Create a team relationship with the community in support of effective schools.

■ *Help people more, hassle people less.* Be sensitive to those who need help. Try not to be bureaucratic.

■ *Demonstrate a sense of direction.* Let everyone know that your schools have a sense of direction—and that direction is educational excellence for students.

■ *Be an educational leader in the community.* Be sure the schools are involved in every major community endeavor.

■ *Create substantive themes.* Develop themes to cover substantive efforts to make education more effective. A good theme can serve as a rallying cry for staff and community.

■ *Be an effective communicator.* A districtwide or buildingwide communications program will be effective only if the people involved are effective communicators themselves.

■ *Have confidence in yourself.* Unless we are confident in ourselves, we will have a hard time building confidence in others.

These steps in building confidence also constitute a public relations plan aimed at improving the quality of education and building support at the same time.

Source: Don Bagin, Donald Ferguson, and Gary Marx, *Public Relations for Administrators* (Arlington, VA: American Association of School Administrators, 1985), p. 29.

Figure 6-5

Sample Public Relations Project Outline

Project: Principals' advisory groups will be formed in each school.

Objectives:

- To act as a sounding board for ideas, and to aid the principal in presenting educational programs to the community.
- To determine what concerns representatives of the community have.
- To listen to the publics' questions about the schools and their programs and to use those questions to provide answers.
- To gain creative suggestions for dealing with problems or opportunities facing the school.
- To increase group members' knowledge of the school and its programs.

Procedures:

Who	Does What	By When
Principal and PTA President	Review guidelines for an advisory group and appoint seven parents, three school staff members, and two nonparents to the group.	By June 15
Principal and PTA President	Survey appointees to determine best meeting times. Set agenda; identify possible agenda items for future meetings. Distribute agendas in advance of meetings.	By August 28
School Secretary	Make calls to remind members of the meeting.	First week in September
Advisory Group	Hold first meeting	By September 10
Principal	Prepares minutes; copies to group members and district communications office.	By September 20
PTA President	Presents brief report on advisory group activities at a fall PTA meeting.	September or October

Resources Needed:

- Postage for mailing agendas, minutes
- Refreshments for meetings
- Assistance of school secretary and volunteer help
- Printing of materials
- Training to ensure productive meeting
- Information packets about the school

Evaluation:

- Ask each participant to complete an evaluation form.
- At a meeting, review accomplishments in relation to objectives.

Source: Don Bagin, Donald Ferguson, and Gary Marx, *Public Relations for Administrators* (Arlington, VA: American Association of School Administrators, 1985), p. 27.

Figure 6-6

7

Networking,
Mentoring, and Sponsoring

Networking, mentoring, and sponsoring are specific cases of communications. They imply close interpersonal relationships.

Networks Among Individual and Groups or Institutions

The network is an increasingly popular means to disseminate information and create change. Prominence of the network was one of ten megatrends cited by John Naisbitt in *Megatrends* which was appropriately subtitled "Ten New Directions Transforming Our Lives." Naisbitt (p.192) defines networks as "people talking to each other, sharing ideas, information, and resources." He calls our attention to networking as a verb — the process of getting to the network (the noun—the finished product) — the communication that creates the linkages between people and clusters of people. In fact, horizontal linkages account for the growing popularity of networks. The networks deliver what bureaucracies cannot. They link each individual in the network to all others either directly or indirectly. Marilyn Ferguson in *The Aquarian Conspiracy* identified numerous ways networking is done: conferences, phone calls, air travel, books, phantom organizations, papers, pamphleteering, photocopying, lectures, workshops, parties, grapevines, mutual friends, summit meetings, coalitions, tapes, newsletters. Networks are said to be the equivalent of the ancient tribe and to fulfill the high-touch need for belonging. Put in this context, we can begin to see the influence of networks.

Deal and Kennedy refer to a special form of network called the cabal. The cabal has been defined as a "group who secretly join together to plot a common purpose — usually to advance themselves in the organization" (p.94). This is a narrow form of networking. What the cabal has in common with other networks is common purpose — usually to foster the advancement of someone or something. Shared values and experiences nurture the network. Trust and loyalty is assumed. It is okay to borrow one another's ideas and, in fact, some networks are intended primarily for sharing information.

Some cabals are formal groups. For example, participants in the Columbia or Harvard Invitational Superintendent groups can be considered as forms of cabals with whom participants want to be identified. Professional groups like Phi Delta Kappa, AASA, ASCD, and others serve similar functions. In addition to the professional reinforcement or advancement functions a network might serve, it is also — and perhaps most importantly — a way of cultivating friends. Friends in networks keep us tuned to what is going on that might be important personally or relevant to the job situation. Friends represent us favorably to others in the culture. They back us up when we are down. They laugh with us when things seem hopeless. They run interference when they can and when we need it. We can even see this kind of networking among students in SADD, Youth to Youth, Just Say No, Peer Counseling, and Peer Tutoring programs.

It is important to distinguish networks and networking, as used here, from the "New Girl Network" or "Old Boy Network." The new network is widespread, egalitarian, and essential. On the other hand, the old network was not widespread, protected the self-interest of a few, and was not created out of necessity. Information is the equalizer in the network and members are considered peers. Networks function across institutions that create or store information. Networks put people in direct contact with the person or resource they seek.

While informal networks have always existed, they have come into prominence as networks during the information age. Since *Sputnik* heralded the age of global communications in 1967, the new information economy has come into prominence. Rigid hierarchical structures have found information flow slowed down. Rigid structures had difficulty in staying in tune. Centralized institutions which relied on hierarchies were crumbling in the 1960s and 1970s. Centralized institutions were replaced with smaller, decentralized units linked informally. Competition in the workplace led us into quality circles — clusters of small, decentralized work groups who make work decisions. Quality circles were described in more detail in Chapter 2. As we got more high tech, we wanted more high touch. Naisbitt noted that more robots resulted in more quality circles. The more word processors and computer terminals, the greater the need to network laterally within an organization. In addition, as the teenagers of the 1960s and 1970s have filled the workplace, this more rights-conscious work group found notions of hierarchy and pyramids contrary to their ideas of democracy.

Hierarchies, of course, remain; but our lack of belief in their efficacy has led to the formation of networks in attempts to solve problems ourselves. People began talking to one another as hierarchies crumbled. Coalitions of educator groups — the administrators, the teachers, the school boards, the parent-teacher groups, and others — and other networks began paying attention to each other to unite to make a difference. Networking has become a powerful tool for social actions. Those who would effect change have begun networking locally, in clusters of like-minded people with a single purpose.

Teleconferencing and other high-tech mediums have allowed for knowledge networking. For example, the Executive Council and other committees and groups within the ASCD (Association for Supervision and Curriculum Development) are linked by a teleconferencing network which permits the exchange and creation of information. These are examples of the use of networks that function to select and acquire only needed information as quickly as possible.

Networks that the superintendent can access are many and varied. The local Chamber of Commerce and superintendents' groups are two among many groups that operate in most districts or counties. The professional organization and the coalitions or caucus within the organization are networks of another kind. Many universities and school districts have organized together to form consortia, usually designed as a way to provide research sites and sources of employment for university personnel while facilitating growth and change within the district. Businesses and schools have recently organized to form partnerships to promote excellence in the schools and sources of skilled employees for the workplace. The Boston Plan for Excellence in Massachusetts and the Corridor Partnership for Excellence in Illinois are two examples of school-business partnerships whose purpose is to promote quality education.

Formal and Informal Networks

Deal and Kennedy in *Corporate Cultures* refer to the "cultural network" and discuss its importance.

> As the primary (but informal) means of communication within an organization, the cultural network is the "carrier" of the corporate values and heroic mythology. Storytellers, spies, priests, cabals, and whisperers form a hidden hierarchy of power within the company. Working the network effectively is the only way to get things done or to understand what's really going on. (p. 15)

Corporations with a cultural network are characterized by Deal and Kennedy as "human institutions," institutions that provide meaning for people on or off the job. The culture is established or the individual identity is cultivated by "shaping values, making heroes, spelling out rites and rituals, and acknowledging the cultural network." (p. 15) The key is to use the activities of the cultural network in your favor.

Corporations that have, acknowledge, and utilize cultural networks are reported by Deal and Kennedy to "have the edge." They are the kinds of companies recognized for their excellence in *In Search of Excellence* and *Passion for Exellence.* The culture provides heroes for others in the corporation to emulate. People are managed by the cues of a culture; a strong culture guides behavior in two ways:

> A strong culture is a system of informal rules that spells out how people are to behave most of the time . . . A strong culture enables people to feel better about what they do so they are more likely to work harder. (pp. 15-16)

The formal network in a corporation or school district is the organization chart. An organization for small- and large-city school districts and county districts might look something like those shown in Figures 7-1 to 7-3. Figure 7-1 is unusual in that the chart is labeled, "Organization for Instruction." Students and learning are the focus and are shown at the top of the chart. All other positions shown support student learning. Figure 7-2 shows an organization for a local district where solid lines depict lines of authority and dotted lines depict lines of consultation and cooperation. Figure 7-3 shows a county school district organization. As is typical in such charts, the vertical lines identify line relationships while horizontal lines identify staff positions or positions at the same level in the hierarchy.

Unlike the titles shown in formal organization charts, the informal network is constituted by various characters who Deal and Kennedy describe as spies, storytellers, priests, whisperers, and cabals. The informal network provides the links between and among various parts of the company. It is the primary means of communication regardless of titles or positions. The informal network both transmits and interprets information for employees. For example, the Notice of Position Vacancy may say that the Administrative Assistant resigned for personal reasons when the network has circulated the real reason — dishonesty or some other offense.

Much of what goes on in the organization has nothing to do with formal events. Yet managers continue to issue memos, letters, reports, and policy statements. Managers hold meetings and use flip charts, decision trees, and statistical analysis. Even in a highly structured meeting, informal communications of bonding, glances, innuendos, and other signals are going on. As in most organizations, the processes of making decisions, gathering support, developing opinions, happen before the meeting — or after.

Sometimes working the network is the *only* way to get the job done. We have repeated examples of this in Bexley. Teachers will, for example, resist ideas of an administrator until some "E.F. Huttons" or key communicators get behind the idea and make it their own. The superintendent can use the network to reinforce the basic beliefs of the district, to pass on stories of the deeds and accomplishments of heroes, set a climate for change, and maintain a tight structure of influence. As in *Passion for Excellence*, people make the difference! The following are characters in the cultural network (Deal and Kennedy, pp. 87-98):

Storytellers

The storyteller changes reality to suit his or her perceptions. The best storytellers have access to a great deal of information and are at the center of activity. The story is the most powerful way to convey information and shape behavior, to get all going in the same direction. The storyteller can serve to preserve the district and its values by imparting legends and what it takes to get ahead to new employees. The storyteller also carries stories about the heroes and outlaws, sometimes one and the same. "Stories are parables that motivate others and extend the power of the effective storyteller." (p. 89).

Priests

The priests guard the values of the organization. They worry about the "religion" and keeping the "flock" together. They always have time to listen to a "confession" and always have a solution to a dilemma. Priests are like storytellers, but they deal in allegories, relating current events back to other events. Their principal duty is to provide historical precedent for planned action. The priestly figure is able to do this because he or she is a human encyclopedia on matters of the district's history. Another duty of the priest is to aid people in event of defeat, frustration, and disappointment. The priest is frequently invisible in the formal organization but has enormous power.

Whisperers

Whisperers are characteristically powers behind the throne — movers and shakers without portfolio. They may climb high in the organization or be buried in an obscure post. The boss's ear is their source of power. They are frightening people who get loyalty. The critical skills of the whisperer are to be able to read the boss's mind quickly and accurately with few clues and have a vast support system of contacts throughout the organization for staying current with what transpires. They are intensely loyal to the boss and have a symbiotic relationship with him or her.

Gossips

Gossips are described as the "troubadors" of the culture. While the priest is an expert on the past, the gossip is the know-it-all about present names, dates, salaries, and events taking place in the district. Their function is to entertain — not to be serious or right. The gossip plays a vital role in reinforcing the culture by embellishing the heroes' past feats and spiffing up the news of their latest accomplishments. By doing so, the gossip can serve to increase or decrease one's stature. Unlike the storyteller or priest who deals one-to-one, the gossip talks in groups at lunch or coffee break, and therefore spreads the news faster.

Secretarial Sources

Clerical workers operate at a different level and are frequently more observant than managers. They are frequently relatively noninvolved and, therefore, unbiased; as such they can tell it like it really is. They usually have excellent judgment and sometimes play the "priestess" role. Similarly, they can pass stories of their boss's deeds through the gossip network.

Spies

A spy is a loyal buddy who keeps you informed about what is going on. The best spies are well-liked and have access to many different people. They are usually unthreatening because they are not likely to get ahead, but they know they will always be taken care of as long as they keep the channels of information open. They don't attempt to color the organizational climate, only to keep their fingers on its pulse. New workers are frequently cultivated as spies.

Cabals

A cabal was defined earlier in the chapter as "a group of two or more people who secretly join together to plot a common purpose — usually to advance themselves in the organization." One of the more common forms of the cabal is where two individuals appear in public and each promotes the other, usually resulting in both getting advancements. The cabal may also be unconscious — a way of reinforcing one's ideas and positions. A cabal is usually understood to be an undesirable network, a conspiracy. The organization can foster a strong subculture among a group in the organization, to weld members together and get them moving in a common direction. Used by management effectively, the cultural network can create a sense of shared purpose and cohesiveness in the organization. Knowing the players in the network is the first step to being able to tap the network. It is important to know what people are really thinking and to influence their behavior day-to-day. Deal and Kennedy (pp. 101-103) prescribe the following pattern for the effective manager to work the cultural network to his or her best advantage: Recognize the network's existence and importance. Cultivate a network of appropriate contacts among key storytellers and priests to be part of the cultural network. Pay respects to the subculture of the people in the network. Put yourself into situations where you can make use of anecdotes and stories you care about. Seek out friendships. Believe that the cultural network can carry your communications effectively.

Mentoring and Sponsoring

The terms mentoring and sponsoring, as used here, are related but different. Both should infer building on strength. Mentoring is defined by Peters and Austin in terms of a "follow my flag" relationship; when the mentor dies, so does the one or ones mentored. While, ideally, this is not so, practically it is. How many of us have had professors or employers who wanted to make us in their own image. If this image was bright and shining and untarnished, it was, for the most part, okay. But when, for whatever reason, we may have felt used or the mentor fell from the limelight or his or her image became tarnished, we may have either been cut off from the kind of help that that relationship afforded or we may have chosen to sever the relationship ourselves to preserve our integrity. Either way, for a time — and perhaps forever — we were deprived of the benefits that the previous relationship held. Sponsoring, on the other hand, is viewed as occurring within the context of the organization's philosophy and needs. The sponsor is responsible for the development, or skill-building, of the person being sponsored. In addition, the sponsor is responsible for selling the person being sponsored laterally and up.

Both are seen as being potentially helpful and useful as well as being fraught with risk. Mentors are important precisely because of their interest in the development and advancement of the individual. There are times when this kind of relationship is not only helpful but necessary outside of the organization context.

Perhaps rather than demeaning the value of the mentoring relationship, we should place responsibility on the person being mentored to seek the kind of person as mentor and the kind of mentoring that will facilitate the attainment of worthwhile, personal goals. If these coincide with those of the mentor, fine. If they don't, the person being mentored needs to make his or her own goals clear and invite help to reach personal goals. Many mentors will want the best for those being mentored.

The problem of dying when the mentor dies, is another problem which is too often real. You may be the Dean's golden boy or girl and be left out in the cold with the demise or leaving of the Dean. You may be being groomed for an advanced administrative position and, again, be left out in the cold with the demise or leaving of the superintendent.

The important point in the mentoring relationship is to seek a mentor who will be interested in you for what he or she can do for you or for the profession and who will help you develop confidence and competence that you and your colleagues can recognize. You may choose to follow the mentor's flag, but the mentoring relationship need not require this response.

Sponsoring involves making the values of the organization explicit. Sponsors are important because they challenge the person being sponsored to take charge of their environment and facilitate their doing so. They may review the process of particular decisions and analyze why decisions succeeded or failed. Sponsoring assumes coaching has been done well and the employee is now ready for the socialization process of knowing the subtle norms — how to understand them, take them into account, and use them to achieve. The sponsor will know when the person being sponsored is ready for increased responsibility and autonomy and will grant these at the appropriate times. Guidance is assumed.

Sponsoring is leaders developing other leaders! Our most important role as leader is identifying and developing leadership. Call it mentoring or sponsoring.

Getting and Giving Help

Networks and mentoring, or sponsoring, are two ways of getting and giving help. Both imply an empowering of the individual and people who nurture each other. In these ways, network and mentoring relationships are liberating. Within the organization, the group will probably be an informal network within the formal structure of the organization (probably a hierarchy). Outside of work, there is opportunity for getting connected with like-minded people. The Columbus Metropolitan Club is such a group that was formed initially to allow a forum for professional women to get together, since they were excluded from professional men's groups. However, as membership grew into the hundreds, equal numbers of men and women were attracted to the variety of informational forums planned by and for its members.

There is a saying in the Positive Mental Attitude literature, "Whatever my mind can conceive and believe, I can achieve." We may need to get help to achieve if we have insufficient power to help ourselves. Someone may have the power of expertise or understanding needed to be helpful. If we are giving help, we need to have a fair estimate of our ability to help. We need to clarify our helping power so those whom we are helping have expectations that are realistic and appropriate.

As superintendents, our helping powers are many. We possess special information about the school system, about instructional and management strategies that can strengthen the system's effectiveness and employees' ability to cope with problems. We control access to material and referral resources that others may need. We have the indirect power to influence how others perceive and respond to difficulties. We have direct power of decision over demands we make of and responses we give to others.

There may be situations when helping agendas conflict. For example, a person we are helping may want to be relieved of responsibility — have us take over the problem. We, on the other hand, may be helping the other person cope with the situation. In such cases, the superintendent may want to negotiate — to help conditionally. The superintendent may get the person who needs help to try alternative approaches as a condition for receiving help.

The superintendent may also compromise. We may agree to take over the problem temporarily while the person being helped develops and tries coping and problem-solving strategies.

It is important that helping is not unilateral. This is why we have named this section, "Getting and Giving Help." The helper has the power to give help, and the person being helped has the power to receive or refuse assistance.

To gain cooperation in helping, the superintendent or person helping must be willing to negotiate. That is, each side applies conditions and agrees to compromise as individuals build a contract both can accept. The person being helped also has power, since refusing to accept the help makes the giver helpless to help. So the helping relationship is a joint responsibility.

Aspiring and new superintendents, particularly, need to realize that no man (or woman) is an island. We may be unwilling to admit that we need help because that infers that we have insufficient power to help ourselves. We may want to project an image of self-sufficiency and strength and may not want to appear weak or unable to cope with problems. First of all, we need to be willing to admit helplessness in the face of a problem; similarly, as helper we need to create a safe environment for our employees to admit helplessness.

Discussing the superintendent's need for help is an opportunity to note the need for all employees to have access to help. Today it is becoming popular to offer help in the form of coaching or peer coaching. Bruce Joyce and Beverly Showers were among the first to use the term coaching to refer to teachers learning new skills.

For coaching to be successful, a climate for risk-taking, a safe environment, is needed. But more is needed. Coaching requires training. Joyce and Showers advocate continued training and the coming together at regular intervals to get more input or share experience. As in other successful learning, *time* — allowing time for people to think and reflect on experience — helps build success.

If coaching is to be successful, it must be practiced. Thinking about it is not enough. In this regard, Joyce and Showers advocate corraling anyone to provide opportunity for practice.

Persons in schools have a tendency to work in isolation. Recent research has shown that a teacher's isolation is frequently by choice. So the employer may be knocking the tendency toward isolation and may need to actively break this down.

As the helper manager, we can assume responsibilities. For example, if we are creating or anticipating change, we can predict the help employees will need and what problems will be created by the changes. Second, we can follow up on help given to see if what we have suggested works and what difficulties may have arisen. It is important, however, not to assume too much responsibility in the helping relationship. There may be a dependency if too much or the wrong kind of help is given or received.

The goal is giving help to empower the person being helped so that he or she will rely on personal power. Similarly, your goal in receiving help is to become more, not less, self-reliant.

Helping is complex and demanding. It necessitates committing energy and making complicated judgments. We expect to see some results whether we are the person giving or receiving help. We may need to modify our expectations and get enough diversity so that we are not always in helping relationships. If we are giving help, we need to avoid taking resistance personally. In other words, acknowledge the need to get positive reinforcement from helping efforts. Peckhardt says, "Reinforcement nourishes power. Helping is an act of power. Without reinforcement, power is lost; and without power, there is no help." If this is true, then we may also want to be sure to thank our helpers and let them know solutions to problems made possible because of their help.

One of the more problematic areas in giving help occurs when an employee is in contractual difficulty. The more help received, the more evidence of incompetence. If help is not received, it is reported that the employee is unwilling to be helped. To minimize the difficulty in these situations, the superintendent can develop an assessment of the problem that both the helper and person receiving help can accept; specify a limited number of behavior changes expected; establish a growth that is realistic; and establish a clear criterion for acceptable performance.

At all times, but particularly when a person feels his or her job is in jeopardy, the conference is critical to receiving help. The superintendent needs to use human feelings, attitudes, perceptions, and predispositions productively. Allay undue anxiety and convince the other being helped that you are there to support and that you share a common purpose. Be totally present to the person in the conference and keep the purpose of the conference foremost.

REFERENCES AND RESOURCES

Deal, Terrence E., and Allan A. Kennedy, *Corporate Cultures: The Rites and Rituals of Corporate Life.* Reading, MA: Addison-Wesley Publishing Company, 1982.

Educational Leadership, February, 1987.

Ferguson, Marilyn, *The Aquarian Conspiracy: Personal and Social Transformation in the 1980s.* Los Angeles, CA: J. P. Tarcher Publishing Co., 1981.

Naisbitt, John, *Megatrends: Ten New Directions Transforming Our Lives.* New York, NY: Warner Books, 1982.

Peters, Thomas J., and Robert H. Waterman, Jr., *In Search of Excellence: Lessons from America's Best-Run Companies.* New York, NY: Harper and Row, Publishers, 1982.

Peters, Tom, and Nancy Austin, *A Passion for Excellence: The Leadership Difference.* New York, NY: Warner Books, 1985.

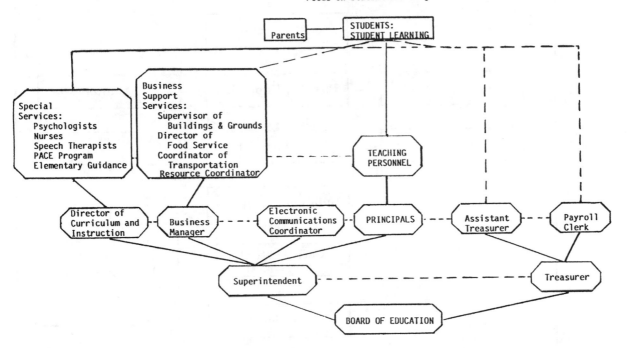

Courtesy of Bexley City Schools.

Figure 7-1

249

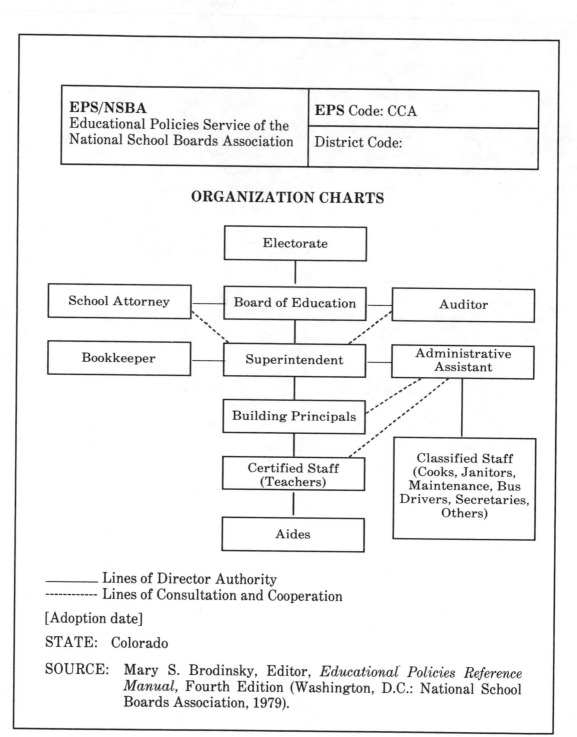

EPS/NSBA Educational Policies Service of the National School Boards Association	EPS Code: CCA
	District Code:

ORGANIZATION CHARTS

Electorate

School Attorney — Board of Education — Auditor

Bookkeeper — Superintendent — Administrative Assistant

Building Principals

Certified Staff (Teachers)

Classified Staff (Cooks, Janitors, Maintenance, Bus Drivers, Secretaries, Others)

Aides

———— Lines of Director Authority
------------ Lines of Consultation and Cooperation

[Adoption date]

STATE: Colorado

SOURCE: Mary S. Brodinsky, Editor, *Educational Policies Reference Manual*, Fourth Edition (Washington, D.C.: National School Boards Association, 1979).

Figure 7-2

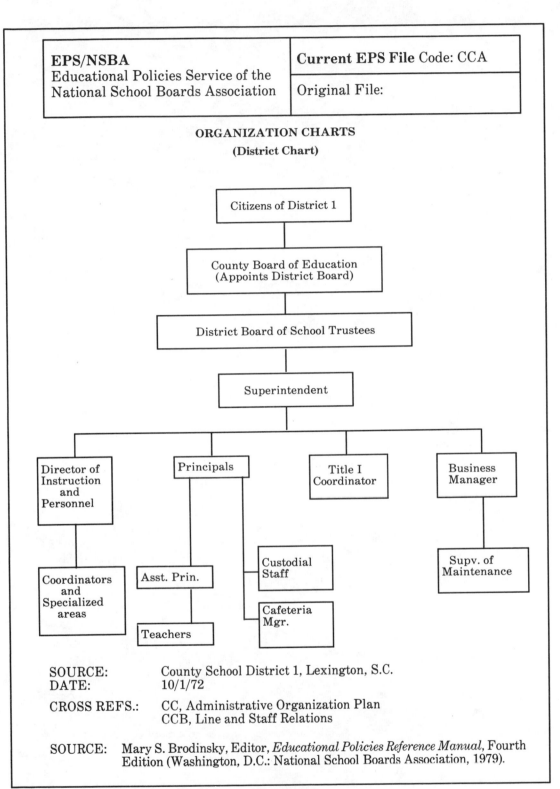

| EPS/NSBA Educational Policies Service of the National School Boards Association | Current EPS File Code: CCA |
| | Original File: |

ORGANIZATION CHARTS
(District Chart)

```
                    Citizens of District 1

              County Board of Education
              (Appoints District Board)

              District Board of School Trustees

                    Superintendent

  Director of      Principals      Title I        Business
  Instruction                      Coordinator    Manager
  and
  Personnel

                                   Custodial      Supv. of
                                   Staff          Maintenance
  Coordinators   Asst. Prin.
  and
  Specialized                      Cafeteria
  areas                            Mgr.
                 Teachers
```

SOURCE: County School District 1, Lexington, S.C.
DATE: 10/1/72

CROSS REFS.: CC, Administrative Organization Plan
             CCB, Line and Staff Relations

SOURCE: Mary S. Brodinsky, Editor, *Educational Policies Reference Manual,* Fourth
         Edition (Washington, D.C.: National School Boards Association, 1979).

Figure 7-3

251

8

Reporting

Reporting is a special form of communicating. As with certain other aspects of communications, the nature and importance of the subject dictates separate treatment.

Required and Voluntary Reporting

There is probably nothing that will impact upon the first-time superintendent more weightily and quickly than the realization that there is a never-ending need to report information and results to various and sundry publics. Even though the volume of required reports may seem in itself overwhelming, the superintendent will more than likely also want to prepare and disseminate reports that are not required.

Required reports may allow room for creativity. Many do not, but are merely forms that require completion and submission, generally to a county or state unit of government of the Department of Education. In some cases, standard forms are required to be completed and published in newspapers. To give an example of the volume of reports required, the timetable, or Calendar of Forms for the State of Ohio for a single year, is shown in Figure 8-1. Suggestions for assuring that these get processed in a timely manner are offered in a later section. What is important to stress here is that this Calendar of Forms represents only a fraction of the total number of reports that will require completion within a single year. Agencies, institutions, and groups of various types will continually make demands on the superintendent's time to complete surveys and supply information. The advantage of keeping or preparing such a Calendar is that the superintendent can anticipate resource needs and allocations for assuring the completion of forms in a timely manner. Looking at the Calendar in Figure 8-1, it is easy to see that July and October in Ohio are particularly demanding months. For the first-time superintendent, looking up files of past years' reports and talking in advance to other professionals will assist in getting a handle on demands. If processing is to be done by the superintendent, appropriate scheduling can be estimated in advance of receipt of the forms. If processing is to be delegated, the superintendent may want to alert the person who will be responsible so that he or she can provide for timely completion. In addition to merely completing the forms, it is important to know if board approval and signatures are required, if publication or filing by a certain date is required, and other sometimes vitally important information about the forms.

For example, referenda and elections have very specific timetables that must be followed to assure that the information is placed on the appropriate ballot for voting. Similarly, in some states — Illinois for example — a Certificate of Tax Levy must be filed annually by the last Tuesday in December. Board action is required for the dollars requested on the levy. Further, if the amount requested, otherwise referred to as the extension, is more than 5% greater than the previous year's dollar request, a Truth in Taxation notice must be published in the newspaper. This notice has specific reporting requirements in terms of time and format. If both of these requirements are not met, the school district will not receive its revenue. The point is that careful attention needs to be paid to reporting requirements. Anticipating reporting requirements is helpful and agencies and colleagues are available to help.

Whether reporting is required or voluntary, when specific information does not need to be reported in a specific way, there is opportunity for creativity. The first rule is to keep the reporting as jargon-free as possible. Second, the format should be as attractive as possible. Finally, graphics should be used whenever possible to assist the reader in interpreting and understanding the information presented.

Forbes magazine has been touted for its ability to make complex information understandable to the lay person. This is a worthy goal for all superintendents. I have included some examples of graphic reports from *Forbes* to illustrate. Figure 8-2 uses simple line graphs to illustrate the complex matter of the failure of the Rooney, Pace Group in light of the regulatory checks and balances of the New York Securities and Exchange Commission, supposedly in operation to protect the public and prevent such a situation. The story is about a corporate culture that took securities violations lightly. In jargon-free language, with illustrations to clarify and support the content, the *Forbes* article shows how easy profits proved the undoing of Randolph Pace and Patrick Rooney. A second example of *Forbes* reporting is shown in Figure 8-3. There are nine bar graphs with positive and negative indicators to reflect percent change in nine consumer stock areas.

There are any number of uses of graphs similar to those shown in Figures 8-2 and 8-3 that can be used by the creative superintendent in reporting data to various publics. The effect of a bond referendum on taxes, the level and percent change in test scores, the level and percent change in various categories of revenues and expenditures are only a few. Some illustrations are included.

Figure 8-4 graphs millage in an Ohio school district. In Ohio, after the voters approve a certain millage rate, it is reduced by a legislated rollback to keep the dollars collected constant as property values increase. Graphing the voted and collected millage gives a clear understanding of the growing gap between the two types of millage and the resulting problem for financing education in the district. Figure 8-5 illustrates the percent of revenue from various sources. It forces the startling realization that property owners must bear nearly 72% of financing the city's education. Figure 8-6 portrays the extent to which education is a labor-intensive business. The pie graph shows that nearly 78% of General Fund expenditures are comprised of salaries and benefits. Figure 8-7 can be used to make the point that resources are appropriately allocated — with nearly 70% of the expenditures for instruction. Bar graphs illustrate California Achievement Test results in Figure 8-8. The graph shows the extent to which all sub-test scores are above the national average and above anticipated outcomes according to the test publisher's correlation of achievement with cognitive ability.

To return to the *Forbes* presentations of information, a third way used by the magazine to graph data is shown in Figure 8-9. By looking at the cost of various items in Russia in U.S. dollar equivalents, it is easy to make comparisons without having the comparisons explicitly represented. For example, when we see from the chart that it costs $20 in U.S. money for a month's rent, this information speaks for itself. Or when we see that a 23″ TV costs $878.75, jeans, $85.66, or a small car, $12,553 — these figures reveal information showing cost of living in a reverse direction. Such a chart could prove useful to the superintendent in a small district who does not benefit from economies of scale and to a superintendent in an area with a comparatively high cost of living, to name two examples.

Finally, a *Forbes* report using no graphics is presented in Figure 8-10. The purpose in using the illustration is to show how information can be presented in an interesting manner clearly, concisely, and coherently. A similar example from Bexley City Schools is presented in Figure 8-11.

Curriculum and Instruction Reports

Information pertinent to curriculum and instruction matters can be presented in as interesting a manner and as clearly, concisely, and coherently as does *Forbes*. For example, in recent years, *Phi Delta Kappan* magazine has been making use of graphics in presenting information from the Gallup Poll. Figure 8-12 is an example of the use of a bar graph to show problems confronting public schools over a five-year span. All of the issues impact on curriculum and instruction. Similar graphics can be used to report percent of students who mastered critical objectives, etc.

Financial Reports

Financial reports can be understandable to those without sophisticated training. As superintendent, it should be our goal to make them readable and understandable. Presentation of comparative data and the use of graphics will help. For example, Figure 8-13 shows the costs and benefits of a preschool program. In addition to the data being very understandable, it can be used strategically in a public relations program to gain support for the program.

A very simple pie graph was used in a small district to show components of revenue and expenditure categories. The simple illustration was part of a National School Public Relations Association award-winning in-house newsletter.

Keeping a Forms Box

The thought of keeping a forms box may sound tacky, but it can be a great way of organizing for reporting requirements. This is particularly true for the superintendent who cannot delegate his or her preparation. Suggestions include:

- Make a file folder for each month of the year.

- As forms are received, place them in the appropriate folder. Be sure to allow for preparation time and board approval and publication time where necessary. For example, if a form requiring board approval is due the 10th of the month and the board meets only monthly the third or fourth week of the month, the form should be placed in the folder of the month preceding the month when actually due. Similarly, if publication in the newspaper is a requirement for submitting the form, it will be necessary to find the requirements for submitting information to be published and then placing the form in the appropriate folder to fulfill all requirements in a timely manner.

- Prepare a tickler file so that timely reviews can be made. It is customary for states to send batches of forms simultaneously, and a tickler file can be used to identify those that are due in the near future.

- Write the name of the form on the outside of the folder where it is placed, specifying its due date and other information pertinent to its completion, such as requirements for board approval or publication. Much of this information can be useful in subsequent years.

An Annual Report to Citizens

The annual report, in some states referred to as the report card, may be required or voluntary. In either case, publishing an annual report to be sent to all taxpayers in the community should be considered, even if it is not required. In states where the report card, or progress report, is required, the Department of Education may issue guidelines for reporting. Such guidelines for the district and buildings are shown in Figures 8-14 and 8-15.

As in other presentations of information and data, the annual report should be interesting, attractive in format, with information stated clearly, concisely, and coherently.

Figures 8-16 through 8-20 show some examples of information presented in annual reports of city school districts. Figure 8-16 presents tabulations of various staff data for The Delaware City Schools (Ohio) for 1985-1986. Figure 8-17 presents tabulations of district pupil data from the same annual report. Figure 8-18 represents financial data for the Bexley City Schools General Fund for 1985. Figure 8-19 shows a simple line graph representation of projected enrollments for the Twinsburg City Schools (Ohio) for 1983-1984. Figure 8-20 uses a simple bar graph to show percent of spending in the General Fund by category from the same annual report.

With the introduction of computers and such software as "Desktop Publishing," graphics can be done as easily as word processing. Superintendents need to be aware of and use to the fullest innovations in computer hardware and software capabilities for producing reports that command reading.

RESOURCES

The Chief State School Officers provide useful reporting resources. Names and addresses are provided below:

CHIEF STATE SCHOOL OFFICERS

ALABAMA
Wayne Teague
Superintendent of Education
State Department of Education
501 Dexter Avenue
481 State Office Bldg.
Montgomery, Alabama 36130
(205) 261-5156

AMERICAN SAMOA
Fuaileleo Pita Sunia
Director of Education
Department of Education
Pago Pago, Tutuila 96799
(OS 633-5159)*

ALASKA
William G. Demmert
Commissioner of Education
State Department of Education
Alaska Office Building, Pouch F
Juneau, Alaska 99811
(907) 465-2800

ARIZONA
C. Diane Bishop
Superintendent of Public Instruction
State Department of Education
1535 West Jefferson
Phoenix, Arizona 85007
(602) 255-4361

* Overseas Operator

ARKANSAS

Ruth Steele
Director of Department of Education
Little Rock, Arkansas 72201
(501) 371-1464
(Officially becomes Director 8/01)

CALIFORNIA

Bill Honig
Superintendent of Public Instruction
State Department of Education
721 Capitol Mall
Sacramento, California 95814
(916) 445-4338

COLORADO

William T. Randall
Commissioner of Education
State Department of Education
201 East Colfax
Denver, Colorado 80203
(303) 866-6806

CONNECTICUT

Gerald N. Tirozzi
Commissioner of Education
State Department of Education
165 Capitol Avenue
Room 308, State Office Bldg.
Hartford, Connecticut 06106
(203) 566-5061

DELAWARE

William B. Keene
Superintendent of Public Instruction
State Dept. of Public Instruction
Post Office Box 1402 — Townsend Bldg.
Dover, Delaware 19901
(302) 736-4601

*Overseas Operator

DISTRICT OF COLUMBIA

Andrew E. Jenkins III
Acting Superintendent of Public Schools
District of Columbia Public Schools
415 Twelfth Street, N.W.
Washington, D.C. 20004
(202) 724-4222

FLORIDA

Betty Castor
Commissioner of Education
State Department of Education
Capitol Building, Room PL 116
Tallahassee, Florida 32399
(904) 487-1785

GEORGIA

Werner Rogers
Superintendent of Schools
State Department of Education
2066 Twin Towers East
Atlanta, Georgia 30334
(404) 656-2800

GUAM

Rosa Salas Palomo
Director of Education
Department of Education
P.O. Box DE
Agana, Guam 96910
(OS 477-8902)*

HAWAII

Charles Toguchi
Superintendent of Education
Post Office Box 2360
Honolulu, Hawaii 96804
(808) 548-6405

IDAHO

Jerry L. Evans
Superintendent of Public Instruction
State Department of Education
650 West State Street
Boise, Idaho 83720
(208) 334-3300

ILLINOIS

Ted Sanders
Superintendent of Education
State Board of Education
100 North First Street
Springfield, Illinois 62777
(217) 782-2221

INDIANA

H. Dean Evans
Supt. of Public Instruction
State Department of Education
State House, Room 229
Indianapolis, Indiana 46204-2798
(317) 232-6612

IOWA

William Lepley
Acting Director of Education
State Department of Education
Grimes State Office Building
Des Moines, Iowa 50319-0146
(515) 281-5294

KANSAS

Lee Droegemueller
Commissioner of Education
State Department of Education
120 East Tenth Street
Topeka, Kansas 66612
(913) 296-3201

KENTUCKY

John Brock
Superintendent of Public Instruction
State Department of Education
1725 Capitol Plaza Tower
Frankfort, Kentucky 40601
(502) 564-4770

LOUISIANA

Thomas G. Clausen
Superintendent of Education
State Department of Education
Post Office Box 44064
Baton Rouge, Louisiana 70804-9064
(504) 342-3602

MAINE

Eve M. Bither
Commissioner of Education
Department of Educational and
    Cultural Services
State House, Station #23
Augusta, Maine 04333
(207) 289-5800

MARYLAND

David W. Hornbeck
State Superintendent of Schools
State Department of Education
200 West Baltimore Street
Baltimore, Maryland 21201
(301) 333-2200

MASSACHUSETTS

Harold Raynolds, Jr.
Commissioner of Education
State Department of Education
Quincy Center Plaza
1385 Hancock Street
Quincy, Massachusetts 02169
(617) 770-7300

MICHIGAN

Gary D. Hawks
Interim Supt. of Public Instruction
State Department of Education
Post Office Box 30008
115 West Allegan Street
Lansing, Michigan 48909
(517) 373-3354

MINNESOTA

Ruth E. Randall
Commissioner of Education
State Department of Education
712 Capitol Square Building
550 Cedar Street
St. Paul , Minnesota 55101
(612) 296-2358

MISSISSIPPI

Richard A. Boyd
Superintendent of Education
State Department of Education
Post Office Box 771, High Street
Jackson, Mississippi 39205
(601) 359-3513

MISSOURI

Robert E. Bartman
Commission of Education
Department of Elementary & Secondary
    Education
Post Office Box 480
Jefferson State Office Building
Jefferson City, Missouri 65102
(314) 751-4446

MONTANA

Ed Argenbright
Superintendent of Public Instruction
State Office of Public Instruction
State Capitol
Helena, Montana 59620
(406) 444-3654

NEBRASKA

Joseph E. Lutjeharms
Commissioner of Education
State Department of Education
Post Office Box 94987
301 Centennial Mall, South
Lincoln, Nebraska 68509
(402) 471-2465

NEVADA

Eugene T. Paslov
Superintendent of Public Instruction
State Department of Education
400 West King Street, Capitol Complex
Carson City, Nevada 89710
(702) 885-3100

NEW HAMPSHIRE

John T. MacDonald
Commissioner of Education
State Department of Education
101 Pleasant Street
State Office Park South
Concord, Hew Hampshire 03301
(603) 271-3144

NEW JERSEY

Saul Cooperman
Commissioner of Education
State Department of Education
225 West State Street
Trenton, New Jersey 08625
(609) 292-4450

NEW MEXICO

Alan Morgan
Supt. of Public Instruction
State Department of Education Bldg.
300 Don Gaspar
Sante Fe, New Mexico 87501-2786
(505) 827-6516

NEW YORK

Thomas Sobol
Commissioner of Education
State Education Department
111 Education Building
Albany, New York 12234
(518) 474-5844

NORTH CAROLINA

A. Craig Phillips
Superintendent of Public Instruction
State Dept. of Public Instruction
Education Building, Room 318
Edenton & Salisbury Streets
Raleigh, North Carolina 27603-1712
(919) 733-3813

NORTH DAKOTA

Wayne G. Sanstead
Superintendent of Public Instruction
State Dept. of Public Instruction
State Capitol Building, 11th Floor
600 Boulevard Avenue East
Bismarck, North Dakota 58505-0164
(701) 224-2261

NORTHERN MARIANA ISLANDS

Henry I. Sablan
Superintendent of Education
Commonwealth of the Northern Mariana
Islands
Department of Education
Saipan, CM 96950
(OS 933-9812)*

OHIO

Franklin B. Walter
Superintendent of Public Instruction
State Department of Education
65 South Front Street, Room 808
Columbus, Ohio 43266-0308
(614) 466-3304

*Overseas Operator

OKLAHOMA

John M. Folks
Superintendent of Public Education
State Department of Education
Oliver Hodge Memorial Education Bldg.
2500 North Lincoln Blvd.
Oklahoma City, Oklahoma 73105
(405) 521-3301

OREGON

Verne A. Duncan
Superintendent of Public Instruction
State Department of Education
700 Pringle Parkway, S.E.
Salem, Oregon 97310
(503) 378-3573

PENNSYLVANIA

Thomas K. Gilhool
Secretary of Education
State Department of Education
333 Market Street, 10th Floor
Harrisburg, Pennsylvania 17126
(717) 787-5820

PUERTO RICO

Awilda Aponte Roque
Secretary of Education
Department of Education
Post Office Box 759
Hato Rey, Puerto Rico 00919
(809) 751-5372

RHODE ISLAND

J. Troy Earhart
Commissioner of Education
State Department of Education
22 Hayes Street
Providence, Rhode Island 02908
(401) 277-2031

SOUTH CAROLINA

Charlie G. Williams
Superintendent of Education
State Department of Education
1006 Rutledge Building
1429 Senate Street
Columbia, South Carolina 29201
(803) 734-8492

SOUTH DAKOTA

Henry Kosters
State Superintendent
Dept. of Education & Cultural Affairs
Division of Elementary & Secondary
   Education, Kneip Bldg.
Pierre, South Dakota 57501
(605) 773-3243

TENNESSEE

Charles E. Smith
Commissioner of Education
State Department of Education
100 Cordell Hull Building
Nashville, Tennessee 37219
(615) 741-2731

TEXAS

William N. Kirby
Commissioner of Education
Texas Education Agency
William B. Travis Building
1701 N. Congress Avenue
Austin, Texas 78701
(512) 463-8985

TRUST TERRITORY OF THE PACIFIC ISLANDS

Office Closed

UTAH

James R,. Moss
Superintendent of Public Instruction
State Office of Education
250 East 500 South
Salt Lake City, Utah 84111
(801) 533-5431

VERMONT

Stephen S. Kaagan
Commissioner of Education
State Department of Education
State Street
Montpelier, Vermont 05602-2703
(802) 828-3135

VIRGINIA

S. John Davis
Superintendent of Public Instruction
State Department of Education
Post Office Box 6Q
James Monroe Bldg.
Fourteenth & Franklin Sts.
Richmond, Virginia 23216
(804) 225-2023

VIRGIN ISLANDS

Linda Creque
Commissioner of Education
Department of Education
44-46 Kongens Gade
St. Thomas, Virgin Islands 00802
(809) 774-2810

WASHINGTON

Frank B. Brouillet
Superintendent of Public Instructions
State Dept. of Public Instruction
Old Capitol Building
Mail Stop FG-11
Olympia, Washington 98504
(206) 586-6904

WEST VIRGINIA

W. Thomas McNeel
State Superintendent of Schools
State Department of Education
1900 Washington Street
Building B, Room 358
Charleston, West Virginia 25305
(304) 348-3644

WISCONSIN

Herbert J. Grover
Superintendent of Public Instruction
State Dept. of Public Instruction
125 South Webster Street
Post Office Box 7841
Madison, Wisconsin 53707
(608) 266-1771

WYOMING

Lynn O. Simons
State Supt. of Public Instruction
State Department of Education
Hathaway Building
Cheyenne, Wyoming 82002
(307) 777-7675

CCSSO OFFICE

Gordon M. Ambach
Executive Director
Council of Chief State School Officers
379 Hall of the States
400 North Capitol Street, N.W.
Washington, D.C. 20001
(202) 393-8161

OHIO DEPARTMENT OF EDUCATION

CALENDAR OF FORMS SUBMITTED TO AREA OFFICE   8/85

DUE DATE	FORM NO.	REPORTING PERIOD	NUMBER OF COPIES TO SUBMIT (ORIGINAL)	PURPOSE
10th of month	SF-410	Monthly	2	Subsidy claim for driver education & list of pupils completed & certificates issued
July 15	SF-14	Jan.-June	3	Nonhandicapped tuition (3313.64)
July 15	T-7	Preceding school yr.	2	Report of actual expense of DH (EMR) transportation by conveyance other than school bus
July 20	T-1 S	Preceding school yr.	2	Transportation to NP and JVS on days when public schools are not in session
July 20	T-2	Preceding FY	2	Report of transportation operating expense for preceding fiscal year
July 20	T-11	Preceding school yr.	2	Report of expense for special transportation of handicapped
July 31	SM-2	Quarterly	1	Quarterly "Spending Plan" status report
July 31	SF-230& district check	LAST YEAR BIENNIUM ONLY-Preceding FY	2	To report unencumbered balance in auxiliary services funds and return unencumbered balance to Treasurer, State of Ohio, by check
July 31	CERTIFICATION OF DR. ED. COSTS	Preceding FY	2	Report of driver education annual program costs
Aug. 15	SF-6	Preceding school yr.	3	Certified excess cost for pupils in special classes for handicapped (3323.14 ORC)
Sept. 15	SF-24	Current school yr.	2	Certification of compliance with mandated non-teaching salary increase (Am.Sub.IIB 291)
Sept. 15	T-5	Current school yr.	3	Application for approval to transport DH (EMR) by conveyance other than school bus
Sept. 30	SF-400 S	Current FY	2	Driver education teacher list
Oct. 15	CS-1	Current school yr.	1	Report of certificated personnel. Replaces old SF-1. SEND TO AREA COORDINATOR OFFICE
Oct. 15	ADM-1	Current school yr.	1	Report of average daily membership for 1st full week Oct. SEND TO AREA COORDINATOR OFFICE
Oct. 15	OCCD-6	Current school yr.	1	Superintendent's opening report — DIRECT TO COMPUTER SERVICES
Oct. 15	SF-2 (C)	Current school yr.	2	Report of contract vocational FTE in a comprehensive high school

Figure 8-1

Oct. 15	T-1	Current school yr.	2	Report of pupil transportation service (Count taken any day of 1st week in Oct.)
Oct. 30	No no. Letter	Current FY	1	Application for supplemental payment printout letter (Am. Sub. H.B. 291)
Oct. 30	T-6	Current school yr.	2	Report of DH (EMR) pupils transported by and conveyance used other than school bus
Oct. 30	SM-2	Quarterly	1	Quarterly "Spending Plan" status report
Nov. 15	SF-230	Preceding FY	2	Reports of receipts from state and actual expenditures for auxiliary services
Nov. 17	SF-28 & SF-28A	Current FY	2 ea.	For districts needing to file for supplemental payment per SF-24 & printout letter
Jan. 15	SF-14	Sept.-Dec.	3	Nonhandicapped tuition (3313.64)
Jan. 30	SM-2	Quarterly	1	Quarterly "Spending Plan" status report
Feb. 15	Amended T-1	Current school yr.	2	Amended report of pupil trans. service, if eligible. Data for 1st week in Feb.
Apr. 8	SM-1	Calendar yr.	1	Annual spending plan
Apr. 19	31a	Calendar year	1 ea. 1 ea.	Annual appropriations resolution & Co. Aud. Am. Official Cert. of Estimated Resources
Apr. 30	SM-2	Quarterly	1	Quarterly "Spending Plan" status report
Apr. 30	SF-20	Next FY	1	Projected ADM and vocational and special units for July estimate SF-12
May 20	SF-28 & SF-28A	Current FY	2 ea.	For districts needing to file for supplemental payment per SF-24 & printout letter
May 20	T-8 Abstract		1 ea.	School bus driver physical exam report & abstract of driving record
TBA	SF-169	June-Dec.	2	169 Board tuition

Source: Ohio Department of Education.

Figure 8-1 Cont'd.

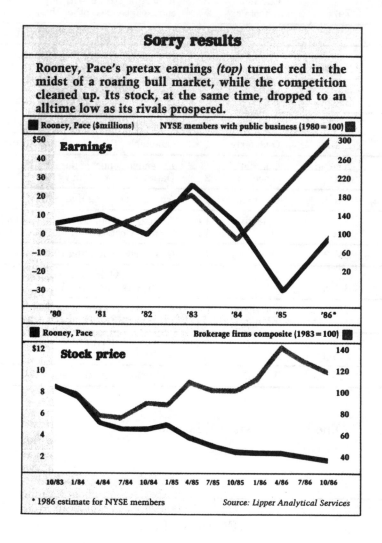

Reprinted by permission of *Forbes* magazine, December 1, 1986. © Forbes Inc., 1986.

Figure 8-2

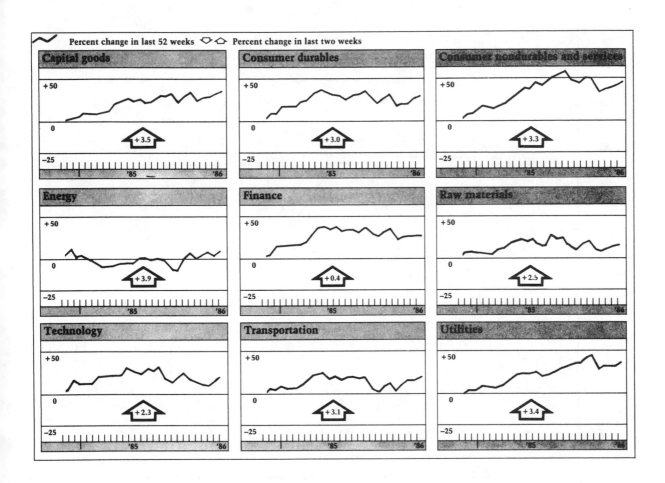

Source: Wilshire Associates, Santa Monica, CA.

Figure 8-3

267

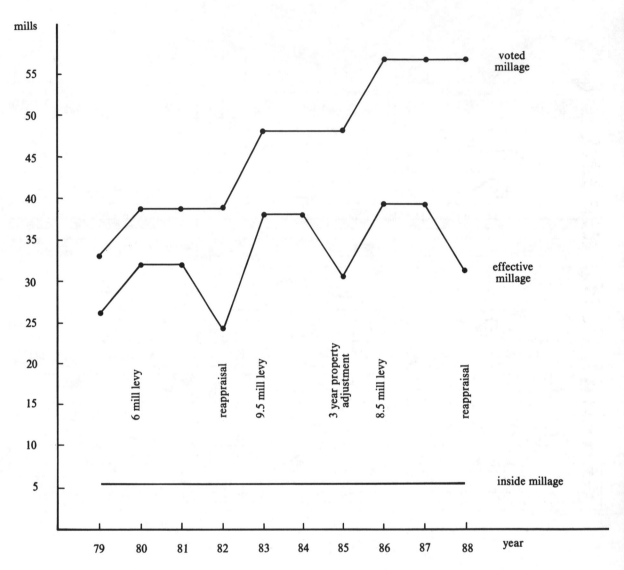

BEXLEY CITY SCHOOL DISTRICT

MILLAGE GRAPH

Voted millage is the rate approved by the voters. Voted millage is reduced after reappraisal of property. This revised millage is called effective millage.

Effective millage is the millage rate actually collected on property.

Inside millage is assigned by the Ohio Constitution. Bexley receives 5.7 mill. This millage is never reduced by reappraisal.

Courtesy of Bexley City Schools.

Figure 8-4

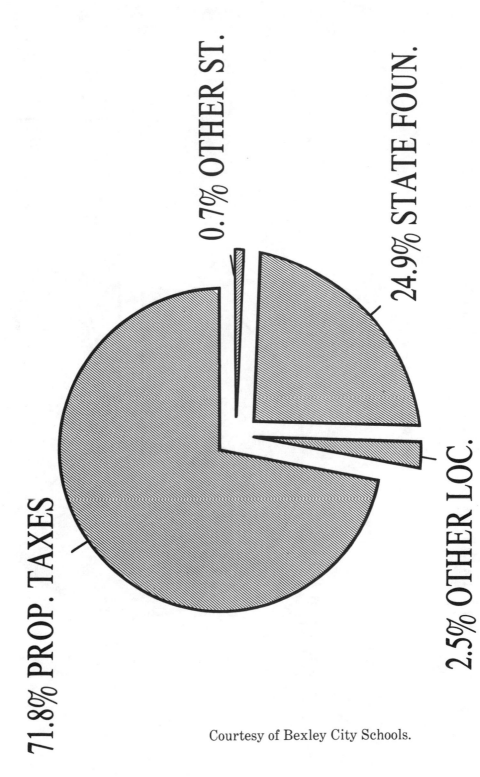

GENERAL FUND REVENUE
1987-1988

71.8% PROP. TAXES

0.7% OTHER ST.

24.9% STATE FOUN.

2.5% OTHER LOC.

Courtesy of Bexley City Schools.

Figure 8-5

GENERAL FUND EXPENDITURE

1987-1988

BY OBJECT LEVEL

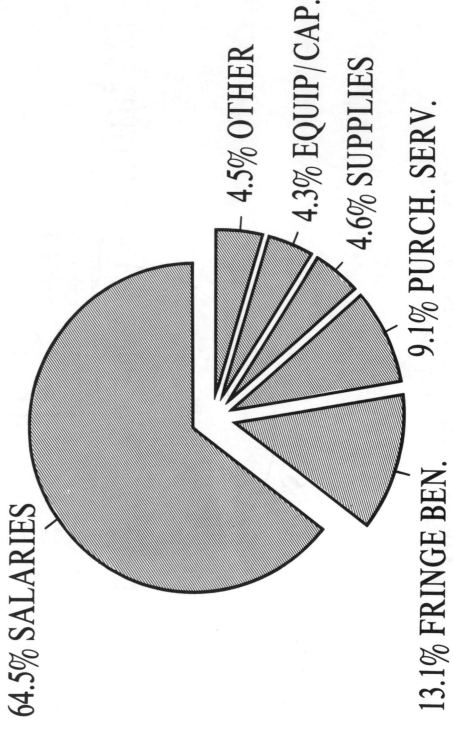

4.5% OTHER

4.3% EQUIP/CAP.

4.6% SUPPLIES

9.1% PURCH. SERV.

13.1% FRINGE BEN.

64.5% SALARIES

Courtesy of Bexley City Schools.

Figure 8-6

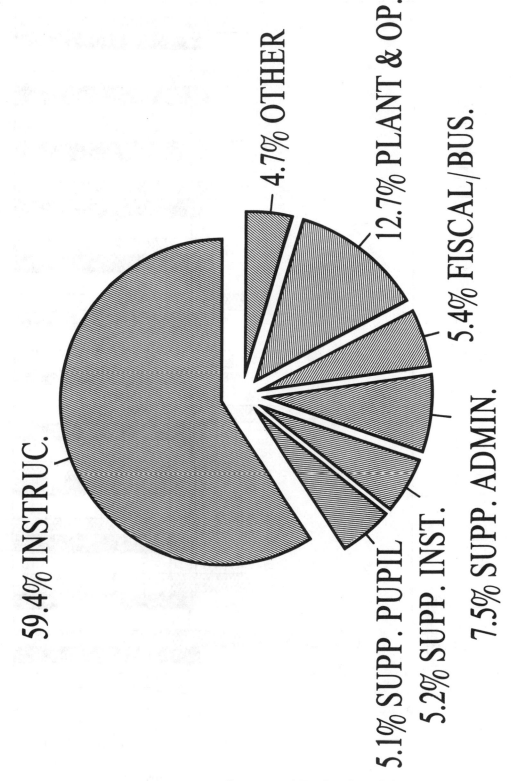

GENERAL FUND EXPENDITURE

1987-1988

BY FUNCTION LEVEL

59.4% INSTRUC.

5.1% SUPP. PUPIL

5.2% SUPP. INST.

7.5% SUPP. ADMIN.

5.4% FISCAL/BUS.

12.7% PLANT & OP.

4.7% OTHER

Courtesy of Bexley City Schools.

Figure 8-7

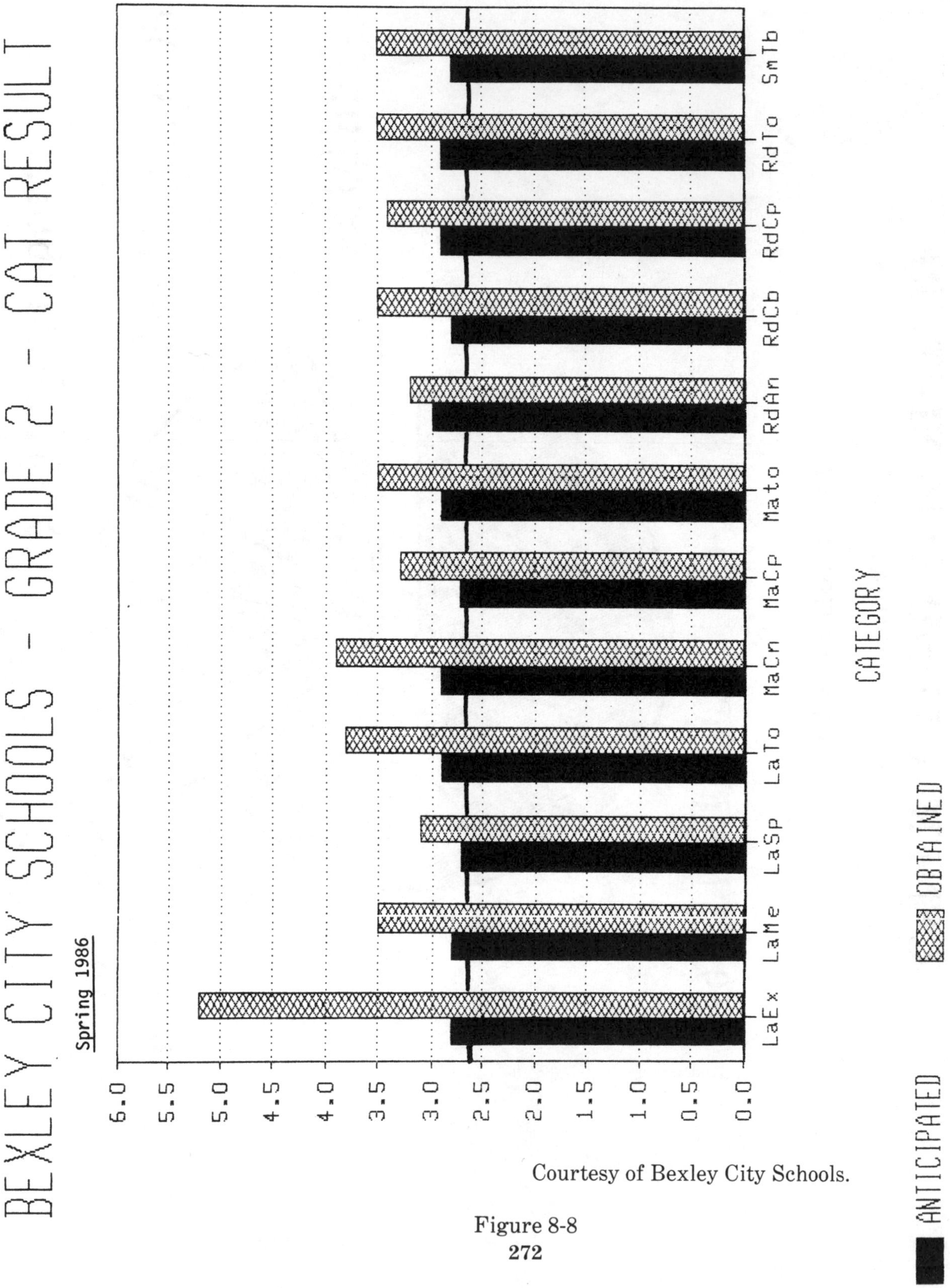

BEXLEY CITY SCHOOLS - GRADE 2 - CAT RESULT

Spring 1986

CATEGORY

OBTAINED

ANTICIPATED

Courtesy of Bexley City Schools.

Figure 8-8

272

An expensive place to live

Below are recent retail prices in Moscow for selected items, expressed both monetarily (at the official, though unrealistically high, rate of 1 ruble: $1.48) and in terms of the working time required to buy these items, using average industrial monthly take-home pay of $260 for Soviet workers, vs. $1,365 in the U.S. The numbers result from the invaluable work of Radio Liberty Research's Keith Bush, who warns of the many pitfalls inherent in such East-West comparisons. Among them: poor quality and availability of goods in Russia, where the consumer is a very low priority.

Consumer items	Rubles	Converted U.S. $	Work hours equivalent
white bread (2.2 lbs.)	0.30	0.44	18 minutes
frozen chicken (2.2 lbs.)	3.40	5.02	3 hours, 24 minutes
ice cream (2.2 lbs.)	1.92	2.84	1 hour, 55 minutes
butter (2.2 lbs.)	3.80	5.61	3 hours, 30 minutes
potatoes (2.2 lbs.)	0.20	0.30	12 minutes
tea (3.5 oz.)	0.76	1.12	46 minutes
red wine (1.1 qts.)	4.60	6.79	4 hours, 29 minutes
vodka (1 pt.)	2.32	3.43	2 hours, 12 minutes
small car (Zhiguli)	8,500.00	12,553.00	48.4 months
regular gasoline (2.6 gals.)	3.00	4.43	3 hours
jeans	58.00	85.66	58 hours
men's shirt	10.00	14.77	10 hours
men's shoes	45.00	66.46	45 hours
color television 23 in.	595.00	878.75	595 hours
monthly rent subsidized, unfurnished	13.50	20.00	13 hours, 30 minutes
VCR	1,200.00	1,772.26	1,200 hours

Source: *Forbes*, December 1, 1986, p. 164.

Figure 8-9

What's Ahead for Business

Edited by Howard Banks

UNCERTAIN TIMES = UNCERTAIN POLICY

Half-truths and consequences

THE CHIEF REASON FOR RECENT JITTERS IN THE BOND MARKET is that traders had overbought. Dealers were stuffed with inventory in anticipation of lower U.S. rates. When it didn't happen, they cut prices, creating bargains for the fleet of foot. That's how markets are supposed to work.

You probably heard otherwise. After the minutes of the September meeting of the Federal Reserve's policymaking open market committee were released, reams of copy were written ("thumb suckers," bored editors call them) speculating that not only was the Fed not about to ease interest rates, but that rapid money growth might force it to tighten, for fear of fueling inflation a year or so ahead.

The incident is important because it shows—again—that when the economy's direction is unclear, as it seems for the first two or three quarters of 1987, markets will wobble on rumors and half-truths.

Gossip that has some plausibility

AS PART OF THIS PATTERN, WASHINGTON HAS BEEN FLOODED with stories that Federal Reserve Chairman Paul Volcker is about to go. The nearer we get to August 1987, when his term as chairman is up, the more these stories will appear.

The rumor comes complete with possible successors. One frequently cited in the gossip is Donald Regan, presently the combative (and increasingly influential, internally) White House chief of staff. Another is George Shultz, the embattled Secretary of State.

Inevitably, too, when the President does send his nominee to the Democrat-controlled Senate for confirmation, the cry "Politicizing the Fed" will be heard.

It will ring true to many ears. "The economy is the number one issue for the 1988 election, and the Administration is laying the groundwork for that election," believes Allen Sinai, chief economist for Shearson Lehman.

Little or no help from the dollar's fall

TRUE OR FALSE, THE CHARGE CAN'T HELP, and might even damage, the authority Volcker's Fed has developed around the world. It needs all the authority it can get.

Japan finally cut interest rates to prod its economy, but it won't help much: Each 1% growth in Japanese GNP would suck in only $400 million of U.S. exports. And the West Germans, after vacillating in early fall, now say that, however hard the U.S. pushes, they won't ease.

What can the Fed do? Its chief short-run concern now is preventing recession. Yet it is staring at better-sounding economic statistics (2.6% third-quarter GNP) and the prospect of consumers in large numbers buying big-ticket items to beat year-end tax changes.

The Fed has to be worried that any significant pause could turn into recession, depressed further by still-rising personal and corporate debt. But until trade takes a turn for the better, the Fed dare not cut U.S. interest rates by much, for fear hot money will pour abroad. Once again it's fence-sitting time.

Figure 8-10

THIS IS BEXLEY

ISSUE NO. 1
NOVEMBER, 1986

BEXLEY CITY SCHOOLS
Dr. Patricia C. Conran
Superintendent
Mr. Brian Freeman
Board of Education
President

Students at Bexley excel in academic achievement, athletic activity and the arts. Scores on such nationally used and recognized tests as the SAT, the ACT and the California Achievement Test far surpass national averages and local school systems. Athletic records continue to be broken as individuals and teams set and achieve tougher standards for themselves. While there is much more than winning to be gained from participation in competitive sports, all appreciate victories. The visual and performing arts are given strong emphasis in the Bexley City Schools from kindergarten through senior year in high school. Many students attain prominence by exhibiting art works or performing professionally outside of school as well as sharing their talents in school productions.

CHAMBER OF COMMERCE
Mr. John Loehnert
President

The Bexley Area Chamber of Commerce is organized to advance the general welfare and prosperity of the Bexley area so that its citizens and all areas of the business community shall prosper. All necessary means of promotion shall be provided and particular attention and emphasis shall be given to the economic, civic, commercial, cultural, industrial and educational interests of the area.

POLICE DEPARTMENT
Mr. Thomas W. Tobin
Chief of Police

Bexley, as a village in 1908, hired its first Marshal for police protection. Today, Bexley has a police department, second to none, providing 24-hour service to its residents. Our major areas of concern are public relations, crime prevention and enforcement. In future newsletters you will be provided with indepth information in each of these areas. If you would like to talk to me about any concern you may have or just to visit, please stop in at my office. My door is always open to you. Until next time, be alert, be safe.

CITY OF BEXLEY
Mr. David Madison
Mayor

I would like all our residents to know that I strongly encourage an "Open Door" policy for anyone to come in or call me regarding their complaints, comments, suggestions, criticism or compliments. It is people such as you who make this city great, and I feel it is important that we hear your concerns. City Hall is open Monday through Friday from 8:00 a.m. to 4:30 p.m. If you would prefer to make an appointment to come in and talk with me, please contact my office at 235-8694. Any information pertaining to city safety, services, water and sewage charges, the Auditor's Department or the Mayor's office can be obtained by contacting City Hall.

Bexley, Ohio: A Special Place To Live

Courtesy of Bexley City Schools.

Figure 8-11
275

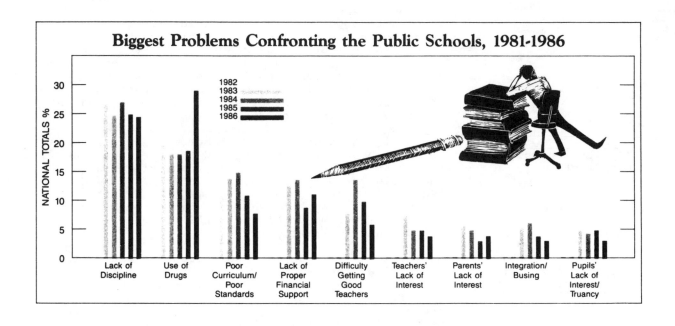

Biggest Problems Confronting the Public Schools, 1981-1986

Source: *Phi Delta Kappan*, September, 1986, p. 45.

Figure 8-12

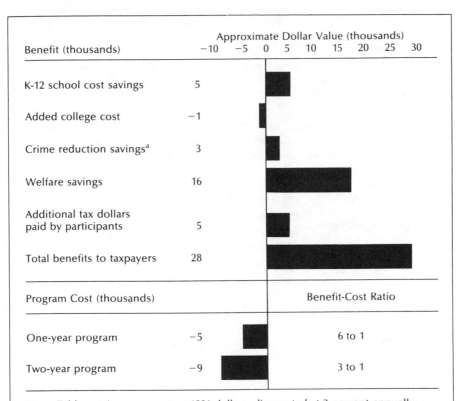

Benefit (thousands)		Approximate Dollar Value (thousands)
		−10 −5 0 5 10 15 20 25 30
K-12 school cost savings	5	
Added college cost	−1	
Crime reduction savings[a]	3	
Welfare savings	16	
Additional tax dollars paid by participants	5	
Total benefits to taxpayers	28	
Program Cost (thousands)		Benefit-Cost Ratio
One-year program	−5	6 to 1
Two-year program	−9	3 to 1

Note: Table entries are constant 1981 dollars, discounted at 3 percent annually. Adapted from John R. Berrueta-Clement, Lawrence J. Schweinhart, W. Steven Barnett, Ann S. Epstein, and David P. Weikart. *Changed Lives: Effects of the Perry Preschool Program on Youths through Age 19,* Monographs of the High/Scope Educational Research Foundation, 8 (Ypsilanti, Mich.: High/Scope Press), 1984, p. 91.

[a]Savings to citizens as taxpayers and as potential crime victims.

Perry Preschool Program Per-Child Costs and Benefits to Taxpayers

Source: Lawrence J. Schweinhart and David P. Weikart, "Early Childhood Development Programs: A Public Investment Opportunity" in *Educational Leadership,* November 1986, p. 9. Reprinted with permission of the Association for Supervision and Curriculum Development. Copyright (c) by ASCD. All rights reserved.

Figure 8-13

3301-11-02 CITY, EXEMPTED VILLAGE, AND LOCAL DISTRICT REPORTS

A

(1) Each school district shall devise a procedure for releasing to the public on a yearly basis data including the achievements, problems, plans and improvements made by the district in meeting the educational goals, established by either: (a) the State Board of Education, (b) the district board of education, or (c) the individual buildings.

(2) This narrative report may deal with the areas of attendance, budget, curriculum, extra curricular activities, facilities, staffing, staff development, special services, transportation, etc.

B. In addition to the preceding information, the Annual Progress Reports for each city, exempted village and local school district shall include the following statistical information:

(1) Financial Data, including:

(a) Average Per Pupil Costs. Percentage of total expenditures from local tax revenue and percentage of expenditures from other revenue sources.

(b) For the first report, total dollars and percentages of general fund operating expenditures in either: (i) the six major reporting categories as designated in the Department of Education's publication entitled "Cost Per Pupil," or (ii) the following categories:

(a) School Building Personnel
   I Teaching
   II Principals and Assistants
   III Pupil Service
   IV Custodial
(b) Central Office Personnel
   I Instruction
   II General Administration
   III Finance and Business

(c) General Services and Supplies
(d) Teaching Services and Supplies
(e) Maintenance
(f) Transportation
(g) Utilities

If the latter method is used, the definitions in 3301-11-01(B) of the Administrative Code should be utilized along with any special instruction provided by the Department of Education. In sub-subsequent years, the method outlined in (ii) shall be utilized showing two year trends.

(c) Information on interest debt retirement, motor vehicles and capital outlay expenditures as defined in the Department of Education "Cost Per Pupil" Report.

(2) Staff Data, including:

(a) Number of full-time equivalent regular, special education and vocational education teachers per 100 students.

(b) Number of full-time equivalent special resource teachers per 100 students.

(c) Number of full-time equivalent administrative, supervisory and pupil personnel staff per 100 students.

(d) Number of full-time equivalent paid instructional aides per 100 students.

(e) Average classroom teacher experience and training based on data reported in Form SF-1, "Report of Certificated Employees."

(f) Average classroom teacher salary based on data reported in Form SF-1, "Report of Certificated Employees."

(g) Percentage breakdown of teachers and administrative, supervisory and pupil personnel staff by race based on data reported in Form SF-1, "Report of Certificated Employees."

(h) Percentage breakdown of teachers and administrative, supervisory and pupil personnel staff by sex based on data included in school district records.

(3) Pupil Data, including:

(a) Enrollment figures including race and sex data.

(b) Average daily attendance based on data reported in Form SF-2, "Report of Certified Average Daily Membership."

Source: OAC 3301-11-02 from the Approved Edition of the *Ohio Administrative Code*. Reproduced with permission of the publisher and copyright owner, Banks-Baldwin Law Publishing Company, Cleveland, OH.

Figure 8-14

3301-11-03 BUILDING REPORTS

A.

(1) Each building, in accordance with the procedure established by the district board of education, shall report to the public on a yearly basis, data indicating the achievements, problems, plans and improvements made by the building in meeting the educational goals established by either: (a) the State Board of Education, (b) the district board of education or (c) the individual building.

(2) This narrative report may deal with the areas of attendance, budget, curriculum, extra curricular activities, facilities, staffing, staff development, special services, transportation, etc.

B. In addition to the preceding information, the Annual Progress Reports for each building shall include the following statistical information:

(1) Staff Data, including:

(a) Full-time equivalent regular teacher, special education teacher and vocational teacher/pupil ratio

(b) Number of full-time equivalent special resource teaching staff.

(c) Number of full-time equivalent administrative, supervisory and pupil personnel staff.

(d) Number of full-time equivalent instructional aides.

(e) Number of full-time equivalent volunteers.

(f) Average classroom teacher experience and training based on data reported in Form SF-1, "Report of Certificated Employees."

(g) Percentage breakdown of teachers and administrative, supervisory and pupil personnel staff by race based on data reported in Form SF-1, "Report of Certificated Employees."

(h) Percentage breakdown of teachers and administrative, supervisory and pupil personnel staff by sex based on data included in school records.

(2) Pupil Data, including:

(a) Total enrollment, including (i) sex of students, as reported in the Elementary Principal's Report Form-22 or the Secondary Principal's Report Form-23, whichever is applicable, and (ii) race of students, as reported in forms collected through the Ohio Educational Data System.

(b) Average daily attendance for the same period reported in Form SF-2 for the total district.

(c) Student mobility.

(d) Total expenditures for the past three years for library-media center materials including library books, periodicals, newspapers and nonprint materials. When a central library serves the particular school only, information describing the total times students used the library-media center during the past year should be presented. This may include class use of the facilities, individual use of the facilities; the number of times materials are circulated for student use, etc.

(e) Economic status. One or more of the following indices may be reported: rate of unemployment, percentages receiving public assistance, percentages receiving free or reduced price lunches.

C. Annual Progress Reports shall include a statement describing the standardized test data which are available on individual students in the building and describe the procedure by which parents may review those data for their own children.

Source: OAC 3301-11-03 from the Approved Edition of the *Ohio Administrative Code*. Reproduced with permission of the publisher and copyright owner, Banks-Baldwin Law Publishing Company, Cleveland, OH.

Figure 8-15

District Staff Data

1. The full time equivalent teacher-pupil ratio was:

   Carlisle   = 1 to 22.4
   Conger   = 1 to 20.5
   Smith   = 1 to 21.1
   Woodward = 1 to 24.5
   Willis   = 1 to 22.4
   Hayes   = 1 to 21.3

2. The number of full time equivalent special resource teaching staff was:

   Carlisle   = 4.7 persons
   Conger   = 6.3 persons
   Smith   = 4.9 persons
   Woodward = 7.0 persons
   Willis   = 9.9 persons
   Hayes   = 9.1 persons

3. The number of full time equivalent administrative, supervisory, and pupil personnel staff was:

   Carlisle   = 2.6 persons
   Conger   = 2.5 persons
   Smith   = 2.4 persons
   Woodward = 2.8 persons
   Willis   = 6.4 persons
   Hayes   = 9.5 persons

4. The number of instructional aides was:

   Carlisle   = 1.5 aides
   Conger   = 2.3 aides
   Smith   = 1.8 aides
   Woodward = 1.8 aides
   Willis   = 10.0 aides
   Hayes   = 8.0 aides

5. The number of volunteers who provided service to the school:

   Carlisle   =   73 persons
   Conger   = 119 persons
   Smith   = 205 persons
   Woodward =   62 persons
   Willis   =   91 persons
   Hayes   =   14 persons

6. Average classroom teaching experience:

   Carlisle   = 10.2 years
   Conger   = 11.7 years
   Smith   = 13.0 years
   Woodward = 11.8 years
   Willis   = 11.9 years
   Hayes   = 11.2 years

7. Teacher training (average):

   Carlisle   = 4.9 years
   Conger   = 5.3 years
   Smith   = 5.3 years
   Woodward = 5.1 years
   Willis   = 5.3 years
   Hayes   = 5.7 years

8. Degree status of professional staff:

	No Degree	BA	5 Year	M.A.	Ph.D.
Carlisle	0	9	10	1	0
Conger	0	6	8	5	0
Smith	0	7	3	7	0
Woodward	0	6	10	4	0
Willis	0	11	10	14	1
Hayes	0	13	18	25	0

9. Race of professional staff:

   Carlisle   =100% white - 0% black
   Conger   = 96% white - 4% black
   Smith   =100% white - 0% black
   Woodward = 93% white - 7% black
   Willis   = 98% white - 2% black
   Hayes   = 97% white - 3% black

10. Sex composition of professional staff:

    Carlisle   = 2% male 98% female
    Conger   = 8% male 92% female
    Smith   =14% male 86% female
    Woodward = 8% male 92% female
    Willis   =28% male 72% female
    Hayes   =50% male 50% female

Figure 8-16

District Pupil Data

1. Average daily attendance and average daily membership:

	ADA	ADM
Carlisle	423	428
Conger	366	383
Smith	345	359
Woodward	467	489
Willis	747	795
Hayes	1069	1157

2. District pupil data — 1985-86:

School	Male	Female	ADM Total	Amer. Indian	Asian	Black	Hispanic	White
Carlisle	228	200	428	0	0	9	2	417
Conger	202	182	384	0	0	15	1	368
Smith	181	178	359	0	2	8	0	349
Woodward	262	227	484	1	3	93	10	382
Willis	398	397	795	0	2	52	2	739
Hayes	594	566	1160	0	4	65	2	1089

3. Student mobility rate (transiency)

Carlisle	= 17.3%
Conger	= 19.3%
Smith	= 19.0%
Woodward	= 25.0%
Willis	= 14.5%
Hayes	= 13.2%

4. Amount of money per pupil spent for library materials in 1985-86:

Carlisle	= $24.03 per pupil
Conger	= $22.23 per pupil
Smith	= $29.00 per pupil
Woodward	= $26.84 per pupil
Willis	= $28.72 per pupil
Hayes	= $26.13 per pupil

5. Average daily use of library:

Carlisle	= 160 students
Conger	= 126.6 students
Smith	= 100 students
Woodward	= 196 students
Willis	= 310 students
Hayes	= 447.3 students

6. Economic status of school as determined by the percentage of free or reduced price lunch:

Carlisle	= 28 students or 6.5%
Conger	= 91 students or 23.8%
Smith	= 70 students or 19%
Woodward	= 194 students or 39.7%
Willis	= 159 students or 20%
Hayes	= 93 students or 8%

Source: Delaware City Schools, Delaware, Ohio.

Figure 8-17

BUDGET

Basic Financial Data
January 1, 1985 to December 31, 1985

Sources of District Revenue

	Amount		Percent of Total Receipts
Beginning Balance January 1, 1985		$ 438,242	
Local Taxes:			
Real Estate	$4,631,454		62.04
Personal Property	112,206		1.50
		4,743,660	63.54
State Aid:			
Basic Foundation Support	$1,846,741		24.74
Rollback/Homestead Taxes	652,845		8.75
Other	53,005		.71
		2,552,591	34.20
Other Local Sources:			
Interest	$ 124,277		1.66
Student Fees, Tuition	17,705		.24
Other	27,000		.36
		168,982	2.26
Total Receipts		$7,465,233	100.00
TOTAL OPERATING REVENUE		$7,903,475	

Uses of District Revenue

	Amount		Percent of Total Expenditures
Salaries:			
Certified Staff	$4,534,354		59.54
Classified Staff	663,032		8.71
Total Salaries		$5,197,386	68.25
Fringe Benefits		$1,175,060	15.43
Purchase Services:			
Utilities	265,619		3.49
Tuition to Other Districts	86,302		1.13
Other	369,946	721,867	4.86
			9.48
Supplies			
Instructional, Textbooks	173,628		2.28
Other	155,288	328,916	2.04
			4.32
Capital Outlay and Equipment		120,206	1.58
Other		72,107	.94
TOTAL EXPENDITURES		$7,615,542	100.00
Ending Balance December 31, 1985		$ 287,933	

Source: Form 4502 Annual Report to the Auditor of State of Ohio.

Courtesy of Bexley City Schools.

Figure 8-18
282

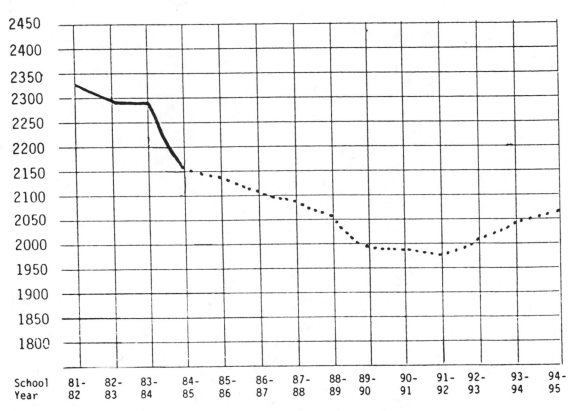

Figure 8-19

283

Source: Twinsburg City Schools, Twinsburg, OH.

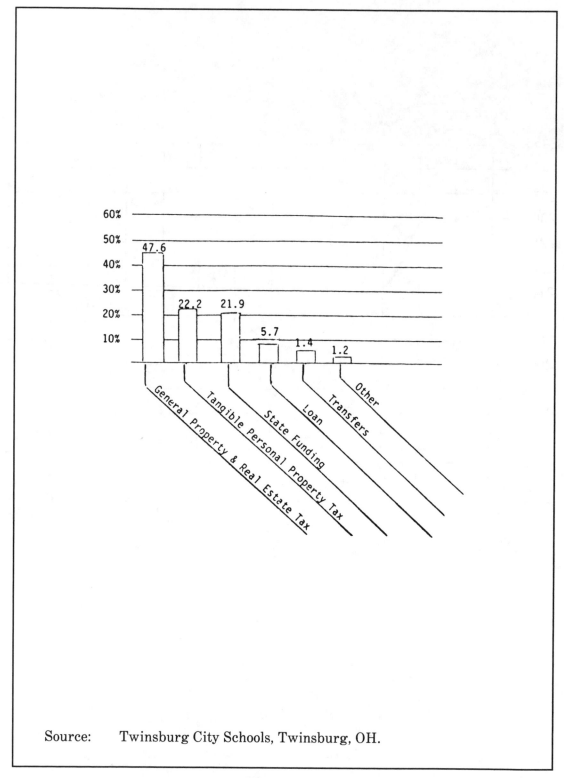

Source: Twinsburg City Schools, Twinsburg, OH.

Figure 8-20
284

III

MANAGING CHANGE

9

Planning
for Best Results

Planning is needed if the superintendent is to steer the direction of change. This chapter deals with related aspects of planning for today's reality which has only change as a constant. The process can be likened to taking an automobile trip. Conventional planning was like going from Point A to Point B where traveling certain roads and following certain directions would assure arrival at a desired destination. Planning today is more like traveling a route frought with hazards of various kinds. Each hazard requires continued processing of new information and continued redirection toward Point B, based on minute-to-minute assessments using the new information. Coping effectively today requires strategic planning, or issues management.

Assessing Needs

There is probably little question that assessing needs is an important part of the planning process. In strategic planning, or issues management, assessment is called "scanning." Assessments, or scanning, is done internally, inside the school system, and externally, outside the school system. This section explores a variety of means for learning the needs of those who will benefit from the planning process.

The Illinois Department of Education led State Departments of Education in the area of needs assessment by producing two processes: The Illinois Problems Index and the Illinois Quality Schools Index. The first, better known as the IPI, used existent or emergent problems as descriptors in the assessment process. The second, better known as IQSI, used descriptors from the effective schools research. Figure 9-1 shows the 51 categories of descriptors in the IPI.

About half of the categories deal directly with curriculum and instruction. Once categories of importance are identified, followup instruments focus on more specific problem statements within a particular category. For example, Figure 9-2 shows the problem statements within the category Reading.

Many users of the IPI thought that focusing on problem statements inferred there was a sickness in the school district. For this reason, the Illinois Department of Education eventually developed a second, alternative process with a more positive focus, eight effective schools characteristics. Figure 9-3 illustrates the eight categories of descriptors in the IQSI.

Each IQSI category uses an instrument with specific statements to identify the extent to which characteristics named apply. Ratings are then compared to a second set of ratings about the perceived importance of the characteristic to quality schooling. Figure 9-4 shows the problem statements within the category School Personnel.

The two processes named, the IPI and IQSI, are only two among a vast number of available instruments and processes to provide very different foci in needs assessment. Both were designed to be comprehensive in assessing strengths and weaknesses of the internal environment. Following are descriptions of the actual processes recommended for using the instruments.

The IPI calls for five meetings, each approximately two hours in length. The author, in using the process, added a sixth to enable committee members to become acquainted and to begin working together. Each meeting can be spaced about two weeks apart to allow for data collection and processing. This means that the entire process can be carried out in a matter of two months. To enable the reader to visualize the IPI process, the means of selecting a committee and the activity of each of the meetings is described. These steps are also visually presented in Figure 9-5.

Step 1 — Organize the I.P.I. Program

Selecting the committee is among the most important tasks of the needs assessment process. It is recommended that size first be determined. A group of 24 to 30 persons is thought to be manageable while allowing for representation of all in the school district. A group of 24 to 30 allows for breaking out into smaller groups of five or six depending on the task to be performed or the kind of communication desired. Perhaps most important, is the selection of the director of the process or the group facilitator. The process works best if the facilitator has no predetermined expectations or conclusions. An open mind and no hidden agenda are important criteria for the director or facilitator. Of course, it goes without saying that the better communication skills and group skills the director or facilitator possesses, the more likely that the process will be productive and satisfying to its members. Once the director or facilitator has been decided, the committee can be chosen. Volunteers are thought to work best. The knowledge that there are a limited number of meetings and each of these is defined in length, makes it easy to secure volunteers for the process. The author's criteria for committee selection were always that members were willing to commit to perfect attendance at meetings and that they were willing to give serious thought to the issues. It did not matter whether they were positive or negative about the school or school district. As a matter of fact, participating in the IPI or a similar needs assessment process can frequently convert a negative person into a supporter.

Depending on the size of the district, more than one committee of 24 to 30 may be desired. Each committee may consist of teacher representatives across the grades, teachers in special areas, representatives of special services personnel, administrators, board members, parents, community members who do not have children attending the schools, and representatives of the business community and churches or synagogues. Calling key communicators and organizations such as Rotary, the Chamber of Commerce, Lions Club, Kiwanis, and other groups can be helpful in selecting respected leaders who will be willing to serve for this important cause.

Key to the success of the committee effort is that members feel they are doing important work, that they feel they are a contributing member to the group effort, and that the product of the group effort will be valued and used. To accomplish this an overview of the effort can be given at every meeting. This is the total process; this is where we are; this is where we need to go; and this is what will happen when we have finished. It is not redundant to share this overview at every meeting while reinforcing how important the group effort is. The author always used the results of the needs assessment process as input into determining board-adopted, long-range goals. There was no question, then, that the effort was deemed to have importance.

Step 2 — First Meeting

This can be one meeting, but the author has chosen to have two meetings to accomplish the objective. First, an inexpensive supper can be used as a way to get the committee together for purposes of becoming familiar with each other. The author followed such a buffet with a group activity that allowed for the opportunity of members to work together and to get familiar with the task. Members will look forward to being present and to participating fully when there is a touch of enjoyment and sense of mystery as to what they will do next.

A follow-up to the supper can be the meeting to accomplish the first objective of the committee. The goal of the activity at the first meeting in the IPI process is to have the committee identify the categories of problems that will provide the focus of group activity in subsequent meetings. The director can have the committee preassigned to subgroups, each having a broad representation. Thinking through the composition of groups is an important task for the director. To the extent possible, each group should be planned so that it contains at least one leader who will serve as a catalyst for discussion.

The director can also lay ground rules for discussion; for example, all persons should feel free to say what they believe is important without feeling the need to take it back or rephrase it to be more acceptable. That is, every member and every contribution is valued. Working in small groups allows for greater communication, the most important part of the needs assessment process.

After moving into small groups of five or six, members review the categories and their definitions to make sure each member understands the terms and how they apply to the school system. Once this understanding has been created, members individually complete Instrument I. Between this and the next meeting, the data are processed.

Step 3 — Second Meeting

The goal of the activity in Step 3 is to identify priorities that will provide a focus for district improvement efforts and to identify the specific problem statements within priority categories by completing Instrument II.

The results of completing Instrument I can be presented in a format as shown for the category of Health/Safety/Nutrition/Drugs and Alcohol in Figure 9-6. The committee can then agree on what ratings they will use to include the category in subsequent committee activity. It is recommended that the categories for focus be limited to four to six. This recommendation is made because the volume of work will get too cumbersome if more are selected. Should the committee have more than six and really not want to let go, it can be agreed that the group will work with the top four to six. Then a subsequent process, perhaps occurring the following year, can work with the next items given importance. Once the four to six categories of most importance have been identified, members individually complete Instrument II (Figure 9-2) for each category identified. Once again, between this and the next meeting, the data are processed.

Step 4 — Third Meeting

The goals of the third meeting are twofold: a) to identify specific problems by reviewing an analysis of responses to Instrument II; that is, the percentage of individuals agreeing on specific problems; and b) to discuss validating evidence; that is, the identification of data the committee will accept as evidence documenting the existence of specific problems.

First, the results of completing Instrument II can be presented in a format as shown for individual items in the category of Communication Skills/Language Arts in Figure 9-7. The committee can then agree on what ratings they will use to include the problem statement in subsequent committee activity.

Once the problem statements have been identified, the group or subgroups can begin to agree on what they will accept as evidence that the problem exists. For example, standardized and criterion-referenced tests may provide evidence of achievement. National, state, and local reports may provide information for staffing and budget line item comparisons, among others. And so on. There is virtually no limit to what the group may suggest as providing evidence. The director can facilitate the actual decision as to what will be used as some suggestions may be more practical or possible than others. Between this and the next meeting, the evidence is gathered and prepared for presentation to the committee. It is important that the evidence is presented as jargon-free as possible with use of graphics to assist in interpretation of the data.

Step 5 — Fourth Meeting

The goals of the fourth meeting are again twofold: a) to review the evidence for the purpose of validating the problem, and b) to order priorities among the problem statements. The IPI process provides Instrument III as shown in Figure 9-8 for this purpose. In lieu of the instrument provided, the author substituted the Phi Delta Kappa process for ordering priorities. The PDK process will not be described in detail here. The PDK process was used because it provides for a rating of importance from 1 to 10, rather than the more limited range in Instrument III. Further, the Phi Delta Kappa process forces choices among items so that there is a clearer ordering of priorities. Finally, the results are known the same evening as the meeting, rather than waiting to process the data. Figure 9-9 shows the results of ranking 22 highest priority problem statements. Note that the mean rankings vary from a high of 8.17 to a low of 1.83 on a scale of 1 to 10.

Step 6 — Fifth Meeting

If the IPI Instrument III was used, the fifth meeting is used to feed back the results of the data collection. If the Phi Delta Kappa process was used, the fifth meeting can be postponed until such time as it has been decided what will be done with the results. For example, if the data is to be used as input into long-range planning or board-adopted goal statements, the final meeting can be used to share such plans with the committee and to thank them for their efforts. A final word is in order. The author had the Board officially recognize the contributions of the needs assessment committee and sign certificates of appreciation that were framed and presented to individual committee members.

Step 7 — Define Potential Solutions and Interact with Program Service Team to Determine Support and Timeliness

This step is recommended by the Illinois Department of Education, who provides the IPI instruments and data analysis. The understanding is that IDE staff can be supportive of the district to assure that the committee product is carried further.

The above steps were presented to give the reader a better understanding of the process used in the one needs assessment effort. By the time the IQSI was developed, computer graphics were being used to present results. For example, Figure 9-10 shows a line graph depicting the importance of leadership to quality schools (top line) and the extent to which leadership is demonstrated in the schools (bottom line). If the two lines merged, the desired and the real would be congruent. The measure of congruence for the leadership line graphs is shown in Figure 9-11. The extent to which the bars in the graph approach zero measures the congruence; a bar being at zero would equate to the two lines merging on the line graph. Specific instructions accompany the materials used in the IPI and IQSI processes. All suggestions may be adapted to suit the specific style of the director and the needs of the committee.

There is a wide variety of needs assessment instruments. The North Central Association and other such groups across the country utilize a planning process that may be less structured as far as instrumentation, but provide an equally comprehensive look at the school or district using the process. Less comprehensive instruments could include specific purpose surveys that could be used in isolation or in combination with a comprehensive needs assessment. The following Figures 9-12 through 9-15 are samples of some survey instruments that have proven useful in assessing schooling needs. Figure 9-12 can be used with citizens to rate school effectiveness. Figure 9-13 for General Curriculum is one of a set of instruments the Ohio Department of Education has written to assist districts in conducting self-evaluation. Figures 9-14 and 9-15 are adaptations of parts of forms used to evaluate learning media services for North Central Association self-studies at the high school and elementary levels respectively. Figure 9-14 rates a small portion of the total learning media services. The figure rates the environment on a scale of 1-5. Contrast this with the portion of the learning media services instrument for elementary schools in Figure 9-15. There are no ratings of the environment and other aspects of services. Rather, there are ratings of guiding principles, and both the desired and present states are rated.

Strategic and Other Planning Models

Strategic Planning Defined

Strategic planning is a system for identifying emerging issues and for planning to deal effectively with emerging issues. Alternatively, strategic planning can be considered a process for identifying appropriate responses to change and acting upon them. Strategic planning implies long-range planning on a continuing basis in a context of changing conditions. Strategic planning, therefore, requires a clear concept of mission and an agreed upon vision.

The superintendent plays a key role in developing or disseminating a vision, or mission statement, that can rally the support of all. The superintendent needs to articulate as an individual and with others: "What kind of school district do we want to become? What should we be doing? For whom should we be doing it? What should be the result? Who will benefit?"

Donald L. Ferguson prefers the title "Issues Management" to strategic planning. Whatever the process may be called, it is important to note that we are concerned with critical issues. Donald Ferguson has defined an issue as "a trend or condition, internal or external, which may, will, or does affect the successful accomplishment of your organization's objectives."

Strategic Planning Compared with Conventional Planning

Strategic planning is proactive; conventional planning is reactive. Conventional planning calls for identifying long-range goals and developing implementation and evaluation procedures. Conventional planning assumes that internal and external forces acting on the school system are static. Strategic planning is dynamic and builds in provisions for change.

Purpose of Strategic Planning

Strategic planning helps the superintendent develop a comprehensive plan to anticipate and shape the future. Strategic planning allows the superintendent to initiate, not merely manage, change. Where strategic planning is employed, the superintendent is able to access continually updated and reliable information as a basis for decisions to accomplish present and future objectives. Changing forces have left the superintendent with no choice but to respond, and strategic planning allows the superintendent to avoid visceral or emotionally charged actions.

Central to strategic planning, or issues management, is the notion that the organization is setting the agenda for the future rather than reacting to special interest group agendas or already current issues. Strategic planning, or issues management, keeps the organization focused and consistent in its actions. Further, by having such a focus, the organization can be consistent in its communications regarding the issues affecting it.

By using strategic planning methods and managing issues, the school district can become an active part, rather than merely a reactive part, of the change process. The process allows the organization to effectively convey its position on issues before these can impact on the organization in a threatening manner and endanger the health of the organization. For example, the superintendent can identify new programs and services necessary to address emerging needs. Such new programs and services can adequately prepare students for the 21st Century. Early identification of needs and effective responses to those needs can help insure adequate resources for implementation of plans.

Issues Impacting Education

Some issues facing education on a recurring basis are teacher negotiations, evaluation of personnel, program evaluation, declining enrollment, school closings, and effective staff development. Other significant issues are the effect of federal policies on schools, fundamentalism, school finance, tuition tax credits, impact of technology on the curriculum, and global education. Still others may include diminishing resources, aging community populations, single parenting, and changing job markets, choice, and restructuring.

Issues are categorized as *current* (e.g., tuition tax credits), *emerging* (e.g., coming teacher shortage, shifting demographics, choice, and restructuring) and *ongoing*. The superintendent is in a defensive posture with a current issue. At best the final outcome can be impacted and lessened. With emerging issues, the superintendent can shape them in the direction they take or diffuse them. Ongoing issues recur year-after-year; the goal is to manage them through periods of more or less prominence without much hope for a final solution.

Strategic planning, or issues management, deals with requirements and use of capital and the quality of the institution's product. It deals specifically with issues as defined above. Megatrends, as described earlier, can be one source of identifying issues having significance for the school system. More generally, special interest groups or individuals can be key sources of issues when such persons or groups hold positions different from the mainstream.

Once identified, issues attract media coverage. In the case of megatrends, these were analyzed according to the amount of coverage given by the media. An issue can die for lack of interest or it can attract supporters. Frequently issues receive the attention of someone in the institution or an elected official. In these ways, they receive public attention.

The focus here is on learning to identify and deal with emerging issues, rather than reacting to current issues. In this way, strategic planning allows for taking advantage and making the most of opportunities. In this regard, Don Ferguson said, "In a reactive posture we seldom manage the issue. . .we manage our position within the dynamics of the issue's evolution." He refers to this posture as "damage control."

Before strategic planning, school districts generally focused upon a small number of issues that were impacting upon them in the present. Management then commonly concentrated resources on the issue or issues to affect its course. By having such a limited focus and putting available resources to work on a single issue or limited number of issues, we are prevented from becoming rapidly involved in new or emerging issues.

Benefits

There are several benefits to be derived from strategic planning, or issues management. Benefits are illustrated in Figure 9-16. The superintendent gets involved early in the process. Through the coordination of positions, all in the organization can speak with a unified voice on the issue. Information that becomes available in the strategic planning process can be made available to all involved in managing the issue, which may include all in the organization, particularly the best experts in the organization.

By focusing on the future and what is not-yet-a-problem, there is less time spent in "putting out fires." The district can focus on goals and set priorities to maintain that focus, despite day-to-day demands and pressures. By having a common focus, we are better able to cope with competing demands on our time. It follows that strategic planning is a time-saving device since eliminating the extraneous, or less important, can save time. Also, by having a clear direction, the organization can shape media coverage and support those speaking for the organization.

By having all focused on common objectives thought by all to be important, objectives are more effectively accomplished and employees are more appropriately involved. Agreement on what is important identifies content that serves as a basis for forming and guiding support groups and individuals. Other benefits include the better use of resources; that is, all key resources to accomplish the district's objectives are coordinated.

Problems

If all of the above benefits are to be derived from strategic planning, we may ask why it is not more popular? The answer is that there are problems in implementing strategic planning, or issues management. Figure 9-17 illustrates some of these problems. People resist change. In addition, the control of information changes so that it is available horizontally rather than controlled hierarchically. Time spent in planning may be viewed as wasted when it may appear more important to jump into problem solution or reacting to at-hand issues or crises. Some who will be affected by the change may fear being left out of the decision process. The traditional image of public relations may hamper this up-front, see-it and tell-it-like-it-is approach. There may be initial confusion in dealing with broader objectives and audiences. The process appears simple and will produce skeptics that it can work. Finally, there is a lingering conception that if we ignore a problem it will go away.

Steps in Strategic Planning, or Issues Management

Having enumerated some benefits and problems, it is well to look at the steps in the process as shown in Figure 9-18 and 9-19. Strategic planning involves identification, analysis, and ordering priorities of issues. Next, strategies for dealing with issues are developed; the strategies are implemented; an analysis and evaluation of the process are completed; any necessary corrections are performed; and a post-analysis is completed.

Any number of individuals or groups can be involved in the identification of issues: individuals, a management team, board members, advisory groups, representatives of selected publics, staff, and students. Figures 9-20 through 9-24 illustrate who is involved in each of these steps and how individuals and groups are involved. Individuals and groups use listening, reading, and other scanning devices to obtain information from other individuals and groups.

Data collected by using the checklists shown below can be helpful in external and internal scanning (McCune, pp.70-74 and 77-80):

External Scanning Data Checklist
    Economic Data and Trends
        Economic Structure
        Employment
        Income
    Demographic Data and Trends
        Population
        Age
        Race/Ethnicity
        Families and Households
        Sex Role Patterns
    Social Data and Trends
        Health
        Welfare
        Housing
        Transportation
        Crime
        Government
    Education Data and Trends

Internal Scanning Data Checklist
    Economic Data and Trends
        School Finance
    Social/Demographic Data and Trends
        Students
        Human Resources (Staff)
        Pupil Personnel Services
        Student Needs
    Educational Data and Trends
        Achievement
        Curriculum
        Organization and Management
        Support Services
    Technology Data and Trends
        Technology Plans
    Political and Public Relations Data and Trends
        Labor, Legal, and Legislative Affairs
        Community Relations
        Governance

Once the data has been gathered, the ad hoc committee, or task force, then weights the issue from high to low in terms of its impact on the organization, its probability of occurring, and the importance of developing a strategy for dealing with the issue. Then the top four to six issues are selected.

As in identifying issues, any number of individuals or groups can be involved in strategy development. Broadly speaking, the involvement should include everyone affected by the issue and those who must ultimately approve the strategy. In the case of a school district, representatives of employees to be affected by the strategy as well as representatives of students and external publics, in some cases can be included in an ad hoc task force that can make recommendations to the strategic planning, or issues management task force, and, in turn, the board of education.

The individuals and groups will take the priority issues and break them down, analyzing them in terms of positive and negative consequences for the organization, their strength or weakness, policy and legal implications they have, key communicators, and organizations who will be involved in the strategy implementation and identification of key coalitions. Positions for resolving the issues will be formulated and communications activities, internal and external to the organization, essential to winning or resolving the issue, will be formulated.

Once a strategy has been developed for dealing with an issue, all key individuals and groups necessary to its implementation will be identified and set to work. Individuals and groups will be responsible for interpersonal and media communications. Objectives for measuring the achievement and effectiveness of the strategy will be determined. Clear identification of who does what by when will be made, and strategy attainment will be monitored. In the post-analysis, various individuals and groups will determine what components worked or did not work, and they will provide a guide to developing future strategies.

Starting the Planning Process

There are steps to take in starting the strategic planning, or issues management process. Figure 9-25 itemizes several steps that can be followed. First, it is important to "sell" the idea by becoming knowledgeable about and stressing the benefits to the organization. Next, it is important to gain support for the idea, especially at the top management and board levels. Develop, review, and revise a plan. Determine what hardware and software are needed to support the data base; secure and test these. Communicate support for the planning process. Establish the groups who will be involved in ad hoc and standing committees. Identify the issues and set priorities. Assign responsibilities for developing strategies and have the responsible individuals and groups develop plans and issue papers. Do whatever work is needed to assure that positions are legal and consistent with policy. Get the board involved in reviewing and revising the draft plan and then get the appropriate individuals and groups working on the top four to six priority issues as described above. Monitor issues and keep these current.

The Dallas Independent School System has used the issues management process with success. Figures 9-26 through 9-29 illustrate the manner in which issues management is used in the Dallas School System, an urban district of 130,000 students. Figure 9-26 traces the route of an issue through the system, beginning with its identification as a potential issue through referring priority issues to appropriate staff for development of a strategic plan. Figure 9-27 names the key players in Dallas' issues management program. Figure 9-28 lists the seven accomplishments Dallas has experienced to date. Figure 9-29 shows key points to keep in mind for those interested in developing an issues management system. Key points include securing of top-level commitment, allocation of time and resources, initial staff resistance, delayed recognition of benefits, early determination of standards but flexibility in these, a communication plan, selecting equipment to meet local needs, selecting staff for key roles, getting outside help, and using the system. More recently, smaller districts have begun to use strategic planning, or issues management. Three in the Columbus, Ohio area are Upper Arlington, Worthington, and Westerville.

Upper Arlington and Worthington are examples of two suburban school districts in the Columbus, Ohio area who cooperate to do joint strategic planning. Figure 9-30 shows the strategic planning process of the Upper Arlington School District. The process was begun with scans of the internal and external environments. Next, a broad involvement of district and community persons was used to develop a mission statement. Succeeding steps call for writing and assessing a plan, writing a plan for implementation, and implementing the plan.

ASCD, Association for Supervision and Curriculum Development, is a professional organization that does strategic planning on a regular basis. Figure 9-31 illustrates the steps in ASCD's strategic planning process. Five-year action plans are developed to support the Organization's mission statement, "Developing Leadership for Quality in Education for All Students." ASCD has the entire governance structure engaged in the planning process. The planning process includes, at the grass-roots level, some 200 members of the Board of Directors who represent their state affiliates and members at large.

Those working in the area of strategic planning emphasize the importance of constantly listing and refining a strategic plan. Martisko and Ammentorp applied strategic planning in nine Minnesota Educational Cooperative Units (*American School Board Journal*, March, 1986). Based on their experience, the two offered advice in the four steps they identified in the strategic planning process: 1) Setting Goals. Call on as many community members as possible — i.e., board, administrators, principals, teacher representatives, P.T.O. representatives, and student council members to list specific goals for schools. Then, edit, eliminate duplication, and ensure clarity of meaning of the goals. 2) Developing Programs. Have groups "free sort" goal statements into groups that have something in common for program implications. Then use the computer to perform a cluster analysis to determine which are most important for the most people. 3) Setting Priorities. Rank individual items and clusters to determine which items are most important to one's schools. 4) Implementing and Evaluating. Board allocates resources for priority clusters. Clusters and goal statements can be used to assess whether programs have met the district's needs and what programs should be implemented in the future.

Costs and Opportunity Costs

Essential to the planning process is the realization that every choice for action has a cost and an opportunity cost. The cost may be in terms of time and energy of human resources or it may be in terms of utilization of space or expenditures of monies. The choice to select any or all of these to utilize also involves a giving up or postponing of other choices; what we give up are opportunity costs.

When we are dealing with scarce or limited resources, it is important to identify the opportunity costs — what we need to give up when we make certain choices. In order to determine opportunity costs, it is important to use a planning model that involves identifying alternative solutions to problems or issues. Once alternatives are identified, criteria for selecting an alternative can be identified and weighted. Then the criteria are progressively applied to the alternatives until the best single or combination of alternatives are identified. A simple grid can be used in this process. List the alternatives down the left side and the criteria across the top. Fill in the grid and then select — maximize opportunity and minimize cost.

REFERENCES AND RESOURCES

Albert, Kenneth, ed., *The Strategic Management Handbook*. New York, NY: McGraw-Hill, 1983.

Baldridge, J. Victor, and Terrence F. Deal, eds., *The Dynamics of Organizational Change in Education*. Berkeley, CA: McCutchan Publishing Corporation, 1983.

Brandt, Steven, *Strategic Planning in Emerging Companies*. Reading, PA: Addison-Wesley Publishing Company, 1984.

Chase, W. Howard, *Issue Management: Origins for the Future*. Stamford, CT: Issue Action Publications, 1984.

Cooper, Harry, *Strategic Planning in Education: A Guide for Policymakers*. Alexandria, VA: National Association of State Boards of Education, 1985.

Cope, Robert, "A Contextual Model to Encompass the Strategic Planning Concept: Introducing a Newer Paradigm," *Planning for Higher Education* 13, no. 3 (Spring, 1985), 13-20.

Strategic Planning, Management, and Decision-Making. Washington, D.C.: American Association for Higher Education, 1981.

Kanter, Rosabeth Moss, *The Change Masters.* New York, NY: Simon and Schuster, 1983.

Lewis, James, Jr., *Long-Range and Short-Range Planning for Educational Administrators.* Newton, MA: Allyn and Bacon, Inc., 1983.

Mace-Matluck, Betty J., *Research-Based Strategies for Bringing About School Improvement.* Austin, TX: Southwest Educational Development Laboratory, 1986.

Martisko, Les, and William Ammentorp, "Take Five Strategic Planning Steps, and Turn School Goals into Realities," *The American School Board Journal* (March, 1986), 38-39.

McCune, Shirley D., *Guide to Strategic Planning for Educators.* Alexandria, VA: Association for Supervision and Curriculum Development, 1986.

Neill, Shirley Boes, ed., *Planning for Tomorrow's Schools: Problems and Solutions.* Arlington, VA: American Association of School Administrators, 1983.

Paine, Frank, and Carl Anderson, *Strategic Management.* New York, NY: CBS College Publishing, 1983.

Patterson, Jerry L., Steward C. Purkey, and Jackson V. Parker, *Productive School Systems for a Nonrational World.* Alexandria, VA: Association for Supervision and Curriculum Development, 1986.

Pfeiffer, J. William, Leonard D. Goodstein, and Timothy M. Nolan, *Understanding Applied Strategic Planning: A Manager's Guide.* San Diego, CA: University Associates, Inc., 1985.

Steiner, George A., *Strategic Planning: What Every Manager Must Know.* New York, NY: The Free Press, 1979.

Other Resources

The Chief State School Officers provide useful planning resources. Names and addresses are listed at the end of Chapter 8.

National School Public Relations Association, 1501 Lee Highway, Arlington, VA 22209.

National Study of School Evaluation, 5201 Leesburg Pike, Falls Church, VA 22041.

District Name

County — District

- ☐ Board Member ☐ Parent
- ☐ Administrator ☐ Community Member (non parent)
- ☐ Teacher
- ☐ Student ☐ Other

ILLINOIS PROBLEMS INDEX INSTRUMENT I: GENERAL PROBLEM CATEGORIES

Circle "Y" for "Yes" if the problem category listed below represents a current problem area. Circle "E" if the category represents an emerging or future problem area. Circle "N" for "No" if it is not an important problem for the school district to consider at this time. Circle "U" if you are undecided. (Circle one per problem category.)

If you circled "Y" or "E", circle the number below that represents how important the problem area is relative to all of the problem areas for which you circled "Y" or "E"

CODE	PROBLEM CATEGORY	CURRENT PROBLEM AREA	EMERGING PROBLEM AREA	NOT A PROBLEM AREA	UNDECIDED	VERY LITTLE IMPORTANCE	LITTLE IMPORTANCE	SOME IMPORTANCE	CONSIDERABLE IMPORTANCE	VERY GREAT IMPORTANCE
	Curriculum and Instruction in Basic Skills									
01	Reading	Y	E	N	U	1	2	3	4	5
02	Mathematics	Y	E	N	U	1	2	3	4	5
03	Communication Skills/Language Arts	Y	E	N	U	1	2	3	4	5
04	Readiness Skills	Y	E	N	U	1	2	3	4	5
	Curriculum and Instruction in Science									
05	Science	Y	E	N	U	1	2	3	4	5
06	Environmental Education	Y	E	N	U	1	2	3	4	5
	Curriculum and Instruction in Home and Health Science									
07	Consumer Education/Family Life/Home Economics	Y	E	N	U	1	2	3	4	5
08	Health/Safety/Nutrition/Drugs and Alcohol	Y	E	N	U	1	2	3	4	5
09	Physical Education	Y	E	N	U	1	2	3	4	5
10	Interscholastic and Intramural Athletics	Y	E	N	U	1	2	3	4	5
	Curriculum and Instruction in Cultural and Social Studies									
11	Social Studies	Y	E	N	U	1	2	3	4	5
12	Citizenship	Y	E	N	U	1	2	3	4	5
13	Foreign Language	Y	E	N	U	1	2	3	4	5
	Curriculum and Instruction in the Arts									
14	Visual Arts	Y	E	N	U	1	2	3	4	5
15	Music	Y	E	N	U	1	2	3	4	5
16	Literature	Y	E	N	U	1	2	3	4	5
17	Theatre	Y	E	N	U	1	2	3	4	5
18	Dance/Movement	Y	E	N	U	1	2	3	4	5
	Intercurricular Concepts									
19	Vocational and Career Education	Y	E	N	U	1	2	3	4	5
20	International Studies and Cross-Cultural Education	Y	E	N	U	1	2	3	4	5
21	Responsibility/Character Education	Y	E	N	U	1	2	3	4	5
22	Critical Thinking/Problem Solving/Decision Making	Y	E	N	U	1	2	3	4	5
23	Study Skills	Y	E	N	U	1	2	3	4	5
24	Arts in General Education	Y	E	N	U	1	2	3	4	5
	Special Programs									
25	Early Childhood	Y	E	N	U	1	2	3	4	5
26	Gifted	Y	E	N	U	1	2	3	4	5
27	Minority/Disadvantaged	Y	E	N	U	1	2	3	4	5
28	Neglected/Delinquent/Dropout	Y	E	N	U	1	2	3	4	5
29	Adult Education	Y	E	N	U	1	2	3	4	5
30	Special Needs	Y	E	N	U	1	2	3	4	5

Figure 9-1

County   District

☐ Board Member ☐ Parent
☐ Administrator ☐ Community Member
☐ Teacher   (non parent)
☐ Student   ☐ Other

ILLINOIS PROBLEMS INDEX INSTRUMENT I:
GENERAL PROBLEM CATEGORIES

Circle "Y" for "Yes" if the problem category listed below represents a current problem area. Circle "E" if the category represents an emerging or future problem area. Circle "N" for "No" if it is not an important problem for the school district to consider at this time. Circle "U" if you are undecided. (Circle one per problem category.)

If you circled "Y" or "E", circle the number below that represents how important the problem area is relative to all of the problem areas for which you circled "Y" or "E".

CODE	PROBLEM CATEGORY	CURRENT PROBLEM AREA	EMERGING PROBLEM AREA	NOT A PROBLEM AREA	UNDECIDED		VERY LITTLE IMPORTANCE	LITTLE IMPORTANCE	SOME IMPORTANCE	CONSIDERABLE IMPORTANCE	VERY GREAT IMPORTANCE
	Resource and Support Services										
31	Media and Library Services	Y	E	N	U		1	2	3	4	5
32	Food Services	Y	E	N	U		1	2	3	4	5
33	Transportation Services	Y	E	N	U		1	2	3	4	5
34	Health and Medical Services	Y	E	N	U		1	2	3	4	5
35	Counseling and Guidance Services	Y	E	N	U		1	2	3	4	5
36	Psychological and Social Work Services	Y	E	N	U		1	2	3	4	5
37	Coordination of Pupil Personnel Services	Y	E	N	U		1	2	3	4	5
	Program Planning and Development										
38	Educational Programming	Y	E	N	U		1	2	3	4	5
39	Educational Planning	Y	E	N	U		1	2	3	4	5
40	Pre-service Education	Y	E	N	U		1	2	3	4	5
41	In-service Education	Y	E	N	U		1	2	3	4	5
42	Teaching Methods and Techniques	Y	E	N	U		1	2	3	4	5
	Educational Administration and Policy										
43	Finance and Staffing	Y	E	N	U		1	2	3	4	5
44	Individual Rights and Responsibilities	Y	E	N	U		1	2	3	4	5
45	Physical Plant and Facilities	Y	E	N	U		1	2	3	4	5
46	School-Community Relations	Y	E	N	U		1	2	3	4	5
47	Administrative Organizations	Y	E	N	U		1	2	3	4	5
	Research and Evaluation										
48	Research and Utilization	Y	E	N	U		1	2	3	4	5
49	Selection and Evaluation of Personnel	Y	E	N	U		1	2	3	4	5
50	Evaluation of Students	Y	E	N	U		1	2	3	4	5
51	Evaluation of Education Programs	Y	E	N	U		1	2	3	4	5

Source: Illinois State Board of Education.

Figure 9-1 (Cont'd.)

County   District

☐ Board Member   ☐ Parent
☐ Administrator   ☐ Community Member
☐ Teacher   (non parent)
☐ Student   ☐ Other

ILLINOIS PROBLEMS INDEX INSTRUMENT II:
READING

Circle "Y" for "Yes" if the statement represents a current or emerging problem in your school district. Circle "N" for "No" if the statement does not represent a problem. Circle "U" if you are undecided. Add additional problem statements at the end of the list if necessary.

If you circled "Y", indicate the grade level(s) at which the problem occurs:

1 = Grades K-3	4 = Grades 9-12
2 = Grades 4-6	5 = All Grades
3 = Grades 7-8	6 = Other

If you circled "Y", circle the numbers below that describe the best evidence you are using to document that a problem exists.

CODE	PROBLEM STATEMENT	IS A PROBLEM	IS NOT A PROBLEM	UNDECIDED	GRADE LEVEL(S)	CLASSROOM/SCHOOL CONDITIONS	STUDENT(S) I KNOW	RESEARCH STUDIES/ EXPERT OPINION	TEST SCORES	BUDGET	CURRICULUM MATERIALS	OTHER
0101	Students cannot read.	Y	N	U		1	2	3	4	5	6	7
0102	Students do not comprehend what is read.	Y	N	U		1	2	3	4	5	6	7
0103	Students do not analyze what is read.	Y	N	U		1	2	3	4	5	6	7
0104	Students do not reason logically from what is read.	Y	N	U		1	2	3	4	5	6	7
0105	Students do not make judgments about what is read.	Y	N	U		1	2	3	4	5	6	7
0106	Students do not have skills for learning new words.	Y	N	U		1	2	3	4	5	6	7
0107	Students do not analyze word root, prefixes and suffixes to determine the meaning of words.	Y	N	U		1	2	3	4	5	6	7
0108	Students do not discriminate between fact and opinion.	Y	N	U		1	2	3	4	5	6	7
0109	Students do not draw conclusions, generalizations, and inferences from what is read.	Y	N	U		1	2	3	4	5	6	7
0110	Students cannot use reference materials efficiently (e.g. dictionaries, encyclopedias).	Y	N	U		1	2	3	4	5	6	7
0111	Students cannot use indexes, table of contents, and glossaries.	Y	N	U		1	2	3	4	5	6	7
0112	Students cannot read graphic materials (e.g., maps, tables, graphs).	Y	N	U		1	2	3	4	5	6	7
0113	Students do not read aloud in an effective manner.	Y	N	U		1	2	3	4	5	6	7
0114	Students do not adapt the style and speed of their reading to particular purposes.	Y	N	U		1	2	3	4	5	6	7
0115	Students do not vary their reading materials.	Y	N	U		1	2	3	4	5	6	7
0116	Students do not choose to read on their own.	Y	N	U		1	2	3	4	5	6	7

Figure 9-2

County   District

☐ Board Member   ☐ Parent
☐ Administrator   ☐ Community Member
☐ Teacher   (non parent)
☐ Student   ☐ Other

ILLINOIS PROBLEMS INDEX INSTRUMENT II:
READING

Circle "Y" for "Yes" if the statement represents a current or emerging problem in your school district. Circle "N" for "No" if the statement does not represent a problem. Circle "U" if you are undecided. Add additional problem statements at the end of the list if necessary.

If you circled "Y", indicate the grade level(s) at which the problem occurs:

1 = Grades K-3	4 = Grades 9-12
2 = Grades 4-6	5 = All Grades
3 = Grades 7-8	6 = Other

If you circled "Y", circle the numbers below that describe the best evidence you are using to document that a problem exists.

CODE	PROBLEM STATEMENT	IS A PROBLEM	IS NOT A PROBLEM	UNDECIDED	GRADE LEVEL(S)	CLASSROOM/SCHOOL CONDITIONS	STUDENT(S) I KNOW	RESEARCH STUDIES/ EXPERT OPINION	TEST SCORES	BUDGET	CURRICULUM MATERIALS	OTHER
0117	Students do not follow written directions.	Y	N	U		1	2	3	4	5	6	7
0118	Students, ranging from remedial to gifted, are not provided with appropriate curriculum alternatives.	Y	N	U		1	2	3	4	5	6	7

Source: Illinois State Board of Education.

Figure 9-2 (Cont'd.)

ILLINOIS QUALITY SCHOOLS INDEX
EIGHT EFFECTIVE SCHOOLS CHARACTERISTICS

1. Mission

2. Climate

3. Leadership

4. Expectations

5. Time on Task

6. Basic Skills

7. Monitoring

8. Parent/Community Participation

Source: Illinois State Board of Education.

Figure 9-3

ILLINOIS QUALITY SCHOOLS INDEX
(Scales A and B)

County — District

Name of School or District

☐ Board Member   ☐ Parent
☐ Administrator   ☐ Community Member (non-parent)
☐ Teacher
☐ Student   ☐ Other

Address   City   Zip

CHARACTERISTIC:
EXPECTATIONS
In a quality school, both staff and students are expected to do their best work in everything they do. This affects the learning climate of the school. Teachers have confidence in their ability to teach and in the students' ability to learn. When high expectations are evident, all members of the school system know what is expected of them. Administrators know what parents, teachers, and students expect them to do. Teachers know what they are expected to teach. Students know what they are expected to learn. Parents know what is expected of them and their children.

SCALE A. Rate the extent to which your school demonstrates this characteristic by circling the appropriate number from a column below.

SCALE B. Rate the importance of this characteristic to quality schooling by circling the appropriate number from a column below.

School personnel demonstrate their expectations by:

CODE	ITEMS	UNDECIDED	NONE	VERY LITTLE	LITTLE	SOME	CONSIDERABLE	VERY GREAT	NONE	VERY LITTLE	LITTLE	SOME	CONSIDERABLE	VERY GREAT
0301	Believing that students will do their best work.	0	1	2	3	4	5	6	1	2	3	4	5	6
0302	Helping students to develop their abilities to their highest potential.	0	1	2	3	4	5	6	1	2	3	4	5	6
0303	Believing that students can succeed.	0	1	2	3	4	5	6	1	2	3	4	5	6
0304	Seeking opportunities to praise all students.	0	1	2	3	4	5	6	1	2	3	4	5	6
0305	Letting students and parents know that high achievement is expected of students.	0	1	2	3	4	5	6	1	2	3	4	5	6
0306	Stressing the importance of educational achievement to parents and students.	0	1	2	3	4	5	6	1	2	3	4	5	6
0307	Requiring students to behave.	0	1	2	3	4	5	6	1	2	3	4	5	6
0308	Encouraging parents to support the educational process at home and at school.	0	1	2	3	4	5	6	1	2	3	4	5	6
0309	Praising low-achieving students as much and as often as high-achieving students.	0	1	2	3	4	5	6	1	2	3	4	5	6
0310	Rewarding good student work through recognition.	0	1	2	3	4	5	6	1	2	3	4	5	6
0311	Featuring student accomplishments in the school or community newspaper.	0	1	2	3	4	5	6	1	2	3	4	5	6
0312	Trying new teaching methods and materials when students are not learning.	0	1	2	3	4	5	6	1	2	3	4	5	6
0313	Performing all tasks to the best of their professional abilities.	0	1	2	3	4	5	6	1	2	3	4	5	6
0314	Providing growth opportunities for each other.	0	1	2	3	4	5	6	1	2	3	4	5	6
0315	Seeking opportunities to increase professional knowledge and skill.	0	1	2	3	4	5	6	1	2	3	4	5	6

Figure 9-4

County — District

Name of School or District

Address | City | Zip

☐ Board Member   ☐ Parent
☐ Administrator   ☐ Community Member (non parent)
☐ Teacher
☐ Student   ☐ Other

CHARACTERISTIC:
LEADERSHIP — Few activities in the school automatically happen. Leaders make things happen. In effective schools this leader may be the building principal, curriculum director, a department chairperson, lead teacher, team of teachers, or interested parent. An effective leader has a dynamic, often charismatic, personality, gets things done because of organizational skills, and influences others to accomplish certain goals. Basically, leadership is two-fold, involving people and tasks. The concept of leadership has meanings as varied as the people involved and the tasks to be done. A leader determines the tasks and the ways to accomplish them, either self-directed or directing others. Effective leadership comes from energetic persons who initiate activities and inspire the involvement of others.

PART A. Rate the extent to which your school demonstrates this characteristic by circling the appropriate number from a column below.

PART B. Rate the importance of this characteristic to quality schooling by circling the appropriate number from a column below.

School personnel:

CODE	ITEMS	UNDECIDED	NONE	VERY LITTLE	LITTLE	SOME	CONSIDERABLE	VERY GREAT	NONE	VERY LITTLE	LITTLE	SOME	CONSIDERABLE	VERY GREAT
0315	Support and encourage each other.	0	1	2	3	4	5	6	1	2	3	4	5	6
0316	Set high standards for themselves and others	0	1	2	3	4	5	6	1	2	3	4	5	6
0317	Believe in the competence of themselves and others.	0	1	2	3	4	5	6	1	2	3	4	5	6
0318	Attend to their own and students' needs.	0	1	2	3	4	5	6	1	2	3	4	5	6
0319	Show concern for self growth and growth of others (staff and students).	0	1	2	3	4	5	6	1	2	3	4	5	6
0320	Consult periodically with each other.	0	1	2	3	4	5	6	1	2	3	4	5	6
0321	Consult frequently with parents.	0	1	2	3	4	5	6	1	2	3	4	5	6
0322	Involve students and parents in relevant decisions.	0	1	2	3	4	5	6	1	2	3	4	5	6
0323	Are forceful and dynamic.	0	1	2	3	4	5	6	1	2	3	4	5	6
0324	Are highly motivated.	0	1	2	3	4	5	6	1	2	3	4	5	6
0325	Motivate others.	0	1	2	3	4	5	6	1	2	3	4	5	6
0326	Are available to students for help beyond class time.	0	1	2	3	4	5	6	1	2	3	4	5	6
0327	Provide reward structures for positive achievement and learning.	0	1	2	3	4	5	6	1	2	3	4	5	6
0328	Deal positively with any pressures.	0	1	2	3	4	5	6	1	2	3	4	5	6
0329	Keep the community informed about various school activities.	0	1	2	3	4	5	6	1	2	3	4	5	6
0330	Use resource materials from all available sources.	0	1	2	3	4	5	6	1	2	3	4	5	6

Source: Illinois State Board of Education.

Figure 9-4 (Cont'd.)

THE ILLINOIS PROBLEMS INDEX – THE PROCESS

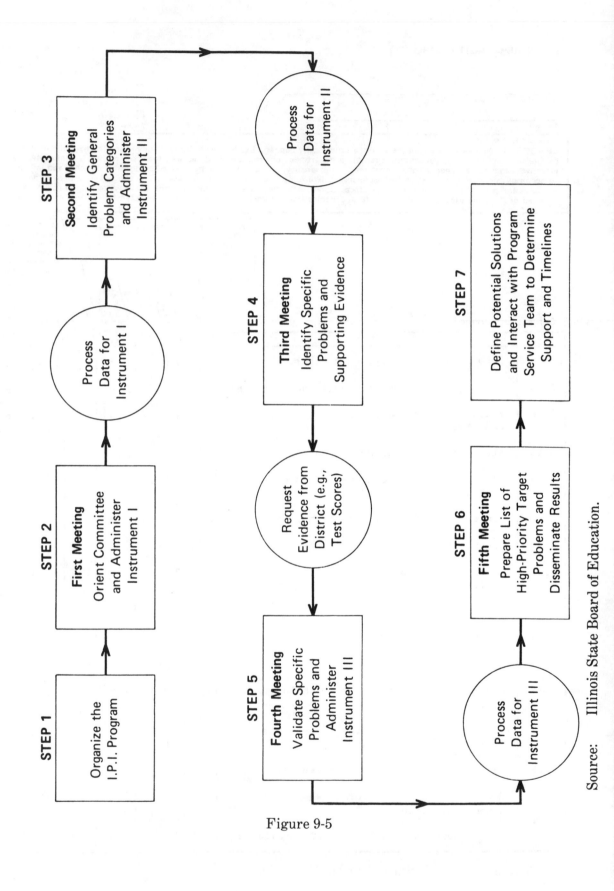

Figure 9-5

Source: Illinois State Board of Education.

Illinois State Board of Education

Code	Problem Category Description	Is This Important Area in Which to Identify Problem?				Total Respondents 21	
		% Yes	% Emerge	% Undecided	% No	Current Problem Av.Rating of Importance	Emerging Problem Av.Rating of Importance
08	Health/Safety/Nutrition/Drugs & Alcohol	57.14	19.04	4.76	19.04	4.41	3.75
23	Study Skills	57.14	19.04	14.28	9.52	3.50	3.75
22	Critical Think/Prob Solv/Dec Mkng	38.09	28.57	14.28	19.04	3.50	3.66
31	Media and Library Services	33.33	23.80	0.00	42.85	4.28	3.60
28	Neglected/Delinquent/Dropout	33.33	19.04	14.28	33.33	4.00	3.25
46	School-Community Relations	33.33	33.33	9.52	23.80	3.57	3.71
43	Finance and Staffing	33.33	52.38	0.00	14.28	3.42	4.00
03	Communication Skills/Language Arts	33.33	19.04	9.52	38.09	3.85	3.50
01	Reading	33.33	4.76	9.52	52.38	4.28	4.00
32	Food Services	28.57	23.80	0.00	47.61	4.33	3.20
33	Transportation Services	28.57	9.52	0.00	61.90	3.50	3.50
26	Gifted	28.57	28.57	14.28	28.57	4.00	3.33
21	Responsibility/Character Education	23.80	28.57	19.04	28.57	3.60	3.33
19	Vocational and Career Education	23.80	9.52	9.52	57.14	3.60	4.50
45	Physical Plant and Facilities	23.80	38.09	9.52	28.57	4.00	3.37
02	Mathematics	23.80	9.52	9.52	57.14	4.80	4.00
09	Physical Education	23.80	9.52	0.00	66.66	3.40	3.50
05	Science	19.04	14.28	14.28	52.38	3.75	4.33
49	Selection and Evaluation of Personnel	19.04	9.52	19.04	52.38	4.25	4.00
51	Evaluation of Education Programs	19.04	23.80	19.04	38.09	4.00	4.00
20	Internat'l Studies & Cross-Cult Educ	19.04	9.52	38.04	33.33	3.25	1.50
27	Minority/Disadvantaged	19.04	4.76	23.80	52.38	3.75	4.00
34	Health and Medical Services	14.28	4.76	9.52	71.42	3.33	3.00
35	Counseling and Guidance Services	14.28	19.04	9.52	57.14	3.00	3.75

Source: Illinois State Board of Education.

Figure 9-6
309

Total Respondents 20 ·

Is This a Problem			% Chkng Grade Level Based on Yes Ans						% Usng Evid Category Based on Ttl Yes Responses						
%Yes	%No	%Und	1	2	3	4	5	6	1	2	3	4	5	6	7

0301 Students Do Not Have Listening Skills
40.00 30.00 30.00   25.00   12.50 62.50   37.50 37.50 25.00

0302 Students Are Not Required to Practice Listening Skills
20.00 50.00 30.00   25.00   25.00 50.00   50.00 25.00   25.00

0303 Students Do Not Have an Adequate Vocabulary
35.00 30.00 35.00   14.28 14.28 14.28 71.42   14.28 100.00 14.28

0304 Students Do Not Have Creative Oral Expression
15.00 55.00 35.00   100.00   100.00

0305 Students Do Not Enunciate Clearly
25.00 45.00 30.00   20.00 20.00   80.00   20.00 80.00   20.00

0306 Students Are Not Required to Practice Speaking Skills
30.00 55.00 15.00   16.66 33.33 16.66   50.00   16.66 66.66   33.33

0307 Students Do Not Express Their Thoughts Orally So Others Can Understand
25.00 65.00 10.00   20.00 20.00   60.00 20.00   100.00

0308 Students Do Not Write Legibly
40.00 30.00 30.00   12.50 12.50 25.00 62.50   12.50 100.00

0309 Students Do Not Use Correct Punctuation
30.00 30.00 40.00   16.66 83.33   16.66 100.00   16.66

0310 Students Do Not Use Correct Grammar
35.00 25.00 40.00   14.28 14.28   14.28 71.42   14.28 100.00   14.28

0311 Students Do Not Spell Correctly
40.00 25.00 35.00   37.50 12.50   62.50   25.00 87.50   12.50

0312 Students Do Not Express Their Thoughts in Writing So Others Can Understand
50.00 35.00 15.00   40.00 20.00 20.00 40.00 10.00   30.00 90.00   20.00

0313 Students Do Not Have Creative Written Expression
40.00 35.00 25.00   25.00   25.00 50.00   25.00 62.50   12.50

0314 Students Are Not Required to Practice Writing Skills
20.00 55.00 25.00   50.00 25.00   25.00   25.00 50.00 25.00   25.00

0315 Students Are Not Aware of Nonverbal Communication Techniques
10.00 50.00 40.00   100.00   50.00   50.00

0316 Students Are Not Aware of Techniques Used in Mass Media and Advertising
60.00 40.00

Source: Illinois State Board of Education.

Figure 9-7

COUNTY — DISTRICT

ILLINOIS PROBLEMS INDEX INSTRUMENT III:

SELECTED PROBLEM STATEMENTS

The following problem statements represent problems that have been shown to exist in your school district.

Circle the number below that represents the extent to which you would like your district to allocate resources toward solving these problems.

CODE	PROBLEM STATEMENT	Not at All	To a Small Extent	To Some Extent	To a Large Extent	To a Very Large Extent
		1	2	3	4	5
		1	2	3	4	5
		1	2	3	4	5
		1	2	3	4	5
		1	2	3	4	5
		1	2	3	4	5
		1	2	3	4	5
		1	2	3	4	5
		1	2	3	4	5
		1	2	3	4	5
		1	2	3	4	5
		1	2	3	4	5
		1	2	3	4	5

Source: Illinois State Board of Education.

Figure 9-8

COMMUNITY CONSOLIDATED SCHOOL DISTRICT NO. 146
1978 NEEDS ASSESSMENT COMMITTEE PRIORITY
CONCERNS BY CATEGORY AND PROBLEM STATEMENT

Problem Statement	Code	Category	Range (1-10) High	Low	Median	Mean
1. Students cannot comprehend what is read.	0101	Reading	10	6	8.5	8.17
2. Students cannot analyze what is read.	0102	Reading	7	4	6.0	5.83
3. Students cannot reason logically from what is read.	0103	Reading	7	1	4.5	4.50
4. Students cannot follow written directions.	0115	Reading	7	1	4.0	4.00
5. Students do not use correct punctuation or grammar.	0305	Communication Skills/Language Arts	10	4	4.5	5.67
6. Students cannot spell well enough.	0306	Communication Skills/Language Arts	9	3	4.0	5.00
7. Students do not have effective writing organization.	0307	Communication Skills/Language Arts	10	4	5.0	5.67
8. Students do not have good listening skills.	0312	Communication Skills/Language Arts	6	2	4.5	4.17
9. Students have not learned strategies for processing information (e.g., coding, analyzing, retrieving).	1904	Critical Thinking/Problem-Solving, Decision-Making	6	1	4.0	4.00
10. Students have not acquired habits of critical judgment.	1907	Critical Thinking/Problem-Solving, Decision-Making	7	1	4.5	4.33
11. Students cannot think logically and critically in solving problems.	1910	Critical Thinking/Problem-Solving, Decision-Making	8	1	5.0	5.00

Figure 9-9

	Problem Statement	Code	Category	Range (1-10) High	Low	Median	Mean
12.	Students have not developed the ability to apply knowledge and skills to the solutions of real-life problems.	1911	Critical Thinking/Problem-Solving, Decision-Making	8	5	5.5	6.00
13.	Students have not developed decision-making skills.	1913	Critical Thinking/Problem-Solving, Decision-Making	8	3	5.0	5.17
14.	Students cannot outline material.	2003	Study Skills	3	2	2.5	2.33
15.	Students cannot summarize material.	2004	Study Skills	4	2	3.0	3.17
16.	Students have not developed the ability to plan their study time effectively.	2009	Study Skills	5	1	3.0	2.83
17.	Students have not developed the ability to study independently.	2010	Study Skills	6	2	3.0	3.50
18.	Students do not assume responsibility for their own learning.	2012	Study Skills	5	1	4.5	3.67
19.	There are not enough non-teaching personnel. (i.e., Aides)	4002	Finance and Staffing	8	3	6.5	6.17
20.	Salaries of teachers are not high enough.	4005	Finance and Staffing	8	5	7.0	6.50
21.	Measurable objectives against which to judge student achievement have not been set.	4701	Evaluation of Students	3	1	2.0	1.83
22.	Tests that show how the student learns, and not what the student has learned, are not used.	4709	Evaluation of Students	5	1	1.5	2.00

Figure 9-9 (Cont'd.)

313

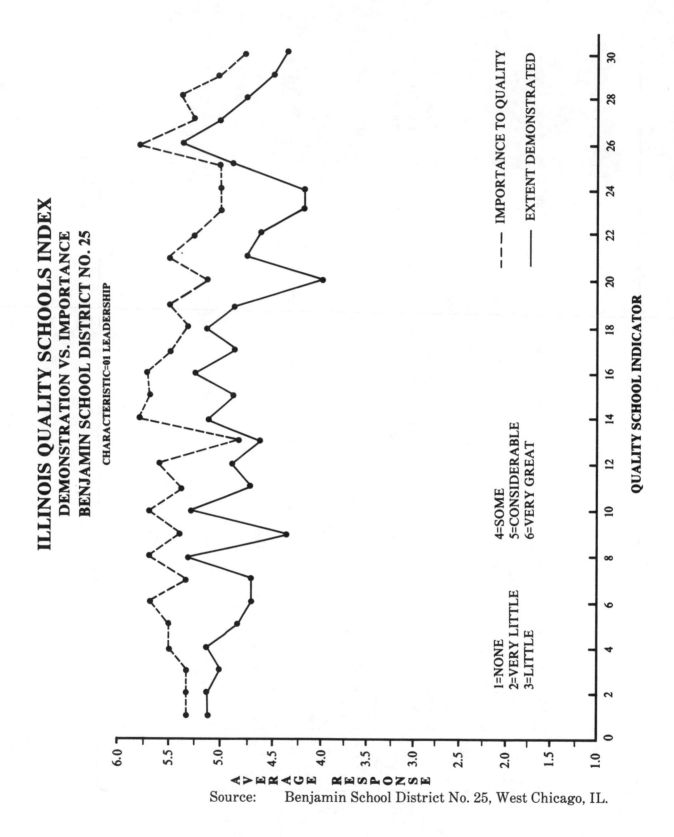

ILLINOIS QUALITY SCHOOLS INDEX
DEMONSTRATION VS. IMPORTANCE
BENJAMIN SCHOOL DISTRICT NO. 25

CHARACTERISTIC=01 LEADERSHIP

1=NONE
2=VERY LITTLE
3=LITTLE

4=SOME
5=CONSIDERABLE
6=VERY GREAT

- - - IMPORTANCE TO QUALITY

——— EXTENT DEMONSTRATED

QUALITY SCHOOL INDICATOR

AVERAGE RESPONSE

Source: Benjamin School District No. 25, West Chicago, IL.

Figure 9-10

314

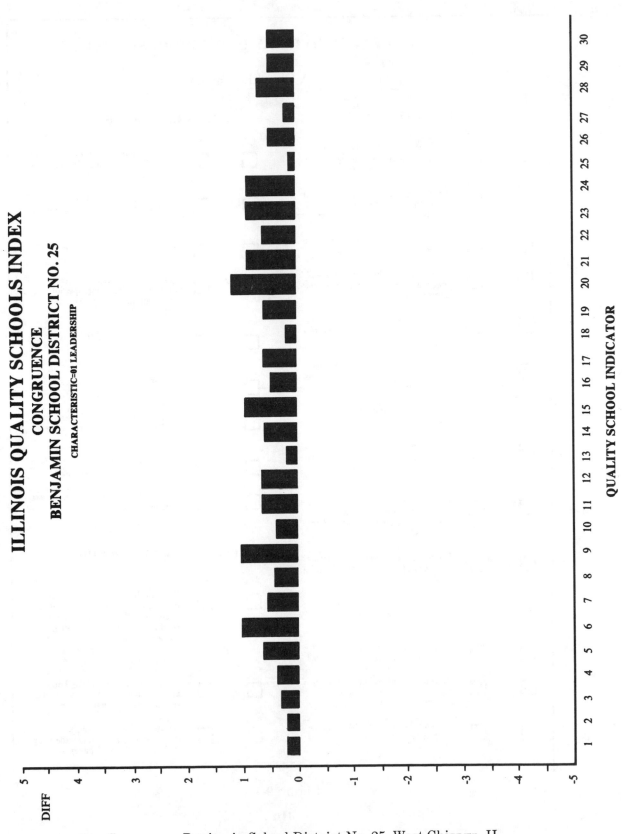

Source: Benjamin School District No. 25, West Chicago, IL.

Figure 9-11

HOW EFFECTIVE ARE OUR SCHOOLS?

☑   **A Checklist for Citizens**

LEADERSHIP

Yes	No	
☐	☐	Does the school district have a clear, well-written, concise statement of instructional goals?
☐	☐	Do you believe the superintendent is providing authoritative, decisive leadership for the district?
☐	☐	Do you believe the principals are authoritative, decisive, and firm?
☐	☐	Do you believe the principals seek ideas and suggestions from the community?
☐	☐	Do you believe the principals seek ideas and suggestions from the teaching staff?
☐	☐	Do you believe the principals fairly enforce rules and decisions for everyone?
☐	☐	Do you believe the budget is spent effectively?
☐	☐	Do you believe the principals visit classes regularly and work with teachers — as a response to the visits?
☐	☐	Do you believe the principals hold high expectations of academic achievement for the staff and the students?
☐	☐	Do you believe the principals are well-grounded in the basic subjects?

EXPECTATIONS

Yes	No	
☐	☐	Do you believe teachers are confident that all children can learn?
☐	☐	Do you believe teachers are enthusiastic about teaching and learning the basic subjects?
☐	☐	Do you believe teachers agree with curriculum policies and priorities?

EXPECTATIONS (CONT'D.)

Yes	No	
☐	☐	Do you believe teachers agree on the school district's educational philosophy and approach?
☐	☐	Do you believe teachers are good models of conduct and academic commitment?
☐	☐	Do you believe hiring practices yield well-educated teachers?
☐	☐	Do you believe teachers are available to students for special help on academic or personal problems?
☐	☐	Do you believe teachers are well-prepared for class? Do they start and end class promptly?
☐	☐	Do you believe teachers write well?
☐	☐	Do you believe teachers are cooperative and supportive of each other?
☐	☐	Do you believe the superintendent is supportive of the teachers?
☐	☐	Do you believe the principals are supportive of the teachers?

CURRICULUM & INSTRUCTION

Yes	No	
☐	☐	Do you believe the curriculum includes requirements in all the basic subjects: English (including reading, writing, literature, and speech), mathematics, science, history, government, geography, foreign languages, and the arts?
☐	☐	Do you believe elective subjects are supplements to, rather than substitutes for, basic subjects?
☐	☐	Do you believe academic priorities are clearly understood by staff, students, and parents?

Figure 9-12

CURRICULUM & INSTRUCTION (CONT'D.)

Yes   No

☐   ☐   Do you believe homework is regularly assigned and checked?

☐   ☐   Do you believe academic problems are diagnosed early and dealt with promptly?

☐   ☐   Do you believe learning results are stressed over teaching methods?

☐   ☐   Do you believe there are checks for student mastery of basic skills and knowledge?

☐   ☐   Do you believe the standards for promotion and graduation are understood by all?

☐   ☐   Do you believe promotions are based on scholastic achievement rather than time spent at one grade level?

☐   ☐   Do you believe there are programs for more able and less able students?

☐   ☐   Do you believe curricular and classroom distractions from academic achievement are recognized and minimized?

☐   ☐   Do you believe the early elementary reading program is sound?

☐   ☐   Do you believe all courses require students to write?

☐   ☐   Do you believe there are writing courses for all children?

☐   ☐   Do you believe textbooks are selected to meet predetermined curricular objectives?

☐   ☐   Do you believe the staff coordinates instruction from grade-to-grade and plans the curriculum sequentially?

☐   ☐   Do you believe inservice training improves the academic background of teachers?

CLIMATE OF ORDERLINESS

Yes   No

☐   ☐   Have the schools published statements of expectations and norms for the conduct of staff and students?

CLIMATE OF ORDERLINESS (CONT'D.)

Yes   No

☐   ☐   Do you believe such statements are widely understood and accepted?

☐   ☐   Do you believe the school is a cohesive social organization?

☐   ☐   Do you believe the school cooperates with parents and with civic agencies?

☐   ☐   Do you believe students have positions of responsibility for student activities, conduct, and school property?

☐   ☐   Do you believe students and staff have numerous opportunities to work jointly on school projects?

☐   ☐   Do you believe the staff displays consistent values and practices throughout the school, as opposed to having individual norms in each classroom?

☐   ☐   Do you believe students are praised for good performance?

☐   ☐   Do you believe students sense that staff members genuinely care about their well-being?

☐   ☐   Do you believe the tone of the staff is business-like and professional yet interested in students?

☐   ☐   Do you believe the staff spots disorders early and responds quickly and firmly?

☐   ☐   Do you believe reprimands are delivered quietly, without disrupting class?

☐   ☐   Do you believe senior teachers who are skilled in keeping order should act as mentors for less experienced teachers?

☐   ☐   Do you believe parents are notified of discipline problems with their children?

☐   ☐   Do you believe the school keeps useful records for delinquency, truancy, disruption, vandalism, tardiness, and other kinds of anti-school behavior?

Figure 9-12 (Cont'd.)

PUBLIC RELATIONS (CONT'D.)

Yes No

☐ ☐ Do you believe parents, school board members, and other citizens have access, as appropriate, to school records, teachers, administrators, and classes?

☐ ☐ Do you believe policies on relations with parents and the community are clearly stated? For example, do parents understand the importance of study time free from TV and other distractions, of reading aloud to children?

☐ ☐ Does the school have a handbook for parents?

☐ ☐ Does the school teach parents about the uses and abuses of standardized testing?

☐ ☐ Do you believe parents receive enough informational publications which stress academic achievement?

☐ ☐ Do you believe the school district's information is stressing academic achievement?

☐ ☐ Are parents and other citizens encouraged to exercise their legitimate shares of authority over school policies, priorities, and curriculum?

☐ ☐ Do you believe there is constructive citizen participation in teaching, administration, and governance?

☐ ☐ Do you believe enough of the district's budget is spent on public relations and the dissemination of information?

ASSESSMENT

Yes No

☐ ☐ Do you believe there is a coherent plan for regular assessment of students, individually and collectively, especially in the basic subjects?

☐ ☐ Do you believe the purposes of testing are clearly understood?

☐ ☐ Do you believe test results tell all concerned what they want to know?

☐ ☐ Do you believe students are tested only on what is actually taught, which is not always identical to the written curriculum?

Additional are welcome. Please attach extra sheet.

ASSESSMENT (CONT'D.)

Yes No

☐ ☐ Do you believe several criteria are used in making important decisions (e.g., for promotion, remediation, graduation)?

☐ ☐ Do you believe the school seeks useful comparisons with other schools?

☐ ☐ Do you believe impartial outsiders are asked to evaluate the school?

☐ ☐ Do you believe students, parents, teachers, board members, and citizens are satisfied with academic achievement in the school?

EXTRA-CURRICULAR

Yes No

☐ ☐ Do you believe appropriate extra-curricular activities are provided in the high school?

☐ ☐ Do you believe appropriate extra-curricular activities are provided in the junior high school?

☐ ☐ Do you believe appropriate extra-curricular activities are provided in the elementary school?

☐ ☐ Do you believe there is an appropriate balance between athletic and nonathletic extra-curricular activities?

☐ ☐ Do you believe there is too much emphasis on athletics?

☐ ☐ Do you believe there is too little emphasis on athletics?

CAFETERIAS

Yes No

☐ ☐ Do you believe the schools provide an adequate lunch program?

☐ ☐ Do you believe the school lunch program provides opportunities for a nutritional lunch — whether it be through a plate lunch or ala carte offerings?

☐ ☐ Do you believe the preparation of food served in the cafeteria is at a desirable level?

☐ ☐ Do you believe the selection of offerings for ala carte lunches is at a desirable level?

☐ ☐ Do you believe the plate lunch menus provide enough variety to satisfy most desires?

☐ ☐ Do you believe the attitudes and actions of the cafeteria staff are conducive to a proper lunchroom atmosphere?

Figure 9-12 (Cont'd.)

CURRICULUM AND INSTRUCTION

B. CURRICULUM AND INSTRUCTION

1. GENERAL CURRICULUM

For each of the statements, circle the number to the left, which best reflects your judgment as to the current status of the practice (1-low, 5-high). To the right of the statement, circle the number which indicates the status desired for the practice in your district. Provide a summary of changes and resources required to bring about a better match in each instance where a discrepancy exists between the current and desired status.

Note: The general curriculum instrument is to be used in combination with any of the curriculum area instruments.

Current Status		Desired Status
1 2 3 4 5	1. Courses of study reflect a balanced, integrated curriculum. Changes ———————————— ———————————————— Resources Required —————— ————————————————	1 2 3 4 5
1 2 3 4 5	2. The curricular programs reflect ongoing assessment and refinement. Changes ———————————— ———————————————— Resources Required —————— ————————————————	1 2 3 4 5
1 2 3 4 5	3. Time allocations indicate a balanced curriculum. Changes ———————————— ———————————————— Resources Required —————— ————————————————	1 2 3 4 5
1 2 3 4 5	4. All faculty members understand the district's competency based programs. Changes ———————————— ———————————————— Resources Required —————— ————————————————	1 2 3 4 5

Figure 9-13

GENERAL CURRICULUM

	Current Status		Desired Status

Current Status

Desired Status

1 2 3 4 5 **5.** Staff members are trained to use a variety of assessment techniques that are appropriate to a specific subject area. 1 2 3 4 5

Changes _____

_____

Resources Required _____

_____

1 2 3 4 5 **6.** Teachers have been provided inservice and materials which assist in their understanding of guidelines governing the use of assessment results. 1 2 3 4 5

Changes _____

_____

Resources Required _____

_____

1 2 3 4 5 **7.** Staff members use a variety of intervention procedures in competency based programs. 1 2 3 4 5

Changes _____

_____

Resources Required _____

_____

8. Teachers are in touch with state and national trends and research in their curricular area, through

1 2 3 4 5 **8.1** conferences 1 2 3 4 5

1 2 3 4 5 **8.2** membership in curriculum organizations 1 2 3 4 5

1 2 3 4 5 **8.3** professional study 1 2 3 4 5

Changes _____

_____

Resources Required _____

_____

Figure 9-13 (Cont'd.)

GENERAL CURRICULUM

Current Status

Desired Status

1 2 3 4 5   **9.** Lesson plans are viewed as an important component of instructional preparation.   1 2 3 4 5

Changes _____

_____

Resources Required _____

_____

1 2 3 4 5   **10.** Lesson plans clearly indicate the content that is found in the adopted course of study.   1 2 3 4 5

Changes _____

_____

Resources Required _____

_____

1 2 3 4 5   **11.** Teachers make use of a variety of media for learning through many senses.   1 2 3 4 5

Changes _____

_____

Resources Required _____

_____

1 2 3 4 5   **12.** Adapted programs are provided in any curricular area for students whose needs are not met in the general program.   1 2 3 4 5

Changes _____

_____

Resources Required _____

_____

1 2 3 4 5   **13.** Progress reports encourage increased communication between parents and teachers.   1 2 3 4 5

Changes _____

_____

Resources Required _____

_____

Figure 9-13 (Cont'd.)

GENERAL CURRICULUM

	Current Status			Desired Status

Current Status

Desired Status

1 2 3 4 5   **14.** There are established procedures for articulation among teachers of individual curriculum areas at various grade levels.   1 2 3 4 5

Changes _____

_____

Resources Required _____

_____

1 2 3 4 5   **15.** Staff members uniformly apply promotion and retention procedures.   1 2 3 4 5

Changes _____

_____

Resources Required _____

_____

1 2 3 4 5   **16.** Parents and students understand the district's graduation requirements.   1 2 3 4 5

Changes _____

_____

Resources Required _____

_____

1 2 3 4 5   **17.** Provision may be made for students below the ninth grade to participate in high school courses.   1 2 3 4 5

Changes _____

_____

Resources Required _____

_____

1 2 3 4 5   **18.** High school students taking subjects meeting for more than the required hours are being awarded proportionately more than one unit of credit.   1 2 3 4 5

Changes _____

_____

Resources Required _____

_____

Figure 9-13 (Cont'd.)

GENERAL CURRICULUM

Current Status		Desired Status

1 2 3 4 5 | **19.** Curriculum requirements are continually reassessed in accordance with new curricular needs. | 1 2 3 4 5

Changes _____

_____

Resources Required _____

_____

20. There is annual evaluation of

1 2 3 4 5 | **20.1** the length of the school day | 1 2 3 4 5
1 2 3 4 5 | **21.2** the length of the school year | 1 2 3 4 5

Changes _____

_____

Resources Required _____

_____

- **What statements should be added to those identified?**

1 2 3 4 5 | **1.** _____ | 1 2 3 4 5

_____

_____

Changes _____

_____

Resources Required _____

_____

1 2 3 4 5 | **2.** _____ | 1 2 3 4 5

_____

_____

Changes _____

_____

Resources Required _____

_____

Source: Ohio Department of Education.

Figure 9-13 (Cont'd.)

LEARNING MEDIA SERVICES

Directions: Please circle the one response that most closely reflects your feeling about the items below. Please circle only one response for each item.

Key:
5 = high
1 = low
na = not applicable

FACILITIES AND EQUIPMENT
Environment

1. The location of the media center provides easy access to all in the school.   5 . . 4 . . 3 . . 2 . . 1 . . na

2. The size of the media center is adequate for the various programs that are carried out there.   5 . . 4 . . 3 . . 2 . . 1 . . na

3. The arrangement of the media center is adequate for the various programs that are carried out there..   5 . . 4 . . 3 . . 2 . . 1 . . na

4. The space allocations are adequate for **each** of the functions listed below.

   a. instruction   5 . . 4 . . 3 . . 2 . . 1 . . na
   b. circulation and distribution   5 . . 4 . . 3 . . 2 . . 1 . . na
   c. viewing and listening by students   5 . . 4 . . 3 . . 2 . . 1 . . na
   d. reading, viewing, and listening by students 5 . . 4 . . 3 . . 2 . . 1 . . na
   e. technology use   5 . . 4 . . 3 . . 2 . . 1 . . na
   f. processing resources   5 . . 4 . . 3 . . 2 . . 1 . . na
   g. producing materials   5 . . 4 . . 3 . . 2 . . 1 . . na
   h. conferences   5 . . 4 . . 3 . . 2 . . 1 . . na
   i. professional materials collection   5 . . 4 . . 3 . . 2 . . 1 . . na
   j. professional materials use   5 . . 4 . . 3 . . 2 . . 1 . . na
   k. staff work areas   5 . . 4 . . 3 . . 2 . . 1 . . na
   l. materials and equipment repair   5 . . 4 . . 3 . . 2 . . 1 . . na
   m. storage   5 . . 4 . . 3 . . 2 . . 1 . . na
   n. other (specify)   5 . . 4 . . 3 . . 2 . . 1 . . na

5. The construction of the media center is adequate in the areas listed below.

   a. access by the handicapped   5 . . 4 . . 3 . . 2 . . 1 . . na
   b. security   5 . . 4 . . 3 . . 2 . . 1 . . na
   c. level of lighting   5 . . 4 . . 3 . . 2 . . 1 . . na
   d. control of lighting   5 . . 4 . . 3 . . 2 . . 1 . . na
   e. control of heating   5 . . 4 . . 3 . . 2 . . 1 . . na
   f. control of air conditioning   5 . . 4 . . 3 . . 2 . . 1 . . na
   g. electric outlets and electrical supply   5 . . 4 . . 3 . . 2 . . 1 . . na
   h. control of noise level   5 . . 4 . . 3 . . 2 . . 1 . . na
   i. water supply and sinks   5 . . 4 . . 3 . . 2 . . 1 . . na
   j. other (specify)   5 . . 4 . . 3 . . 2 . . 1 . . na

6. The media center is inviting and aesthetically pleasing.
                                                  5 . . 4 . . 3 . . 2 . . 1 . . na

7. Other (specify)   5 . . 4 . . 3 . . 2 . . 1 . . na

Figure 9-14

LEARNING MEDIA SERVICES

Directions: Please circle the one response that most closely reflects your feeling about the items below. Please circle only one response for each item.

Key: 5 = high
         1 = low

	What Should Be	What Is
1. Teachers stimulate students' use of media center materials and equipment.	5..4..3..2..1	5..4..3..2..1
2. Teachers evaluate and recommend media center materials and equipment for acquisition	5..4..3..2..1	5..4..3..2..1
3. The media center is staffed with certified personnel.	5..4..3..2..1	5..4..3..2..1
4. The media center staff is adequate to service needs of students and teachers.	5..4..3..2..1	5..4..3..2..1
5. Administration is supportive of media center use by students and staff.	5..4..3..2..1	5..4..3..2..1
6. The media center financial resources are adequate.	5..4..3..2..1	5..4..3..2..1
7. Policies and procedures have been developed for objecting to media center materials.	5..4..3..2..1	5..4..3..2..1
8. Media center staff facilitates group learning.	5..4..3..2..1	5..4..3..2..1
9. Media center staff facilitates individual learning	5..4..3..2..1	5..4..3..2..1
10. Media center staff promotes independent use of facilities by students for accomplishing learning objectives.	5..4..3..2..1	5..4..3..2..1
11. Media center services are accessible to students and staff.	5..4..3..2..1	5..4..3..2..1
12. Teachers are helped to use materials and equipment appropriately.	5..4..3..2..1	5..4..3..2..1
13. Students are helped to use materials and equipment appropriately.	5..4..3..2..1	5..4..3..2..1
14. Teachers are helped to use media center services effectively.	5..4..3..2..1	5..4..3..2..1
15. Media center materials and equipment are selected to meet program and individual needs.	5..4..3..2..1	5..4..3..2..1
16. Media center materials are adequate in quantity.	5..4..3..2..1	5..4..3..2..1
17. Media center equipment is adequate in quantity.	5..4..3..2..1	5..4..3..2..1

Figure 9-15

	What Should Be	What Is
18. Media center materials are adequate in quality to meet program objectives.	5..4..3..2..1	5..4..3..2..1
19. Media center equipment is adequate in quality to meet program objectives.	5..4..3..2..1	5..4..3..2..1
20. Materials are easily accessible to students and staff.	5..4..3..2..1	5..4..3..2..1
21. The arrangement of the media center is adequate for the various programs carried out there.	5..4..3..2..1	5..4..3..2..1
22. Other (specify)	5..4..3..2..1	5..4..3..2..1

Figure 9-15 (Cont'd.)

BENEFITS OF ISSUES
MANAGEMENT

Helps the organization set priorities and focus on its goal(s) amid day-to-day demands and pressures.

Gets early involvement from Chief Executive.

Assures broad involvement by all stakeholders in an issue, specifically the best experts of the organization.

Sets clear responsibility, time schedule, evaluation criteria.

Coordinates all key resources toward accomplishing the organization's objectives.

Identifies issues, trends early enough to become significantly involved — proactive rather than reactive [or damage control].

Leads the change process rather than follows it.

Paper flow can be kept at a minimum using modern technology.

Coordination of positions ... speaking with one voice.

Availability of all information to all involved management.

Less time putting out fires.

Keeps us focused — goal-oriented — amid a wide variety of demands on our time.

Saves time.

More effective media response and initiatives.

Speakers' support and briefing materials.

Helps us accomplish our objectives more effectively.

Assures appropriate involvement within the organization.

Guides development of constituency support groups and individuals.

Increases trade and professional association involvement opportunities.

Better use of financial and human resources.

Source: Donald L. Ferguson.

Figure 9-16

PROBLEMS IN IMPLEMENTING
AN ISSUES MANAGEMENT SYSTEM

1. Resistance to change.
2. Hierarchy of information control changes to horizontal information availability.
3. Time — at the start of a new system — will be viewed negatively and without perspective of benefits downstream.
4. The crisis of the moment prevents us from addressing top priorities.
5. Concern over being left out of the decision-making process.

6. Traditional image of Public Relations as a "Things and Stuff" or media shop.
7. Confusion over government relations and effective communications strategy with broader objectives and audiences.
8. Freedom of Information Act and letting "outsiders" know.
9. The system looks too simple to be effective (looking at the "product" not the process).
10. If we avoid the issue it will go away.

Source: Donald L. Ferguson.

Figure 9-17

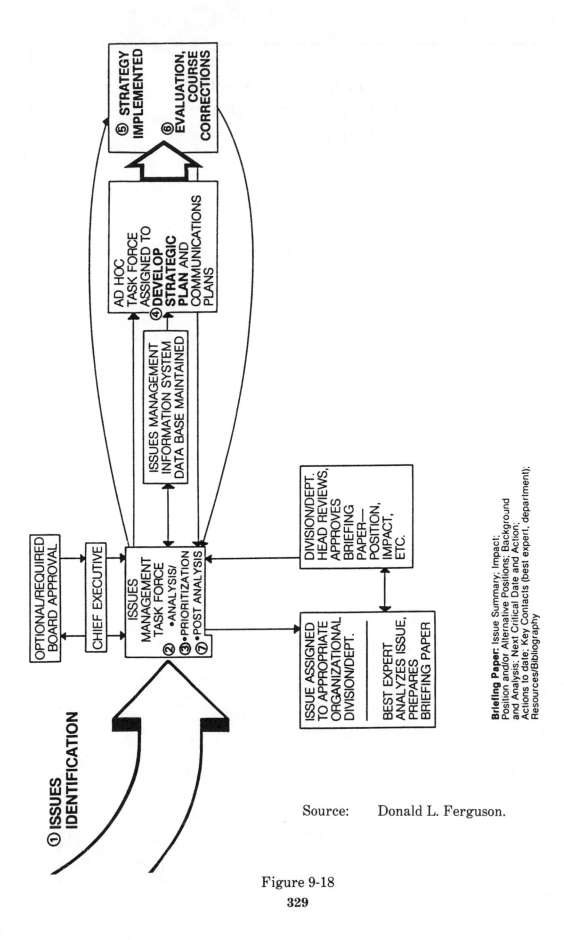

Source: Donald L. Ferguson.

Figure 9-18

329

**GENERAL STEPS IN THE
ISSUES MANAGEMENT
PROCESS**

1. Identification

2. Analysis

3. Prioritization

4. Strategy Development

5. Implementation

6. Analysis, Evaluation,
    Course Corrections

7. Post-Analysis

Source: Donald L. Ferguson

Figure 9-19

ISSUE IDENTIFICATION

WHO:

- Individuals

- Management team

- Board members

- Advisory groups

- Representatives of selected

  publics

HOW:

- Scanning

- Sensing

  ... feedback

  ... surveys

- Task forces

- Audit interviews

- Workshops

- Individuals

Source: Donald L. Ferguson

Figure 9-20

331

ANALYSIS
PRIORITIZATION

WHO:

- Issues Management Task Force

HOW:

- Weight each issue 1 (high) to 5 (low) considering

  ...impact of the issue on the organization

  ...probability of it occurring

  ...importance of developing a strategy to manage the organization's position on the issue

- Select top (4-6) issues within high priority list

Source: Donald L. Ferguson.

Figure 9-21

STRATEGY DEVELOPMENT
for Top Priority Issues

WHO:

- Ad Hoc Issue Task Force on each top issue (4-6)

  ...representing all stakeholders within the organization

  ...may involve external publics

- Issues Management Task Force review, approval

- Senior Management (Board) approval

HOW:

- Break the issue into its sub-issues

- Analyze all sub-issues

  ... pros and cons; strengths and weaknesses

  ... policy and legal implications

  ...players — key communicators, organizations

  ...potential coalitions

- Develop plan

  ...how the issues are to be resolved — positions

  ...communications activities — internal and external — essential to "win" on the issue

Source: Donald L. Ferguson.

Figure 9-22

STRATEGY IMPLEMENTATION EVALUATION: COURSE CORRECTIONS

WHO:

- Department(s), key individuals implement components of plan under direction of key Issue Manager

- Issues Management Task Force monitors implementation activities

HOW:

- Media/interpersonal communications

- All appropriate departments

- Variety of components available

- Coalitions; constituency groups

- Set measurements (objectives) for strategy

- Clearly determine who does what by when

- Monitor

Source: Donald L. Ferguson.

Figure 9-23

POST-ANALYSIS

WHO:

- Ad Hoc Issue Task Force

- Issue Manager

- Issues Management Task Force

- Senior Management (Board)

HOW:

- Determine what components worked or did not work to guide development of future strategies

Source: Donald L. Ferguson.

Figure 9-24

STEPS TO TAKE IN STARTING
THE ISSUES MANAGEMENT
PROCESS

1. Become knowledgeable; develop a proposal stressing benefits to your organization.
2. Secure top management approval and support.
3. Draft a policy plan of action for a) development, and b) operation of your organization's system.
4. Review the draft plan with all top management, make changes as needed.
5. Determine hardware needed and begin to develop software for the information system... test the system.
6. Communicate top management support and policy for operating the issues management program for your organization.
7. Establish a working group of program liaisons — a task force representing all key elements of the organization's structure.
8. Identify issues.
9. Set preliminary priorities.
10. Assign responsibilities to best experts in the organization for drafting briefing (position) papers on all number 1 priorities, consolidating background and resource files.
11. Information system briefing papers are drafted ...position papers and alternative courses of action may be needed for some issues.
12. Issue papers approved by appropriate management level.
13. ISSUES MANAGEMENT TASK FORCE reviews papers and elements (accepts or refers back for change).
14. Legal and policy checks may be needed.
15. Boards, if involved, and/or top executive, reviews and makes changes as required.
16. Task force begins operation.
17. Top 4-6 issues are selected as priorities for the Issues Management Task Force and process.
18. Begin to develop briefing (position) papers on priority 2, 3, 4, and 5 issues to complete issues management information system.
19. New issues are added as they are identified and flow into the system ... all issue briefs are kept current and monitored.

Source: Donald L. Ferguson.

Figure 9-25

ISSUES MANAGEMENT — DALLAS STYLE

Route of an Issue Through the System

1. It is identified as a potential issue.

2. It is referred to the task force for consideration.

3. It is sent to the appropriate staff liaison person (called a key link in the DISD) who represents one of the 12 issue categories.

4. The liaison person identifies the best available expert who drafts a recommended position paper (based on a brief standard format).

5. The draft is reviewed by the appropriate department head and returned to the task force.

6. The task force accepts, rejects, or asks for modifications in the paper.

7. The paper becomes part of the electronic monitoring system and is reviewed on key dates.

8. If considered a top priority, the issue is referred to appropriate staff for development of a strategic plan which also becomes part of the tracking system.

Source: Donald L. Ferguson, *NSPRA Scanner*, vol. 2, no. 7, Summer, 1985 (Arlington, VA: National School Public Relations Association).

Figure 9-26

ISSUES MANAGEMENT — DALLAS STYLE

Key Players

1. The liaisons (link) who keep the issue papers updated.

2. The experts who draft papers, maintain related files, and develop strategies.

3. The system manager (the PR person) who oversees the operation.

4. The system operator who inputs and maintains the software program.

5. The issues management task force.

Source: Donald L. Ferguson, *NSPRA Scanner*, vol. 2, no. 7, Summer, 1985 (Arlington, VA: National School Public Relations Association).

Figure 9-27

ISSUES MANAGEMENT — DALLAS STYLE

Major Accomplishments to Date

1. An electronic anticipation and tracking system (via IBM Displaywriter word processing) is in place.

2. Management is "forced" to deal with issues by the system.

3. A "common" position has been developed on key issues.

4. Staff has a "party line" to follow on key issues.

5. Files on key issues are readily available.

6. Issues that may have otherwise gone ignored are being addressed.

7. A true "bottoms up" opportunity exists for all staff.

Source: Donald L. Ferguson, *NSPRA Scanner*, vol. 2, no. 7, Summer, 1985 (Arlington, VA: National School Public Relations Association).

Figure 9-28

ISSUES MANAGEMENT — DALLAS STYLE

Key Points to Keep in Mind

1. Don't start unless there is top-level commitment.

2. It's hard work and requires time and resources.

3. Initial staff resistance is great.

4. Benefits aren't obvious until the system is up and running.

5. Determine standards early (procedures, format, etc.), but be flexible in the development range.

6. Develop a communications plan.

7. Select equipment that is available and meets local needs.

8. Carefully select staff for key roles.

9. Get outside help in the development stage.

10. Use the system!

Source: Donald L. Ferguson, *NSPRA Scanner*, vol. 2, no. 7, Summer, 1985 (Arlington, VA: National School Public Relations Association).

Figure 9-29

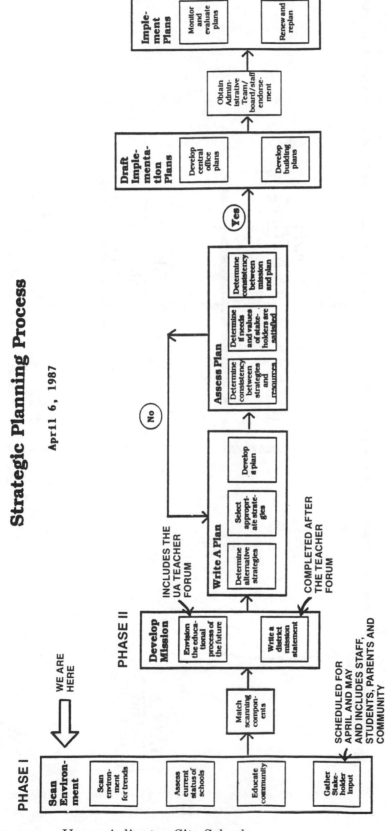

Source: Upper Arlington City Schools.

Figure 9-30

STRATEGIC PLANNING PROCESS

ENVIRONMENTAL SCAN EXTERNAL ANALYSIS

- Social Trends
- Economic Trends
- Political Trends
- Demographic Trends

PROGRAM INTERNAL ANALYSIS

- Achievement
- Dropouts
- Climate
- Standards

ORGANIZATION INTERNAL ANALYSIS

- Strengths
- Weaknesses

ESTABLISH:

- Mission Statement
- General Objectives

CREATE ACTION PLANS

- Specific Objectives
- Action Steps
- Schedule
- Resource Requirements

TASK 1:
RESEARCH AND ANALYSIS

TASK 2:
STRATEGIC PLANNING

TASK 3:
OPERATING PLANS

Source: Association for Supervision and Curriculum Development.
Figure 9-31

10

Coping with Growth, Decline, and Changing Demographic Conditions

At any point in time in a school system, the focus is on what is happening in the system. As we saw in the previous chapter, however, school system effects are continually being affected by external forces. Knowing the forces — issues and trends — is required today, if the superintendent is to steer desired change.

Determining Trends and Their Implications

External scanning of the environment, a step in the strategic planning, or issues management, process is one means used to determine trends and their implications. Strategic planning was discussed in the previous chapter. In this chapter, other means of knowing trends are discussed. For this section, the framework of Naisbitt's *Megatrends* is used to look at trends and their implications. Naisbitt used a media analysis to determine ten megatrends listed in Figure 10-1. Not all agree with Naisbitt's findings, but the megatrends are useful for their implications for education.

Megashift to an Information Society from an Industrial Society

The year 1957 is identified as the beginning of the era of global satellite communications. The year 1957 saw the launching of *Sputnik* and the turning of the world inward upon itself. Among our contemporaries, Marshall McLuhan perhaps best understood the reality of the global village. Today the first largest employment category is clerk; the second is professional. Both of these categories are information worker categories. In other words, the creation, processing, and distribution of information *is* the job for most today.

The nature of work and the power that drives work and society has been altered dramatically. Initially the physical strength of humans and animals were *the* power sources. Then the steam engine, gasoline motor, and generation of electricity caused human and animal power to be replaced by coal and oil. Finally, nuclear power and the microchip have risen to prominence in scientific and technological developments. The microchip is preeminent in the information age (McCune, pp.4-6). The time orientation in the information age is the future; hence, the need for ongoing strategic planning for health and survival of the organization.

As superintendents, we need to assure that schools are preparing students in *all* ways for the reality of the information age and its resultant world of work. In terms of technology; we are still in the infant stage of the new technology; for example, using the computer as a tool for learning. In the future we will be creating things suggested by the technology itself. This shift will require a transformation in our thinking and educational programming.

Our challenge as superintendents is to provide for the maintenance of the work force and professional activity that rely on high-tech skills. We will need to make expanded and more sophisticated use of technology for instruction and management. Similarly, we will need to prepare our students for higher levels of educational achievement (McCune, pp. 66-67).

> Cognitive Goals
> >   Stronger higher-order skills
> >   Generalizable skills
> >   Right to excel
> >   Global education
> >   Many literacies, more than one language
> Affective Goals
> >   Small-group skills
> >   Independent, entrepreneurial
> >   Support group orientation
> Curriculum
> >   Interdisciplinary programs
> >   Varied program options
> >   Computer as learning tool in all programs
> >   Varied program options
> Job Preparation
> >   Multiple career preparation
> >   Early skill development
> >   Career/vocational education as integral part of educational
> >   community experience

A further implication that we have heard for some time is the difference in *where* students will learn. We are reminded that tomorrow's students may wish to work at home. However, this possibility raises concerns about the achievement gap of disadvantaged children. Will expanded use of technology continue to increase this gap? Other questions can be raised. Will learning at home create a balance for the predicted shortage of qualified teachers?

High Tech/High Touch Response to New Technology

High touch is described by Naisbitt as the counterbalancing human response to forced technology. High touch is said to have been growing since the 1950s, the period of the highest number of union members. A highly personal value system compensates for the impersonal nature of technology. Hence, there has been a growth of self-help and personal-growth movements advocating discipline and responsibility; these movements became popular and evolved into the human potential movement. The more technology is introduced the more, it is predicted, people will want to be with each other. Evidence of this desire to be in touch is the popularity of rock concerts, shopping malls, camping, and going to the sea shore. In a similar vein, soft shapes and vibrant color have grown with high tech.

Implications for superintendents come from the feeling that technology will liberate us from personal discipline and responsibility. The current epidemic of AIDS cautions against this belief. The challenge for superintendents is to keep students from developing the attitudes and immoderate lifestyles where people feel they can eat and do anything and be spared ultimately by some technological breakthrough. On the other hand, technology threatens ultimate annihilation through nuclear warfare. This threat presents a challenge to superintendents to assist students to develop the necessary knowledge and wisdom to guide the exploration and uses of technology.

Movement to a World Economy from a National Economy

We live in a global economy. Whereas once there was trade among countries, we now live in interdependent communities. Peter Drucker predicts that production sharing, similar to that in the automobile industry, will be the prevailing form of worldwide economic integration. Products may be shipped to several countries before they are completed. The United States no longer sets the pace for the world economy. Probably no single country will ever do so again. Americans find the transition difficult and mourn the loss of what was.

McCune (p. 75) identified several economic national planning assumptions. Those that apply here are shown below.

Greater international competition
Increase in foreign business ownership and investment in the United States
Offshore movement of U. S. jobs, markets, and industries

Moderate growth in U. S. Gross National Product (GNP)
Growth in U. S. productivity
Possible continued cycles of recession
Varying economic conditions in geographic regions
Continued growth of small, entrepreneurial business
Growth of education and training to the major U. S. industry
Slowdown in growth of U. S. labor force
Increased use of robots in industrial and household settings
Growing problems of workers displaced by technological
   advances

Superintendents need to assure that students are prepared for a deindustrialized society. Our two economies have been described as sunrise and sunset. The sunset economy consists of traditional industries; the sunrise economy consists of such innovations as gene-splicing and robotics. Superintendents need to assure that students understand this dual economy to cope with the future. Similarly, students need to understand the need to understand a world culture and embrace world interdependency as a means to economic survival and world peace. Shirley McCune (p. 11) predicts that our schools will shift from institutions that train and socialize to institutions essential to economic survival and well-being.

Movement to Thinking Long Term from Thinking Short Term

The importance of strategic planning, or issues management, was stressed in the previous chapter. Naisbitt reminds us that strategic planning must proceed from strategic vision. Only one company in ten in America was found to have long-term incentives; therefore, a dramatic shift is required. Short-term objectives are achieved at the expense of long-term objectives.

Naisbitt proposed the most important question to answer in developing strategic vision is, "What business are we really in?" The answer requires completely rethinking our purpose in light of the changing world. Railroads are cited in *Megatrends* as an example of the principle, called the "law of the situation." Railroads should have known they were in the transportation business, the business of moving goods. The nonresponse of railroads is contrasted with the response of banks, who knew they were in the business of information in motion.

In schools the notion of life-long learning is already accepted by most. Complete rethinking is needed. Superintendents need to be alert to changes and to anticipate the impact of changes. We must reconceptualize either what business we are in or what business it would be useful to be in. For example, with businesses offering lifetime employment, the call for generalists, rather than specialists is already being heard. Superintendents play a key role in developing and articulating a strategic vision for their schools.

Decentralization Has Caused Centralized Structures to Crumble Across America

Decentralization in politics has resulted in a power shift from the state to the local levels. Decentralization in business has resulted in diminished top-down national strategies. Geography and architecture of a region recognize and celebrate diversity.

The collapse of *Life*, *Look*, and *Saturday Evening Post* were used by Naisbitt as examples of mass audience interests giving way to special interests. We are cautioned that the leading TV networks may go the same way, giving way to cable. School districts can go the same way. Many have.

The power shift away from centralized structures energizes decentralized structures. Bottom-up strategies are replacing top-down strategies. Limited, individual solutions that grow naturally out of a particular set of circumstances are becoming the norm. In schooling, superintendents need to be more responsive to local initiatives since these are probably what will work. Many school districts, the largest being in Florida, have already restructured their systems as decentralized units. For decades, educational theorists have advocated decentralization and building-level autonomy. That is, once the district has identified what is to be done, the building can decide how it is to be accomplished.

The notion of decentralization has gained more credibility for two reasons: a) the effective schooling results have grown in acceptance; and b) reforms have shifted from courses and credits to developing personnel and restructuring the organization.

The Disengagement by Individuals from Institutions That Have Disillusioned Them Has Led to a Reliance on Self-Help, or Self-Reliance and Personal Responsibility

Disillusionment with education as we know it has led to parental activism, questioning of the school system, and massive numbers choosing home instruction or private education.

In other areas, the disillusionment has been manifest by questioning the omnipotence of science. A cure for cancer has not been found and now AIDS and other fatal diseases await a cure. Individuals assume more responsibility for self with diet and exercise programs.

In business there is a shift from macro- to micro-economics. Growth of entrepreneurs and venture capital indicates increased self-reliance.

For social change SADD, MADD, AA, and other groups rely on individuals helping others. In schools, demand for peer counseling among students, peer coaching among teachers and administrators, group counseling or staff and student groups, and cooperative learning has grown.

A word of caution is in order, however, before moving toward decentralization or school-based management. Shirley McCune (p. 25) notes that "Decentralizing programs or moving to school-based management is likely to succeed to the degree that overall district systems (mission, goals, curriculum, instruction, staff development, facilities, budget, etc.) are in place and district goals can be coupled or coordinated with those of the building."

A crisis in confidence frequently results when individuals are confronted with what seems to be an overwhelming change in lifestyle or accomplishment. Superintendents can help teachers regain confidence by freeing them to act, helping teachers feel effective and productive without feeling someone is hovering over their shoulders, or searching for ways to prevent them from doing something. Teachers need to feel challenged. New, more challenging roles than doing study hall supervision or other nonprofessional duties might include group counseling, peer coaching, tutoring in subject-area laboratories, coordinating a subject area, to name some examples. As the superintendent helps the school become a center of authority and autonomy, he or she can help the building principal recognize that both the principal and the team of certified and noncertified, or classified, staff within that building *are* the unit. Superintendents can facilitate an environment where people who have confidence in their ideas and their abilities would take initiative without being penalized and would be judged on their success or failure. Superintendents can encourage principals and teachers to help students gain that confidence by giving them all work they can do while simultaneously challenging them to "ski the outer limits." Schools can help students in the visualization process, a part of the goal-setting process, so they can affirm, "Whatever my mind can conceive and believe, I can achieve."

Participatory Democracy Has Replaced Representative Democracy

People who are affected by a decision must be consulted about and be part of the decision process. Quality circles is one way to have participatory democracy in the workplace, including schools.

Representative democracy in the form of unionism is still strong in education, although it has suffered dramatic decline in business. In schools, most employees are now covered by comprehensive collective bargaining laws which guarantee employees a right to bargain wages, salaries, and working conditions. In addition such laws give employees the right to impact bargaining. The reality of the situation is that superintendents recognize that there will be a demand to bargain everything. Listening to Al Shanker, we know that we have seen only the tip of the iceberg. Mr. Shanker has helped school employees redefine their roles and rights. Employees want and may have it all. However, a monster may be created along with the genie.

Informal Networks Are Replacing Hierarchies, or the Pyramid Structure in Organizations

The concept of informal networks replacing more formal structures was discussed more thoroughly in the chapter on networking. As defined earlier, networks are people talking to each other, sharing ideas and information and resources. It is worth reiterating here that the important part is the process of getting to the network — the communication that creates the linkages among people and clusters of people. Networks empower individuals and networkers nurture one another.

Fostering self-help, increasing productivity, sharing resources, and creating change are some of the reasons for the existence of networks. Networks are structured to communicate information in ways that are more high touch and more energy efficient than any other. New networks are being formed to provide various service functions to educators — for example, new services for finding personnel.

Naisbitt attributes the popularity of networks as a critical social forum to three fundamental reasons: "the death of traditional structures, the din of the information overload, and the past failure of hierarchies." Simultaneously, the strength of traditional networks like family, church, and neighborhoods is dissipating. The new networks put people in direct contact with the person or resource sought. There are horizontal and overlapping linkages as well as vertical linkages. Information sharing in networks is lateral, diagonal, and bottom up.

The superintendent is a member of networks, since these exist in organizations as formal or informal. The superintendent can exert power and influence to create or help shape networks that help all in the organization — to focus on the district's mission and to accomplish district goals. A principal way the superintendent can use networks to the advantage of all in the district is to facilitate a learning culture. A positive school climate with an open and caring staff doesn't just happen; it requires the participation and openness of the superintendent — always working the network, knowing which employees are key and knowing how.

Migration to the South and West Has Created a Massive Shift in Population and Economic Activity from North and East

The massive shift has caused a restructuring of America. The shift is rooted in other shifts, such as the shift to information and global societies and decentralization, as examples. The shift means sunrise, or boom, for one area and sunset, or decline for another. This megashift and its ripple effects have had drastic implications for educators. While some areas are growing faster than schools can keep pace, others have declined or are declining to a small fraction of their previous size and wealth. The shift calls for strategic planning for resources, program, and other areas.

Movement to Multiple Options and a Wide Variety of Choices and the Need for Many Decisions from Either/Or, the World of Few Decisions

Americans are discovering new alternatives in work styles; family life; celebration of racial, cultural, and ethnic diversity; and other areas that impact on the lives of our students and their performance in our schools. We know from statistics that there is no such thing as a typical family. Only 7% of families have been found by researchers to fit the traditional profile where father is the breadwinner and mother stays home to care for the house and children.

The superintendent is faced with the need to expand programs of early childhood development. Early childhood is a critical time when children develop their self-concept and framework for intellectual functioning, form language skills, and develop social skills. With demographic shifts that show increases in the disadvantaged (that is, the dramatic increase in single-parent households where the head is a female teenager), many children will develop fewer of the intellectual, language, and social skills needed for successful and responsible functioning in society at home. Where the school doesn't provide preschool programs directly, the superintendent can cooperate with area providers of services and influence providers so that services important for later functioning in school and society are fostered. Similarly, the superintendent will be faced with the need to provide or cooperate with providers for before- and after-school child care for children of working families.

A second trend that educators need to pay particular attention to is the multiple option variety of conservative churches. The latter have and will result in demands on educators to change or eliminate certain programs and materials.

Increased heterogeneity in our school populations creates the need for more responsive curriculum and instruction. Teachers need a repertoire of teaching behaviors and knowledge of content and processes sufficient to allow flexibility in the teaching process to intervene in individual students' learning as appropriate. Increased heterogeneity will also require more options for students. The recent educational reports and reformers call for conformity and uniformity. This runs contrary to trends of multiple options and diversity in student groups. Rather, more options in curriculum and instruction and other organizational variables seem to be needed.

The greater opportunity for self-expression means more variety for the superintendent to cope with and plan for. Strategic planning is called for to cope effectively with the results of the movement to multiple options.

Rather than looking at all these shifts on the down side, we should acclaim with Naisbitt, "What a fantastic time to be alive!"

Trends relating directly to curriculum and schooling were identified in 1987 by Gordon Cawelti, Executive Director of ASCD (Association for Supervision and Curriculum Development). Cawelti chose the top five media stories in 1986 and discussed the implication of each for what is taught in school. Briefly, the five stories and their implications are

1. *Textbooks Give Scant Attention to Religious Treatment of History and Other Subjects; Lower Court Rules for Objecting Parents*

   Cases in Alabama and Tennessee allowed for parents to "opt out" of curriculum for religious objections. Topics are likely to be expanded so that board-adopted curriculum can be fragmented and not common to all students.

2. *Schools Called Upon to Teach More About Sex and Drug Education*

Concern over drug abuse and fear of an AIDS epidemic led to increased demands for schools to include these topics in the curriculum. The demands placed on the schools shows confidence in the schools; however, to retain that confidence, the schools will need to have a unified community approach to the problems.

3. *Appropriate Use of Native Language Important Element of Effective Bilingual Education*

The call for native language instruction as an aid to learning English challenged the "English only" supporters. The goal is to move limited-English-speaking children into the mainstream as productive citizens rather than continue alarming dropout rates.

4. *Evidence on Power of Early Childhood Education Continues to Mount*

Evidence in support of early childhood education claims that children from early childhood programs achieved better in later years; were more likely to enroll in college or be employed after high school; and were less likely to be involved in crime, delinquency, welfare, and teenage pregnancy. Evidence also favored developmental programs with "child-initiated learning" over direct instruction approaches. Schools are responding with before- and after-school child care and programs for three- and four-year-olds.

5. *Student Writing Ability Remains Unsatisfactory in U.S. Schools*

Studies have shown students do not express themselves adequately in writing. Poor writing skills have been linked to the lack of emphasis on higher-order thinking skills throughout the curriculum. Student composition skills and higher-order outcomes (critical thinking, creativity, problem-solving, etc.) need to be high-priority school-improvement activities.

Planning for Growth

Assuring adequate resources for students entering the school system at some future date requires strategic planning. Some of the variables to be considered in such planning are reviewed here.

In growth areas, the superintendent will need to know the maximum density projected for the area and the timeline for growth. There are four categories of the information the superintendent needs to know to project maximum density: 1) the location, size, and zoning for undeveloped property in the district; 2) the type, dollar value, and timeline for development of properties; 3) the estimated density per unit constructed and the estimated number and ages of children per unit; and 4) any tax abatement or other incentives for building that may impact on district resources.

Location, Size, and Zoning for Undeveloped Property in the District

Aerial photography and physically traveling to identify undeveloped property are two ways to know the location and size of undeveloped property. City and regional planning groups may also exist to facilitate this identification.

Once the parcels have been identified, current zoning practices will dictate land use. It is not uncommon for these to be developing and changing in growth areas. The superintendent needs to have a mechanism, therefore, to keep updated on zoning of particular parcels. Zoning can be residential. In this case, it will be single-family or multiple dwelling units. Zoning can be retail, commercial, research/office, and industrial, to name other examples of use. Zoning decisions will have implications for assessed valuation, inventory projections, and student enrollments. All of these impact resources or the need for resources in the district.

In addition to attending to undeveloped property, the superintendent needs to be alert to redevelopment. For example, in this superintendent's school district, a university located within the city is discussing plans for expansion. Purchasing and demolishing of at least 17 homes is planned. The rezoning of the residential property for university use will cause the schools to lose assessed valuation and students. Further, residents in the immediate vicinity of the university are concerned that the takeover will cause a decrease in property values; should the suspected depreciation occur, the project further impacts on district resources.

Type and Dollar Value of Properties to Be Developed

As noted above, zoning guides the type of development of property. Local government bodies, working in concert with the district superintendent and board members will normally develop detailed projections of the dollar value of a project, expected earnings and employment figures, and numbers of children at various age and grade levels expected from various size and dollar value and type of housing. The timeline for development then becomes critical. For example, one builder may be able to construct 80 units per year in a development. If the zoning allows for 400 units, the superintendent can project that it will take five years for that one builder to complete the project. There may be several such building projects going on simultaneously, each involving a different number of units and each with a different estimate of time for completing units. Such projections will help the district balance availability against need for resources.

Estimated Density per Unit and Estimated Number and Ages of Children per Unit

In growth areas consultants and developers usually can estimate the density per unit based on the type, location, and cost of the dwelling and current trends in population growth. The cost will frequently determine the age of the owner and, hence, consultants and developers are able to estimate the ages of the children.

Information on density, including the number and ages of children per unit, is frequently available from assessor's offices or other county agencies. In areas of rapid growth, neighboring school districts may have performed studies that apply.

When the density is known and the projected timeline for growth for the area has been established, the superintendent can begin planning for resources — personnel and facilities — needed to adequately serve students.

Tax Abatement or Other Incentives Impacting on Resources

It is common for states and cities or other local government units to make deals that impact district resources. State governors are frequently courting business and industry representatives with the promise of lower taxes or other incentives to locate in the state. Cities and local government units offer tax abatement and other incentives to encourage business and industry to move into or remain in the area, to renovate property, to expand operations, and other reasons.

The superintendent needs to keep abreast of legislation and negotiations in areas where incentives to business and industry will impact on the district. Sometimes the deal may include annexation to or deannexation from property in the school district. Such a battle presently exists in Columbus, Ohio for a proposed large, affluent development to be included in the Columbus Public Schools. Frequently the vigilant superintendent can influence the deal culminated or incentive offered.

Beyond the decisions concerning how business or industry is attracted to move into, remain, or expand in the area, the superintendent needs to be concerned with the expected wealth resulting from operations. Projections are generally made by business or industry, consultants, government, and others. Comparisons can be made for the present projected growth compared to projections made in similar situations to obtain as accurate a projection as possible. Estimating conservatively for revenue projections is always recommended.

Planning for Decline

As it does in the case of planning for growth, assuring adequate resources for students in the school system in a period of decline requires strategic planning. First of all, the decline must be anticipated as far in advance as possible. The decline can be in the numbers of students enrolled or in resources or both.

Decline can be caused by a variety of reasons. The most generalized form of decline in the last two decades has been caused by the fall in birth rates. The superintendent needs to monitor trends in birth rates and adjust trends for the particular area, using census and other data. In addition to national census data, the superintendent is advised to take the census locally every three years.

As far in advance as possible, the superintendent needs to assess possible alternative use of space or rental or sale of facilities. In addition, the superintendent needs to assess how the reduction in numbers will impact class sizes, school organization, and programs (including extracurricular and athletic programs). Beyond these considerations, the superintendent will need to assess the need for staff, staffing patterns, and possible reduction in force.

Regional decline has been caused by the sunset economy phenomenon. Schools in the north, east, and midwest have been particularly affected by business and industry growth in the south and west. The decline of an industry, such as steel or automobile manufacturing, can devastate a large area, sometimes even an entire state. Such decline will certainly impact district wealth and may impact on student enrollments and the ability to attract outstanding candidates for positions.

Where a business or industry dominates, the superintendent will need to keep careful watch on what is happening locally and nationally to the business or industry. This vigilance needs to be in terms of general economic conditions and what is happening specifically within the business or industry. Take for example, the oil industry. When the price per barrel of oil dropped significantly, oil rich states were severely impacted.

Locally decline can be caused by a shift in demographics or by a business or industry local to the area suffering a decline, by takeovers of local firms, and resultant sale of the firms, and by rezoning of property in ways not favorable to district revenues. Many local situations cannot be anticipated. A business or industry may decide overnight to close its doors. A takeover can be culminated and overnight a decision is made to sell the firm or to relocate. Nontaxable property may be dramatically expanded. External scanning of the environment is the best way to keep as up-to-date as possible.

Planning for Demographic Shifts

Demographic shifts may be toward or away from the particular superintendent's district. Shifts will bring changes in school district enrollments and resources. Many of the initial changes caused by demographic shifts have ripple effects. Some shifts and their implications are explored here.

In the last decade, an area in Illinois leading west from downtown Chicago out to Aurora has expanded dramatically. Whereas there was only scattered development and farmland, today more than 25% of the country's *Fortune*

500 companies are headquartered along the corridor. This is an example of a shift that has resulted in incredible growth in many area suburbs. Direct effects are increased wealth and increased enrollments for districts in the path of the growth. Some ripple effects include: 1) the need for understanding of multiple cultures new to the district; 2) the need to provide second language instruction for the ethnic groups new to the district; and 3) the opportunity to start a large-scale school and business partnership known as the Corridor Partnership for Excellence.

A move out of the area of a business or industry may be followed by retooling of the town. Recently the author was in Boekelo in The Netherlands where such retooling had taken place. The town for centuries had been dominated by the textile industry. Following the decline of the textile industry in the town, high tech and automobile sales became dominant. A similar phenomenon is occurring in Columbus, Ohio as the city experiences dramatic growth, primarily in information and other services. Ripple effects in such shifts include: 1) changing expectations for the level of education students will pursue; 2) changing expectations for program quality; 3) changing expectations for involvement in the decision-making in schools; 4) increased opportunities for sharing resources and others.

The need to assess the adequacy of facilities and resources due to demographic shifts is obvious. Less obvious is the discerning of the ripple effects caused by the shift. A district that had large personal property revenue may lose this or vice-versa. The value structure of the new or remaining cohorts may differ significantly from values of cohorts before the shift. Birthing patterns of the new or remaining cohorts may differ significantly from birthing patterns before the shift. Instead of new opportunities for school and business partnerships, there may be significant losses in these resources. Numbers remaining may not warrant sustaining the previous academic and athletic programs. Districts may be taxing at a legislated maximum and not have the freedom to sell bonds for new facilities. Alternatively districts can be saddled with buildings that they are not able to sell or lease due to legal limitations. The list could go on and on. Of importance to the superintendent is the need to look beyond the obvious implications of a demographic shift. Planning methods need to include assessing all foreseeable implications of change.

REFERENCES AND RESOURCES

Brodinsky, Ben, *Declining Enrollment . . . Closing Schools.* Arlington, VA: American Association of School Administrators, 1981.

Hodgkinson, Harold L., *All One System: Demographics of Education, Kindergarten Through Graduate School.* Washington, D.C.: Institute for Educational Leadership, Inc., 1985.

McCune, Shirley D., *Guide to Strategic Planning for Educators.* Alexandria, VA: Association for Supervision and Curriculum Development, 1986.

Naisbitt, John, *Megatrends: Ten New Directions Transforming Our Lives.* New York, NY: Warner Books, 1982.

United Way of America, *What Lies Ahead — A Mid-Decade View: An Environmental Scan Report.* Alexandria, VA: United Way of America, 1985.

MEGATRENDS

Ten New Directions Transforming Our Lives

The Megashift:

1. From an Industrial to an Information Society
2. From Forced Technology to High Tech/High Touch
3. From a National to a World Economy
4. From Short Term to Long Term
5. From Centralization to Decentralization
6. From Institutional Help to Self-Help
7. From Representative Democracy to Participatory Democracy
8. From Hierarchies to Networking
9. From North to South
10. From Either/Or to Multiple Option

Reprinted by permission of Warner Books/New York from *Megatrends.* Copyright © 1982 by John Naisbitt.

Figure 10-1

11

Putting Research
into Practice

Advocating Practice with a Research Base

Not too long ago we were frequently able to implement or to ignore research in education without much effect. One exception has been the extent to which research on organizations has been put to productive use in school systems. Today much of the research in education, both qualitative and quantitative, commands our attention. Practitioners have found that putting research into practice can bring desired results.

The change over the years is due to many factors. Studies in cognition have resulted in our knowing more about how we learn. Using the implications of how we learn led to implications about how we should teach. Other studies have suggested means to motivate learning and to apply other principles of effective instruction. Studies that showed schools did not make a difference were followed by those which found some did and all could. Research methods and the use of technology made it possible to work with many variables simultaneously so as to simulate a complex and continually changing system.

Research has demonstrated what is effective in teaching and learning. Brain research that has helped us to know how we learn and to understand learning styles has led to research that helps us to know what, when, why, and how to teach for best results. Beyond these areas there is research in each of the subject areas that helps us to understand that different content approached differently for different children can help specific individuals be more productive in learning. Effective schools research has helped to identify characteristics of schools that make a difference in students' learning. The research has led to interventions that help develop effective schools. There are beginning studies of first year teachers and administrators to help understand the change process. These are only a few examples of research that has helped the superintendent make a positive difference in schooling.

In addition to having better research available, this is now available to us in usable forms. Phi Delta Kappa regularly issues a "Research into Practice" article. The Ohio State University has for years published *Theory into Practice*. The Kelwyn Group continues to bring the good news of the effective schools research. Madeline Hunter's effective instruction principles and steps are available in visual and easy-to-read book forms. The Association for Supervision and Curriculum Development (ASCD) and other professional organizations continue to develop practical and easy-to-use videotapes and other materials designed with a practitioner point of view.

The Role of Professional Organizations and Journals

Professional organizations and the journals they and others produce play a vital role in bringing research results to the practitioner in a form that can be understood and used. Some of these possibilities have been named above.

Professional organizations afford a forum for professionals to get together and exchange learnings and viewpoints face-to-face. Through local and national meetings, members get exposure to a wide variety of ideas that have failed or have been successful. It is important to know what worked or didn't work and why. The professional organization allows such exchanges to take place. In addition, professional organizations will frequently have a research component where select individuals focus on identifying or doing pertinent research that can be shared. Most professional organizations have a variety of means for bringing research on issues and emerging issues to readers.

Research departments of professional organizations, such as ASCD (Association for Supervision and Curriculum Development) and Phi Delta Kappa, also can be helpful in performing the scanning needed in strategic planning. That is, computer searches can be done to identify issues affecting the organization.

Some professional organizations regularly engage leadership in identifying critical issues and ordering these according to priorities. For example, Phi Delta Kappa has delegates at its regional or international meetings prepare lists of critical educational issues. From these lists, Phi Delta Kappa plans its focus and takes its direction for activity and publications. Similarly, ASCD will have its international Board of Directors debate critical issues and determine focus areas for the organization's activity.

Using the Experts

Reading what the experts have written is certainly one way to use them to achieve desired results. Listening to them on tape or viewing them on videotape are two additional ways. Hearing or viewing Drucker, Peters, or

Naisbitt on tape or TV adds a dimension and emphasis lacking in the printed word — like hearing a poem read by its author.

Finally, we can work with the experts in person. Conferences where experts are used as keynote speakers and are available for discussion following the presentation helps with understanding what the expert has to say and the expert's particular frame of reference or point of view. For example, having the opportunity to hear and speak with E. D. Hirsch has enabled the author to understand what led Hirsch to write *Cultural Literacy*.

Work conferences can provide in-depth work in an area over a short or long time period with the benefit of having an expert as facilitator. As an alternative to going to the expert, the person can be brought on site to work with limited numbers or an entire staff in a building or district, parents and other community members, personnel from neighboring district, or others.

In working with experts it is important to have the district's mission and goals clearly in mind so that the expert is helping fulfill that mission or attain the goals. Otherwise the expert will do his or her own thing and, at a minimum, cause confusion and dissatisfaction. Even more, the expert can undo benefits already produced. Upsetting the apple cart is more likely to occur when the superintendent brings in dog-and-pony shows that appear, do their thing, and leave. Best results come when a trusted expert works overtime to achieve mutually agreed upon goals. Whatever the expectation of the district is for the expert, it should be made clear from the beginning.

Since experts have been using audiovisuals to deliver their message, many more of the experts have become available to the practitioner. People like Madeline Hunter, Jack Frymier, Ralph Tyler, and others in education can be viewed for comparatively little cost. To have any of these persons work personally with our staffs is frequently prohibitive from a cost perspective. Creative superintendents, however, can find ways to get the expert in. For example, the superintendent may sponsor and pay for the expert but invite other districts to send employees and share the cost. Or there may be various organizations, networks, or consortia in the area who will assume sponsorship to benefit a number of superintendents.

Experts can be helpful in learning desirable alternatives and in developing a structure for training. There may be less costly, yet effective, trainers who can be brought in to work with groups and individuals to accomplish desired results.

Many of the nationally recognized experts are familiar with the gamut of possibilities of schooling situations and can easily identify with your particular situation. Similarly, such a person can make suggestions and guide practice for increased productivity in students' learning. However, it is important that the practitioner discern whether the expert is familiar with and can assist in the particular setting.

Experimenting

Experimenting is both necessary and difficult to accomplish. It is needed because without the vision that experimenting implies, the schools will perish. It is difficult because Americans want it all and want it now.

Benefits

Unless we experiment, we cannot try new theories or test new practices to see if these bring desired results. Alternatively, if we have practices that are producing undesirable results, we need to experiment to find out what was responsible for the effect so an intervention can be planned. Similarly, if we want to assure that desirable results can be repeated, we need to experiment to know what produced the desired result.

Benefits to be derived from experimenting, then, include: 1) the opportunity to try a practice on a small scale to see if it works or does not work; 2) the ability to study what about practices make them work or not work; 3) the opportunity to design and try selective interventions to see which brings about desired results; 4) the ability to test something on a small scale, thereby, limiting the impact on students' learning and on district resources; and 5) employee motivation to try new things and, thereby, to grow professionally and enable the profession to grow.

Problems

Each of the benefits has a potential down side that may be viewed as a problem with experimenting. Some problems are suggested:

1) Experimenting with a small group creates an elite cohort that may be undesirable in some districts. Everyone wants to be invited to the party.

2) We may think we know what accounts for success or failure, but this can change because of the instruction, time of day or year, culture of the school or district, cognitive function of the group, or other factors.

3) If the experiment is expected to work for the small group, it should be made available to all. Alternatively, if we cannot predict that the experiment will be a success, no one should have the exposure to the failure. Very few of us want to be guinea pigs and very few of our clients want their children to be guinea pigs in the learning process. Designing an intervention that works with one group may not work with others.

4) The district may be unwilling to risk any chance that students will be harmed or that there will be a period when learning progress is not made. And the district may be unwilling to risk any use of resources when success does not seem an apparent outcome.

5) Employee morale may suffer if the experiment does not succeed.

Fortunately, recent research has made experimenting less ambiguous and hazardous than it has been until recent years. If the superintendent plans the innovation and thinks through what will potentially make the innovation succeed or fail, it will be easier to produce the desired results.

Examples

It is frequently helpful to know the thinking that led to an innovation or experiment. Following are examples of modest experiments and the thinking behind them.

One example of an experiment is the foreign language program being introduced to students for the first time at a middle school or junior high school level. It is likely that those who have strong language skills in place will do better in the foreign language than those who have weak skills. Now there are two trains of thought on this subject — both right. One concept is that strong language skills are needed. The other is that learning a foreign language helps to develop strong language skills. The latter works if the foreign language teacher is prepared to teach the language skills and does not expect that these be at the mastery level when beginning the study. However, if this is the first time the program is being taught, and we want to be able to advertise success, it might be well to begin the program with students who have mastered the English language while developing ways to extend the program to those who have not.

A second example of an innovation in one school district was the introduction of Control Data hardware and Plato software for use in the learning disabilities resource rooms. The reasons for choosing the particular hardware and software were as follows: 1) Control Data, with its touch screen, made it easy for the learning disabled student to respond to cues; 2) the Plato system, was sequenced to allow backing up or moving forward to match the student's entry skill level; 3) the program used many graphic materials so that a representational mode of instruction introduced a strong visual element; 4) student names were used during the computer instruction which added a personal element; and 5) immediate and nonjudgmental feedback was given after response tries.

The underlying belief in the innovation of using the computer with learning disabled students was that at least as much learning would take place as with traditional instruction. If this were true, using the computer would prove cost effective instruction since fewer teachers would be needed to service students. The district used pre- and post-tests to demonstrate that students achieved higher levels of learning for the two years after computers were introduced than for the two years preceding the use of computers.

Evaluating Results of the Experiment

Of paramount importance in experimenting is to identify the desired results and then to monitor the program and adjust as necessary along the way to assure that the desired results are achieved. This means that an evaluation of the program must be built into the planning. For example, if the superintendent is going to test the effectiveness of the use of computers in learning disabilities classrooms, what is expected in the way of student attitude and self-concept changes as well as what is expected in the way of achievement should be identified in advance. Then data should be gathered before the experiment or innovation begins and at regular intervals afterwards. If the experiment does not work, and everything possible has been done to rethink and redesign it, the experiment should be dropped. If a decision is made to extend the innovation, such as use of computers to other areas of instruction, a new experiment is begun. The superintendent should know what results are expected from the expanded innovation and then monitor and adjust activity to assure that results are achieved. Once again, if things do not work out, and everything possible has been done to rethink and redesign the experiment, it should be limited in scope or dropped.

Allowing for Failure

Educators, unlike other areas of business and government, find it hard to admit that an experiment did not work and then move to something that will. Recently the British government gave up on building their own specialized defense planes after sinking billions into the try with unsatisfactory results; they acknowledged their lack of success when announcing that they were moving to the purchase of American-made Boeings.

It takes guts to admit that we are not always right, but reasonable people know that this is not always possible. What should be avoided in experiments, if possible, is doing damage to the situation or learner. That there are no demonstrated results at times should be expected.

The recognition that time to experiment is necessary and that experiments do not always work has recently been demonstrated in the efforts of one professional organization. The Executive Council of the Association for Supervision and Curriculum Development (ASCD) has given the Publications Department a sum of money with which to experiment; that is, Publications will develop a concept to the point of making a determination as to the need for and marketability of a certain product to develop higher levels of productivity in students' learning. "Where there is no vision, the people perish." Vision and acting on vision lead to productive results.

REFERENCES AND RESOURCES

American Education
American Educational Research Journal
Educational Leadership
Educational Researcher
Elementary School Journal
Harvard Educational Review
Journal of Negro Education
Journal of Teacher Education

Mitzel, Harold, *Encyclopedia of Educational Research* (5th ed.). New York, NY: Macmillan Publishing Co., 1982

NASSP Bulletin

Phi Delta Kappan.

Review of Educational Research

School Review

Today's Education

Urban Education

Wittrock, M.C., ed., *Handbook of Research on Teaching* (3rd ed.). New York, NY: Macmillan Publishing Co., 1986.

Other Resources

The Chief State School Officers provide useful research resources. Names and addresses are shown in Chapter 8.

Educational Research Service, 2000 Clarendon Boulevard, Arlington, VA 22201.

IV

UTILIZING RESOURCES

12

Budgeting

Budgeting in most school systems is done on a cash or modified accrual basis. This means that, for the most part, only *cash transactions* are recorded. The accrual basis of accounting is common to most other businesses. In the accrual system, expenses *incurred* and income *earned* for a particular period are shown, whether or not actual cash payments and receipts have been made or received during the period.

Knowing How Much

There is no magic to knowing how much is available to spend or how much should be spent. Revenues in education are, at best, ambiguous. And expenditures are usually cut back to available revenues. Few districts enjoy the luxury of unlimited revenue and all should be mindful that expenditures are cost effective.

It is important to recognize the ambiguity in school finance. Educators frequently think, however, that schools are the only agencies or businesses with such a plight, and this is not so. Most businesses depend on some form of sales which are always ambiguous. What we need to do is to discern the best indicators of both revenues and expenditures to make the budget process more palatable and professional.

Different states have different formulae for determining what monies will go to schools. An illustration of the application of Ohio's formula for one school district is shown in Figure 12-1. Examples of sources of revenue the state distributes include income and sales taxes and lottery revenue. Since California's Proposition 13, there have been varieties of rollbacks to limit school revenues. Figure 12-2 illustrates how the legislated rollback in Ohio has reduced the collected millage in one district to nearly 50% of that voted. The illustration shows the voted millage as 56.80 and the collected millage as 31.4979. The graph shown in a previous chapter as Figure 8-4 illustrates the growing gap between voted and collected millage for this same district. Each superintendent needs to learn what system for determining school revenue is being used in his or her particular state.

In Illinois, for example, districts must guesstimate yearly in December what will be needed for the next fiscal year that will begin the following July. In between the December and July dates, the real estate assessed valuation figures are made known. If one guesses too low in an area where the assessed valuation is increasing at a rapid rate, the district may lose important revenue. But assuming the guesstimate was high enough so that the dollar extension met or exceeded what would be available by multiplying the legal tax rate by the assessed valuation, the district would have access to whatever that amount was. As the assessed valuation increases, so do the revenues.

Contrast the above example in Illinois with Ohio where voters must approve a levy in mills at a particular point in time when the assessed valuation is at a particular amount. For succeeding years the monies received stay pretty much the same as the millage is rolled back. This means that in real dollars, the district has less to spend over time even though the assessed valuation for the district is increasing. Alternatively, the district must repeatedly return the voters for additional millage.

State funding formulae are also different. Most have a weighting to favor the urban poor, a higher cost of living, or districts with more educated, and consequently higher salaried, staff. Some have a fixed guaranteed amount so that even wealthy districts get some funding. Others have a percent increase built into yearly funding to allow for inflation. In hard times, the state usually reconsiders so that all districts receive less than they may budget to receive. Similarly, in hard times, some may not pay real estate taxes and this will impact on school revenue from local sources.

Districts vary in the sources of their revenue so the superintendent needs to know how much is expected from what source and how much variance there can be in what is expected. In some states, 80% or more is received from state funds, in other states districts can receive less that 20% in state funds. The graph shown in an earlier chapter as Figure 8-5 illustrates the percent of revenue from various sources. An alternative means to illustrate revenue by source for this same district is shown in Figure 12-3.

Studying Variances

Assuming that the budget is viewed as a planning document, it is important to perform ongoing analyses to keep track of how much actual receipts and expenditures vary from what were predicted. There are many ways to do this in terms of how it is done and how often.

Based on a history of revenues and expenditures, the annual budget can be broken down into percent of revenues expected and percent of estimated expenditures by line item or category for any period of time. Figure 12-4 shows a district's yearly appropriations and expected expenditures by category for a partial year. A monthly financial statement to the board, as shown in Figure 12-5, accounts for variances by category of spending. When the budget is on a computer, variances can be shown at any time by budget line item as illustrated in Figure 12-6. A monthly comparison by clusters of line items within each category of revenues and expenditures is generally satisfactory to the board. The board statement can be supplemented by monthly expenditure statements to individuals who are responsible for funds — school principals for example.

Careful accounting for resources on an ongoing basis assures that there are no surprises and it helps to predict and plan cash flow. Even if funds are transferred into a particular budget category or line item to assure that there are no negative balances, it is important to keep track of the actual expenditures for the various budget line items and to compare actual expenditures to the proposed budget or appropriations. This enables those responsible for budget preparation to study the reason for the variance and to adjust thinking as necessary in preparing future budgets.

Zero Base by Program

For the past 15 or more years, program accounting in schools using zero-based budgeting has been popular. This means that all that is done in the school is given program function and object numbers. All related expenses are charged against their respective function and object numbers. Figure 12-7 illustrates the significance of various parts of the numbering system used in Ohio schools.

The zero base means that an analysis of needs is undertaken yearly rather than assuming that one will start with an amount in relation to the previous budget amount. Rather than saying so much will be spent per pupil for art or another program, those preparing budget requests look at needs in relation to the prescribed course of study and materials and supplies available to determine future needs. Rather than saying that each classroom teacher will have a dollar amount to spend for his or her classroom, the teacher must project what will be needed in relation to the course of study, the next year's specific program, and available materials and supplies.

Zero-base budgeting has the potential for making expenditures cost effective. That is, if teachers and others in the school system must analyze and justify what it is that they want to accomplish and think through how this will be done and what will be needed, there is the potential that expenditures will be put to more effective use for more productive learning than if such thought was not expected.

Program accounting, when used with zero-base budgeting, enables the superintendent to see at a glance how much a particular program or service at each site or, alternatively, how much the total program by site is costing. Such information enables the superintendent to make equity decisions as well as other determinations as to how monies should be expended to achieve desired results. Program accounting also enables the superintendent to monitor expenditures in terms of what planning groups have said are district priorities.

Alternatively if budget is managed at the school site level, comparisons of expenditures by building facilitates principal/superintendent discussions around employment decisions, building and grounds maintenance, ordering of priorities in the curriculum, and equity issues.

Being Precise

Errors in budgeting inevitably come back to haunt. It may be during contract negotiations. It may be when a cash flow shortage appears unexpectedly. It may be when independent or state auditors come to verify revenues and expenditures against budget figures. But at some time, errors reveal themselves. Hence, it is worthwhile to be precise and do things right the first time.

Building in checkpoints by categories and clusters of revenues and expenditures will assure that errors made along the way are caught before an extensive search for the error becomes necessary. Similarly, taking time to proof entries after these are made by hand entry or on a computer, can save literally days of checking and cross-checking when it comes time to balance accounts.

Aside from auditors demanding exact accounting for revenues and expenditures, there are other reasons for being precise. First, budget affects all in the school system. When errors are made in an individual's account or accounts, this causes a morale problem that can be more or less serious and last for a brief or long time. Second, budget preparation and administration affects how the Board and school publics view the district. If there are large and continued variances that could be avoided; if there are continual errors that need correction; if budget is presented in obtuse terms that cannot be understood by any except the treasurer, people get upset or confused and alienated. Third, errors inevitably need correction which causes additional time to be spent in nonproductive ways. Doing it right the first time and presenting budget in such a way that it can be understood by all, will increase everyone's morale and confidence in the system and in those responsible for its preparation.

Cutting the Pie

Deciding who gets what is the difficult part of budgeting when there are limited resources. Education is a labor-intensive, or personnel-heavy business. It is not uncommon to have 75% to 80% of the total budget in personnel costs. Pie graphs shown in a previous chapter as Figures 8-6 and 8-7 illustrate how expenditures can be clustered in alternative ways to show expenditures by function and object. Figure 12-8 presents similar data for the same district using a bar graph. The graph shows that salaries and benefits in the district have fluctuated from under 70% to almost 90% of total expenditures. Since school districts have begun declaring bankruptcy, states have begun to generate guidelines as to what percent of the budget is reasonable to expect for different items.

In some states, monies must be levied for specific funds and the monies in the various funds cannot be comingled. For example, in Illinois funds can be levied for Education; Operations Building and Maintenance; Bonds and Interest; Transportation; Retirement Funds; Site and Construction; and other purposes. Each fund has definite guidelines and limitations for expenditures and for transfer of monies from one fund to another.

Strict accounting by fund makes it easy to keep track of monies received and expended for specific purposes; it makes it more difficult to allocate funds according to need. Other states are less restrictive and permit funds collected to be spent for education and buildings and grounds as well as other purposes. The latter system, while allowing for more flexibility and discretion as to the use of funds, generally results in funds being reduced for maintenance and capital expenditure items when resources are scarce. It is important for the superintendent to know what rules govern budget for his or her school district.

Being Conservative

Coming as close as possible to predicting actual revenues and expenditures is desirable in budgeting. Making long-range projections and continually updating these will assist in making accurate predictions. Figure 12-9 shows a three-year projection for a district. Amounts were budgeted conservatively, but realistically.

Short of making perfect predictions, being conservative in budgeting is recommended. That is, underestimating revenues and overestimating expenditures to allow a safe margin can provide the needed cushion against surprises. Preparing figures for the purposes of concealing or fooling others is not what is recommended here.

As an example of being conservative, if you know that 95% to 98% of real estate taxes are normally collected, then what is reasonable to expect as collectable should be budgeted rather than what the levy extension might show. If history shows that only a portion of state funds will be collected or that the legislature will withhold one or more payments, then only the expected should be bugeted rather than what the district may have been led to believe could be expected. If interest rates are fluctuating, then rates that tend to be on the low side of a swing in rates should be budgeted rather than what rates may be at the time of preparing budget figures.

Expenditures can be treated in a manner similar to revenues. If an analysis of variances shows that expenditures in general or particular expenditures are regularly underestimated, items should be increased enough to avoid surprises. If expenditures are likely to occur, it is reasonable to budget for them even if they don't actually occur. If items regularly show increases each year or if an item is long overdue to show an increase, even though an exact figure is not known, a reasonable estimate of the increased amount can be made and used in the budget process. And so on.

Wherever shortfalls are likely or possible, revenue should be estimated on the low side. Wherever excesses are likely or possible, expenditures should be estimated on the high side. With luck, you will balance or be close.

Dealing with the Unexpected

The unexpected occurs all too often in schooling. However, with strategic and other long-range planning, the effects of the unexpected can be minimized.

Acts of God and nature can wreak havoc in a school system by making costly rebuilding and repair necessary. However, with accurate records and a plan for dealing with emergencies, the effects of tragedies can be minimized.

Knowing the value of property, having an inventory of all property, and keeping track of replacement costs on all property can facilitate the rebuilding, repairing, or replacing made necessary by the unexpected. Such recordkeeping is also required in cases of theft and vandalism.

Without adequate recordkeeping, unnecessary delays occur when tragedy strikes. To assure the safety and availability of records when these are needed, it is important to keep backup records in a second location; in school districts where there is only one building, the second site can be a county or state office or a neighboring school district. Keeping backup records is particularly important in the information age when tapes or other means for storing electronic data can be inadvertently destroyed.

Whatever the emergency happens to be, there can be persons designated to be in charge of restoring normalcy. This may be a media specialist who will take charge of assessing damage or loss to inventory. It may be the building principal who will take charge of assessing any loss within the building. It may be the business manager who will be responsible for communicating with other district personnel to assess loss and to arrange for rebuilding, repairing, or replacing.

At the time an unexpected tragedy occurs, it is the opportune time to reassess if planning should take place to do things differently. If rebuilding a structure is needed, it may be that a new design would better serve students' needs at that particular time and for the future. If repair is necessary, it may be that new materials or methods of installation will issue in a better product than previously. If replacement is necessary, it may be that new equipment or materials will be desired for more and better student achievement. Ongoing strategic planning and other long-range planning programs will assure that a data base for assisting in the assessment efforts is in place.

To some extent the unexpected should be expected or its consequences should be anticipated. For example, if a district is in deficit spending going into a levy, strategies for dealing with and reducing or eliminating the deficit should be part of the planning that goes into the attempt to pass the levy. All eggs cannot be placed in the expectation that the levy will pass. Similarly, one can guess by age and general condition of construction and equipment that it is vulnerable to problems or failure.

In short, to the extent the superintendent can foresee the unforeseeable and anticipate consequences of the unexpected, the more manageable budgeting will be.

REFERENCES AND RESOURCES

Greenhalgh, John, *School Site Budgeting*. Lanham, MD: University Press of America, Inc., 1984.

Hymes, Donald L., *School Budgeting . . . Problems and Solutions*. Arlington, VA: American Association of School Administrators, 1982.

Other Resources

American Association of School Administrators, 1801 N. Moore St., Arlington, VA 22209-9988. (Publishes *The School Administrator* magazine.)

Chief State School Officers provide useful budgeting resources. Names and addresses are shown in Chapter 8.

National School Boards Association, 1680 Duke St., Alexandria, VA 22314.

Ohio Department of Education-Division of School Finance
Form SF-12 Fiscal Year 1983-84 June Calculation   (AM.SUB.H.B.291)

Bexley City S.D.   Franklin County

A. Basic Program Support:
    1.   153 Kindergarten ADM
    2.   1,939 Grades 1-12 (Excludes FTE on Line 14, ADM on Line 16
                     and 75% of Joint Vocational and Contract ADM)
    3.   2,016 Basic ADM (One-half Line 1 Plus Line 2; Sec 3317.02)
    4.   126,833,498 Assessed Valuation; Valuation Per Pupil = 62,913
    5. Basic State Aid (Section 3317.022)
       (A) ($1835 X 1.041) X Line 3   3,851,043.84
       (B) Assessed Valuation X .02   2,536,669.96
    6. Line 5A Minus Line 5B   1,314.373.88
    7.
    8. Larger of Line 6 or Line 7   1,314,373.88
    9. Adjustments (Section 3317.023)
       (A) Number of Classroom Teachers
       (B) Training and Exp of Classroom Teachers (50% of Total)   23,215.34
       (C) Educational Service Personnel
       (D) County Board Deduction (See Line 23)
   10. Current Basic State Aid (Line B Plus or Minus Line 9)   1,337,589.22
   11. FY83 Guarantee (If Valuation Per Pupil Less Than 91750,
       105% of FY83 Basic Aid Per Pupil X Line 3 ADM*.
       If Valuation Per Pupil Equal to or Greater Than 91750,
       103% of FY83 Basic Aid Per Pupil X Line 3 ADM*.   956,350.08
   12. Larger of Line 10 or Line 11   1,337,589.22
   13. Disadvantaged Pupil Impact Aid
   13A.FY84 Basic Program (Line 12 Plus Line 13)   1,337,589.22

B. Categorical Program Funding:
   14. Approved Vocational Units: 1.92; FTE 18.16
       (A) Salary Allowance + 15% $7325   51,894.53
           (Includes Proprietary ADM of   X $1,815.86)
                              or
       (B) (Line 12/Line3) X 105% X FTE   12,651.36
       (C) Larger of Line 14A or 14B X 1.000   51,894.53
   15. Approved Child Study, Occupational or Physical
       Therapy, Speech and Hearing, Supervisors and Coordinators
       of Special Education Units: 1.80
       Salary Allowance + 15% + $1215 X 1.0000   38,829.45
   16. Approved DBECN and EMR Units:
       (A) Salary Allowance + 15% + $6500   132,505.15
           DBECN Units   5.00 DBECN ADM   73
           EMR Units   .00 EMR ADM
                   or
       (B) (Line 12/Line3) X 105% X Spec. ADM 50,856.26
       (C) Larger of Line 16A or 16B X 1.0000   132,505.15
   17. Gifted Units: 1.00 Gifted Allowance   23,798.70
   18. Approved Extended Service   4,277.52
   19. Approved Transportation   16,022.65
   20. Total Categorical Program Funding (Sum of Lines 14C,15,
       16C, 17, 18 and 19)   267,328.00
   21. Line 13A Plus Line 20   1,604,917.22
   22. Other Guarantees (Specify)
       (A) Reappraisal (Section 3317.04)
       (B) Consolidation (Section 3317.04)
   23. Total State Support (Larger of Line 21 Minus
       Line 9D or Line 22) $1,604,917.22

Bexley City S.D.   Franklin County
     JVS and Contract ADM Excluded from Calculation   12
     Total ADM as Reported on SF-2   2,196

     Formula District

*June 1983 SF-12, Reduced line 12/Line 3ADM

Courtesy of Bexley City Schools.

Figure 12-1
374

BEXLEY TAX RATES SINCE 1979

YEAR	UNVOTED INSIDE MILLAGE	TOTAL VOTED OPERATING MILLAGE	OPERATING VOTED EFFECTIVE MILLAGE RESIDENTIAL	TOTAL VALUATION
1979	5.7	32.80	26.3125	$ 96,025,475
1980	5.7	38.80	32.3120	96,519,330
1981	5.7	38.80	32.3120	98,470,367
1982	5.7	38.80	24.3926	126,833,180
1983	5.7	48.30	33.8637	126,392,848
1984	5.7	48.30	33.8637	127,207,150
1985	5.7	48.30	30.6450	139,860,256
1986	5.7	56.80	39.150	140,910,682
1987	5.7	56.80	39.1448	141,847,121
1988	5.7	56.80	31.4979	173,455,843

Courtesy of Bexley City Schools.

Figure 12-2

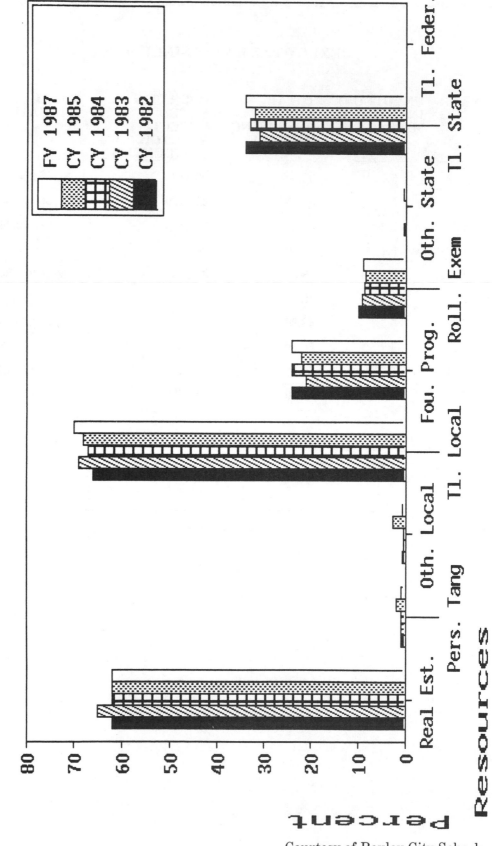

Figure 12-3

376

Form SM-1
Revised 5/86

OHIO DEPARTMENT OF EDUCATION - OFFICE OF SCHOOL MANAGEMENT ASSISTANCE
ANNUAL SPENDING PLAN (O.R.C. 5705.391)

SCHOOL DISTRICT BEXLEY CITY SCHOOLS
COUNTY FRANKLIN
YEAR 1988
IRN # 043620

	(1) FY APPROPRIATIONS	(2) JULY	(3) AUGUST	(4) SEPTEMBER	(5) OCTOBER	(6) NOVEMBER
BEGINNING CASH BALANCE	$1,675,735	$1,675,735	$2,340,255	$2,605,413	$2,209,219	$1,677,173
RECEIPTS FROM AMENDED CERTIFICATE						
From Local Sources						
1. Real Estate Tax	5,540,000	1,171,200	759,968	00	00	00
2. Tangible Personal Property Tax	125,000	00	00	00	64,000	00
3. Investment Earnings	150,000	12,766	16,889	8,000	24,000	10,000
4. Proceeds from Borrowing	00	00	00	00	00	00
5. Other	50,000	6,131	121	5,000	5,000	2,000
From State Sources						
6. Foundation Program	2,166,000	176,954	176,954	176,954	196,954	196,954
7. Rollback and Homestead Exemption	850,000	00	00	396,710	00	00
8. Other	68,000	00	00	00	00	10,000
From Federal Sources						
9. Public Law 874	00	00	00	00	00	00
10. Other	00	00	00	00	00	00
From All Transfers						
11. Transfers and Advances In	4,000	00	00	00	00	4,000
12. TOTAL RECEIPTS (Lines 1-11)	8,953,000	1,367,051	953,932	586,664	289,954	222,954
13. TOTAL RECEIPTS PLUS CASH BALANCE	10,628,735	3,042,786	3,294,187	3,192,077	2,499,173	1,900,127
EXPENDITURES & PRIOR YEAR ENCUMBRANCES						
14. Salaries & Wages	6,322,250	453,667	453,273	501,650	530,000	545,000
15. Fringe Benefits	1,309,220	102,117	119,624	100,108	100,000	100,000
16. Purchased Services	882,000	85,252	19,821	71,000	70,000	78,000
17. Materials, Supplies & Textbooks	446,216	26,388	37,293	103,000	55,000	25,000
18. Capital Outlay (incl. Replacement)	333,793	32,573	14,117	202,100	40,000	20,000
19. Repayment of Borrowing (Prin. + Int.)	00	00	00	00	00	00
20. Transfers and Advances Out	142,106	00	00	5,000	26,000	1,000
21. Other	156,150	2,534	44,646	5,000	1,000	1,000
22. TOTAL EXPENDITURES (Lines 14-21)	9,591,735	702,531	688,774	982,858	822,000	769,000
ENDING CASH BALANCE (Lines 13 minus 22)	1,037,000	2,340,255	2,605,413	2,209,219	1,677,173	1,131,127

NOTE: Circled numbers are for Department use only.

Courtesy of Bexley City Schools.

Figure 12-4

BEXLEY CITY SCHOOLS
JUNE FINANCIAL STATEMENT
1987

	MONTH ESTIMATE	MONTH ACTUAL	MONTH DIFFERENCE	YR TO DATE (ESTIMATE)	YR TO DATE ACTUAL	OUTSTANDING ENCUMBRANCE	YR TO DATE DIFFERENCE
BEGINNING CASH BALANCE	$1,118,822	$1,812,677	$693,855	$1,596,932	$1,596,932		$ 00
RECEIPTS							
FROM LOCAL SOURCES							
1. Real Estate	$ 542,907	$ 320,500	(222,407)	$ 5,334,000	$ 5,377,483		$ 43,483 (A)
2. Personal Tangible	12,000	11,460	(540)	112,000	127,822		15,822 (B)
3. Investment Earnings	8,793	20,019	11,226	125,000	157,331		32,331 (C)
4. Other	4,000	21,186	17,186	46,300	79,369		33,069 D
FROM STATE SOURCES							
5. Foundation Program	170,014	174,273	4,259	2,080,000	2,088,934		8,934 (E)
6. Rollback & Homestead Ex.	00	00	00	792,000	793,357		1,357 (E)
7. Other	00	00	00	15,000	20,163		5,163 (E)
FROM ALL TRANSFERS							
8. Transfers & Advances in	00	00	00	3,000	4,137		1,137
9. Total Receipts (Lines 1-8)	737,714	547,438	(190,276)	8,507,300	8,648,596		141,296
10. Total Receipts plus Cash Bal.	1,856,536	2,360,117	503,581	10,104,232	10,245,528		141,296
EXPENDITURES							
11. Salaries and Wages	528,500	487,801	40,699	5,979,900	5,775,540	00	204,360 (F)
12. Fringe Benefits	115,038	98,204	16,834	1,210,180	1,165,689	518	43,973 (F)
13. Purchased Services	100,000	63,146	36,854	867,360	740,317	27,547	99,496 (G)
14. Materials, Supplies, & Textbooks	22,057	10,674	11,383	372,115	334,177	22,332	15,606 (H)
15. Capital Outlay — Inc. Replacement	28,214	(514)	28,728	201,800	109,506	110,035	(17,741)
16. Transfers & Advances Out	00	16,500	(16,500)	328,000	318,242	00	9,758 (I)
17. Other	00	8,570	(8,570)	82,150	126,322	700	(44,872) (J)
18. TOTAL EXPENDITURES Lines 11-17	$ 793,809	$ 684,381	109,428	$ 9,041,505	$ 8,569,793	$161,132	$310,580
ENDING CASH BALANCE Lines (10-18)	$1,062,727	$1,675,735	613,008	$1,062,727	$ 1,675,735		$451,876 (K)

Figure 12-5   Courtesy of Bexley City Schools.

378

USA521

BEXLEY CITY SCHOOL DISTRICT

DATE 01/22/88

A P P R O P R I A T I O N   T O T A L S   B Y   A C C O U N T

ACCOUNT CODE	OBJECT	SUBJECT	OPERATIONAL	LV JOB ASSIGNMENT	PRCNT1
DATE	PREVIOUS APPROPRIATION	ORIGINAL APPROPRIATION	APPROPRIATION ADJUSTMENTS	FUNCTION	YEAR-TO-DATE EXPENDITURE	UNEXPENDED BALANCE	OUTSTANDING ENCUMBRANCE	UN INSTRUCTION	UN ENCUMBERED BALANCE	PRCNT2
FED PROJECT	PREVIOUS EXPENDITURE	CARRY OVER PURCHASE ORDER	APPROPRIATION BALANCE		MONTH-TO-DATE EXPENDITURES				

Account / Date					
001-C000-1110-513-11000000-400-00-000 11/11/87	ELEM INSTRUC TEACHING AIDS MATHEMATICS MARYLAND ELEME	$.00 / $250.00 / $.00 / $186.80 / $63.20	$63.20	74.72	74.72
$.00 / $.00 / $250.00 / $.00				$.00	$63.20
001-C000-1110-513-11000000-500-00-000 10/23/87	ELEM INSTRUC TEACHING AIDS MATHEMATICS MONTROSE ELEME	$.00 / $1,500.00 / $60.00- / $1,387.65 / $52.35	$52.35	96.36	96.36
$.00 / $.00 / $1,440.00 / $.00				$.00	$52.35
001-C000-1110-513-12040000-300-00-000 12/17/87	ELEM INSTRUC TEACHING AIDS VOCAL MUSIC CASSINGHAM	$785.00 / $800.00 / $.00 / $716.59 / $83.41	$83.41	89.57	89.57
$778.28 / $.00 / $800.00 / $68.99				$.00	$83.41
001-C000-1110-513-12040000-400-00-000 10/21/87	ELEM INSTRUC TEACHING AIDS VOCAL MUSIC MARYLAND ELEME	$634.83 / $445.00 / $36.21- / $126.13 / $282.66	$282.66	30.85	30.85
$552.58 / $.00 / $408.79 / $.00				$.00	$282.66
001-C000-1110-513-12040000-500-00-000 12/31/87	ELEM INSTRUC TEACHING AIDS VOCAL MUSIC MONTROSE ELEME	$720.00 / $930.00 / $.00 / $696.83 / $233.17	$27.17	97.08	97.08
$708.65 / $.00 / $930.00 / $.00			$206.00	$27.17
001-C000-1110-513-12051000-000-00-000 07/02/87	ELEM INSTRUC TEACHING AIDS MUSIC BAND	$.00 / $150.00 / $.00 / $.00 / $150.00	$150.00	.00	.00
$.00 / $.00 / $150.00 / $.00				$.00	.00
001-C000-1110-513-12052000-000-00-000 10/23/87	ELEM INSTRUC TEACHING AIDS STRING-ORCH	$.00 / $160.00 / $.00 / $247.56 / $87.56-	$87.56-	154.73	154.73
$.00 / $.00 / $160.00 / $.00				$.00	$87.56-
001-C000-1110-513-13010000-300-00-000 01/14/88	ELEM INSTRUC TEACHING AIDS SCIENCE CASSINGHAM	$894.73 / $1,703.00 / $106.36- / $1,053.02 / $663.90	$584.25	65.97	65.97
$715.56 / $120.28 / $1,716.92 / $20.34			$79.65	$584.25
001-C000-1110-513-13010000-400-00-000 12/31/87	ELEM INSTRUC TEACHING AIDS SCIENCE MARYLAND ELEME	$434.39 / $1,300.00 / $150.00- / $168.27 / $981.73	$815.93	29.05	29.05
$434.39 / $.00 / $1,150.00 / $.00			$165.80	$815.93
001-C000-1110-513-13010000-500-00-000 01/14/88	ELEM INSTRUC TEACHING AIDS SCIENCE MONTROSE ELEME	$430.83 / $1,000.00 / $180.00 / $1,169.39 / $23.22	$.47	99.96	99.96
$421.28 / $12.61 / $1,192.61 / $.00			$22.75	$.47
001-C000-1110-513-15000000-300-00-000 11/24/87	ELEM INSTRUC TEACHING AIDS SOC SCI-SO STU CASSINGHAM	$.00 / $357.00 / $106.36 / $428.14 / $35.22	$4.22	99.09	99.09
$.00 / $.00 / $463.36 / $.00			$31.00	$4.22
001-C000-1110-513-15000000-400-00-000 07/08/87	ELEM INSTRUC TEACHING AIDS SOC SCI-SO STU MARYLAND ELEME	$.00 / $100.00 / $.00 / $.00 / $100.00	$80.00	20.00	20.00
$.00 / $.00 / $100.00 / $.00			$20.00	$80.00

Figure 12-6
379

ACCOUNTING SYSTEM EXPLANATION

REVENUE

FUND NUMBERS 001-xxxx-xxx

The first series of numbers are the fund numbers. They are the same as fund numbers under the expenditure explanation.

SPECIAL COST CENTER xxx-8384-xxxx

The second series of numbers are the special cost center numbers. See Special Cost Center under expenditures.

RECEIPT xxx-xxxx-1110

The third series of numbers are the receipt numbers. They are used to separate the source of the revenue. The 1000 numbers are local revenue, 3000 numbers are revenue from state sources, and 4000 numbers are revenue from federal sources. 5000 numbers are interfund revenue.

OPERATION UNITS xxx-xxxx-xxxx-900

See Page 4 under expenditures.

ACCOUNTING SYSTEM EXPLANATION
EXPENDITURES

FUND NUMBERS 001-xxxx-xxxx-xxx-xxxxxxxx-xxx

The first series of numbers are the fund numbers. Examples are General Fund (001), Bond Retirement Fund (002), Food Service Fund (006), and Chapter I (572). Funds are used to segregate specific activities of the district in accordance with special regulations, restrictions, or limitations. The general fund (001) is used to show all ordinary operations of the school district. The fund numbers between 001 and 099 are local funds. Fund number (200) is for student activity funds and fund number (300) is for the athletic fund. (400) fund numbers are for state funds and (500) funds are federal funds.

SPECIAL COST CENTER xxx-8283-xxxx-xxx-xxxxxxxx-xxx

The second series of numbers are the special cost center. They are used in conjunction with the fund numbers. The purpose of these numbers are to separate the different federal and state projects and separate the different student activity accounts. An example is Chapter I fund (572)

Figure 12-7

380

which would have a special cost center number of 8283 to designate the 1982-83 fiscal year project from the 1983-84 project. Another example would be the Activity Fund (200) with a special cost center number 1984 which would separate out the class of 1984 activity from all other Student Activity accounts.

FUNCTION xxx-xxxx-1110-xxx-xxxxxxxx-xxx

The third set of numbers is the function. Function numbers are used to show the action a person takes or the purpose for which a thing exists or is used. The activities of a school district are classified into six broad areas or functions: Instruction, Supporting Services, Extracurricular Services, Debt Services, Nonprogrammed Charges, and Contingencies. Functions are further broken down into subfunctions and service areas. Specific explanation of each function is listed under the function numbers in the appropriation document.

OBJECTS xxx-xxxx-xxxx-111-xxxxxxxx-xxx

The fourth set of numbers are the object numbers. Object numbers show the service or commodity obtained as a result of a specific expenditure. The eight major object categories are:

100	Salaries and Wages —	Amounts paid to employees of the school district who are considered to be in the position of a permanent nature or hired temporarily.
200	Retirement and Insurance Benefits —	Amounts paid by the school district on behalf of the employees for retirement and all fringe benefits such as insurances and unemployment insurances.
300	Other Benefits —	This series of objects is a part of the total 100 object appropriation salaries. This object would include sick leave, personal leave, and any other fringe benefits not included in the retirement and insurance benefits.
400	Purchase Services —	Amounts paid for personal services rendered by personnel who are not on the payroll of the school district, and other services which the school district may purchase.
500	Supplies and Materials —	Amounts paid for materials of an expendable nature that are consumed, worn out, or deteriorated in use; or items that lose their identity through

Figure 12-7 (Cont'd.)

381

		fabrication or incorporation into different or more complex units or substances.
600	Capital Outlay —	Expenditures for the acquisition of fixed assets or additional fixed assets. Included are expenditures for land or existing building improvement of grounds; remodeling of buildings; initial equipment; and additional equipment and furnishing and vehicles.
700	Capital Outlay-Replacement —	Expenditures for replacement of any item covered under the 600 series.
800	Other Objects —	Amounts paid for goods and services not otherwise classified.

SUBJECT AREA xxx-xxxx-xxxx-xxx-10060000-xxx

The fifth set of numbers are the subject area. The subject area is used to break expenditures into specific instructional subjects as taught in the school district.

OPERATION UNITS xxx-xxxx-xxxx-xxx-xxxxxxxx-100

Operation units are the last group of accounting numbers the district is currently using. These numbers break the expenditures down to the building level. These numbers are: High School (100); Junior High (200); Cassingham (300); Maryland (400); Montrose (500); Central Office (600); Athletic Fields (601); District (700); Tennis Courts (701); Columbus School for Girls (800); and St. Charles (900). Expenditures for each school bus is also broken down by using the specific school bus number as the operational unit number.

JOB xxx-xxxx-xxxx-xxx-xxxxxxx-xxx-xx-603

This dimension groups into general categories the kind of work staff members perform. Examples are 702, maintenance workers and 902, custodian.

Figure 12-7 (Cont'd.)

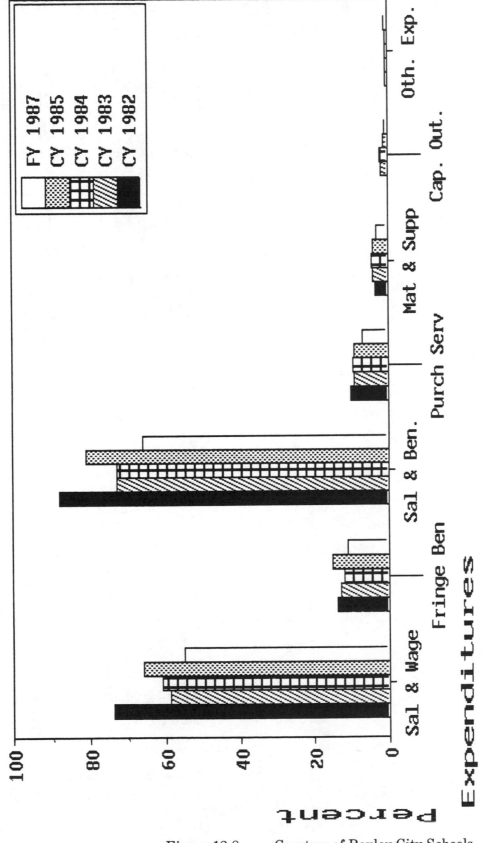

Figure 12-8   Courtesy of Bexley City Schools.

GENERAL FUND
THREE-YEAR PROJECTION

2/1/88

	ACTUAL July 85 thru June 1986	ACTUAL July 86 thru June 1987	PROJECTED July 87 thru June 1988	PROJECTED July 88 thru June 1989	PROJECTED July 89 thru June 1990	PROJECTED July 1990 thru June 1991	PROJECTED July 1991 thru Dec. 1991
REVENUE							
PROPERTY TAXES (INCLUDES ROLLBACK)	$6,641,417.45	$6,298,662.33	$6,536,000.00	$6,808,300.00	$6,856,800.00	$6,945,000.00	$2,674,000.00
OTHER LOCAL REVENUE	207,209.95	240,836.63	230,000.00	240,000.00	245,000.00	250,000.00	130,000.00
STATE FOUNDATION	1,937,016.95	2,088,933.63	2,266,000.00	2,270,000.00	2,285,000.00	2,290,000.00	1,650,000.00
OTHER STATE	29,646.40	20,163.37	68,000.00	20,000.00	20,000.00	20,000.00	10,000.00
TOTAL REVENUE RECEIVED	$8,815,289.90	$8,648,595.96	$9,100,000.00	$9,338,300.00	$9,406,800.00	$9,505,000.00	$4,464,000.00
EXPENDITURES							
SALARIES	$5,406,453.02	$5,775,539.93	$6,330,000.00	$ 6,820,000.00	$ 7,230,000.00	$ 7,664,000.00	$4,062,000.00
FRINGE BENEFITS	1,134,214.40	1,165,688.84	1,285,000.00	1,403,500.00	1,525,000.00	1,650,000.00	891,000.00
PURCHASE SERVICES	784,909.81	740,316.83	890,000.00	890,000.00	925,000.00	962,000.00	485,000.00
SUPPLIES	298,866.39	334,177.15	450,000.00	425,000.00	425,000.00	450,000.00	225,000.00
EQUIPMENT/CAPITAL OUTLAY	89,278.40	109,506.18	425,500.00	250,000.00	250,000.00	250,000.00	125,000.00
OTHER	111,978.56	144,564.24	140,000.00	150,000.00	160,000.00	170,000.00	90,000.00
TRANSFER TO P.I.	300,000.00	300,000.00	.00	156,060.00	312,120.00	312,120.00	156,060.00
TRANSFER TO FOOD SERVICE/ATHLETIC/OTHER	.00	.00	30,000.00	60,000.00	40,000.00	40,000.00	20,000.00
TOTAL EXPENDITURES	$8,125,700.58	$8,569,793.17	$9,550,500.00	$10,134,560.00	$10,867,120.00	$11,498,120.00	$6,054,060.00
Receipts Less Expeditures	(689,589.32)	78,802.79	(450,500.00)	(796,260.00)	(1,460,320.00)	(1,993,120.00)	(1,590,060.00)
BEGINNING BALANCE 7/1/00	907,342.78	1,596,932.10	1,675,734.89	1,225,234.89	1,235,284.89	1,387,584.89	1,007,084.89
(ENDING BALANCE 6/30/00)	$1,596,932.10	$1,675,734.89	$1,225,234.89	$ 428,974.89	$ (225,035.11)	$ (605,535.11)	$ (582,975.11)
Revenue from 9.3 mills collected				806,310.00	1,612,620.00	1,612,620.00	806,310.00
Starting 1/1/89 at $173,400 per mill							
ENDING BALANCE 6/30/00							
WITH NEW MILLAGE				$1,235,284.89	$1,387,584.89	$1,007,084.89	$ 223,334.89

Courtesy of Bexley City Schools.

Figure 12-9
384

13

Getting the Most for Your Dollar

To get the most for the district's dollar, the superintendent needs to work in concert with the business manager and treasurer. Careful budgeting, close approximations of when revenues will be received and expenditures will be made, accurate recordkeeping, and thoughtful investing are all needed.

Investing

School district investments are governed by state statutes and board policy. While there is not broad flexibility in the instruments to be used in investing, there is room for creativity and initiative to maximize earnings within prescribed limits.

What to Invest When

Ideally all available funds will be earning maximum interest daily. An assertive cash management plan can realize significant additional revenues for the district. For example, in one district, when excess balances were transferred to certificates of deposit from the checking account, where they had been needlessly kept, up to 4% increases were realized.

All cash should be deposited on a daily basis. This should be done in a timely manner to earn interest for the day deposited. And all cash balances should be earning interest in some form on a daily basis. Balances earning low interest should be transferred in a timely manner to higher interest-bearing instruments. To come as close to the ideal as possible, cash flow will need to be estimated accurately and monitored continually. This is where careful budgeting can assist. By estimating cash flow, maximum funds can be invested for periods at maximum interest rates.

While striving for the ideal, it is important to acknowledge that less than ideal conditions will always exist for a variety of reasons. For example, it is generally desirable to keep an account at a local bank which may or may not give the highest available interest rate. But the goodwill and services of the local banker are needed. To illustrate, if tax anticipation warrants or notes will be needed, more than likely it will be the local banker who is called upon to deliver.

How to Invest

Legal restrictions dictate the variety of investments a district can make. There is flexibility within limits, however. When relations are developed with a banker, a bank messenger will frequently be willing to deliver certificates of deposit and other records to facilitate investing.

Following the fluctuating market can help to determine the type of investment to be made for the long and short term. Investment and other bankers will also be happy to be of assistance. To assure that you are getting objective advice, talk to more than one banker initially and monitor advice in an ongoing manner.

Shopping Around

Reading the financial statements of institutions where you plan to invest will help you know if your investment is safe. Of course, few investments are 100% safe, but states generally have guidelines for investing to assure that safety precautions are taken. Beyond what is required, the superintendent can use the same means that private investors use to assure safety to the greatest extent possible.

The type of institution may help in the determination. Savings and loan institutions generally offer a higher rate of interest than do banks, but this is not always true. It helps to have a list of institutions for which interest rates can be monitored on a regular basis, especially shortly before and at the time large sums of monies are due either from taxes, sale of bonds, or other sources.

In shopping, it is important to obtain the rate on investments of various sizes and varying lengths for which funds are to be invested. A combination of investments may result. For example, on a sale of bonds where millions are expected, it may be that one institution will give the best rate up to a certain investment period and/or for a certain dollar amount. At some point, it may pay to invest in a second or third institution if rates are higher for a longer investment period or for larger sums of money.

When districts have surpluses, banks are usually willing to put together packages that will make it desirable to leave funds in one bank rather than moving them around frequently. It can be costly to the district to wire transfer funds. Furthermore, a loss of interest may occur as a penalty for transferring funds in some cases. Having the bank work for the district can be to the advantage of both the district and the banker, since it gets the bank doing the work of the district while allowing the bank to depend on investments or other services.

Once money is invested, getting the best deal continues to be an effort as long as there are funds to be invested. There should be a tickler file to alert the investor when funds need to be reinvested. At these times, it is important to once again check the list of institutions to compare rates. Keeping a track record long term can be useful to check fluctuating rates and to avoid needless switching of funds.

Purchasing

The superintendent may recommend policy and develop procedures to guide purchasing. Figure 13-1 shows administrative procedures for purchasing. Figure 13-2 supplements these procedures with regulations for requisitioning materials and supplies. By including such procedures in policy manuals, general knowledge of the procedures can be assumed. New or forgetful employees can be referred to the procedures to assure correct procedures are followed for smooth functioning of the business office. In addition, there are some procedures which the auditor will insist be followed.

The Purchase Order and Procedures

Use of the purchase order and following clearly defined procedures are necessary for sound business management. Figure 13-3 is a sample purchase order. Companion forms to assist in the procurement of materials and supplies are shown in figures 13-4 and 13-5. Figure 13-4 is a completed requisition for office and classroom supplies ordered from a central warehouse. Figure 13-5 is a completed requisition for instructional materials to be ordered from a vendor.

Working with staff to teach them correct completion of the purchase order and holding staff accountable for adhering to the purchasing procedures will serve two purposes: 1) Receiving properly completed purchase orders will save the superintendent or business office time; and 2) holding staff accountable for correctly completing the purchase order will increase others' interest in and responsibility for budget.

To increase staff interest and responsibility, the superintendent will want to involve staff in budget preparation. Following the development of budget or appropriations, the superintendent should hold staff accountable for portions of expenditures for which the individual has responsibility; for example, the building principal will typically have several building accounts. In some districts where site-level management is practiced, principals are responsible for all budget line items charged to the individual school.

To assure that persons who share in the responsibility for purchasing have adquate information, it is important to keep them apprised on a regular basis of the status of the accounts for which they have responsibility. One way of doing this is shown in Figure 13-6. While the computer printout shown gives a variety of information, the basic purpose is to show what has been budgeted for individual budget line items, what has been encumbered and expended, and what remains unencumbered, or available to expend.

Note that differentiation was made between amounts encumbered and expended. When a purchase order is submitted, the superintendent or business office will generally encumber the amount shown as the total on the purchase order or the total plus an added amount for estimated shipping charges. However, the actual invoice frequently differs from the amount encumbered for several reasons. Such reasons may include: 1) the cost of the item may have changed; 2) one or more of the items ordered may no longer be available; 3) shipping charges may be different from estimated or they may be added to a purchase order total which did not provide for shipping charges; 4) discounts may apply or may differ from what were estimated.

Some states require the treasurer or another responsible individual to certify that funds are available at the time the purchase order is approved. The form shown in Figure 13-3 requires such a certification. Even where this is not mandated by law, it is a sound business management practice to have a person designated to check unencumbered balances and to certify that funds are available when approving each and every purchase order.

While using the purchase order consistently and correctly is one step toward sound purchasing practices, the latter assumes that purchasing procedures are also in place and are being followed consistently.

Developing Relationships

The superintendent or designee responsible for purchasing will want to develop friendly and helping relationships with staff and with vendors. The purchasing process should be viewed as a service. All district procedures are in place to facilitate the learning process. The business office exists to serve student learning. This means that the superintendent or designee in purchasing must develop working relationships with staff who are responsible for assessing needs that will facilitate teaching and learning.

There need not be a strained relationship between the individual responsible for purchasing — whether this be the superintendent or a designee — and staff in the area of budget and purchasing. If the superintendent stresses the business office as a service function, staff may interpret this as meaning that the person who fills the purchasing role should serve them or be their servant. To avoid mistaken notions, the focus should be that all in the school system are there in the interest of students' learning. It is then encumbent on staff to make clear what is needed and to act as a cheerleader in assuring that what is needed is received.

A second area where relationships can be strained is scarcity of resources that prevents a request from being granted in total. The superintendent should then discuss the individual items and amounts in question with the person submitting the purchase order or the person responsible for the budgeted amount. Unilateral assumptions about need and priorities should not be made. A basis for making such assumptions should be worked out between the superintendent or business manager and the individual submitting requests. The person submitting the request must ultimately be informed and given reasons for the rejection. It will frequently be necessary to make adjustments in teaching plans when something expected is not received.

Therefore, the person submitting the request needs to know whether or not to expect the item. Similarly, there should be opportunity for a person to make a case for an emergency and to be heard. These kinds of considerations are what we mean by developing friendly and helping relationships with staff.

In addition to relations in the school system, the superintendent and business official need to develop relationships with vendors outside the system. To receive information on new products and best price quotes, it is important for the superintendent to develop working relationships with vendors.

Relationships with vendors require openness. These should be businesslike and without strings. A well-intentioned vendor will respect that the superintendent is busy and will come well-prepared to discuss a particular request or suggestion. The superintendent can expect that the vendor will be clear and concise. Time availability will dictate the kind and amount of information to be shared.

In order to maintain vendors' interest in offering competitive quotes, it is frequently necessary to allow them a forum periodically. There are not too many persons who will stand ready to jump to the superintendent's assistance if common courtesies are not afforded in between such opportunities.

The superintendent of the small district is especially hard-pressed to find time to relate to vendors. The superintendent may be the only person responsible for the purchasing function as well as all other central office functions. In such cases, it is imperative that the superintendent's secretary be helped to assist in screening persons who will be scheduled to meet with the superintendent, in asking questions that will be helpful to the superintendent, in knowing whether or not the superintendent needs to meet with the vendor, and in being pleasant with vendors as well as being helpful in letting them know that the superintendent's time is scarce and must be used efficiently. A mutual respect and openness between the school personnel and vendors will usually suffice to assure that healthy and productive relationships can be sustained.

I would be remiss if I did not discuss the matter of vendor gifts. Whether or not there is a state law or board policy to mandate action in this regard, it is advisable never to accept gifts. I remember a well-known superintendent search consultant, Carroll Johnson, using as the guideline: "If you would not want it brought up during a town meeting, don't do it." It is frequently not easy to discern what is a gift. Some would not approve of taking gifts of money or products, but would accept outings at the country club or other intangibles. Accepting nothing is advised. Vendors will come to know your position in such matters and will respect this.

Comparing Apples and Apples

When obtaining price quotes from vendors, it is important that specifications be prepared in sufficient detail so that each bidder is clear as to the item being bid. Brand names should be specified as well as other qualities and quantities that may make a difference in bidding. It should be made clear that quotes should be submitted on the specifications and that, when a substitute is being bid, that details of the substitute item be made known by the vendor.

One area that is difficult to assess for comparisons is insurance. Frequently insurance companies will not have identical services. Generally it is advisable to have a consultant compare insurance packages; when it is clear what is needed and what is being offered for the money, a decision can then be facilitated.

Fulfilling Legal Requirements

The legislature frequently has issued mandates to guide investing and purchasing. As in other aspects of job performance, it is important that legal requirements be met.

For example, in the area of investments, the kind of investment is frequently restricted by state statutes. For instance, savings accounts, checking accounts, certificates of deposit, and treasury bills are generally accepted forms of investments for school districts. Speculative investments are generally not permitted. Dealing in commercial paper generally has restrictions which limit the amount and time of investments.

In addition to the kind of investment that is permitted, some states require that the board approve depositories on a regular basis, usually annually, while other states allow for the board to give the treasurer freedom in this regard. In addition to regular forms of investing, many states are now developing pooling arrangements. In the latter cases, district monies are deposited with a state-approved agency and monies are pooled with those of other districts.

Assuring that investments are safe is the primary concern of the legislature in placing legal requirements on investing. While formerly it was necessary for a bank or savings and loan institution to collateralize investments when monies invested exceeded the insured amount, states have in some cases relaxed this requirement. It is, therefore, imperative to monitor the financial condition of institutions where funds will be invested. State departments of education and financial institutions, themselves, may offer guidelines for checking an institution's soundness.

Having developed a relationship with a banker can be helpful in that the banker will frequently know the law and can guide investing so that the superintendent stays within the limits of the law. The banker can also monitor interest rates and advise when debt refunding is advised and how this can best be accomplished within legal limitations.

There are frequently legal requirements in the area of purchasing as well. Usually the statutes specify an amount for which a contract can be issued without publishing a legal notice inviting bids. When the contract price of some purchase is expected to exceed the amount that can be purchased without legal notice to bid being published, the process of publishing and accepting sealed, competitive bids is required.

When a legal notice is required, there are usually legal specifications regarding the publication. The superintendent should check state statutes to determine when publication of a legal notice to bid is required, contents of the notice, and the form this should take.

Legal notices are costly so just enough information to make your message known should be given. Full specifications can be available to be picked up. The notice should specify when and where specifications can be obtained. Specifications need not always be picked up in the district offices. For example, in bidding new facility construction, it may be efficient for contractors to pick up specifications at the architect's office. In doing so contractors can have technical questions pertaining to the specifications answered or obtain additional information that may be helpful in the bidding process. Time and place of the bid opening should also be published in the legal notice. There should also be a disclaimer to permit the board to reject any and all bids.

While most states require that the board accept the lowest responsible bid, this does not mean that the lowest bidder must be awarded the bid. There can be many reasons for rejecting the lowest bidder or the lowest few bidders. Since a lawsuit may result, especially when the bid is large, it is important to have a reason for rejecting low bids.

The author served in a district where a multimillion dollar construction bid was rejected. The lowest bidder had done only one school construction job and the evaluation of performance from that one district was not glowing. While the rejected bidder involved a lawyer and threatened suit, delaying construction, ultimately the contractor accepted not getting the award. In the same case, the second lowest bidder was still involved in an uncompleted project with the district; unsatisfactory performance of the first contract was used as justification for not awarding a second contract to the same bidder. The point is that refusing to award a contract to the lowest bidder cannot be arbitrary and capricious; however, a district need not be victim to less than satisfactory performance merely because a bid is low.

Frequently vendors or contractors may make errors or claim after an award that an error was made in the bidding process. For example, in a construction bid, the total of the bid may differ from the sum of its parts. A contractor may list a lower amount to get the bid and later claim that an error was made; or the contractor may later lower the amounts bid on the various parts so that the total remains the same. The superintendent may want to seek legal counsel in cases where it appears that low bids should be rejected.

There are many ways that vendors and contractors can err intentionally or unintentionally. Hence, it is common to announce the apparent low bidder when opening bids. Then the superintendent or another, such as the architect, can verify bids and the probability of the bidder completing the work before the contract is awarded.

Unless the vendor or contractor has established a record of performance in the district or area, it is good to verify with the bidder that the bid is correct and that the job can be expected to be completed or delivery made on a desired date. Of course there are legal requirements on the part of the vendor or contractor who bids, but it may save the superintendent much time and grief to do the checking himself, rather than filing suit and waiting for the vendor or contractor to deliver on promises.

The Spread Sheet

Once bids have been invited, a spread sheet listing all items bid and known bidders should be prepared. This is usually in a grid format with bidders listed vertically down the left side and items bid listed horizontally across the page in columns.

The spread sheet is usually presented as an exhibit to the board. In large bids, the board will generally want to know that an effort was expended to get a reasonable number of bidders. For example, in million or multimillion-dollar construction projects, it is reasonable to expect six to eight bona fide bidders. In small bids, just over the legal limit, two or three competitive bids are probably sufficient to assure quality at the lowest price.

Cooperative Bids

Cooperative bids were mentioned above. Many states organized cooperative bidding procedures for large scale purchases of computers in the 1970s and following. Some more progressive states have extended this practice to the purchase of gas, insurance, and many items, particularly larger and more costly items. However, the burden still generally rests with the district superintendent to initiate cooperative bidding.

Small districts may want to consider cooperative bidding. Generally board authorization is needed and vendors will need to know at the time bidding occurs who are cooperating in the bidding process. One alternative for the small district is to do cooperative bidding with a neighboring larger district. The superintendent of the larger district is usually more than willing to accommodate the needs of the smaller district. Again, board authorization and the vendors need to know this when bids are secured.

A word of caution is in order when doing cooperative bidding. When purchase orders are issued, be sure that all orders for individual districts are separate. That is, pooling of orders for various districts on a single purchase order is not recommended.

Bookkeeping

To the greatest extent possible, new technology should be utilized in performing bookkeeping functions. Duplications of effort should also be avoided.

Using Computer Hardware and Software

All districts can benefit from using the computer to keep track of investing and purchasing operations. The size of the district will probably dictate the most efficient and effective computer operation. A small district will in all probability benefit most from either a district-owned microcomputer or district time sharing on a terminal that is hooked into a remote main frame. For example, a district of approximately 1,000 students can probably have its needs met by either the microcomputer or by sharing time on another district's main frame. A large district will most likely have a main frame computer, varying in size to suit the district's needs.

The important point to note in thinking about using a computer is to be sure that software is available or can be developed readily to serve schooling needs. Horror stories abound in districts who have been convinced that a larger-than-necessary computer should be purchased or leased. Frequently maintenance or service costs on the larger computer exceed what a microcomputer would cost and the larger computer serves the district's needs no better than a microcomputer. Or the district may be sold on hardware with the promise that software is being developed, only to find out later that the developers did not have the needs of the school in mind.

Fortunately, computers have been used long enough that many states have done research on what is being used, for what purposes, and with what degree of satisfaction. Colleagues can also be a useful source of information to learn satisfaction or dissatisfaction with particular hardware or software.

Getting It Right the First Time

Anyone who has done bookkeeping need not be warned about the value of accuracy. The reality is that sloppy procedures or time pressures frequently result in errors. And errors either cause inconvenience to others in the system or result in time wasted in correcting errors or both.

Care should be taken to assure accuracy. All bookkeeping entries should be checked, and totals should be run frequently enough to catch mistakes when these can be corrected easily. A system of checks and balances should be developed to assure that a mistake is not repeated in several areas or on several reports.

The Value of Fund and Program Accounting

States have varying requirements for maintaining records of district receipts and expenditures. Within broad, general guidelines for governmental accounting, there is flexibility for naming funds to suit district needs. Figure 13-7 shows the various distinct funds used in one school district in the State of Ohio. Earlier budget illustrations were from the General Fund, one of 17 distinct funds in the district.

Generally there are some restrictions against comingling of funds, even though restrictions may differ from state to state. In addition to keeping funds distinct, there are usually restrictions in transferring funds. Therefore, the superintendent will need to get a firm grasp on what is required and permitted in a particular state.

Program accounting has grown in popularity in the past two decades. States generally have budget report forms that require some form of program accounting. However, there is generally much room for discretion on the part of individual districts in breaking out accounts. The superintendent needs to decide what information is important to have and then set up funds and function and object numbers to serve the purpose.

Minimizing Miscellaneous

The budget is generally considered a planning document. There are probably few boards, however, who do not expect close adherence to the budget as presented. In order to best predict revenues and expenditures, minimizing budget line items entitled "miscellaneous" is advised.

Periodic checks of variances between budgeted and actual amounts is one way to obtain realistic information that can be used in subsequent budgeting procedures. Also, scrutinizing the revenues and expenditures to identify the unpredicted and unlikely to reoccur is also helpful.

Hiding amounts, whether in miscellaneous or other categories, is not advised. To maintain honest and open relationships with the board, the union and various publics, the superintendent is advised to be up front and as precise as possible in budgeting. This does not preclude budgeting conservatively. That is, to allow for the unpredicted, it is advisable to budget for revenues on the low side of what are expected and to budget for expenditures on the high side.

RESOURCES

American Association of School Administrators, 1801 N. Moore St., Arlington, VA 22209-9988.

Association of School Business Officials, 1760 Reston Ave., Suite 411, Reston, VA 22090.

The Chief State School Officers provide investing and business management resources. Names and addresses are shown at the end of Chapter 8.
National School Boards Association, 1680 Duke St. , Alexandria, VA 22314.

402   PURCHASING PROCEDURES

All supplies, materials, or equipment needed by any staff member, with the exception of those items stored in central supply, shall be submitted on a general requisition form following the procedures outlined in 401, above.

A purchase order, based on the requisition, shall be developed by the central office. Usually these are sent out within the next few days. Staff members should allow at least a three week period before expecting to receive any items that need to be ordered.

Requisitions which cannot be honored due to lack of funds within the appropriation, or due to lack of funds within departmental budgets shall be returned to the building principal or central staff member.

Purchase orders shall be priced before they are issued. Orders may, however, be issued verbally when necessary and confirmed by mail.

Special Departmental Allocations

While requisitions may be submitted by any staff member at any time, there will be times when requisitions will be requested by a specific date. There are annual departmental allocations given each year, shortly after January 1, and requisitions based upon these departmental allocations are required to be in by a specific date, usually by mid March. The reasons for requiring these requisitions to be in, and the purchase orders processed, is that; first of all, we are able to get ahead of many of the other school districts across the country, and that allows us to receive priority and fewer backorders; and secondly, by ordering early in the Spring, we can usually receive about 90 percent of the departmental requests before the current school year is out. This allows individual departments to store their materials and know what they have in the way of supplies throughout the summer and not have to be concerned with shuffling cartons and cases of supplies, materials and equipment that are received during the summer.

The following departments and special areas receive specific allocations, or budgets, for their use throughout the year:

    Home Economics
    Physical Education
    Industrial Arts
    Science
    Music
    Libraries (Books & AV Software)

(continued)

CROSS REF.

| REV. NO. | I | JUNE 1984 | II | | **Bexley City Schools** |
| III | | IV | | V | | **Bexley, Ohio** |

Courtesy of Bexley City Schools.

Figure 13-1

402   PURCHASING PROCEDURES

(continued)

> Clinics
> Professional Periodicals/Books
> Audio-Visual Equipment
> Art
> Psychological
> Gifted Classes
> Learning Centers
> Tutors, Title I
> Guidance
> Speech/Language

Deliveries

In most cases, all purchase orders issued direct tht delivery of the supplies, materials, or equipment on those purchase orders to the central receiving area for the district. The goods are then checked in at that location, and forwarded to the appropriate building or staff member. Centralized receiving is advantageous in that fewer people are receiving material, it keeps many cases and cartons out of the building principal's offices, it helps to centralize the knowledge of what has been delivered, and creates less confusion at the individual building level. Receiving copies of the purchase order are sent to the treasurer's office.

Direct Purchasing

There shall be no direct purchasing by individual staff members, unless given special permission by the central office. As required by Section 5705.41, Revised Code of Ohio, no expenditure of public monies may be made until a purchase order has been prepared to cover same and the treasurer has certified thereon that monies to cover the expenditure have been appropriated or are in the process of collection.

Staff members may investigate, secure prices, discuss availability, etc., of items which they desire to request, but this information shall then be submitted to the central office on the general requisition form and follow the normal procedure in the issuing of a purchase order. Staff members may not go ahead and obligate funds of the district by purchasing directly from any source.

CROSS REF.

REV. NO.	I	JUNE 1984	II		**Bexley City Schools**
III		IV		V	**Bexley, Ohio**

Figure 13-1 (Cont'd.)

405   OUTSTANDING WARRANTS

In keeping with good business policy, any warrant outstanding for a
period of six months will not be carried as an outstanding warrant.
The treasurer will stop payment on the warrant through the bank and
cancel the expenditure on the financial records of the district.
If the payment is requested at a later date, the treasurer will issue
a new warrant.

406   REQUISITIONS

There are three basic requisitions with which each staff member should
be familiar:

1.   The office and classroom supplies requisition which has a
      detailed listing of various kinds of office and classroom
      supplies stocked in the central storage area.

2.   The art supplies requisition which has a detailed listing
      of the various kinds of art supplies needed by most
      staff members are stocked in the central storage area.

3.   A general requisition form which should be used for all
      other types of supplies or equipment needs. This would
      also include all office and classroom supplies, and art
      supplies, which are not on the detailed list as available
      in the central storage warehouse.

Any of these requisitions should be filled out on an as-needed basis
by each staff member, and signed by the principal of the building.

Requisition Procedures

Requisitions from each school shall be submitted through the building
principal to the central office. Central staff members, and those staff
members serving more than one building, shall submit their requisitions
directly to the central office. Only the white and yellow copies of
the requisitions should be sent to the central office; the pink copy
should be maintained either in the building principal's office, or
held by the central staff member.

(continued)

CROSS REF.

REV. NO.	I	JUNE 1984	II		Bexley City Schools
III		IV		V	Bexley, Ohio

Courtesy of Bexley City Schools.

Figure 13-2

<u>406</u>   <u>REQUISITIONS</u>

(continued)

On the <u>office and classroom supply requisition</u> and the <u>art supply requisition</u>, the yellow copy will be returned with the materials requested. Normally, these requisitions are filled within three days. There will be occasions when some items are temporarily out-of-stock, and out-of-stock items will be indicated on the requisition form. The requisition will be filled by the warehouse personnel except for those items temporarily out-of-stock. Items temporarily out-of-stock should then be reordered at a later time.

The <u>general requisitions</u> which are submitted to the central office will be processed, a purchase order issued, and the yellow copy returned to the building principal of central staff member to indicate that the supplies or equipment have been ordered.

<u>407</u>   <u>REPORTS TO THE BOARD OF EDUCATION</u>

Financial reports shall be submitted to the board of education monthly.

Status reports on special projects which may be in process throughout the district each year shall be submitted periodically to the board of education.

Reports of an informational nature shall be presented to the board of education from time to time.

CROSS REF.

REV. NO.	I	JUNE 1984	II		Bexley City Schools
III		IV		V	Bexley, Ohio

Figure 13-2 (Cont'd.)

BUSINESS OFFICE, BOARD OF EDUCATION

BEXLEY CITY SCHOOL DISTRICT

348 S. CASSINGHAM ROAD
COLUMBUS, OHIO 43209

PURCHASE ORDER

NO. **22115**

TO:

DATE _____

REQUISITIONED
BY _____

| DELIVER TO |

SCHOOL _____

REMARKS _____

_____

IMPORTANT: ALL SHIPMENTS MUST COME BY TRUCK OR MAIL. ALL SHIPPING CHARGES MUST BE PREPAID · WE CANNOT ACCEPT COD SHIPMENTS. **PLEASE READ CONDITIONS ON BACK.**

QUANTITY	UNIT	DESCRIPTION (INCLUDE CATALOG NO.)	UNIT PRICE	TOTAL PRICE

FOR SCHOOL USE ONLY

TI	FUND	SCC	FUNC	OBJ	SUBJECT	O. U.	I.L.	JOB	AMOUNT	CONFIRMATION	TOTAL AMOUNT PAID
										DATE P.O. ISSUED	

PURCHASER IS A NON-PROFIT EDUCATIONAL ORGANIZATION (POLITICAL SUB-DIVISION), REGISTERED FOR TAX-FREE TRANSACTIONS UNDER CHAPTER 32 OF THE INTERNAL REVENUE CODE. REGISTRATION NO. A-284087.

THIS ORDER VOID UNLESS TREASURER'S CERTIFICATE IS SIGNED

TREASURER'S CERTIFICATE

ACCT./OBJ. CODE	DEBIT	CREDIT	TOTAL

IT IS HEREBY CERTIFIED THAT THE AMOUNT (\$ _____)
REQUIRED TO MEET THE CONTRACT, AGREEMENT, OBLIGATION PAYMENT OR EXPENDITURE FOR THE ABOVE, HAS BEEN LAWFULLY APPROPRIATED OR AUTHORIZED OR DIRECTED FOR SUCH PURPOSE AND IS IN THE TREASURY OR IN PROCESS OF COLLECTION TO THE CREDIT OF THE _____ FUND FREE FROM ANY OBLIGATION OR CERTIFICATION NOW OUTSTANDING.

BOARD OF EDUCATION

BEXLEY CITY SCHOOL DISTRICT

DATED _____ _____
(TREASURER)

BY: _____
(PURCHASING AGENT)

Courtesy of Bexley City Schools.

Figure 13-3

Bexley City Schools
Office and Classroom Supplies Requisition

School **Cassingham** Teacher **Claydon** Date **Aug. 19**

DIRECTIONS: The following list of items will include most of the different types of supplies that a teacher will use during a school year. For any items not listed fill out the regular requisition (Form F-1) – giving all pertinent information – and allow three to four weeks for delivery, since they must be special orders.

DESCRIPTION	UNIT	QUAN.
DUPLICATOR SUPPLIES		
Master Units, 8½x11½	Bx 100	1
Master Units, 8½x14½	Bx 100	
Paper, White, 8½x11	Ream	
Paper, White, 8½x14	Ream	
Ditto Fluid	Gal	1
MIMEOGRAPH SUPPLIES		
Stencils (Film)	Qr 24	
Stencils, Program (Film)	Qr 24	
Paper, 8½x11, 20#		
White	Ream	1
Buff	Ream	
Pink	Ream	
Green	Ream	
Yellow	Ream	
Blue	Ream	
Paper, 8½x14, 20# White	Ream	
Ink, Black	Tube	
Correction Fluid	Btl	2
Stencil Cement	Btl	
TYPING SUPPLIES		
White Bond 8½x11	Ream	
Copysettes, 8½x11	Ream	
Carbon Paper, Black	Bx 96	1
Typewriter Cleaner	Btl	
Ribbons, Black	Each	4
Ribbons, Red & Black	Each	4
TAPE SUPPLIES		
Adding Machine, 2¼"	Roll	
Adding Machine, 3"	Roll	
Adding Machine, 4"	Roll	
FILING SUPPLIES		
File Folders, Letter, ⅓Cut	Bx 100	2
File Folders, Legal, ⅓ Cut	Bx 100	
File Pockets, Letter	Each	
File Pockets, Legal	Each	
MISCELLANEOUS		
Staplers	Each	5
Staples, Bostitch, B-8	5M	
Staples, Standard	5M	1

DESCRIPTION	UNIT	QUAN.
ENVELOPES		
Coin, 2⅞x5¼, Manila	100	
Clasp, 4⅝x6¾, Manila	100	
Clasp, 9x12, Manila	100	2
Clasp, 10x13, Manila	100	
Clasp, 11x14, Manila	100	
White, 5x7½	100	
White, 6x9	100	
White, #6¾	500	
White, #10	500	
CHALKBOARD SUPPLIES		
Chalk, White	Bx/144	1
Chalk, Yellow	Bx/144	
Erasers, Foam, Complete	Doz	
Erasers, Foam, Refills	Doz	4
Erasers, Felt	Doz	
CLASSROOM PAPERS		
White Newsprint, 9x12	Ream	1
Grade 1, Ruled 1", 9x12	Ream	1
Grade 1, Ruled ½", 10½x 8	Ream	
Grade 1, Story, 18x12	Ream	1
Grade 2, Ruled Paper	Ream	
Grade 3, Ruled Paper	Ream	
Grade 4-6, Ruled Paper	Ream	
White Ink Paper (Theme)	Ream	
Cross Section Paper, ¼"	Ream	
Cross Section Paper ½"	Ream	
Cross Section Paper 1"	Ream	
Tracing Paper 8½x11	Ream	1
Sentence Strips, Oaktag	Ream	
Chart Papers, 24x32,	Sheet	
Ruled Short Way	Pad/38	
THERMAL SUPPLIES		
Spirit Master Units 8½x11	Box/100	
Spirit Master Units 8½x14	Box/100	
Mimeo Master Units	Pkg/25	
Copy Paper 8½x11	Box/100	1
Copy Paper 8½x14	Box/100	
Transparencies, Blackline	Box/100	
Transparencies, Heavy	Box/100	

ITEMS FROM THIS COLUMN MAY BE REQUISITIONED ONLY BY THE SCHOOL SECRETARY.

DESCRIPTION	UNIT	QUAN.
INDEX CARDS		
White 3x5, Ruled	Pkg 100	
White 3x5, Plain	Pkg 100	
White 5x8, Ruled	Pkg 100	
White 5x8, Plain	Pkg 100	
White 4x6, Plain	Pkg 100	
TAPE SUPPLIES		
Scotch, Magic Mending, ½"	Roll	
Scotch, Magic Mending, ¾"	Roll	
Masking, ¾"	Roll	
Masking, 1"	Roll	
Scotch Dispensers, Plastic	Each	
PEN/PENCIL SUPPLIES		
Ballpoint Pen, Fine, Red	Doz	
Ballpoint Pen, Fine, Blue	Doz	
Felt, Fine, Red	Doz	
Felt, Fine, Blue	Doz	
Pencil, #2 W/Eraser	Doz	
Pencil Sharpeners	Each	
Kindergarten Pencils	Doz	
MISCELLANEOUS		
Paper Clips	Bx 100	
Fasteners, Paper, 1"	Bx 100	
Fasteners, Paper, ½"	Bx 100	
Legal Pads	Doz	
Rubber Bands, Asst	¼ #	
Thumb Tacks, ⅜"	Bx 100	
Notebooks, Steno	Doz	
OTHER		

Principal ....

WHITE and YELLOW copies to Central Office. PINK copy remains in Principal's Office. YELLOW copy returned with supplies

Courtesy of Bexley City Schools.

Figure 13-4

BEXLEY CITY SCHOOLS

REQUISITION

Name ___ ST. CHARLES PREPARATORY SCHOOL ___ Date ___ 10-27-87 ___

☒ High School   ☐ Maryland   ☐ Office of Superintendent   ☐ Business Office

☐ Cassingham   ☐ Montrose   ☐ Junior High   ☐ Special Services

INSTRUCTIONS: When requisitioning books, supplies, or equipment, file this form in triplicate with your principal. If approved, he will transmit the first two copies to the Central Office. Please use a separate requisition for each firm or company.

NAME OF COMPANY (Where available) AMERICAN REFERENCE P.O. BOX 1777 TOPEKA, KS 66601	FOR OFFICE USE ONLY *004029* Account No. _____ P.O. # *21369* Requisitioned By _____ School _____ Remarks _____

QUANTITY	DESCRIPTION	COST PER UNIT	EXTENDED AMOUNT
	<u>E.C.I.A. CHAPTER II, 1987-88</u>		
1 set	WORLD TODAY (7 books) #5900386	$93.25	$ 93.25
	BOOK PROCESSING @99¢ ea.	.99	6.93
1	BENJAMIN FRANKLIN AUTHOR: McMASTER, J.	9.95	9.95
	BOOK PROCESSING #0913673	.99	.99
1	CRAZY HORSE and CUSTER AUTHOR: AMBROSE, S.	13.95	13.95
	BOOK PROCESSING #0916650	.99	.99
	TOTAL (does not include shipping)		$126.06
	**THE ENCLOSED CATALOG CARD KITS AND PROCESSING FORM MUST BE ENCLOSED WITH THE ORDER TO INSURE PROPER PROCESSING OF THE CATALOG CARDS. THANKS, NANCY.	*EST FRT*	*7.00* *133.06*

Approved by _____ (Central Office)   Approved by _____ (Principal)

WHITE and YELLOW copies to Central Office, PINK copy remains in Principal's Office.

Courtesy of Bexley City Schools.

Figure 13-5

BEXLEY CITY SCHOOL DISTRICT

EFFECTIVE DATE 12/31/1987   APPROPRIATION REPORT BY OBJECT & FUNCTION   CURRENT DATE 01/22/88

FUN-SPCC	OBJ	FUNC	OBJECT-DESC	FUNCTION-DESC	APPROPRIATION BALANCE	MONTH-TO-DATE EXPENDITURE	YEAR-TO-DATE EXPENDITURE	OUTSTANDING ENCUMBRANCE	UNENCUMBERED BALANCE	PERCENT
001-0000	516	1110	SOFTWARE MAT	ELEM INSTRUC	1,745.45	0.00	117.44	0.00	1,628.01	6.728
001-0000	516	1120	SOFTWARE MAT	JR HIGH INSTR	2,138.90	228.51	337.21	0.00	1,801.69	15.765
001-0000	516	1130	SOFTWARE MAT	HIGH SCH INST	3,774.50	0.00	822.73	22.00	2,929.77	22.379
001-0000	516	1190	SOFTWARE MAT	OTHER REGULAR	20,000.00	79.00	12,810.45	6,026.68	1,152.87	94.185
001-0000	516	2120	SOFTWARE MAT	GUIDANCE SERV	0.00	0.00	0.00	0.00	0.00	0.000
			OBJECT TOTAL		27,658.85	307.51	14,087.83	6,048.68	7,522.34	72.803
001-0000	519	1190	OTHER GEN SU	OTHER REGULAR	15,500.00	211.20	1,990.15	2,735.08	10,774.77	30.485
001-0000	519	2220	OTHER GEN SU	LIBRARY SERVI	2,026.56	304.28	1,129.89	136.46	760.21	62.487
001-0000	519	2929	OTHER GEN SU	NORTH CENTRAL	1,000.00	38.75	38.75	335.50	625.75	37.425
			OBJECT TOTAL		18,526.56	554.23	3,158.79	3,207.04	12,160.73	34.360
001-0000	520	1110	TEXTBOOKS	ELEM INSTRUC	19,700.00	38.85	16,399.44	643.75	2,656.81	86.513
001-0000	520	1120	TEXTBOOKS	JR HIGH INSTR	12,000.00	0.00	1,761.45	430.92	9,807.63	18.269
001-0000	520	1130	TEXTBOOKS	HIGH SCH INST	27,149.49	625.00	18,690.15	1,140.10	7,319.24	73.041
001-0000	520	2220	TEXTBOOKS	LIBRARY SERVI	0.00	0.00	0.00	0.00	0.00	0.000
			OBJECT TOTAL		58,849.49	663.85	36,851.04	2,214.77	19,783.68	66.382
001-0000	523	1110	REBINDING TE	ELEM INSTRUC	500.00	0.00	500.00	0.00	0.00	100.000
001-0000	523	1120	REBINDING TE	JR HIGH INSTR	500.00	0.00	500.00	0.00	0.00	100.000
001-0000	523	1130	REBINDING TE	HIGH SCH INST	2,000.00	0.00	1,612.62	0.00	387.38	80.631
			OBJECT TOTAL		3,000.00	0.00	2,612.62	0.00	387.38	87.087
001-0000	524	1110	WORKBOOKS	ELEM INSTRUC	19,300.00	0.00	18,681.61	691.37	72.98-	100.378
001-0000	524	1120	WORKBOOKS	JR HIGH INSTR	10,000.00	0.00	7,637.18	0.00	2,362.82	76.371
001-0000	524	1130	WORKBOOKS	HIGH SCH INST	10,000.00	50.00	7,815.41	330.71	1,853.88	81.461
			OBJECT TOTAL		39,300.00	50.00	34,134.20	1,022.08	4,143.72	89.456
001-0000	530	2220	LIBRARY BOOK	LIBRARY SERVI	17,226.23	15.21	7,770.82	3,005.23	6,450.18	62.556
			OBJECT TOTAL		17,226.23	15.21	7,770.82	3,005.23	6,450.18	62.556
001-0000	533	2220	BOOK REBINDI	LIBRARY SERVI	1,054.00	0.00	319.76	0.00	734.24	30.337
			OBJECT TOTAL		1,054.00	0.00	319.76	0.00	734.24	30.337
001-0000	539	2220	LIBRARY SOFT	LIBRARY SERVI	7,360.00	0.00	5,799.70	685.11	875.19	88.108
			OBJECT TOTAL		7,360.00	0.00	5,799.70	685.11	875.19	88.108
001-0000	540	2120	PERIODICALS-	GUIDANCE SERV	241.09	0.00	36.86	0.00	204.23	15.288
001-0000	540	2134	PERIODICALS-	NURSE SERVICE	630.00	12.00	273.75	31.95	324.30	48.523
001-0000	540	2140	PERIODICALS-	PSYCHOL SERVI	164.80	0.00	92.78	13.95	53.27	66.706
001-0000	540	2210	PERIODICALS-	CURRICULUM IM	1,164.80	16.75	659.72	448.08	57.00	95.706
001-0000	540	2220	PERIODICALS-	LIBRARY SERVI	4,133.00	78.75	942.65	100.00	3,090.35	25.227
001-0000	540	2310	PERIODICALS-	BOARD OF EDUC	860.00	38.00	489.58	0.00	370.42	56.927
001-0000	540	2410	PERIODICALS-	SUPERINTENDEN	2,036.00	93.00	459.29	89.56	1,487.15	26.957
001-0000	540	2421	PERIODICALS-	PRINCIPAL	2,348.70	0.00	582.11	97.68	1,668.91	28.943
			OBJECT TOTAL		11,573.59	238.50	3,536.74	781.22	7,255.63	37.308
001-0000	543	2223	AV MATERIALS	A/V SERVICES	5,048.85	267.77	1,444.79	3,488.46	115.60	97.710
			OBJECT TOTAL		5,048.85	267.77	1,444.79	3,488.46	115.60	97.710
001-0000	545	2220	CASSETTES (V	LIBRARY SERVI	2,000.00	0.00	0.00	0.00	2,000.00	0.000
			OBJECT TOTAL		2,000.00	0.00	0.00	0.00	2,000.00	0.000
001-0000	570	2720	MAINT SUPPLI	CARE & UPDATE	2,000.00	0.00	0.00	0.00	2,000.00	0.000
			OBJECT TOTAL		0.00	0.00	0.00	0.00	0.00	0.000
001-0000	571	2730	LAND MAINT	CARE & UPDATE	3,494.50	0.00	2,467.59	163.07	863.84	75.280
			OBJECT TOTAL		3,494.50	0.00	2,467.59	163.07	863.84	75.280
001-0000	572	2720	CUSTODIAN SU	CARE & UPDATE	42,119.32	266.60	32,230.01	7,095.18	2,794.13	93.366
			OBJECT TOTAL		42,119.32	266.60	32,230.01	7,095.18	2,794.13	93.366
001-0000	573	2640	AV MATERIALS	PRINTING, PUB	40,000.00	0.00	12,559.85	335.00	27,105.15	32.237
001-0000	573	2740	AV MATERIALS	CARE & UPDATE	30,628.24	1,293.85	24,861.91	5,747.66	18.67	99.939
001-0000	573	2960	AV MATERIALS	DATA PROCESSI	2,500.00	0.00	911.22	147.84	1,440.94	42.362
			OBJECT TOTAL		73,128.24	1,293.85	38,332.98	6,230.50	28,564.76	60.938
001-0000	580	2750	WAREHSE-INVE	VEHICLE SERVI	600.00	0.00	30.00	0.00	570.00	5.000

Courtesy of Bexley City Schools.

Figure 13-6

ACCOUNTING SYSTEM
EXPLANATION OF FUNDS

001 General Fund

The General Fund is a set of accounts used to show all ordinary operations of a school system, generally all transactions which do not need to be accounted for in another fund.

002 Bond Retirement

The Bond Retirement Fund is that provided for the retirement of serial bonds and short-term loans. All revenue derived from general or special levies, either within or exceeding the ten-mill limitation, which is levied for debt charges on bonds or loans, shall be paid into this fund.

003 Permanent Improvement

The Permanent Improvement Fund provides for the purchase or construction of capital outlay items involving major expenditures and having an extended useful life.

006 Food Service Fund

The Food Service Fund is used to record financial transactions related to food service operations.

007 Trust Fund

The Trust Fund accounts for money and property held in trust by the school district.

014 Special Rotary Fund

The Special Rotary Fund is provided to carry out a cycle of operations. Amounts expended from this fund are restored from earnings from operations for which the fund is designed.

018 Public Support Fund

The Public Support Fund was formerly called the Principal Fund. The Public Support Fund is used to account for local revenue sources other than taxes or expendable trusts. Expenditures will be made to supplement curriculum activities and will be used to support those activities that may otherwise have been made from the General Fund (001).

Figure 13-7

019 Other Grant Fund

The Other Grant Fund accounts for proceeds of specific revenue sources, except for state and federal grants that are legally restricted to expenditures for specified purposes.

200 Student Activity Fund

The Student Activity Fund is used to account for funds for those student activity programs which have student participation in the activity and have students involved in the management of the Program.

300 District-Managed Student Activity Fund

The District-Managed Student Activity Fund consists of those programs which have student participation in the activity but do not have student management of the programs.

401 Auxiliary Service Fund

The Auxiliary Service Fund is used to account for monies which provide services and materials to pupils attending nonpublic schools within the public school district.

416 Teacher Development Fund

The Teacher Development Fund records receipts and expenditures for providing assistance to local school districts for the development of inservice programs.

422 Excellence in Education Fund

The Excellence in Education Fund provides an accounting for educational excellence for teachers and pupil development. The fund also accounts for excess lottery profits.

514 Title II

Title II Fund monies are provided for strengthening instruction in science, mathematics, foreign language, English, arts, reading, history, and industrial arts.

516 Title VI-B

Title VI-B monies are grants provided to assist states in the identification of handicapped children, development of procedural safeguards, implementation of least restrictive alternative service patterns, and provision of full educational opportunities to handicapped children at the elementary and secondary levels.

Figure 13-7 (Cont'd.)

572 Chapter I

Chapter I is a fund to record receipts and expenditures for the reading program funded by the federal government. Chapter I was formerly Title I.

573 Chapter II

Chapter II provides for selection and purchase of school library resources and other printed and published instructional materials; acquisition of laboratory and special equipment and materials to strengthen instruction in specific subject areas. Chapter II was formerly Title IV-B ESEA Fund.

Figure 13-7 (Cont'd.)

14

Working
with the Experts

Whether superintendent of a large or small district, there will no doubt be occasions when working with experts is either necessary or desirable. This section offers some pointers for getting what you want.

The Importance of Access, Timeliness, and Accuracy

No doubt there could be any number of qualities identified to discuss as important when dealing with experts. The focus here is on three such qualities: access, timeliness, and accuracy. These were selected because of the author's experiences as superintendent when one or more of these qualities were absent, and so, recognized as important and valued.

The mention of needs satisfaction leads to an important point. It is important to have experts with whom you can develop a relationship. This relationship should be one where you make known when it is imperative to get information as quickly as possible; that is, when a situation is an emergency, and when a more casual response is acceptable.

It is not unreasonable to expect a return call within minutes in emergency situations. Under normal conditions, it is reasonable to expect a return call the same or next day. Whether an emergency or not, it is important for the superintendent to make known and make clear whether immediate access is or is not demanded in the situation. Then it is important not to abuse a relationship and treat situations as emergencies when they are not. Generally, in working with a firm with a number of principals or associates, the superintendent can specify who he or she would like to service the district.

Experts understand the importance of a relationship and understand that for whatever reason, individuals can relate better to one or more persons than to others.

The importance of timeliness cannot be underestimated. Building or renovating facilities, improving grounds, processing unfair labor practices, objecting to unemployment compensation claims, meeting required deadlines for referendum or levy issues, and dismissing personnel are a few examples where timely action is critical to success. The responsibility for timely responses or action rests both with the superintendent and the expert. The superintendent must anticipate as much and as early as possible to use experts most efficiently and effectively.

For example, when there is a suspected teacher dismissal or some other serious concern, it is helpful to discuss early on with the attorney aspects of the case so that things can be done right. The attorney usually stands ready to support and defend the actions of the district, but this is a lot easier and less costly when action has been taken according to best legal interpretations.

Similarly, in using experts, when the superintendent can let the expert know early when there is a situation likely to arise when services will be needed, the expert can assist in the planning to prevent costly and time-consuming errors. The superintendent also has the responsibility for reporting situations that actually do occur as soon as possible so that timely filings and other communications can occur.

Assuming that the superintendent has acted in a timely manner, then it is important to work with an expert who is careful to take action as needed. Untimely filing of objections to unemployument compensation cases can be costly. Untimely filing of briefs in teacher dismissal and other important personnel matters can be devastating to the district. I read recently of a teacher dismissal case where the district was ordered at the appellate level to take a terminated employee back with full back pay and benefits because of an untimely filing by the attorney. Similarly in processing unfair labor practices, missing a deadline can be assumed to admit guilt.

It goes without saying that accuracy is demanded when using experts. The superintendent needs to stay alert, however, to be sure that accuracy is delivered. For one thing, the expert acts on information received from the superintendent and other sources. The superintendent needs to work with the expert to assure that information is received and interpreted correctly.

It is important to note here that it is advisable to work with an expert who is familiar with the public sector and, more specifically, with school districts. Public and private sector practice is generally very different, governed by different codes and requirements and limitations.

Personal experience lets me relate an example of the kind of tragedy that can occur when an appropriate expert has not been employed for the situation. A district had terminated its superintendent; the board had done everything right in terms of following the state statutes until a local attorney who was serving the school district brought in a so-called labor expert to advise the board. In the latter case, the private-sector attorney gave ill advice to the board that resulted in the board taking action that led to lawsuits at various levels over the next five years. Such errors are all too common when discretion in choosing and using experts is not exercised.

To the extent that the expert has worked successfully with other school districts in the state and county, accuracy is more likely. It is sometimes advisable to challenge the expert in a respectful way. You may have heard or read something or have firsthand experience with some matter that is different from what is being recommended. It is advisable to raise the difference in understanding for discussion. Even experts cannot know everything, especially as this pertains to every situation. Experts will respect your questioning.

The Importance of Experts Knowing You and Your Situation

Establishing a relationship with the expert was recommended above. The appropriateness of the expert's response or recommendation will frequently require knowledge of you as superintendent and your situation. This knowledge builds as the relationship builds.

Working with the attorney, architect, and investment banker are discussed below as examples of working with experts. The attorney, architect, and investment banker are examples of experts used here to discuss the importance of their knowledge of you as superintendent and your situation.

Working with the Attorney

The attorney, or a group of attorneys with whom you work, will get to know you very quickly. If they know you anticipate situations, they will stand ready to help you think through alternatives for action in the situation and to tell you possible legal outcomes and exposure in the various situations. If they come to know that you do not anticipate when talking through a situation or seeking advice is advisable, they may initiate suggestions and stimulate thinking on important present or emerging issues.

Either way, whether one anticipates or not, the superintendent stands to gain because of the way a trusted attorney views the superintendent as a person and his or her behavior and thinking. Similarly, when the attorney knows how the superintendent thinks and processes information, he or she will know how much detail is needed, when to ask questions for clarification, what such questions should be, when it is necessary or unnecessary to put things in writing, and what amount of detail or research on a matter is required. Saving of time and money can result when the superintendent and attorney are on the same wavelength and the superintendent is alert and anticipates situations.

Working with the Architect

Working with an architect will probably be an inevitability at some point in a superintendent's career. This may be due to reorganization of the district due to declining or increasing enrollments, building new buildings, expanding buildings, doing life safety and other health and safety modifications to buildings as deemed necessary or required by law, program changes that require space modifications, asbestos abatement, or other projects. One or more of these situations is likely to occur over time.

A professional architect can save the superintendent time, the district money, and costly mistakes. Boards are sometimes reluctant to employ the services of an architect, but this reluctance is sometimes penny-wise and pound-foolish. The architect is expected to keep current on area codes, policies, and procedures of local planning and zoning commissions and best materials and practices. Having this knowledge available when planning a construction project is invaluable.

Again, it is important for the architect to know the superintendent as a person and to know the district situation. Similarly, as you work with the architect you can detect whether you are getting the "Cadillac" or "Chevrolet" versions of a plan. In working with the architect, it is important for him or her to know your desires as far as communication and other matters.

For a project to run smoothly, a close working relationship is needed. As with the attorney, an architect who knows you and your situation will know how many questions to ask and what these should be, will know when to proceed with planning and when to hold back for verifications or guarantees, etc. Without such a relationship, there can be unnecessary delays and costly and unnecessary planning and presentations.

Working with the Investment Banker

The investment banker is a third expert you as superintendent are likely to use during your career. This may be merely for investing monies on a regular basis or it may be in selling bonds or restructuring debt. Whatever your situation, it is wise to contact a trusted banker and develop a relationship. For example, frequently districts have debt limits set by the state legislature. An investment banker can help the superintendent look at debt structures long term so that monies can be obtained as needed. This will sometimes mean selling bonds with a shorter term maturity to take advantage of lower interest rates with the intention of restructuring debt in subsequent years as the tax base in the district increases, etc.

In periods when interest rates are declining, your investment banker can be used to watch the market and suggest when it will be beneficial to the district to restructure debt to save interest charges. Since there are costs attached to restructuring debt, the banker can be relied on to judge when it will be cost effective for such action.

Weighing Advice and Counsel

To suggest that the superintendent weigh advice and counsel does not suggest distrust. Only you and your board can judge whether what is being suggested is right for the time and the situation. It goes without saying that if it is the law, there is no choice. But in most situations, there is room for flexibility of action. In such discretionary situations it is important for the superintendent and the board to realize that a recommendation has been made by the expert and the decision rests with the superintendent or board.

To be realistic, experts are offering their service to earn a profit. Some service may be more or less profitable. It is incumbent on the superintendent to assure that the most value is obtained for the least cost. This is one factor that needs to be considered when weighing advice. When should a case be settled or dropped instead of pursuing the matter at all or pursuing it at higher levels? When should alternative architect designs be pursued and how carefully should these be scrutinized to assure the maximum value has been obtained at least cost? How do we know we have obtained the lowest interest rate on bond sales or the highest interest rate on investments? To accept advice and counsel blindly, without understanding or examining this, is never advisable.

How to Work with the Attorney, Architect, and Investment Banker

As noted above, the superintendent stands to benefit from working with the attorney, architect, and investment banker. Each of these experts has valued services to provide.

Attorney Services

The attorney can assist in policy formation, interpreting state statutes in a district's everyday concerns, and in specific situations that pertain to preventing or dealing with pending litigation. Of course it is advisable to be honest at all times; it is especially recommended that the superintendent be honest when working with the attorney. There may be a reluctance to be totally forthright, especially when an error has been made or feared. But by disclosing full particulars about a situation, the superintendent can best be assured that appropriate advice will be received.

It is important that the superintendent be as knowledgeable as possible and learn to anticipate situations that may have legal implications. To the extent that these can be discussed in advance with the district's attorney, it will facilitate prudent decisions. Assuming the attorney is providing quality service, such anticipating of situations, even when suits are later filed, will usually end with victories for the district. Many suits involve personnel; it is therefore advisable to discuss with the attorney and with the person who needs to evaluate personnel, alternative courses of action that will lead to the desired result and discourage a lawsuit or promise victory in the event of suit.

Architect Services

The architect can help in planning and designing space and in suggesting alternative and best uses of space. When working with the architect, it is advisable to have broad staff and community involvement to assure that the best decisions are made. However, it is important that one person be responsible for communicating with the architect in terms of decisions and approving change orders, etc. The architect will want to design something that is aesthetically pleasing to the eye as well as what fits the purpose. Sometimes what is structurally effective needs to be sorted out from aesthetics. A quality architect will want to work with the superintendent and board in making changes that fit the district budget but will not impact on the quality of the structure. This may require looking at every aspect of the proposed construction and working with contractors to determine where modifications can be made.

Investment Banker Services

The investment banker can frequently be relied on, not only to assist in making decisions about bond sales and investments, as mentioned above, but also to help determine strategies for community promotion, to prepare presentations and materials for public relations, and to perform other services. When selecting an investment banker, it is important to know what services the banker can be relied upon to deliver.

Frequently your district attorney or fellow professionals can suggest a banker who delivers a wide variety of services. For example, in one bond sale, the author worked with an investment banker who prepared color line graphs for distribution at a community informational meeting about the bond sale. The graphs showed the effect of the bond sale on tax rates over the life of the bond. The banker also made a presentation at the meeting. He also tracked the calendar to assure that all matters pertaining to the bond sale and appearance on the ballot were performed in a timely manner.

Tasks as noted above usually require close working with the attorney and much last-minute running around to secure proper signatures, etc. In more general matters, if the banker knows what you expect in determining cash flow, when receipts are expected, and when funds are needed — all of which requires communication on a regular basis — the banker will be able to provide quality service.

15

Keeping
Buildings and Grounds
Safe, Secure,
and Eye-Appealing

Buildings

Assuring That Your Buildings Are Safe and Meet Legal Standards

Each of us would probably like to provide the best facilities that could be constructed to facilitate our educational program. Not too many have the opportunity to construct new facilities or redesign existing facilities according to an educator's or architect's dream. We usually need to settle for less. At a minimum, facilities should be safe and meet legal standards.

Working with an architect who knows local codes and has experience in receiving approval locally for designs is probably the most efficient way to assure that buildings are kept hazard-free and conform to life safety, handicapped, and other required modifications.

It is important to utilize the services of an architect who is known and trusted locally. This is so because designs usually must be submitted to a county or some other local agency to be approved prior to obtaining state or other needed approval.

Many factors will enter into estimating costs of the design; for example, whether union laborers from the county must be used on the job, etc. Such factors will enter into the estimated costs which generally need to be submitted for approval and will form the basis for a building bond referendum or another basis for funding the project.

Officials will reject the project if figures appear bloated compared to figures submitted for other projects. And the school district will be the loser if the figures are too low and will not permit getting the job done. It takes an experienced person working with local contractors to be able to guesstimate an appropriate range for a total project by square feet and type of construction or by item in remodeling work.

Once a relationship has been established with an architect, that professional will usually keep the district updated on general change requirements. State and local officials will also send information regularly on required modifications; for example, on asbestos control. Such requirements can then be turned over to the architect for his study and suggestions.

A trusted architect will always distinguish between what is required as a minimum for a safe environment to meet legal requirements and what is desirable from a structural or aesthetic point of view.

Assuring That Your Buildings Operate Efficiently and Are Secure

Efficiency in operation and security are two factors which never cease to be a concern, especially in large school districts.

Today even relatively small districts with five or six buildings can benefit from a computer-controlled operation for heating and cooling buildings. A word of caution is in order, however, to move into computer control cautiously. Many providers will make bloated claims in order to get their foot in the door in educational institutions in the area. They may believe their claims for efficiency in operation and savings in energy costs, but be unable to deliver.

The author is presently in a district where a computerized energy-saving system was installed two seasons previously. Under the agreement, no money was paid and the contractor was to recoup costs and profits out of the district's projected energy savings. To date, no money has been paid to the contractor since the system has not functioned properly. Erratic temperatures ranged on the same date from lows in the 50s to highs in the 90s in various parts of the same building and in various buildings. Now if a substantial part of the heating season has gone by where heat was substantially lower than the previous year due to malfunctioning of the new computerized system, of course there will be energy savings, but not the desired kind. Hence, it is important to check the track record of the contractor under consideration. For the district to be the leader in the local area, state, or nation in something so important as temperature control, is not recommended. Find others with close to the same type buildings and construction dates and other factors that will give you the best chance of having a successful conversion.

It is important to keep in mind that energy-saving measures which change the environment will have an impact on people in the environment, and such impacts need to be considered. For example, will lowering the light level cause halls to appear dreary? Will lowering temperature levels cause discomfort? If planned changes promise undesirable impacts and the changes are still thought to be advisable, it is important to deal with the negative side effects. For example, it may be possible to brighten up halls and other areas where light levels have been reduced by using lighter paint and colorful paintings. Having people wear warmer than normal clothing can offset the effects of a few degrees drop in temperature.

The people factor is an another important consideration in devising more efficient operations. It is important that all in the system and all users of the facility become concerned that buildings operate efficiently. If windows or doors are left open during the operation of pneumatic systems, the operation will be thrown off and will not be energy efficient. Similarly, if people play with thermostats or pneumatic controls, the system will not operate efficiently. It goes without saying, that without proper maintenance, heating and cooling systems will not operate efficiently. Yet it is not uncommon to find untrained maintenance employees and custodians left to care for sophisticated heating and cooling systems. Either hire trained contractors to provide services to the district on a regular basis or see to it that district employees receive adequate training and are held accountable for maintaining a regular schedule.

Security is a second area that affects all districts and becomes more of a problem the more buildings are used by the community and the more buildings in the district. There should be strict control of master keys and keys to the security system; those who have them should be held accountable for not giving them to others or duplicating them.

Most districts rely on some form of security system. In most cases, triggering of an alarm will automatically result in police or fire being dispatched to the district. In some cases, the alarm will need to be processed by a middleman.

All who have authorized access to the building, when it has been secured, need to be schooled in proper entry and leaving procedures. Unless there is an understandable procedure that can be followed operating within the district, there will be a needlessly large number of false alarms set off by accident. It is no exaggeration to say that police and fire departments will frown on repeated calls and may even come to ignore them. The author knows of two different cases involving police and fire departments where so many false alarms were received during a short period that each ignored subsequent calls when they should have responded. While ignoring the alarms cannot be condoned, it is understandable how departments, especially if these are small or volunteer, can get overwhelmed and annoyed by repeated and unwarranted alarms. If someone should set off an alarm in error, this should immediately be reported; generally the police will come out to check but will be more empathetic when a person calls and admits error. The person needing to make such a call and wait for police arrival will also be less prone to repeat the error.

In a large complex, it is important to have a sign-in and -out in a single location when the building is entered and exited during times when the building is secure. This way, it will be easy to tell if someone is still in the building and should be depended on to secure the facility when leaving. Another way of knowing if someone is in the building is to have an outside service that can be called immediately upon entering a secured building and before leaving. The service can then be relied on to keep track of who is in the building. Further, a running record of those entering and leaving the building can also be kept. Such a record can be helpful in planning work schedules and in other planning that may need to take into account building use and access.

Using Experts

The architect as expert has already been discussed. There are other experts who can be relied upon to assist in keeping buildings operating efficiently and secure.

Formerly, opposition from unions frequently discouraged subcontracting, but recent court cases are tolerating this practice. I am not encouraging subcontracting here as a way of doing away with unions. Rather, I am suggesting that frequently district employees are not qualified to perform the kind of sophisticated service needed. When this is so, others should be brought in either to perform the service on a regular basis or to work with district personnel to train them.

Once standards have been set for efficient operation and security, it can be determined whether experts or district personnel can best provide the service. Even when district personnel perform the needed services, it is advisable to have experts tour the facilities on a regular basis to point out emerging and existing trouble spots or other areas needing attention. The roof and heating systems are two areas that come to mind. The superintendent may also want to have tuckpointing and landscaping checked on a regular basis. If the district is in a rural area, well and septic experts should be expected to check the systems on a regular basis and to suggest and perform routine maintenance such as cleaning of the septic or filling air tanks for well systems.

Preventing Vandalism and Creating a Positive Image

Simply not allowing the results of vandalism — however small or great — to exist is the best way to prevent additional and future vandalism. Creating community pride in the schools is the best way to prevent vandalism. Having the community think positively about the schools is the best way to keep vandalism from occurring or reoccurring.

Those systems most plagued by vandalism will confirm that programs that help the community feel ownership in the school system and have pride in their schools, work to reduce or prevent vandalism. Simply by pouring money into cleanup or repair will not work. The attitude toward the schools must be converted to positive for a lasting effect.

Assuming that there is a program being built or in operation to develop pride in the schools, it is important to remove all traces of vandalism immediately or as soon as possible. This may mean a custodian working late or early hours to remove paint from bricks or other surfaces. The payoff is great.

When property is damaged, all must be on guard to attempt to spot vandals and the persons held accountable to pay for or otherwise undo the vandalism. Having an alert staff and community are two ways to discourage vandalism. When this occurs, there should be a plan where concentrated effort is expended to undo the effects of the vandalism immediately, whether this means replacing glass, repainting doors or walls or bathroom stalls, and so forth.

As a general guideline, the goal should be to have a totally litter-free environment inside and outside the school buildings. Only when every person is conscious of this can it be so. It is possible, and any number of schools can be toured and found to be totally litter-free no matter when visited.

Grounds

Access and Traffic Flow

Nothing can be more frustrating when approaching a building than not to be able to find out how to get inside. Similarly, once inside, the second most frustrating thing is to have entered into a place where it is isolated and you do not know how to proceed to your destination.

From the outside of the building, there should be a focal point so that people can easily find the entrance into the principal's office, the entrance to be used for gym activities, adult education classes, etc. This can be done, either with an architectural feature, signage, walkways, location of parking, lighting, or some other feature. With the help of an architect, the focus visitors have when approaching the building and the various destinations for various purposes can be studied for the purpose of devising a plan. This can be as elaborate or as simple as you want or as resources permit.

Approaching the facility and while inside, traffic flow should be designed for safety, to alleviate congestion, and to serve specific traffic patterns.

Whenever possible, it is advisable to have an entrance and exit into a facility with all traffic flowing one way. This flow facilitates safety and speeds traffic flow in heavily congested areas. At a minimum, there should be an entrance and exit for safety reasons, should one entrance become blocked or otherwise not be serviceable.

In districts where there is busing, traffic flow can be devised so that bus, bike, and pedestrian traffic are kept in distinct areas. This facilitates the traffic flow and keeps conditions safe. Whenever possible, a bus loading zone should be devised; buses can then line up in the same place and in the same order daily. This is especially important for smaller children who need the security of a routine. Curbs should be marked so that the bus loading zone prohibits parking or restricts this during loading hours.

Without too much effort it is usually possible to devise routes for children to enter and exit the building in ways that will not interfere with various forms of transportation and will, therefore, provide for the safety of students. Car poolers can be assigned places for dropping off and picking up students and for standing and waiting. Generally parents will cooperate with the principal who enforces such traffic procedures. Police may occasionally be needed to enforce laws concerning school dropoff and pickup areas. Bikers should have another distinct route and should be expected to walk bikes on school grounds. Bike stands or racks should be placed in areas where these can be kept in view for security reasons and in a location that is out of the way from cars and playground for safety reasons.

Special Purpose Landscaping

Most districts will have some landscaping on their grounds. Too often this is done without plan and because a well-intentioned group wants to plant or donate a tree or bulbs or some other form of landscaping.

Landscaping can serve many purposes, in addition to making grounds aesthetically pleasing. Recently, some landscaping has been designed to provide for environmental and outdoor education programs or to provide specimens for the science education programs. This special purpose in some way complements the educational program.

A second special purpose is to clearly mark certain areas, either for designating play areas for various grade levels or for various activities. Landscaping facilitates designating special purpose areas for students.

A third purpose is to provide for wind and weather shields. Various plantings can be designed for maximum heartiness and minimum care. These can provide sun shields in the warm weather while affording protection from severe weather in winter.

Using Experts

A nursery and architect are two expert services the superintendent will want to consider in designing and caring for landscaping. Whether new or existing landscaping, care needs to be exercised to protect plantings and to provide plantings that resist disease and require minimum care.

Generally the superintendent will need to consider some reconstruction of driveways or other construction. Several considerations are important. When plans are made, it is important not to encroach on the drip lines (the lines formed around the tree by the tips of the branches) of existing trees; otherwise the tree will die immediately or after a period. Similarly, if building is to be done in phases, planning will need to include present and future landscaping to avoid uprooting trees. Other considerations are the radius needed for turning vehicles and the degree of incline for ramps and driveways.

Experts may be called in to give advice to district employees or may be employed to provide one or more of a variety of services. For example, it may be less expensive to have a service to provide for fertilizing and weed treatments than it would be to purchase tractors and other expensive equipment. Or the superintendent may want to consider using a service to maintain special areas, such as soccer fields, that require special care to assure adequate playing surfaces to prevent injury and other mishaps.

Experts will know what kind of insect infestations and diseases are common to the area in general or in particular seasons or years; they can recommend treatments or perform treatments that will prevent costly damage and keep trees and shrubs healthy and aesthetically pleasing.

At times, root feeding will be recommended. Pruning and trimming are also necessary both for aesthetic reasons and to prevent shrubbery from topping out. While using the services of experts may appear costly, the alternative — loss or damage of shrubbery — can be devastating.

Preventing Vandalism and Creating a Positive Image

Maintaining well-manicured and litter-free grounds is probably the best way to create a positive image and discourage littering and vandalism. As with controlling vandalism of facilities, vandalism of grounds can be discouraged by creating a sense of community ownership and pride. When grounds are used by the park district or other community groups, it is easier to encourage community responsibility for their appearance and maintenance. Involving the community in installing playgrounds and in plantings will also increase their sense of ownership and responsibility.

Cadres of students can be organized regularly to keep the grounds litter-free. In one district, the author used the entire junior high school student body to prepare a newly planted soccer field for seeding. Rows and columns of students were formed to clear the entire field of small stones and other debris over the lunch hour. While not all situations will lend themselves to such a maneuver, the occasion is used as an example of what can be done. In another school district, the author had students choose theme colors and, with the help of the building custodian, paint trash containers with the building custodian and then place them in strategic locations around the school grounds.

As with the inside of a facility, if all participate in keeping the grounds litter-free, it is easier to maintain aesthetic surroundings. There are strategic times when extra surveillance is needed; after school and on weekends if older students tend to congregate, after athletic and other events when large numbers have congregated, and the last day of school, for example. Each district will have its own special times when more litter tends to accumulate (e.g., the last day of classes, or the day when students empty lockers); it is precisely at those times when extra maintenance attention is needed to restore grounds to perfect order as quickly as possible.

There are guidelines for mowing of the lawn to keep a well-manicured look. The lawn should be trimmed within these guidelines. Generally heavy equipment is used in the mowing; it is therefore imperative not to let the mowing get out of hand so that an extra wet period will prevent mowing at a critical time. Better to mow more often than to risk losing a lawn due to improper care.

When vandalism to grounds or to playground equipment on the grounds does occur, it is imperative to have this restored to normal as quickly as possible. If the superintendent notes that repeated damage occurs, for instance to swings, he or she may want to plan for alternatives to the existing landscaping or equipment. Unless the circumstances are extraordinary, regular and persistent repair or replacing of damaged grounds or equipment will prevent further misuse or vandalism.

RESOURCES

Resources shown at the end of Chapter 13 may be helpful for learning more about upkeep of buildings and grounds.

V

DEMONSTRATING LEADERSHIP
IN EMPLOYEE RELATIONS

16

Hiring, Retaining, and Firing Employees

Doing Things Right the First Time

The most important personnel task of the superintendent is to hire the right employees, whether he or she personally selects those who will be reommended to the Board of Education or delegates selection to one or more persons. Robert Phay stresses that the employment of the best teachers it can recruit is a legal and moral responsibility of a school board. Hence, it is the obligation of the superintendent to recruit and recommend the best. The importance of doing things right the first time cannot be overestimated. Of course, no one can predict for sure the performance of an employee for the job for which he or she has been hired. But certainly there are a number of measures which can be utilized to take away as much chance as possible in the hiring practice.

When publicizing the vacant position, be as clear as possible what qualifications are needed to fill the position. Require demonstrated quality performance in the same or similar jobs. For example, in hiring a first-year teacher, student teaching performance and demonstrated ability in organizing and other qualities can be expected. In sorting through the paper for those who have made application, narrow prospects for interviewing to those who seem to have demonstrated above average performance in job-related responsibilities, if not in the same or similar jobs.

The personal interview is an important opportunity for both the superintendent and candidate. The superintendent or designee gets to interview the prospective employee and the candidate gets to determine whether or not this is a setting where he or she can be happy and successful. It is, therefore, important for both to get maximum benefit from the interview.

This section concentrates on hiring principals and central office personnel since these are positions for which the superintendent will most likely be directly interviewing all candidates. It is advisable that the superintendent work with staff who will be supervised by the prospective employee to determine what qualities seem most desired at the time of hiring. Similarly, it is helpful to have the input of peers who will be a colleague with the prospective employee. Putting comments in perspective with the superintendent's own knowledge of the situation will yield a profile from which questions can be developed.

Figure 16-1 shows a list of categories and questions used in hiring a building principal. Figure 16-2 shows the grid that was developed upon interviewing all candidates for the position. Names have been changed to numbers to protect the privacy of candidates. Criteria for marking the grid were developed and are shown in Figure 16-3. Employees in the building and parents of students attending school in the building each separately prepared questions for a group interview of candidates. After receiving the two sets of questions, the superintendent combined the lists to prepare a limited number of questions for the group interview, designed to take 45 minutes to one hour. The list of 21 questions for the group interview is shown in Figure 16-4. Following the interviews with all finalists, the interview team rated the various candidates and discussed their reasons for the various ratings. The superintendent used the team's input as a basis for deciding a recommended candidate.

A grid process for rating candidates' strengths and weaknesses was used by search committee members during the selection process for the author's present position. Candidates were rated as excellent (+), good (/), or average (0) on seven criteria. The criteria and brief descriptors are presented below:

1. Human Relations — energy, accessibility, well-liked, front person.
2. Management Skills and Team Focus—experience, catalyst, leadership, listening skills.
3. Funding and Levies—Bexley Education Fund, expenditures, building areas and facility.
4. Strength of Character—honesty, taking a hard stand, conflict management skills.
5. Curriculum—depth, experience, innovation, practicality.
6. Special Education (K-12)—meeting individual needs and differences.
7. Credentials and National Profile.

The author has used a similar practice in hiring many building level and central office administrators. The process has always produced satisfactory results. It is important to note that while the superintendent can delegate the actual recommendation to a team of employees who will be supervised by the candidate or to a group of his or her peers, the practice is not recommended. The superintendent will be held accountable for the success and performance of the prospective employee; it is, therefore, encumbent upon the superintendent to make the decision to recommend.

While input has been received in hiring many employees, as noted above, it is important to note also that the choice of those interviewing was not always the choice to be recommended. Most recently, the author needed to recommend a new high school principal. An extensive selection and interview process had been followed with various constituent groups participating. All of the groups except department chairpersons favored two of three finalists; the department chairpersons were united in opposing the person chosen. While the superintendent recommended the nonchoice, she first met with all members of the teaching staff who had participated in the interview process: 1) to attempt to determine why there was such a difference in choices of candidate, and 2) to correct perceptions about what could be expected from a new principal. The superintendent suspected that department chairpersons were needlessly fearing some changes and how changes would be accomplished. The meeting of all staff involved in the interviewing process allowed for airing of expectations and fears and resulted in the absence of resistance to the new principal.

The above is only one of many successful practices. The superintendent needs to find a comfort level in hiring. Checking with colleagues on their practices will enable the superintendent to choose from among several practices. In addition, there are commercial ventures that have identified principal leader qualities and provide training for their development. One such enterprise is Educational Services Institute, Inc. (ESI). ESI identified characteristics of the principal as "intrapreneur." The intrapreneur principal is defined by ESI as: "A visionary educational leader who is a discretionary risk-taker and acts to innovate through the utilization of people, processes, and resources. This person has a sense of timing, coupled with the ability to persuade others to act in concert to achieve success." Characteristics of the intrapreneur are shown below:

1. Vision of what is and what can be.
2. Problem solving skills — with the ability to manipulate all of the variables.
3. Willingness to initiate and motivate.
4. Sensitivity to the internal and external environment.
5. Risk-taking.
6. Common sense.
7. Willingness to learn.
8. Power to think.

9. Dedication.
10. Has high integrity.
11. Dedicated to quality.
12. Can develop leverage.
13. Brings out productive power in others.
14. Stretches the abilities of others.
15. Can get a job done/get it done right.
16. Has need for achievement.
17. A central perceiver of opportunity.
18. Commitment to seeking opportunities.
19. Opportunity scout.
20. Ability to size up an opportunity/produce.
21. Demonstrates confidence.
22. Committed to action.
23. Does more with less.
24. Encourages team performance.
25. Is self-confident.
26. Believes success is possible.
27. Has a belief/commitment to the outcome.
28. Has a mission.
29. Energetic/single-handed.
30. Initiator.
31. Excellent communicator.
32. Discovers or invents.
33. Independent.

The above characteristics were the product of a "think tank" effort sponsored by ESI. One way to use the list in the selection process is to identify a cluster of characteristics believed to be most important in the school setting. Then identify criteria for use by any in the selection process to rate strengths and weaknesses in the various characteristics identified as important. ESI further identified four motivators of intrapreneurs that may also be transformed into questions in the selection process. The four motivators are:

1. The desire to be independent while working toward district goals.
2. The desire to be recognized for accomplishments.
3. The desire for personal recognition.
4. The pure joy of winning; making a difference in what happens in a school where students are learning.

Just as one of the criteria shown above includes getting the job done right, so too in the selection process, doing it right facilitates accomplishing district goals. Putting in time at the hiring level is critical to "selecting in" a team who can work together and who can deliver excellence in performance.

Securing Outstanding Job Applicants

If the top candidates do not already apply for jobs in your school district, you will need to work at procuring the finest in applicants. And you need not have the top salary schedule or the newest or best facilities to secure the best.

The first criterion in securing the best is to put your house in order and to make sure that what you have happening in the district will attract the best to come and to stay. Developing and maintaining a tradition of excellence in education is the best way this superintendent knows of attracting the best. Once the reputation of the school or district begins to be established, this can be touted by the superintendent and community.

Certainly the superintendent will want to make known to quality schools of education the tradition of excellence in schooling of the district. In time, the district will be on the favored list of quality schools of education where colleges and universities will send candidates or information on candidates. Getting on such a roll does not happen overnight, but the author has experienced the phenomenon in more than one district. Location will, of course, determine appeal. For some with less affluence and less desirable locations, the job is tougher but equally possible.

Recently, the author received a brochure for a teacher exchange program from a district in the southwest. This is a creative way to invite quality teachers into the district and to create understanding of the district. Limited time period exchanges and other means can be used creatively to stimulate quality and a reputation for quality. When the reputation grows so too will the interest in persons in applying for jobs in the school or district.

Asking the Right Questions

Applications and interviews can be a waste of time or can provide vitally important information. To obtain useful information that can help sort out candidates, it is important to ask the right questions. Most likely these will be different for each position or for different times, but they will also likely have commonalities.

Earlier in Figures 16-1 and 16-4 lists of questions asked of a candidate for an elementary school principal position were shown. Many of the same questions apply regardless of the school level. Yet, because of the teaching level and environment and other expectations and demands on time, many questions will differ. Using the process described above for identifying the desired qualities and developing the questions to be asked in the interview process will help assure that the right questions are developed.

It is important to note that there are also many "canned" interview processes available to supplement other aspects of the interview process. One process that the author has used for over a decade is Teacher Perceiver, developed by Selection Research Institute. There is also an Administrator Perceiver; however, many of the categories are overlapping. Since training is expensive and the administrator interview is lengthy to give and to score, the author uses many questions from the Teacher Perceiver for administrators as well as teachers. Use of the "canned" approach became popular when affirmative action became an issue in the 1970s. The Teacher Perceiver offered an "objective" approach to interviewing; that is, it was demonstrated over time that using the process produced consistent results. While the superintendent will certainly want to have a multi-faceted selection process, using standardized questions can be recommended to be included in the total process.

Listening Objectively

There is probably no area where the saying, "Beauty is in the eye of the beholder," is more true than in the employee selection process. Physical appearance, similarity in background or experience, knowing mutual friends, and other qualities can cause jaded vision when selecting an employee. It is important, therefore, to determine in advance that one will be as objective as possible in the selection process.

Having a set of questions that are asked of all candidates will provide a basis for comparing responses. It is important to listen as well for how things are said, for what is left unsaid, and for body position and other forms of nonverbal communication.

Certainly having training in interpreting responses to interview questions, such as the Teacher Perceiver, is one way to strengthen the ability to listen objectively. Having various groups involved in the selection process, as indicated earlier, is another way to assure that one's perceptions are accurate. While it may seem superfluous, it is important to caution that, when others are invited to interview prospective candidates, time be allotted for feedback. Such seemingly ordinary expectations can be overlooked in pressing times.

Keeping Desirable Staff

Once desirable staff have been hired, it is incumbent on the district to take some responsibility for keeping them. Most are familiar with the so-called "hygiene factors" and "motivators" that create either satisfaction or dissatisfaction. Factors that can cause extreme satisfaction are achievement, recognition, work itself, responsibility, advancement, and growth. Factors that can cause extreme dissatisfaction are company policy and administration, supervision, relationship with supervisor, work conditions, salary, relationship with peers, personal life, relationship with subordinates, status, and security. It is important to remember the footnote in the theory: the factors that cause dissatisfaction, if removed or changed to be positive factors, will not motivate or satisfy. To keep us humble, Peter Drucker has said, "No one knows how to *kindle*, but know how to *quench*." Mentoring programs for new employees, recognition and professional growth programs, displays of care and concern for employees are some activities that can help new staff become committed to the school district.

In addition to valuing employees and providing for their growth, it is important that a process be set in motion to assure that staff are being evaluated consistently and continually and that timely decisions concerning their retention be made.

Helping Staff Grow

Once employed, the superintendent has an obligation to provide conditions for success, conditions that will help employees grow. We are not suggesting that the district assume the individual's responsibility for growth. Rather, we affirm that individuals are successful *in context*. There are, therefore, factors that facilitate or impede success.

The author arrived in one school district where getting and keeping an outstanding principal for one of its schools had been difficult. There had been four new principals in fewer than ten years. When it came time to hire a new principal, the superintendent involved many groups to determine desirable qualifications. With each group the need for the group to make the principal successful was emphasized. Staff and the parent teacher organization were told that they needed to support the new principal and take responsibility for helping him become successful. As it happened, the frequent turnover had resulted in both staff and parents feeling that there must be something very wrong with them or the school. This was a myth that they were asked to assume responsibility for dispelling. Assuming they were normal served as a basis for being able to get outside themselves to support the new principal. The above story was related to stress the importance of success in a context or culture.

Once the employee is aboard, the superintendent should set aside more time for nurturing the new employee than would otherwise be required for successful veteran employees. Such time can be well spent to: 1) help the employee gain accurate perspectives of the community, school, and staff; 2) exchange philosophical and theoretical thoughts; 3) share short-term and long-term plans and other purposes. Being on the same wavelength with the new employee can save precious time later that might otherwise need to be spent taking corrective action.

The district's staff evaluation system should facilitate employee growth. The systems illustrated earlier in Chapter 3 assume a mutual sharing of goals and action plans by the superintendent and employee being evaluated. Employee self-appraisal is assumed to take place in determining focus areas. The superintendent's input can be in terms of overall district needs or specific building and individual needs. Helping the employee think through plans for growth can facilitate the employee's vision for performing job responsibilities.

Blanchard and Johnson, in *The One Minute Manager,* advocate One Minute Goal Setting as described in Figure 16-5. The purpose of the goal-setting is to make sure employees know what they are being held accountable for and what desired performance is. Clearly the goal process takes more than one minute, but maintaining a goal system can be done quickly and should be done continuously.

Being brief and direct when a change in specific behaviors is desired will facilitate on-the-job growth. Again Blanchard and Johnson have provided one-minute prescriptions for growth. A One Minute Praising is advocated to celebrate success and a One Minute Reprimand is prescribed to facilitate growth when improvement is needed. Details of the praising and reprimand are shown in Figures 16-6 and 16-7. In reviewing performance, we are reminded by Peter Drucker to be sure the employee *can do* the jobs for which he or she is being evaluated. Similarly the employee needs to know expected contributions — objectives, goals, standards, timetables. Then the superintendent must *enable* the employee to do the job and to hold one's self accountable for performance.

Supervising and Evaluating Staff

Growth is the principal reason for supervising and evaluating staff. Our job is to make ordinary people capable of extraordinary performance. We need to teach, help, show, explain. There are many models in use. Two means were described in Chapter 3. Any useful model assumes that the entire scope of duties to be performed will be supervised and evaluated.

Supervising implies coaching. Evaluation implies judging. Coaching and giving feedback on performance, on what has been judged can be and usually is accompanied by praising or reprimand. As shown above in Figures 16-6 and 16-7, Blanchard and Johnson have described when praising and reprimand work well. A key to praising is to catch employees doing something right. If an employee has achieved a goal or any part of a goal, praise the achievement. This process will lead to success. If the employee has the skills to achieve a goal, to do something right, but does not, give the reprimand. Then review, clarify, and agree on the goals and have the employee begin again. Drucker recommends helping employees grow, in between praising and reprimanding, by asking at least twice a year, "What are three or four things I can do to help you get the job done?" and "What are three or four things that hamper you?"

The inability or unwillingness to judge employee's effectiveness frequently inhibits nonrenewal or dismissal when this is deemed necessary. If a judgment of incompetence is made, such a judgment needs to be documented over time in specific and precise language and supported with examples.

Recommending Employment and Dismissal

Putting in the time and effort and doing the right things right in screening candidates are among the most critical tasks a superintendent can do for the success of the system. Recommendations to the board should provide a description of the qualifications of the person for the position, what position the candidate will hold, comments that speak to the strengths of the candidate, and other remarks that help the board obtain a picture of the person and the rationale for the recommendation.

Once the candidate becomes an employee, the superintendent needs to use the principles of fairness, reasonableness, and good faith to judge performance and make future renewal, nonrenewal, or dismissal recommendations. Employees have protections from unjust or arbitrary employment decisions. The superintendent needs to know the specific protections guaranteed employees in the school district and to know how to apply the processes to guarantee the protections.

The superintendent may recommend nonrenewal to release a probationary or nontenured teacher at the end of a contract period. This may require merely notice or there may be other provisions attached, such as those named in a Fair Dismissal provision of a contract as shown in the succeeding chapter.

The superintendent may recommend dismissal to terminate a tenured teacher or a nontenured teacher within the contract period. Dismissal requires procedural protection due to property interests established both by tenure statutes and employment contracts.

Because we are in a litigious society and because unions have a duty to protect, the superintendent should be prepared for a federal suit charging violation of a Fourteenth Amendment right to due process. Therefore, the superintendent needs to take care that elements of procedural due process have been afforded, including notice of charges, timelines of notice, right to a hearing, the impartiality of the school board, evidence, findings and decisions, and post-termination hearings.

While on the subject of dismissal, it should be noted here that states have begun to test for competency as a criterion for certification and recertification. Suits from teacher unions usually result. A case was recently decided in Georgia over teacher testing. The National Education Association fought the state for two years to bar the use of teacher testing as a screening device for certification. The state won but conceded to NEA to revise its subject tests, to provide a free study course for teachers who have to take the tests, and to pay study grants of $6,000 to teachers who failed the examinations in Fall, 1987, and thus lost their certification and their jobs.

There is always some probationary period during which an employer can choose not to renew employment. Once a probationary period has passed, there are usually definite cases when dismissal is allowed and only if specific procedures are followed.

In the case of teaching staff, Robert Phay writes, "The probationary teacher who does not appear to have the potential for excellence should be culled as soon as possible." Phay adds, "most nonreappointment actions should be taken in the first rather than the third year of employment."

Tenure is the bane of all school superintendents. For the past 13 years of the Gallup polls, parents have identified teacher incompetence as one of the biggest problems facing schools. Administrators, too, see tenure as a major problem to be reformed or abolished.

While, technically, tenure statutes were designed to compel procedural due process in dismissal or adverse employment actions, practically the tenure statutes have become a roadblock to dismissing employees whose performance is judged unsatisfactory. Dismissal of a tenured teacher is a rare occurrence. Tenure is considered by Joseph Beckham to be the most substantial property right conveyed to a public school employee. And the burden of proof is on the employer to provide sufficient evidence to warrant an adverse employment decision. When a tenured teacher is dismissed, certain procedural due process rights are guaranteed. Such rights are specified in the state education code.

Evidence of progressive discipline is needed in civil service dismissals. It is advisable to show such a progression even when it is not required, assuming the employee's behavior does not warrant immediate removal. Some effort at remediation is owed morally and, usually, legally.

Following Legal Mandates

States have definite requirements for disciplining and dismissing employees. Such requirements have been designed to safeguard employee rights.

Nonteaching, or classified, staff in Ohio can be disciplined or removed according to the procedures outlined in Figure 16-8.

Tenured, or continuing contract, teaching personnel in Ohio can be terminated according to the provisions shown in Figure 16-9:

Legal advice is recommended whenever the superintendent contemplates removal of a classified personnel after the probationary period or termination of tenured teachers. As soon as the attorney is alerted, timelines and steps leading to successful removal or termination can be developed. If the superintendent is going to go through the pain of removing or terminating employees, assurance that the process will ultimately be successful is warranted.

REFERENCES AND RESOURCES

Beckham, Joseph, and Perry A. Zirkel, eds., *Legal Issues in Public School Employment*. Bloomington, IN: Phi Delta Kappa, 1983.

Bennis, Warren, and Burt Nanus, *Leaders: The Strategies for Taking Charge.* New York, NY: Harper and Row, Publishers, 1985.

Blanchard, Kenneth, and Spencer Johnson, *The One Minute Manager.* New York, NY: William Morrow and Company, Inc., 1982.

Gross, James A., and Thomas R. Knight, *Public Policy and the Arbitration of Tenure Decisions.* Final Report. Ithaca, NY: School of Industrial and Labor Relations, Cornell University, 1981.

Mason, John L., *Ohio Revised Code.* Cincinnati, OH: Anderson Publishing Company, 1985.

Ohio Civil Service Laws and Rules. Cleveland, OH: Banks-Baldwin Law Publishing Company, 1974.

Peters, Thomas J., and Robert H. Waterman, Jr., *In Search of Excellence: Lessons from America's Best-Run Companies.* New York, NY: Harper and Row, Publishers, 1982.

Peters, Tom, and Nancy Austin, *A Passion for Excellence: The Leadership Difference.* New York, NY: Warner Books, 1985.

Other Resources

State statutes applicable to schools, available from the school district attorney or state departments of education.

Bexley City Schools

348 South Cassingham Road • Bexley, Ohio 43209 • Phone (614) 231-7611

Interview questions for Cassingham Principal
July, 1987

LEADERSHIP
1. Tell me about your leadership or management style.

2. How do you view your involvement in the classroom?

3. What do you see as your principal mission as principal?
   How would you accomplish your mission?

MANAGEMENT

4. (Timeliness of decisions/willingness to make unpopular
    decisions)
   You learn that a junior high school student has written a
   note to one of your fifth graders. The note is found in the
   student's desk. What would you do?

5. You have finished all your classroom assignments and a parent
   comes to you insisting that his child be transferred from the
   P.M. to the A.M. Kindergarten. What would you do?

6. The P.T.O. approaches you with the desire to have a school
   talent show which the previous principal would not permit.
   How would you respond?

7. How well organized are you? How important is organization?   Why?

8. Tell me how you would go about setting up meetings? Would
   you feel it important to be present for the meeting? What

Figure 16-1

kinds of meetings have you established? What kind of meetings have you attended that you have not established? How do you feel in terms of your commitment to different kinds of meetings?

COMMUNICATIONS

9. In what ways would you make your presence known to students? to staff? to parents?

PERSONALITY

10. Name 10 words to describe your personality. How would your peers describe you? How would your supervisors describe you?

11. Name the 5 most important qualities of a principal. Which of these are your strongest and which are your weakest qualities?

RELATIONSHIPS

12. Do you feel it is important for students to like you? Why?
Do you feel it is important for staff to like you? Why?
Do you feel it is important for parents to like you? Why?
How would you go about getting students/staff/parents to like you?

KNOWLEDGE/EXPERIENCE

13. The Cassingham School shares facilities with the Junior High and High School. What problems do you foresee with such an arrangement? How would you solve these problems?

14. What part do you feel the areas of art, music and P.E. have in elementary education? How would you go about scheduling these areas?

Figure 16-1 (Cont'd.)

15. How have you been involved in special education? What part do feel the principal should have in providing for students' special needs? How would you assure this?

16. How do you keep professionally up to date? What have you learned recently? How do you go about sharing what you learn?

MULTIPLE AREAS

17. How would you go about developing understanding of your school community? How would you judge if you had positive relations and communications with your school community? How would you develop positive relations/communications?

18. Describe a good listener for me, please. How do you know if you're doing a good job of listening.

19. What are some ways you wouuld use to be accessible to your school community?

20. What percent of your time would you spend in the classroom? How would you assure this?

21. Do you feel you are trustworthy? What basis do you have for your belief?
            Give me an example.

22. What means would you use to build positive morale in your school?

P. Conran

Figure 16-1 (Cont'd.)

Candidate evaluation matrix (hand-drawn). Symbols: + , ‡ (double plus), O , – , ? (uncertain), ⊕ (O with +).

Candidate	1. L STYLE	2. L CLASSROOM	3. L MISSION	4. M DECISION THS>5th	5. M DECISION <Kdg Assign.	6. M DECISION <PTO	7. M ORGANIZ.	8. M MTGS.	9. C PRESENCE	10. P PERSONALITY TRAITS	11. P PRINCIPAL QUALITIES	12. R LIKING	13. k/e SHARED FACILITY	14. k/e SPECIAL AREAS	15. k/e SPECIAL EDUC.	16. k/e PROF GROWTH	17. UNDERSTANDING EL + REL/COM	18. LISTENER	19. ACCESSIBILITY	20. % CLASS TIME	21. TRUST	22. + MORALE	GRADES Avg. or above	REFERENCES	WRITTEN COMMUNICATION	ORAL COMMUNICATION	KNOWLEDGE of CURRICULUM	NONVERBALS
1. AC	+	+	‡	+	+	+	O	+	+	O	O	+	O	O	‡	‡	O	O	+	+	+	+	+	‡	+	+ (FAST)	+	+
2. JS	O	O	O	–	–	–	–	–	O	O	O	–	O	O	+	O	+	O	–	+	–	O						
3. WH	+	+	‡	+	+	+	?O	+	+	+	+	?O	O	+	‡	‡	+	O	+	+	O	‡	+	+	+	+	+	+ (TWITCH)
4. SG	+	+	+	O	+	+	O	O	+	+	O	O	O	O	+	+	+	+	+	+	+	+						
5. DT	+	+	+	+	O	–	+	+	+	+	‡	O	–	O	+	+	+	O	O	+	O	+						
6. EC	?O	?O	+	+	+	+	?O	+	‡	O	+	O	O	+	+	+	‡	+	+	+	‡	+	⊕				O	
7. NK	+	+	+	+	+	O	+	O	+	‡	+	O	O	O	O	+	+	O	O	+	+	+			?	+		+ (SMILE)
8. SH	+	O	+	+	+	+	+	+	‡	‡	+	‡	O	+	+	+	‡	+	+	+	+	+			+	‡	‡	‡ (CLOSE EYES)
9. KD	+	+	+	O	+	+	O	+	‡	+	+	O	O	O	O	+	‡	+	+	O	?O	+			+	+		+
10. CB	‡	+	‡	O	+	+	+	+	‡	‡	‡	O	‡	+	+	+	+	+	+	+	+	+						
11. CO	+	+	+	+	O	+	O	+	‡	+	+	+	O	O	+	+	+	+	+	+	+	O	⊕					
12. PT																												

Figure 16-2

CRITERIA FOR EVALUATING RESPONSES
TO SUPERINTENDENT'S QUESTIONS
7/27/87

Leadership

1. Style

   + Collegial relationship: cooperative, seeks ideas and input from staff, teamwork, working together with take charge attitude, not threatened by competence of others.

   o Not clear or seeks ideas only from administrators.

   - "Drill sergeant" or laissez-faire.

2. Classroom Involvement

   + Many and varied ideas: observe what is; find ways to work with students, teach for teacher; develop with clear idea of acceptable models.

   o Some ideas for supervision, and working with students or teachers.

   - Few ideas, limited involvement, not able to distinguish roles.

3. Mission

   + See that every child, every minute of every day, has a challenging school experience and see that Board-adopted curriculum is implemented with ways to bring about.

   o Some focus on important aspects of scheduling, but not clear focus that the school is for learning.

   - No focus or inappropriate focus.

Management

4. JHS Student Note to Fifth Grader

   + Acts to make timely decisions; seeks additional information and doesn't overreact; involves appropriate persons; corrective action to help.

   o Not clear that follow-through would involve appropriate persons with intention to help and learn and lead to closure.

   - Avoids decision; overreacts and involves others prematurely or unnecessarily; punitive rather than helping attitude.

5. Classroom Assignment Change Request

   + Seeks information, recognizes problem of being arbitrary; flexible with valid reason, willing to make unpopular decisions.

   o Not clear that flexibility is for valid reason or that the principal will take charge.

Figure 16-3

    - Inflexible or unwilling to take stand or unnecessarily involves teacher.

6. Talent Show Request Prohibited by Previous Principal

    + Seeks information, approaches in problem-solving way, seeks to preserve the integrity of the school day while providing opportunities for students, willing to make unpopular decision.

    o No clear indication that preserving learning may be issue or that principal will make decision.

    - Inflexible or unwilling to take stand, no evidence that implications of proposal will be thought through.

7. Organization

    + Important, organization with flexibility allows for reaching goals and gives security to others.

    o Organized and flexible but organization seen as benefit to self only.

    - Not organized or inflexible.

8. Meetings

    + Purposeful meetings planned for benefit of participants and with their input, effort to make meetings worthwhile and enjoyable, commitment to be present.

    o Some sense of flexibility in scheduling, but no clear idea of leadership needed or plan to benefit participants.

    - Avoids meetings or schedules routinely for the sake of meeting, no clear indication that presence is viewed as important.

Communications

9. Presence Known to Students, Staff, Parents

    + MBWA with proven past experience or clear ideas for being visible and involved often and in varied arenas, importance of knowing names.

    o Some ideas and some variety of ways to be involved.

    - Few, if any, ideas or no indication that practice will support ideas.

Personality

10. Ten Words to Describe Personality: Self, Peers, Supervisor

    + Majority of descriptors viewed as important to principal role, consistency in how viewed by self, peers, supervisor.

    o Some descriptors viewed as important to principal role, personality seems inconsistent.

    - Descriptors not viewed as important to principal role.

Figure 16-3 (Cont'd.)

11. Five Most Important Principal Qualities: Strengths, Weaknesses

    + Strong character traits plus clear indication that person can implement curriculum, develop staff, and demonstrate respect for staff and develop teamwork.

    o Some important traits, but no clear indication of ability to develop teamwork or implement curriculum.

    - Qualities not viewed as important to principal role.

Relationships

12. Importance of Liking: Students, Staff, Parents

    + Clear indication that liking is important to help others have positive attitudes, importance of influence of principal on school environment.

    o Substitute respect for liking.

    - Liking not seen as important or expects others to take initiative.

Knowledge/Experience

13. Problems with Shared Facilities.

    + Problems of facilities themselves (noise, competing for space) *plus* student problems (growing up too fast, etc.), but viewed as solvable with understanding, cooperation, sharing.

    o Either facility or student problems foreseen with some ideas for avoiding or overcoming.

    - Either problems not foreseeable or no ideas for avoiding or overcoming.

14. Importance and Scheduling of Art, Music, P.E.

    + Areas seen as basic or very important. Seek input and exert leadership to schedule with focus on what is best for students.

    o Areas of importance. Input sought, but no clear idea of what to do if conflict or lack of focus on what is best for students.

    - Areas not viewed as important. Formula solutions seen as unworkable (e.g., all p.m.) or without seeking input.

15. Involvement in Special Education, Principal's Role.

    + Principal is advocate for student with clear idea of principal as important member of team, need to work with classroom teacher in understanding and serving student needs.

    o Principal as important part of team, not clear idea of advocate role or need to work with teacher and be familiar with I.E.P.

    - No knowledge or involvement.

Figure 16-3 (Cont'd.)

16. Professional Growth and Sharing

    + Many and varied ways to assure continued professional growth, evidence of recent learning and ways to share that will invite others to want to learn, also sees the problem of not getting information firsthand.

    o Some ideas, but no concrete ideas of both growth and sharing.

    - No evidence of effort as continual growth or ways of sharing that improve ideas.

Multiple Areas

17. Understanding and positive relations/communications with school community

    + Many and varied ideas to initiate contact (be positive, questions, involvement in functions, feedback).

    o Some ideas for making contact.

    - No indication person will initiate effort or few, if any, suggestions.

18. Listener

    + Clear indication that listening is to benefit speaker and this is known if speaker is encouraged to continue (many describe in terms of active listening, nonverbals).

    o Either part of question is off mark.

    - Listening is described in terms of hearing and giving back.

19. Accessibility

    + Many and varied ideas such as open door, being available for phone calls, attending events, being out and around.

Figure 16-3 (Cont'd.)

GROUP INTERVIEW QUESTIONS
FOR ELEMENTARY PRINCIPAL POSITION
July 30, 1987

1. Describe your leadership or management style.

2. What is the role of the principal with the ever-increasing demand for specialized services?

3. What basis would you use for making classroom assignments?

4. What would you do if a junior high school student destroyed Cassingham school student work on display in the hall?

5. What kinds of teacher duties do you see as necessary? How would you schedule these?

6. A committee you have appointed comes up with an idea with which you disagree. What would you do?

7. The Cassingham School has a tradition of special activities. How would you be involved in these?

8. What do you expect to see when you walk into a classroom? Suppose parents express concern because not all at a grade level are doing the same thing? How would you go about bringing change to what you viewed as inappropriate?

9. What do you look for in recommending a teacher for employment?

10. How would you help staff become better teachers?

11. What do you see as the role of parent volunteers in the school? How have you involved volunteers in the past?

12. Cassingham parents are free in voicing their opinions. What is your style of dealing with these?

13. Considering the demands on your time, how do you see yourself maintaining contact with students? How would you assure this?

14. When there is conflict between what P.T.O. wants and what the principal or staff thinks is appropriate, what would you do?

15. What are three to five things you feel are important to do your first year as principal? What are your long-range plans for Cassingham?

16. How would you handle a situation where there is conflict between a teacher recommending retention and a parent not agreeing? How would you handle a situation where there is conflict between a parent requesting retention and a teacher not agreeing?

Figure 16-4

17. Name three innovative or unique ways for dealing with students?

18. When you have a student who does not fit the curriculum of a grade level, what do you do to make the curriculum fit the child or to adapt curriculum?

19. Name the most difficult situation you have needed to handle. How did you handle it?

20. How do you discipline, reinforce, and motivate staff and students?

21. Why did you apply for this position? Why should we hire you?

Figure 16-4 Cont'd.

One Minute Goal Setting is simply:

1. Agree on your goals.

2. See what good behavior looks like.

3. Write out each of your goals on a single sheet of paper using less than 250 words.

4. Read and re-read each goal, which requires only a minute or so each time you do it.

5. Take a minute every once in a while out of your day to look at your performance, and

6. See whether or not your behavior matches your goal.

Source: Kenneth Blanchard and Spencer Johnson, *The One Minute Manager* (New York: William Morrow and Company, Inc., 1982) p. 34.

Figure 16-5

The One Minute Praising works well when you:

1. Tell people _up front_ that you are going to let them know how they are doing.

2. Praise people immediately.

3. Tell people what they did right—be specific.

4. Tell people how good you feel about what they did right, and how it helps the organization and the other people who work there.

5. Stop for a moment of silence to let them _"feel"_ how good you feel.

6. Encourage them to do more of the same.

7. Shake hands or touch people in a way that makes it clear that you support their success in the organization.

Source: Kenneth Blanchard and Spencer Johnson, _The One Minute Manager_ (New York: William Morrow and Company, Inc., 1982) p. 44.

Figure 16-6

The One Minute Reprimand works well when you:

1. Tell people <u>beforehand</u> that you are going to let them know how they are doing and in no uncertain terms.

   the first half of the reprimand:

2. Reprimand people immediately.

3. Tell people what they did wrong—be specific.

4. Tell people how you feel about what they did wrong—and in no uncertain terms.

5. Stop for a few seconds of uncomfortable silence to let them *feel* how you feel.

   the second half of the reprimand:

6. Shake hands, or touch them in a way that lets them know you are honestly on their side.

7. Remind them how much you value them.

8. Reaffirm that you think well of them but not of their performance in this situation.

9. Realize that when the reprimand is over, it's over.

Source: Kenneth Blanchard and Spencer Johnson, *The One Minute Manager* (New York: William Morrow and Company, Inc., 1982) p. 159.

Figure 16-7

123:1-31-01 General procedure

The removal, reduction, or suspension of an employee, except as otherwise provided in these rules, shall be made for one or more of the statutory reasons enumerated in Section 124.34, Ohio Revised Code. The employee shall be notified in writing on forms or those equivalent to those provided by the Director or the Personnel Board of Review of the statutory reasons for the action, and the effective date of the action. This form shall advise the employee of his right to appeal. Any such appeal shall be made in accordance with the rules of the Personnel Board of Review.

124.34 Tenure of office; reduction, suspension, and removal; appeal

The tenure of every officer or employee in the classified service of the state and the counties, civil service townships, cities, city health districts, general health districts, and city school districts thereof, holding a position under this chapter of the Revised Code, shall be during good behavior and efficient service and no such officer or employee shall be reduced in pay or position, suspended, or removed, except as provided in section 124.32 of the Revised Code, and for incompetency, inefficiency, dishonesty, drunkenness, immoral conduct, insubordination, discourteous treatment of the public, neglect of duty, violation of such sections or the rules of the director of administrative services or the commission, or any other failure of good behavior, or any other acts of misfeasance, malfeasance, or nonfeasance in office. A finding by the appropriate ethics commission, based upon a preponderance of the evidence, that the facts alleged in a complaint under section 102.06 of the Revised Code constitute a violation of Chapter 102. of the Revised Code may constitute grounds for dismissal. Failure to file a statement or falsely filing a statement required by section 102.02 of the Revised Code may also constitute grounds for dismissal.

In any case of reduction, suspension of more than three working days, or removal, the appointing authority shall furnish such employee with a copy of the order of reduction, suspension, or removal, which order shall state the reasons therefor. Such order shall be filed with the director of administrative services and state personnel board of review, or the commission, as may be appropriate.

Within ten days following the filing of such order, the employee may file an appeal, in writing, with the state personnel board of review or the commission. In the event such an appeal is filed, the board or commission shall forthwith notify the appointing authority and shall hear, or appoint a trial board to hear, such appeal within thirty days from and after its filing with the board or commission, and it may affirm, disaffirm, or modify the judgment of the appointing authority.

In cases of removal or reduction in pay for disciplinary reasons, either the appointing authority or the officer or employee may appeal from the decision of the state personnel board of review or the commission to the court of common pleas of the county in which the employee resides in accordance with the procedure provided by section 119.12 of the Revised Code.

In the case of the suspension for any period of time, or demotion, or removal of a chief of police or a chief of a fire department or any member of the police or fire department of a city or civil service township, the appointing authority shall furnish such chief or member of a department with a copy of the order of suspension, demotion, or removal, which order shall state the reasons therefor. Such order shall be filed with the municipal or civil service township civil service commission. Within ten days following the filing of such order such chief or member of a department may file an appeal, in writing, with the municipal or civil service township civil service commission. In the event such an appeal is filed, the commission shall forthwith notify the appointing authority and shall hear, or appoint a trial board to hear, such appeal within thirty days from and after its filing with the commission, and it may affirm, disaffirm, or modify the judgment of the appointing authority. An appeal on questions of law and fact may be had from the decision of the municipal or civil service township civil service commission to the court of common pleas in the county in which such city or civil service township is situated. Such appeal shall be taken within thirty days from the finding of the commission.

Figure 16-8

§ 3319.16 Termination of contract by board of education.

The contract of a teacher may not be terminated except for gross inefficiency or immorality; for willful and persistent violations of reasonable regulations of the board of education; or for other good and just cause. Before terminating any contract, the employing board shall furnish the teacher a written notice signed by its treasurer of its intention to consider the termination of his contract with full specification of the grounds for such consideration. The board shall not proceed with formal action to terminate the contract until after the tenth day after receipt of the notice by the teacher. Within ten days after receipt of the notice from the treasurer of the board, the teacher may file with the treasurer a written demand for a hearing before the board or before a referee, and the board shall set a time for the hearing which shall be within thirty days from the date of receipt of the written demand, and the treasurer shall give the teacher at least twenty days' notice in writing of the time and place of the hearing. If a referee is demanded by either the teacher or board, the treasurer shall also give twenty days' notice to the superintendent of public instruction. No hearing shall be held during the summer vacation without the teacher's consent. The hearing shall be private unless the teacher requests a public hearing. The hearing shall be conducted by a referee appointed pursuant to section 3319.161 [3319.16.1] of the Revised Code, if demanded; otherwise, it shall be conducted by a majority of the members of the board and shall be confined to the grounds given for the termination. The board shall provide for a complete stenographic record of the proceedings, a copy of the record to be furnished to the teacher. The board may suspend a teacher pending final action to terminate his contract if, in its judgment, the character of the charges warrants such action.

Both parties may be present at such hearing, be represented by counsel, require witnesses to be under oath, cross-examine witnesses, take a record of the proceedings, and require the presence of witnesses in their behalf upon subpoena to be issued by the treasurer of the board. In case of the failure of any person to comply with a subpoena, a common pleas judge of the county in which the person resides, upon application of any interested party, shall compel attendance of the person by attachment proceedings as for contempt. Any member of the board or the referee may administer oaths to witnesses. After a hearing by a referee, the referee shall file his report within ten days after the termination of the hearing. After consideration of the referee's report, the board by a majority vote may accept or reject the referee's recommendation on the termination of the teacher's contract. After a hearing by the board, the board by majority vote may enter its determination upon its minutes. Any order of termination of a contract shall state the grounds for termination. If the decision, after hearing, is against termination of the contract, the charges and the record of the hearing shall be physically expunged from the minutes, and if the teacher has suffered any loss of salary by reason of being suspended, he shall be paid his full salary for the period of such suspension.

Any teacher affected by an order of termination of contract may appeal to the court of common pleas of the county in which the school is located within thirty days after receipt of notice of the entry of such order. The appeal shall be an original action in the court and shall be commenced by the filing of a petition against the board, in which petition the facts shall be alleged upon which the teacher relies for a reversal or modification of such order of termination of contract. Upon service or waiver of summons in said appeal, the board shall immediately transmit to the clerk of said court for filing a transcript of the original papers filed with the board, a certified copy of the minutes of the board into which the termination finding was entered, and a certified transcript of all evidence adduced at the hearing or hearings before the board or a certified transcript of all evidence adduced at the hearing or hearings before the referee, whereupon the cause shall be at issue without further pleading and shall be advanced and heard without delay. The court shall examine the transcript and record of the hearing and shall hold such additional hearings as it deems advisable, at which it may consider other evidence in addition to the transcript and record.

Upon final hearing, the court shall grant or deny the relief prayed for in the petition as may be proper in accordance with the evidence adduced in the hearing. Such an action is a special proceeding within the purview of section 2505.02 of the Revised Code and either the teacher or the board may appeal therefrom.

In any court action the board may utilize the services of the prosecuting attorney or city solicitor or director of law as authorized by section 3313.35 of the Revised Code, or may employ other legal counsel.

Source: John L. Mason, *Ohio Revised Code* (Cincinnati, OH: Anderson Publishing Company, 1985).

Figure 16-9

17

Negotiating a Contract

Win-Win Versus Win-Lose and Lose-Lose Negotiations

Negotiations are by definition adversarial. There are sides: the board, or the management side, and the union side. One side has what the other side wants. The two sides have conflicting goals and aspirations. Negotiations is the contest to determine who will give and who will get. The process implies compromise, concession, and power struggles. Since the union organizer needs to create issues, negotiations will frequently be emotional and divisive.

Speaking technically, the union is an adversary of the board in the bargaining process. That is, the union and board oppose each other in giving and getting. This does not mean that the union is an enemy or that the board needs to feel it is at war. Whatever term is used to define the bargaining process, the superintendent and negotiating team need to deal with the union firmly and honestly, without being devious, deceptive, misleading, or applying overkill. Having credibility should be a goal. To achieve credibility, know what you mean; say what you mean; and mean what you say. If both sides approach the process in the same open manner, a predicted win-win attitude should result.

The superintendent needs to understand the union and deal with it. Negotiating is a game of strategy. The superintendent and the negotiating team need to learn and practice the strategies needed to win the game.

Win-win bargaining infers that both the board and union teams will come to the end of the negotiations game feeling as if they have won. Ideally management gives up as little as possible in the win-win process while making employees feel the district is a good place to work. Win-win bargaining requires being informal and patient. It requires that each practices effective communication and sees the other's point of view. Frequently it requires much more. If the union team is sophisticated and the union representative is tough, win-win bargaining can end with the board giving away the shop in language and benefits. In effect, win-win becomes win-lose.

Winning requires learning the language of the teacher and knowing the difference between what is said and what is meant. The union will attempt to exhaust and harass the board. This is particularly true if the union does not have the power to take employees out on strike.

The union will create the myth of needing a contract that will protect the employee. The board's negotiating team will need to avoid making concessions that will leave the district with a "ball and chain" contract. The key is to give a little rather than a lot. In districts known to have engaged in win-win bargaining in Illinois and Ohio, increases of 15% or greater and language that eliminates evaluation or other important management rights were conceded.

In one Illinois district, win-win bargaining was preceded by a retreat among board members, administrators, union representatives, and negotiators. The retreat theoretically provided the opportunity for each side to understand the other's point of view. In reality, it offered the union a captive audience to air all complaints and, hence, build a case for union demands. The superintendent and board need to know that the union will attempt to intimidate board members and criticize administration. These tactics are designed to gain concessions. Therefore, the superintendent, board, and administrators need to be mutually supportive. While maintaining interactive communication, the board team needs to stand together to stand strong.

Whether through a formal win-win process or merely through opportunities to air concerns, it is best to start at the table without petty concerns that should have been dealt with administratively. If such concerns come up, the superintendent should see that they are addressed and corrected. However, the negotiating team should avoid adding the addressing of petty concerns into the contract.

Prior to any form of bargaining, the superintendent can use committees to allow for free and open exchange and the addressing of concerns. And, of course, the union has the grievance procedure to deal with concerns on a formal basis in an ongoing manner. The superintendent can also find ways during the year to work with the union as a political entity. For example, the superintendent can help union leaders look good by helping the union represent the staff in matters that are not of major consequence for the board. Then the superintendent needs to let the union take the credit.

The author maintains that a win-win atmosphere can be maintained without win-win bargaining techniques as such being applied. The board team can attempt to understand what the union wants by putting themselves in the union team's shoes. Understanding implies listening, not only to what is said, but to how it is said. Applying the communication skills described in Chapter 3, knowing the persons and the process, and knowing when to hold and when to fold are crucial. It is also important to be one's self, whether flamboyant and mean or quiet and reserved.

Size of the Negotiating Team

The size of the negotiating team is mentioned in the context of win-win bargaining because size affects outcome. The smaller the teams, the more informal the process can be and less time is needed for caucus. A minimum of two will assure that what is heard is what was said. If there is concern for broad representation, a team of three to five will suffice. But since continuity is important and administrative time is costly, the smaller the team the better.

Where to Bargain

Advocates of win-win bargaining may recommend off-site bargaining as a positive. And it may be. Recently, the Whitehall District in Ohio bargained for a four-day period in a retreat environment and concluded negotiations.

However, winning requires access to information and the means to process this. For this reason, the superintendent may not want to consider off-site bargaining. Theoretically being away from the district provides a neutral site. On the down side, the team is then removed from data sources and the means to process data. One way to minimize the detractors from such an attempt is to have both teams agree on financial data and other pertinent data in advance of going off-site. Agreement on the accuracy of data and what the data mean in advance of bargaining will also facilitate bargaining on-site.

Timing

Winning is closely tied to correct timing. One aspect of timing is the manner in which concessions are made at the table. The team should avoid making concessions without thinking or deliberation. Otherwise, union negotiators will feel they should have asked for more.

When to begin is another question of timing. If the board is negotiating with more than one unit, staggering the time of negotiating is desirable. Also, the board needs to avoid starting too soon or too late.

Generally, it takes four to six weeks meeting twice per week to bring the negotiations process to closure when renegotiating a previously existing contract which has been administered with little conflict. If the teams are negotiating a contract for the first time or a contract that has been difficult to administer has been in place, a longer period will be needed to provide for education or clarification and understanding. Something to remember is that the longer the process, the more the board will give away.

Some states have labor relations boards that have defined when agreement must be reached. In such cases, the process can be backed up to a reasonable starting date allowing flexibility for vacations and other occurrences that will impede or prevent negotiations.

If the board begins the process too early, comparisons with other districts and general economic conditions may not be known. This will result in wasted time while each side waits to get a clearer picture of what is happening and what to expect. If negotiations begin too late, both sides may feel pressured to make concessions that could mean disaster for the district or permanent ill will among union members.

If the board settles too early or too late, it can mean trouble. For example, if the board reveals its bottom line too early, and other districts are coming in higher, the teachers will not want to settle. Or if the union does settle, it may later feel cheated, a loser. On the other hand, if the board holds back from its final position for too long and by too much, the teachers agitate to strike. The board needs to understand that the only real power of the employees is in their services. To demonstrate power the employees threaten to withhold services. Sometimes it is necessary for the board to let the union reach this position, but it should be acknowledged that strike is a lose-lose proposition.

In traditional bargaining, there are usually no cheerleaders for learning. Both sides may want not to offend. However, each side is usually busy defending its private interests.

It is important to bring interests out into the open and to clarify issues. For example, teachers will want reduced class size. The issue is not whether reduction in class size will improve student achievement, since the claim that it will is debatable. Rather, the issue is whether use of district monies to reduce class size is the best use of those monies. Therefore, the issue is solely the teacher's self-interest. Many other teacher self-interest items are couched in professed teacher concerns for students or the integrity and professionalism of teachers. If you know this and teachers know you know, playing the negotiations game is easier.

It goes without saying that to achieve any kind of win, the confidentiality of the board's position must be maintained. This includes both strategy and tactics. Certainly accurate communication is needed to win. Hearing it right and getting it down right are important. For this reason, one member should take notes in the bargaining sessions. Another aspect of winning is for individuals to feel that they and their concerns have been taken seriously and treated with respect, even if demands appear ludicrous.

Red Flag Words

There are terms that can cause serious problems for management when they get written into contract language. I use the term "fed flag words" to refer to contract language that can spell disaster for the district.

Just Cause

State statutes will probably use the term "just cause" in the section dealing with tenure, or continuing contracts. The union may be advocating strenuously for just cause for just about anything adversely affecting employment. Arbitrators agree that just cause requires the following: 1) adequate warning of the consequences of conduct, 2) a reasonable relation of management's rule or order to efficient and safe operations, 3) investigation prior to administering discipline, 4) a fair and objective investigation, 5) substantial evidence or proof of guilt produced by the investigation, 6) application of the rules, orders, and penalties evenhandedly and without discrimination, and 7) a reasonable relation between the penalty and the seriousness of the offense and the past record. The union may want to have just cause apply even to probationary employees. Management would need to exercise great care, then, to assure that all procedures were strictly followed. In addition to nonrenewal for just cause, the union will advocate having just cause discipline. Recent court decisions have not upheld the requirement that discipline be for just cause.

Fair Dismissal

It would seem that the union is concerned with employees being dismissed fairly with the term fair dismissal. When the term is used, it applies to nonrenewal of limited contract teachers, rather than dismissal of tenured, or continuing contract, teachers. Hence, the effort is to impose standards on nonrenewal that do not normally appear in state statutes. If the term is put into contract language, it should be defined very clearly, recognizing the significance of each word in the language, with differing conditions applying to differing periods of employment.

Fair Share Fee

The fair share or agency shop provision requires that all employees pay union dues. This provision is presently being tested in the supreme court as a violation of employee rights. The union claim is that all employees benefit from union activity on behalf of union employees. The union will attempt to equate the fair share with the total annual dues. In some cases a percent less than 100% has been designated to allow for some portion being allocated for political activity that does not directly benefit the employees. Even when a percent of the total has been identified, this has been contested by employees who feel that fair share violates their constitutional rights.

Other red flags are signaled, not so much by specific terms, but by the lack of specificity of the language. Examples of union demands follow:

1) Notify for personal leave "as far in advance as possible"; that is, there is not a definite time period for application specified. Or the union may wish to have use of personal leave unqualified, rather than giving a reason or assuring that it is for business that cannot be conducted outside the school day. Also, the union may wish to have personal leave unrestricted, rather than assuring that it cannot extend vacations.

2) Expand benefits without a cap. For example, the union may demand that the board pay Medicare employee contributions. Other samples of recent demands are paid lunch periods or day care.

3) Leave grievance undefined, merely the expression of a concern, rather than reducing the concern to writing and naming the specific section or clause claimed to be violated, misinterpreted, or misapplied. In the processing of grievances, the union will want the board to pay for grievance arbitration or will want the costs divided rather than having the loser pay. The union will also resist having restrictions placed on the arbitrator who hears the grievance, regarding substituting his or her own opinion for that of the evaluator or making determinations outside the terms of the contract.

4) Use seniority, rather than the best interest of the district, to determine how job vacancies will be filled. The union may also demand that reassignments be by mutual agreement with the staff member.

5) Specify hours as consecutive. This problem can be compounded if minimum days are specified. For example, bus drivers usually work split shifts. If hours are specified as consecutive and a minimum day is defined as four hours, the resulting problem is obvious.

6) Require that a custodian be present when any group meets.

7) Strive for binding *interest* arbitration by having an arbitrator conduct a hearing on unresolved contract issues during negotiations and having the arbitrator's decision be final and binding.

8) Strive for unlimited days or unlimited use of days provided for union activity.

9) Specify time limits that are the maximum advantage for employees and maximum disadvantage to the employer. For example, the union may specify that a grievant has up to 90 working days to file a grievance; working day may be further defined as days when school is in session. It is easy to see how distant the grievance can be from the alleged grievable act.

10) Demand a seat on the school board! The most recent negotiations with teachers in which the author was engaged included this demand.

11) Restrict reduction in force to make it difficult, if not impossible, for a board to make reductions. For example, the union may not agree that financial reasons can be used to reduce staff.

12) Eliminate evaluation or demand the inclusion of evaluation procedures that make it difficult or impossible to nonrenew teachers. This can be done by severely restricting observation dates, by requiring advance notice of a certain time period, by requiring minimum numbers of visits or length of visits, by requiring post-observation conferences, and by defining a remediation process and time period. The union will also attempt to limit the evaluation of a teacher solely to what was observed during a formal, scheduled observation.

13) Assert the right to academic freedom without limit. The result is that employees could do their own thing without consequence, regardless of the negative consequences on student learning or the work environment.

14) Prohibit public criticism. Taken to the extreme, this could prohibit the board from stating reasons for termination of an employee at a board meeting.

15) Access personnel records or have other services on demand. To avoid problems which would result from "demand" services, specify the conditions under which services will be provided. Such conditions might name the person to deliver the service, that the request be in writing, that an appointment be made, and that hours are limited, at a minimum, to the normal work day. The union may also make unlawful demands, such as those contrary to mandates of freedom of information acts.

To avoid many of the pitfalls indicated by the above demands, do not work off the union language. Have the board attorney or other negotiator skilled in formulating language prepare the language from which the teams will work. Working from the union language can be a problem for various reasons. In addition to the red flag words that the union will include in its demands, as noted above, there may be sections in the existing contract that can be overlooked unless the board works from the existing contract.

In contract formation, brevity is the rule. Every concession to the union, or right conferred on the employee, is a corresponding duty imposed on the employer. The longer the contract or section of the contract, the more duties are imposed on the employer, or the more limitations on management. Also, the longer the contract or section of the contract, the greater is the possibility for disagreement over meaning and application of terms. Be specific, concise, and precise. Achieving the latter is one reason for working from the board's language or counterproposal. The board's language may satisfy the real concern without the excess union language.

New Laws and Collective Bargaining

The trend in the last decade has been toward state-mandated collective bargaining bills. Such comprehensive bargaining bills usually contain wording similar to the following: "All matters pertaining to wages, hours, or terms and other conditions of employment and the continuation, modification, or deletion of an existing provision of a collective bargaining agreement are subject to collective bargaining between the public employer and the exclusive representative, except as otherwise specified."

For mandatory subjects of bargaining in Ohio, the parties to an agreement must: 1) bargain upon request; 2) are ordinarily forbidden to act unilaterally, unless the parties have reached ultimate impasse, because unilateral action undermines the status of the majority bargaining representative; and 3) are prohibited from entering into separate agreements with individual employees.

Ohio's comprehensive bargaining bill further defines what the duty to bargain means. To bargain collectively means to perform the mutual obligation of the public employer, by its representatives, and the representatives of its employees, to negotiate in good faith at reasonable times and places with respect to subjects noted above with the intention of reaching an agreement, or to resolve questions arising under the agreement. The duty includes executing a written contract incorporating the terms of any agreement reached. The obligation to bargain collectively does not mean that either party is compelled to agree to a proposal nor does it require the making of a concession.

In addition to mandated subjects of bargaining, comprehensive bargaining bills usually require that subjects reserved to the management and direction of the governmental unit must be bargained when these affect wages, hours, terms, and conditions of employment, and the continuation, modification, or deletion of an existing provision of a collective bargaining agreement. That is, the *effects* must be bargained.

There are, in addition to the scope of bargaining mandated, permissive subjects of bargaining. For example, in Ohio a public employer need not but may include in the collective bargaining agreement:

1) Matters of inherent managerial policy, standards of services, overall budget, utilization of technology, and organizational structure.

2) The direction, supervision, evaluation, or hiring of employees.

3) Maintaining and improving the efficiency and effectiveness of governmental operations.

4) Determining the overall methods, process, means, or personnel by which governmental operations are to be conducted.

5) Suspending, disciplining, demoting, discharging for just cause, laying off, transferring, assigning, scheduling, promoting, or retaining employees.

6) Determining the adequacy of the work force.

7) Determining the overall mission of the employer as a unit of government.

8) Effectively managing the work force.

9) Taking actions to carry out the mission of the public employer as a governmental unit.

The National Labor Relations Board has ruled that either party may lawfully refuse to bargain permissive subjects. Similarly, neither party may condition bargaining on the inclusion of permissive subjects. However, the language defining the scope of bargaining in a particular comprehensive bargaining bill may dictate that a permissive subject of bargaining is converted to a mandatory subject of bargaining once it is included in the agreement. The latter applies in Ohio. The superintendent should be prepared for the union to want to bargain everything and to assert that anything affects wages, hours, terms, and conditions of employment.

There may also be subjects of bargaining that are prohibited. For example, in Ohio the conduct and grading of civil service examinations, the rating of candidates, the establishment of eligible lists from the examinations, and the original appointments from the eligible lists are not appropriate subjects for collective bargaining. Clearly the scope of prohibited subjects is narrow.

In some cases, state law will provide for the negotiated agreement to supersede the law. For example, in Ohio an agreement between a public employer and an exclusive representative entered into according to provisions of Ohio's Revised Code governs wages, hours, and terms and conditions of public employment covered by the agreement. If the agreement provides for final and binding arbitration of grievances, public employers, employees, and employee organizations are subject solely to that grievance procedure. In such cases, the state personnel board of review or civil service commissions have no jurisdiction to receive and determine appeals relating to matters that were the subject of a final and binding grievance procedure. That is, the agreement may supersede applicable state or local laws or ordinances pertaining to the wages, hours, and terms and conditions of employment for public employees.

All of the above dictates that the superintendent provide leadership and direction to the negotiating team in writing and when agreeing to contract language. To provide leadership and direction, the superintendent needs to keep continually updated on legal mandates and bargaining practices. State school boards associations and other groups regularly sponsor workshops for negotiations updates.

Even more of a problem than *what* is bargained is the composition of the unit. Recently the push has been for wall-to-wall bargaining. With the decline in numbers of teachers, for example, NEA (the National Education Association) has been exerting pressure for wall-to-wall bargaining units. This means that *all* in the district are covered by the same contract. The result is that the district is ruled by the desire of the employee union.

Some of the problems and questions that arise with wall-to-wall bargaining are illustrated below:

1) *Salary problems between cohorts.* Aides are generally paid less than custodians, but they think they are teachers. Secretaries want to get paid more than custodians.

2) *What is full time?* Bus drivers usually have split shifts with fewer hours than other full-time employees.

3) *When do benefits apply?* How many hours are required to be worked to be eligible for benefits? How is overtime compensated? Will benefits be retroactive?

4) *Who gets what raises?* Hourly and salaried employees generally get different raises.

5) *How is seniority decided?* How will promotions and layoffs be decided? Seniority should be within a cohort. Will reductions be decided by percent of time worked?

6) *Will subcontracting be permitted?* The concept of subcontracting may be more acceptable to one cohort than to others.

7) *Will the expiration date be uniform?* If the same date, power issues arise. If different dates, there are different impasse guidelines to be followed. Also, noncertified staff may be on a calendar year for bargaining; whereas, the certified staff may be on a school year.

8) *Who will represent employees?* If the teacher union is the representative, the district can look forward to the same kind of bargaining as the teacher organization. Also, teacher contract language will be included in noncertified proposals.

9) *How will employees be disciplined?* Will there be progressive discipline for all employees? Will there be probationary periods?

10) *What will the grievance procedure be?* How will the days be defined? Will there be binding arbitration? Will this be in conflict with grievance forums for noncertified employees?

11) *What will happen in a strike?* Will all employees honor a strike called by one cohort? Can replacements be hired on a temporary or permanent basis?

12) *What about issues of comparable worth?* The issue of comparable worth will be raised, but superintendents are urged not to grant this.

The above examples are cited to give the superintendent some idea of the variety and number of concerns that need to be thought through when employees demand that the entire work force be a unit or when cohorts join to form new units in nontraditional configurations. The problems of wall-to-wall bargaining become magnified when issues of past practice arise.

Wall-to-wall bargaining may bring additional problems if the representative for the teacher group is not trusted by nonteaching personnel. That is, the nonteaching groups may feel like stepchildren. The nonteaching group will not understand the process, and much of the process may occur in sidebars without input from the employee representatives. Also, an offer acceptable to the nonteaching employee representatives may be turned down by the negotiator for the professional group. There are no easy answers. Since laws allow virtually any configuration of a unit desired by employees, there may be increased demand for wall-to-wall bargaining.

Resource or Firing Line

The question of who will negotiate requires serious consideration and careful study of one's own situation. The negotiations process takes time and requires specific skills, the presence or absence of which severely impact the negotiations process.

Ordinarily it is not recommended to have either the superintendent or board members at the table, on the firing line. But the author has successfully negotiated with a board member experienced in labor negotiations. At the table the superintendent served both teams as a resource while the board member was on the firing line. It was possible in the example for the board member and the superintendent to work as a team. With careful preparation of what was possible to give away and trade off, the board member took the lead, allowing for the superintendent to state implications for practice of various items being discussed.

Reasons why the superintendent may *want* to be on the firing line include: 1) The superintendent is known by and trusted by the teachers; 2) teachers are not militant; 3) teachers are not using the services of a professional negotiator; and 4) contract is policy. Reasons why the superintendent may *not want* to be on the firing line include: 1) The superintendent or teachers have an axe to grind; 2) the teachers are using the services of a professional negotiator; 3) the negotiations process is time consuming and detracts from other administrative functions. Board members should consider the above reasons when deciding whether or not to be on the firing line. In addition, the board member will need to have an appropriate personality and will have difficulty not ratifying a contract that he or she negotiated. Whether directly involved or not, the superintendent needs to provide leadership and direction to the board and negotiating team.

Rather than arbitrarily deciding whether you should or should not be directly involved at the bargaining table, consider the following:

1) The negotiators should know what they are doing. They should know the consequences of what is given away in the negotiations process and the consequences of the contract language. Your state unit of the National School Boards Association and other workshop presenters offer in-depth preparation in negotiating. This training should include a clear understanding of contract language and its importance. The negotiators also need knowledge of administrative practices. The superintendent should be knowledgeable about the negotiations process and should assure that the board and other team members become knowledgeable and skilled in the negotiations process.

2) The negotiators must have authority. The negotiators must know the issues and be able to negotiate them without referring every one back to the board. Aside from such a practice being annoying and a waste of time, the board may get charged with an unfair labor practice. All on the negotiations team must be informed of the board's positions and priorities and limits to the team's authority.

3) The negotiators must know the board's bottom line position in money matters and language proposals. Within the actual dollar limit and the concept

covered by the language, the negotiators need freedom to make concessions, and the board must be willing to stick by bottom lines. If the negotiators are bargaining with bottom-line figures or language in mind and the board changes these when a strike is threatened, the process and board are discredited.

4) The negotiators must be flexible. Agree to procedures that appear to be fair and workable to both sides. Be willing to adjust procedures if they are not working. For example, short-term agreements regarding hours and meetings will probably work best to give flexibility and freedom to change these.

Staying Professional

Whatever occurs during the negotiations process, it is incumbent on the superintendent to remain professional. Stick to the facts. Communicate the district's position and how it will handle the strike. That is, will the schools be open or closed? Will regular programs be maintained? Will there be one-to-one replacements for strikers? Will there be security? Will attending school be dangerous? Will grades on school work done during the strike count?

Answers to all of these questions can raise or lower the anxiety level of community members. Preparation for business as usual will also dampen enthusiasm for a strike. The superintendent needs to communicate that he or she is in charge and in control of the situation.

Tactics that try to split the board and undermine confidence in the board should be expected. Such tactics will be used to get a reaction, to put the board on the defensive. It is important that the superintendent study union tactics, help board members and administrators understand these, and be prepared to respond firmly but professionally. Tactics and the need to respond professionally become exaggerated during a strike, or job action.

In the event of a strike threat or strike, the superintendent will need to hold daily meetings with management and confidential staff to keep them informed, to relate procedures and expectations, and to reinforce their behaviors and boost morale. Staff who have remained on the job will also need to be supported.

Though it would seem obvious that one should not get emotionally involved when unprofessional union tactics are employed, frequently administrators and board members do become extremely upset with teacher behaviors during a difficult negotiations process or threatened job action, or strike. For example, if students are told that grades administered during a strike will not count or that it is dangerous to come to school, the community and, in turn, board and administrators tend to get upset and angry. The superintendent needs to view the process dispassionately and to help other administrators and board members do likewise. Understanding the needs of both management and labor will help.

What to Negotiate

Assume for purposes of bargaining in good faith — or to avoid the accusation of arguing in bad faith — that everything is negotiable. While teachers will want to claim this, the district's position in bargaining can be a firm and consistent, "No," for those items which the board and management want to and are permitted to reserve as policy or management issues. As noted above, many states have passed comprehensive collective bargaining legislation that defines issues that must and may be bargained by employers. Teachers will want to interpret every decision or action as impacting upon the conditions in which employees work.

Disregarding the unknowns that teachers may demand to bargain, there are features that are common to most contracts:

The Contract

The Table of Contents of a contract will most likely appear fairly uniform. Teachers follow the union parent organization's (e.g., NEA) master contract as a wish list. Alternatively, teachers will pick and choose from a variety of local district contracts, most of which reflect the influence of the union's parent organization master contract.

While contract contents may appear similar, there are vast differences in language. Following is a sampling of clauses from an existing contract between an IEA/NEA local district union and the board. The language was written by the district administration with expert assistance from Anthony G. Scariano, a principal in the Chicago firm of Scariano, Kula, Ellch, and Himes. Included with each excerpt is an analysis of pitfalls, undesirable language that either found its way into the contract or was successfully kept out.

Article I — Recognition

Who is in and who is out needs to be defined precisely. Statutes may define who should be included in the bargaining unit. Those categories of employees needing special attention include: full-time, part-time, substitute, regularly employed, and employees who have been paid off the salary schedule. Figure 17-1 shows a recognition clause.

Article II — Employment Conditions

School Calendar, Planning Time, Professional Staff Work Schedule, Personnel File Review, Parent Complaints, and Employee Discipline are topics covered in Figure 17-2.

The school calendar language should specify the number of days teachers will work, not only the number of calendar days that are student attendance days. The district may wish to consult with the union in the construction of the calendar, but the board will want to reserve decision-making authority for itself. The board will also want to reserve the right to decide the need for work and compensation outside of the specified teacher work days.

When planning time is included in the contract, the board will want to retain as much flexibilty as possible. For example, if teachers are provided a minimum of five duty-free planning periods per week, the district is not committed to one each day or to periods of equal length. The more specific, the less flexibility there is for administration of the program and the more costly for the district.

In discussing the professional staff work schedule, the board will want to specify a time period before and after the first bell and dismissal, when teachers are expected to be at the place of their first assignment. In addition, the board will want to gain as much flexibility as possible for the administration to expect teacher participation in outside-of-school events such as staffings, open houses, building and district meetings, etc.

The wording for personnel file review should be such to prevent demand appearances by staff requesting immediate review at any time.

In the area of parent complaints, regular channels of movement from teacher to principal to superintendent to board is assumed. If this has not been the practice, such channeling is recommended.

The wording for employee discipline should be such to avoid having the union present at every conversation between the employee and supervisor. Discipline has been defined in the example for areas not covered by law.

Article III — Association Rights

It is common sense that it is desirable to have a short clause for association rights and a lengthy clause for management rights. Figure 17-3 shows a clause with rather tight language.

Article IV — Grievance

The Grievance and Management Rights clauses are considered by Myron Lieberman and other experts in the field of collective bargaining to be the two clauses that management wants because they are restrictive of union power. A sample grievance clause is shown in Figure 17-4.

Note that the definition calls for the grievance to be written and to refer to specific provisions of the contract. Note also that the individual's right to file or not file a grievance and his or her desire for representation are protected. Only at the level of arbitration does the union have the sole right to file. And at this level it is believed to be advantageous to the board to limit filing to the union to prevent frivolous charges.

The statutes in Illinois require binding arbitration. The pros and cons of binding arbitration can be debated. In states with comprehensive bargaining bills and labor relations boards, it is generally considered advantageous from a management perspective for an arbitrator, rather than the labor relations board, to handle grievances.

The procedure should specify who will bear the cost of arbitration, should limit the power of the arbitrator, and should limit the forums for action to one.

Article V — Wages and Benefits

In the areas of wages and benefits, the area of benefits needs to receive much more attention than it has in the past. From their inception as a fringe, benefits have grown from approximately 5% to 20% or more of stated compensation. Figure 17-5 is a sample wages and benefits clause.

When the board provides life, health, dental, and other insurance coverages, having employees pay for part of the coverage will cause employees who may already be covered by a spouse's insurance to rethink the need. Stating the board's share as a flat dollar amount or an amount with a cap will help control costs and facilitate budgeting.

Sick leave is usually designated as some minimum number of days in state statutes. The number of days is usually in excess of the private sector. Sick leave banks are not recommended. When days are granted in excess of state minimums, a progressive increase corresponding to years of service is recommended. Service should be in terms of full-time equivalency; part-time should be pro-rated.

In addition to sick leave, it is common to grant business or personal leave, and reimbursement for unused sick leave.

When tuition reimbursement is granted and this is tied to movement on the salary schedule, it behooves the board and administration to take a firm stand on what courses will be approved.

Article VI — Leaves and Absences

Specificity in defining leave is especially important. For example, who is covered in the immediate family? Are leaves the board *shall* grant limited to tenured teachers with board having discretion in granting leaves to nontenured teachers? Are advance notice, a time requirement for application, and a duration specified? Figure 17-6 shows language for leaves and absences.

The board may wish to prevent double-dipping by specifying that sick leave not be applicable during maternity or child-rearing leave. Today, contracts should cover maternity and child rearing in leaves and should include adoptive parents.

Statement of intent to return should be included to give the superintendent flexibility in recommending the hiring and possible nonrenewal of employees. Reinstatement should guarantee a position only — one for which the employee is qualified, not the employee's former position.

The board may require a doctor's certificate and continuing consultation when long-term disability is involved.

When specifying religious holiday leaves, a word of caution is in order to avoid discrimination suits. The language illustrated is believed to be legally sound. By allowing the employee the use of business days or alternative employment, the employee is still free to exercise religious freedom.

In the area of jury duty, the district will want to guard against double-dipping. While it is customary to expect salary to continue, the district will want the employee to assign stipends received and to be responsible for expenses.

In granting long-term leaves of absences, the board will want to stay in control.

Article VII — Teacher Evaluation

The language on teacher evaluation shown in Figure 17-7 is about as minimal as possible. Unions today are pressing to get the entire evaluation instrument and procedures into the contract. Superintendents are urged to resist the content of union proposals for evaluation instrument and procedures and to resist having contract language pertaining to the instrument or procedures.

Article VIII — Vacancies and Transfers

As in other areas, the board will want to maintain discretion to the extent possible in filling vacancies or transferring employees (Figure 17-8). While vacancies may be posted, the board retains the right to decide when the vacancy exists. Employee applications may receive first consideration for interview, but not for employment. The board will want to retain the right to reassign as necessary; employees who do not like the reassignment are free to resign or to receive consideration for an interview in a requested transfer for future vacancies.

Article IX — Early Retirement, and Article X — Reduction in Force

Many states have statutes governing early retirement and RIF. Figure 17-9 and Figure 17-10 illustrate language in the latter areas. The board may want to obtain more flexibility or specificity than is written into the law and may, therefore, include early retirement and reduction in force clauses in a contract. For example, the board may want to define its own limits on numbers of employees who are eligible for early retirement. For both early retirement and reduction in force the board will want to define seniority; this definition may differ for different purposes. The RIF clause will also want to set up restrictions for recall.

Article XI — Negotiation Procedures

The contract will want to provide a starting date but will leave ground rules to be determined by the negotiating parties. The language shown in Figure 17-11 is an example of one that got away. The language should state negotiations shall begin no *earlier* than, rather than no *later* than March 1.

Article XII — Subcontracting

Subcontracting rights may be important for the board, particularly when such positions as coaching, supervision, and substitute positions are difficult to fill. Figure 17-12 shows subcontracting language. Again, the board will want to retain flexibility.

Article XIII — Management Rights

The board wants to reserve all rights which are not specifically expressed in the terms of the contract. Figure 17-13 illustrates managements' rights language. The first and last paragraphs would have been sufficient to protect managements' rights.

Article XIV — No-Strike Clause

The goal in no-strike clause language is to obtain safeguards against strike and slowdown. Figure 17-14 illustrates language to provide such safeguards.

Article XV — Effects of Agreement

The effects of agreement clause acknowledges that the negotiated contract is a complete agreement that settles all demands and issues on all matters within the scope of negotiations. If it contains a "zipper" clause as contained in the example in Figure 17-15, each party waives the right to additional bargaining during the life of the contract. Today there are usually clauses added to allow for impact bargaining.

What to Prepare

Thinking about what will make the schools more effective should guide thinking about preparations for negotiations. The superintendent can provide leadership and direction in the preparations.

Whether negotiating for the first time or renegotiating an existing contract, the superintendent and other administrators will want to assess the effectiveness of existing practices.

If negotiating for the first time, contracts of other districts can be helpful in decisions to reject or concede demands. The superintendent should secure and study contracts of other districts.

If renegotiating, determine if an existing contract presented any difficulty to administer. Study grievances and the outcome of grievances to gain insights into the ease or difficulty of administering the present contract. Develop a thorough understanding of teacher proposals and help administrators and the board understand demands. To take a position for or against a proposal, understanding is needed.

For the bargaining process itself, prepare notebooks for the negotiating team with index tabs for the various clauses of the contract. Annotate demands and include board counterproposals and fall-back positions. Designate a spokesperson and decide caucus procedures. Assign a recorder to take notes during negotiations sessions. Determine how tentative agreements will be recorded. The "TA" for tentative agreement should be put only on final language agreeable to both sides; trying to refine language to reach agreement after negotiations are presumed to be completed is extremely difficult.

Identify data needed to respond to the various demands. Decide how information will be presented. Determine the order in which issues will be negotiated.

With the team, work out a suggested meeting time and place. Know schedules of team members to set a schedule for negotiations sessions.

Trading Off Management Rights

Many districts have granted concessions to their employees that make it impossible to manage the district effectively. One has only to read the contract and compare how closely it matches the union master contract to know the limit of managements' rights. Experts suggest a general rule — not to bargain what you cannot live without. Hence, the argument for a strong Management Rights Article.

A sample Management Rights Article was presented in Figure 17-13. Teachers will not want to recognize that the board has rights to hire, dismiss, promote or demote, transfer or reassign, establish programs and courses of instruction, determine class schedules and hours of instruction, determine responsibilities and assignments; but they must. The board needs to retain authority in the above areas. Such rights should not be traded off.

The Grievance Article shown in Figure 17-4 also preserves board authority. This is done in the reverse by decreasing union authority. The grievance article defines grievance narrowly as a violation of specific terms of the contract. It imposes responsibility on the union by requiring the grievance be in writing, by limiting the time for filing after the alleged occurrence for the grievance, by requiring identification of contract provisions alleged to be violated, by requiring that the relief sought be stated, and by restricting the authority of the arbitrator to the scope of the contract.

The board should attempt to get something for what it gives. Know the value of items to each side and trade off something the board wants for something the teachers want. Salaries as well as nonmoney items need to be considered in the trade for management rights. At a minimum, renegotiate what administrators have found difficult to administer.

Assure that the board team controls language. Get rid of fuzzy language. If you have given everything away, get it back gradually.

Plan to have the board team control the substance, process, and outcome of negotiations.

Postscript to Negotiations: Contract Administration

Once the contract has been negotiated it needs to be administered. The Ohio School Boards Association has identified five goals of contract administration: 1) joint adherence to contract terms while fostering an attitude of cooperation and good faith, 2) quick resolution of disputes at the lowest level with a minimum of animosity, 3) protection of management rights, 4) consensus interpretation of the contract by management, and 5) consistent treatment of employees.

Collective bargaining is ongoing. It does not end when the contract has been negotiated. Reaching agreement on one contract signals the beginning of preparations for the next round of bargaining. Some material for preparations for the next round will come from disputes in contract administration that do not get resolved satisfactorily.

Contract administration has been defined as "the continuing effort of management and labor to abide by the terms in the negotiated collective bargaining agreement." During the life of the contract, the contract cannot be set aside. The language of the contract governs the interaction of the parties to the contract. Both sides interpret the contract. Grievances result from different interpretations about what the language means.

There are steps the superintendent can and should take to organize management to administer the contract. These include awareness of the contract and training and recordkeeping. To increase awareness of the contract, keep a record of grievances, involve administrators in ongoing discussions about negotiations, hold a contract workshop for administrators and supervisors, maintain positive relations, be sensitive to employees' viewpoints as represented by the union leadership, communicate with the board's negotiator, and utilize the structure of a labor and management committee.

One of the steps named above was to hold a contract workshop. Management personnel need training to effectively administer the contract. Workshop content should include provisions of the law, study of the contract, attention to new and changed language, instruction on management positions and interpretations of key sections, instruction regarding past grievance settlements and grievance arbitration decisions, and emphasis on the importance of consistency in interpretation and implementation of the contract.

Negotiating the Superintendent's Contract

In addition to looking out for the district's best interests when negotiating teacher or administrator contracts, the superintendent also has a self-interest in his or her own contract. Figure 17-16 shows sample provisions for a superintendent's contract prepared jointly by the Illinois Association of School Boards and Illinois Association of School Administrators.

Terms of the Contract

Obtaining a minimum of a three-year contract is advised for a beginning superintendent. A three-year term gives the superintendent at least one and one-half years to prove his or her effectiveness. Some states will have "windows" restricting the period when a contract can be renewed. It is common to have rollover contracts so that the superintendent contract is renewed the year prior to expiration. Duties should be spelled out in a board-adopted job description and evaluation should be based on the job description. Of course, the superintendent can expect to perform many duties that are not in the job description. Salary should be competitive for the area. The superintendent may or may not want to risk being the highest paid administrator in the area.

The guidelines shown in Figure 17-16 show an April 1 deadline for board evaluation of the superintendent. Many states mandate deadlines, but the earlier the date the better for the superintendent. The author prefers a January superintendent evaluation followed by February evaluation dates for other administrators. This generally allows for concluding administrator evaluations and establishment of salaries prior to the start of other negotiations. Some prefer to set administrator salaries following negotiations with other unions.

Proper certification is always expected. When moving from state to state, different requirements are frequently expected. However, personnel in state departments of education are generally accommodating to facilitate a superintendent candidate in obtaining the proper credentials. Check with the appropriate state office as far in advance as possible to assure you have all the needed paperwork in order when needed. Many superintendents will have some understanding for professional speaking engagements and other professional duties. Personal advice is never to accept compensation for an activity performed on board-paid time.

Protections against discharge and provisions for disability are common clauses in the contract. State codes will have provisions for discharge that may differ from state to state. The guidelines in Figure 17-16 show provisions for a mutual agreement for termination of contract. If you can get a one-sided agreement that favors the superintendent, all the better.

In addition to standard items in most contracts, the guidelines in Figure 17-16 include possible additions. A vacation of at least 20 days per year is common. Sick leave and other benefits should, at a minimum, match that of other professional staff. Life insurance of at least double the annual salary of the superintendent is common. Depending on the number of dependents, the superintendent may wish to negotiate a substantially larger insurance coverage. The guidelines in Figure 17-16 advocate long-term disability insurance benefits to the extent of 60% of the superintendent's annual salary. One consideration in disability insurance is to have the policy specify that the superintendent is considered disabled if he or she is unable to perform the duties of superintendent.

The sample clause referring to provisions for an automobile restrict use to school business. It is common for the superintendent to be able to use the board-provided automobile for personal use as well. However, the superintendent is then responsible for keeping and supplying the district records to support information needed by the Internal Revenue Service.

An attorney skillful in preparing Chief Executive Officer contracts, including those for superintendents, can frequently obtain concessions that offer additional protections and benefits. In addition, administrator associations and other organizations perform surveys of superintendent benefits and disseminate results. Such information can help the superintendent keep abreast of reasonable inclusions to the superintendent's contract.

REFERENCES AND RESOURCES

Cohen, Herb, *You Can Negotiate Anything*. New York, NY: Bantam Books, 1980.

Fisher, Roger, and William Ury, *Getting to Yes*. New York, NY: Penguin Books, 1981.

Other Resources

American Association of School Administrators, 1801 N. Moore St., Arlington VA 22209-9988.

National School Boards Association, 1680 Duke St., Alexandria, VA 22314

Article I
RECOGNITION

1.1 DEFINITION UNIT

The Board of Education of Benjamin School District 25, DuPage County, Illinois, hereinafter referred to as the "Board," hereby recognizes the Benjamin Education Association, hereinafter referred to as the "Association," affiliated with the Illinois Education Association, and the National Education Association as the sole bargaining agent for all full-time and part-time, regularly employed certificated personnel except the Superintendent, other central office professional staff, building principals, assistant principals, substitutes, and the director of special education, the foregoing exceptions being compensated pursuant to Board policy.

1.2 DEFINITION TEACHER

The term "teacher," when used hereinafter in this Agreement, shall refer to all employees represented by the Association in the negotiating unit as determined above.

Source: Benjamin School District 25 — Chicago, Illinois.

Figure 17-1

Article II
EMPLOYMENT CONDITIONS

2.1 SCHOOL CALENDAR

The school calendar shall consist of 185 days or such minimum number of days as may be required by law. Teachers shall work 181 days in consideration of the annual salaries set forth herein. If the teacher works in excess of 181 days as part of a Board-approved assignment (before the commencement of and/or after the conclusion of the regularly adopted school calendar), such teacher shall be compensated for such work at a sum of money equal to 1/181 of such teacher's last annual salary as set forth in the salary schedule herein. The foregoing shall not apply to summer school or attendance at workshops or conventions, the foregoing being voluntary and compensation, therefore, being set by agreement between the Board and the individual teacher. The Association will be consulted in the construction of the school calendar.

2.2 PLANNING TIME

Teachers will be provided with a minimum of five duty-free planning periods per week.

2.3 PROFESSIONAL STAFF WORK SCHEDULE

Teachers shall be present for duty at the place of their first assignment at least 20 minutes prior to the first bell in the morning and at least 20 minutes after the dismissal of school on all days when school is in session. In addition, teachers shall be present for Institute and Inservice Days as scheduled, building and district staff meetings, special education staffings, parent orientation and open house nights, and other district-sponsored events where teacher participation is a requirement as determined by the Superintendent.

2.4 PERSONNEL FILE REVIEW

Each teacher shall have the right to review contents of his/her own personnel file under the following conditions:

2.4.1 WRITTEN REQUEST

Written request is made to the Superintendent prior to inspection;

2.4.2 REVIEW

The Superintendent, upon receipt of such request, shall schedule a review at such time as may be mutually agreeable;

2.4 Continued

2.4.3 CONDITIONS OF REVIEW

Review shall take place during regular business hours of the Administration Center when school is not in session in the presence of the Superintendent or his/her designee;

2.4.4. RIGHT TO REPRESENTATION

The teacher shall have the right, upon request, to have a representative of the Association present during review.

2.5 PARENT COMPLAINTS

Any complaint by a parent of a student directed toward a teacher shall be channeled as follows: a. Teacher; b. Principal; c. Superintendent; d. Board of Education. If the complaint is not resolved between the teacher and parent or if the parent does not bring the complaint to the teacher, the immediate supervisor will inform the teacher about the complaint and schedule a joint meeting among parent, teacher, and supervisor for the purpose of resolving the problem, unless immediate action is necessitated by suspected or actual danger to the welfare and safety of students and other school personnel. In cases requiring immediate action, the conference with the teacher will be held as soon as practicable. Any complaint about school personnel will be investigated by the administration before consideration and action by the Board. The teacher will be consulted should it be deemed necessary for the Board to take action. The teacher who is the subject of the complaint shall have the right, upon request, to have a representative of the Association present at any such conference involving a parent complaint directed toward the teacher and the administration shall have the right to have a representative of its choosing present at any such conference.

2.6 EMPLOYEE DISCIPLINE

Discipline includes: reprimands, suspensions, reductions in rank, and discharges for cause. Reprimands shall be made in writing to the teacher by the Superintendent or by the Superintendent on behalf of the Board of Education. Notice of suspension, reduction in rank, and discharge shall be accomplished within provisions of law. The employee shall have the right, upon request, to have a representative of the Association present at any such conference that involves a disciplinary action.

Source: Benjamin School District 25 — Chicago, Illinois.

Figure 17-2

Article III

ASSOCIATION RIGHTS

3.1 ASSOCIATION MEETINGS

The Board agrees that the Association shall have the right to use school buildings for meetings on school days during hours when the building is open and school is not in session. Requests to use school buildings shall be made to the building principal. Such use shall not interfere with or interrupt school operations or conflict with previously scheduled activities. When special custodial service is required, the Association shall reimburse Benjamin School District 25 for the cost of such service.

3.2 ASSOCIATION NOTICES AND INFORMATION

3.2.1 ASSOCIATION COMMUNICATIONS

The Association shall have the right to post notices of its activities on a teacher bulletin board at a specific location at each site. The use of teacher mailboxes to deposit Association mail shall be made available to the Association for communications. The Association shall be permitted use of a typewriter, computer, and duplicating machine, provided the Association reimburses Benjamin School District 25 for paper, duplicating fluid, and other supplies used.

3.2.2 BOARD COMMUNICATIONS

The Association shall be given copies of agendas prior to meetings of the Board and copies of minutes after approval by the Board.

Source: Benjamin School District 25 — Chicago, Illinois.

Figure 17-3

Article IV
GRIEVANCE

4.1 DEFINITIONS

4.1.1 GRIEVANCE

A grievance is defined as a written complaint or claim by a teacher or the Association that there has been a violation, misinterpretation, or misapplication of specific provisions of the Agreement.

4.1.2 DAYS

Days shall be school days, except that when a grievance is submitted less than ten (10) days before the close of the current school term, time limits shall consist of all weekdays when the business office is open in order that the matters may be resolved before the close of the school term or as soon thereafter as possible. School days for purposes of the grievance procedure shall mean teacher employment days.

4.2 RIGHT TO REPRESENTATION

4.2.1 ASSISTANCE

The Board acknowledges the right of the Association to assist a grievant at any level of the grievance procedure if it obtains the consent of the grievant, and the Association acknowledges the right of any member of the Administration to receive assistance as desired in any step of the grievance procedure.

4.2.2 PRESENCE

At any level of the grievance procedure, the Association will have been given the opportunity to be present.

4.3 TIME LIMITS

Failure of any teacher or the Association to act on a grievance within the prescribed time limits will act as a bar to any further appeal, and an Administration's failure to give a decision within the prescribed time limits shall permit the grievant to proceed to the next step. The time limits, however, may be extended by mutual consent.

4.4 INFORMAL DISCUSSION

Before a grievance can be processed formally, the aggrieved party or parties shall have made an attempt to resolve the problem through free and informal discussion with the immediately involved supervisor. The two parties may agree to an informal

4.4 Continued

discussion with the buidling principal and/or superintendent before going to the next step.

4.5 INITIATING A GRIEVANCE

4.5.1 GRIEVANCE AT BUILDING LEVEL

If a problem cannot be resolved informally, the grievant or the Association shall present the grievance in writing on the Grievance Form, Exhibit Article IV. If the grievance involves the act of an Administrator at the building level, the grievance shall be filed at Step 1.

4.52 GRIEVANCE AT OTHER THAN BUILDING LEVEL

If the grievance involves the act of an Administrator other than at the building level, the grievance shall initially be filed at Step 2 of the grievance procedure after the grievant has first advised the Administrator involved.

4.6 STEP 1 — IMMEDIATE SUPERVISOR LEVEL

If the grievance cannot be resolved informally, the grievant or the Association shall present the grievance in writing on the Grievance Form to his/her immediate supervisor no later than twenty (20) days after the occurrence of the event giving rise to the grievance or should the grievant be absent at the time of the occurrence, no later than twenty (20) days after the grievant's return to work. The supervisor will arrange for a meeting to take place within five (5) days after receipt of the grievance. The grievant, the immediate supervisor, and any such representative(s) as provided for in Section 4.2 of this Agreement shall be present for the meeting. The supervisor will then, within five (5) days after the meeting, provide the grievant, the Association, and the Superintendent with a written memorandum setting forth the disposition of the grievance. Such memorandum shall contain reasons upon which the disposition of the matter was based.

4.7 STEP 2 — SUPERINTENDENT LEVEL

If the grievant is not satisfied with the disposition of the grievance at Step 1, or if Step 1 time limits expire without the issuance of the supervisor's memorandum, the grievant may, within ten (10) days after the Step 1 meeting, refer the grievance to the Superintendent. The Superintendent shall, within ten (10) days conduct a meeting with the same parties being present as may be present in Step 1. Each party to the grievance shall have the right to include in its presentation a counselor if so desired.

Source: Benjamin School District 25 — Chicago, Illinois.

Figure 17-4

473

4.7 continued

Upon the conclusion of the hearing of the grievance, the Superintendent shall have ten (10) days in which to provide his/her written decision to the grievant and the Association.

4.8 STEP 3 — BOARD LEVEL

If the grievant is not satisfied with the disposition of the grievance at Step 2, or if Step 2 time limits expire without the issuance of the Superintendent's decision, the grievant may refer the grievance to the Board. Upon receipt of the request the Board shall, within thirty (30) calendar days, schedule a closed session hearing on the grievance, and shall within ten (10) days thereafter render its decision in writing. Each party to the grievance shall have the right to include in its presentation a counselor if so desired.

4.9 STEP 4 — ARBITRATION

4.9.1 BINDING ARBITRATION

If the grievance is not resolved satisfactorily at Step 3, there shall be available an additional step of impartial, binding arbitration. The Association may submit, in writing, a request to the Superintendent within ten (10) days from receipt of the Step 3 answer. The arbitration shall be selected from the American Arbitration Association in accordance with the *Voluntary Labor Arbitration Rules.*

4.9.2 ASSOCIATION INDEMNIFICATION OF THE DISTRICT

If the Association is grievant, the association shall indemnify the district against Duty of Fair Representation suit for the Association's failure to take a grievance to arbitration.

4.9.3 CONDITIONS OF ARBITRATION

Neither party to the grievance will be permitted to assert grounds not previously introduced in the grievance process. Each party shall be entitled to representation and witnesses. The arbitrator shall have no power to alter the terms of this Agreement.

4.9.4 COST OF ARBITRATION

Cost of the arbitrator shall be borne equally between the Association and the school district. Should either party request a transcript of the proceedings, that party will bear the cost of the transcript. Any additional costs shall be borne by either party incurring the cost.

4.9 Continued

4.9.5 ARBITRATOR DECISION

The arbitrator's decision shall be final and binding upon the parties. His/her decision must be based solely and only upon his or her interpretation of the meaning of application of the express relevant language of this Agreement.

4.10 RELEASE TIME

Should the investigation of any grievance require, in the judgment of the Superintendent, that an employee be released from his/her regular assignment, he/she will be released without loss of pay or benefits.

4.11 NO REPRISALS

The Board agrees not to take any reprisal against any person for his/her participation or refusal to participate in the grievance process. The Association agrees to take no reprisals against any person because of his/her participation or refusal to participate in the grievance process.

4.12 FORUM FOR ACTION

4.12.1 ACTION IN A SINGLE FORUM

Should any member of the bargaining unit commence an action against the Board and/or any of its members individually or collectively, before any State or Federal Administrative Agency, Court or Tribunal, charging the Board or any of its members with a violation of any of the rights granted to or enumerated in this Agreement, said action shall act as a bar to the commencement or further processing of the grievance.

4.12.2 BOARD INDEMNIFICATION OF ASSOCIATION

The Board agrees to indemnify the Association against a suit that claims the Association has negated, abrogated, replaced, reduced, diminished, or limited in any way teacher rights, guarantees, or privileges provided in Illinois statutes enacted by the Illinois General Assembly.

4.13 WITHDRAWAL OF GRIEVANCE

A grievance may be withdrawn at any step without establishing precedent.

Figure 17-4 (Cont'd.)

ARTICLE V
WAGES AND BENEFITS

5.1 COMPENSATION

Teachers will be compensated in accordance with the Compensation Schedule (Exhibit Article V) attached as part of this Agreement.

5.2 INSURANCE

Regularly employed teachers shall be provided the following insurance coverages:

5.2.1 LIFE INSURANCE

Life insurance in the amount of $15,000, 100% Board paid.

5.2.2 HEALTH INSURANCE

Health insurance with coverages as detailed in the individual carrier agreement: 90% Board paid for the individual employee premium and 50% Board paid for the premium differential between individual and family coverage.

5.2.3 DENTAL INSURANCE

Dental insurance with coverages as detailed in the individual carrier agreement: 90% Board paid for the individual employee premium and 50% Board paid for the premium differential between individual and family coverage.

5.3 SICK LEAVE

Regularly employed teachers shall be granted sick leave with compensation each school year as follows: year one, full-time equivalency — 10 days; year two, full-time equivalency — 11 days; year three, full-time equivalency — 12 days; year four and thereafter, full-time equivalency — 13 days. Unused sick leave shall be cumulative to 190 days.

5.4 PERSONAL BUSINESS LEAVE

Regularly employed teachers shall be granted up to two (2) personal business leave days with compensation each school year. Unused personal business leave days shall be cumulative to four (4) after which unused personal business leave days shall be cumulative as sick leave.

5.5 REIMBURSEMENT FOR UNUSED CUMULATIVE SICK LEAVE

Each regularly employed teacher shall receive attendance points annually as follows: year one, full-time equivalency — 10 points; year two, full-time equivalency — 11 points; year three, full-time equivalency — 12 points; year four and thereafter, full-time equivalency — 13 points. One point shall be deducted from the annual total allocation for each sick leave day taken by the teacher. Attendance points shall be cumulative to 190 points. Any teacher who retires, resigns, or is dismissed in accordance with the provisions of Reduction in Force shall be paid $20 for each accumulated attendance point.

5.6 TUITION REIMBURSEMENT

Each regularly employed teacher shall receive $40 reimbursement per graduate semester hour of credit for courses that have the preapproval of the Superintendent.

Source: Benjamin School District 25 — Chicago, Illinois.

Figure 17-5

ARTICLE VI
LEAVES AND ABSENCES

6.1 PERSONAL ILLNESS AND INJURY

6.1.1 NUMBER OF DAYS

The Board shall grant each regular full-time teacher sick-leave with compensation each school year as follows: year one, full-time equivalency, — 10 days; year two, full-time equivalency, — 11 days; year three, full-time equivalency, — 12 days; year four and thereafter, full-time equivalency, 13 days. Regular part-time teachers and individuals employed for a portion of the school year shall have the sick-leave provisions prorated according to the length of service in relationship to the full-time teacher. Sick leave shall be cumulative to 190 days.

6.1.2 DEFINITION

Sick leave shall be interpreted to mean personal illness, quarantine at home, or serious illness or death in the immediate family or household. The immediate family shall include parents, spouse, brothers, sisters, children, grandparents, grandchildren, parents-in-law, brothers-in-law, sisters-in-law, and legal guardians.

6.1.3 DOCTOR CERTIFICATE

The Board may require certification by such doctor(s) as it deems necessary for personnel to continue to serve the District, to receive benefits for absence caused by temporary illness or temporary incapacity, and to be eligible to return to work following termination of a temporary illness or temporary incapacity.

6.1.4 INTENT TO BE ABSENT

When a teacher has advance knowledge concerning the temporary illness or temporary incapacity, he or she shall notify the Superintendent or his/her designee as far as possible in advance of the proposed absence, in writing so that proper plans may be implemented.

6.1.5 INTENT TO RETURN

Notification of intent to return to duties shall be given to the superintendent or his/her designee at least two school days in advance of the date of return in those circumstances where the absence has exceeded one month.

Source: Benjamin School District 25 — Chicago, Illinois.

Figure 17-6

6.1.6 CONTINUE INSURANCE

A teacher who is temporarily ill or temporarily incapacitated may continue membership in the District group insurance programs, provided the premiums are paid in advance monthly by the staff member, when applicable, to the Business Office and provided further that the insurance carrier approves thereof.

6.2 PARENTAL LEAVE OF ABSENCE

6.2.1 CONDITIONS — TENURE TEACHER

A teacher who has entered upon contractual continued service shall be eligible for maternity/child rearing leave without pay or other benefits subject to the following conditions: (As used herein, "teacher" means a tenure teacher except in 6.2.10, which is applicable only to nontenured teachers.)

6.2.2 NOTIFICATION

The teacher shall advise the Superintendent or his/her designee of her pregnancy no later than the fourth month of pregnancy or upon ascertainment of such condition, whichever shall be the later. At such time, she shall provide a written statement from her physician indicating the expected date of delivery.

6.2.3 WRITTEN APPLICATION

Application for such leave shall be made in writing to the Superintendent at least ninety (90) calendar days prior to the anticipated birth of the child.

6.2.4 DURATION

The teacher and the Superintendent or his/her designee shall agree upon a date and plan for the commencement and termination of such leave, taking into consideration maintenance of continuity of instruction and medical factors to the maximum possible degree and the pertinent time factors related thereto. The leave shall begin on agreed upon date, the actual date of delivery, or the date on which the teacher shall be unable to continue in employment, whichever shall first occur. The leave shall not exceed the balance of the school year in which it commences and one additional school year. Every effort shall be made to have such leave terminate immediately prior to the start of a new school term.

6.2.5 SICK LEAVE

Sick leave shall not be applicable during the period of the maternity/child rearing leave. Any accumulated sick leave available at the commencement of the leave shall be available to the teacher upon return to employment in the District.

Figure 17-6 (Cont'd.)

6.2.6 CONTINUE INSURANCE

Any teacher whose leave is to commence during the summer recess shall be eligible for fringe benefits through August 31st of that year. With the consent of the carrier, the teacher may maintain insurance benefits provided the premiums are paid in advance monthly by the staff member to the Business Office.

6.2.7 ADOPTION

A teacher desiring maternity/child rearing leave as a result of becoming an adoptive parent shall notify the Superintendent or his/her designee in writing upon the initiation of such adoption proceedings. Maternity/child rearing leave shall be granted upon written notification to the Superintendent or his/her designee of the date the child is to be received. It shall be the responsibility of the applying teacher to keep the Superintendent or designee informed of the status of the proceedings and, as soon as known, the expected date of delivery of the child. The length of this leave shall be consistent with maternity/child rearing time lines.

6.2.8 INTENT TO RETURN

A teacher on a leave of absence must give written notice to the Superintendent or his/her designee by March 1 of the year the leave expires of the teacher's intention to return or resign. Failure to furnish such written notice shall constitute a notice of resignation.

6.2.9 REINSTATEMENT

Upon reinstatement following leave, the teacher will be reemployed in any position for which he/she is qualified to teach.

6.2.10 CONDITIONS — NONTENURE TEACHER

A maternity/child rearing leave may be granted to a nontenured teacher under unusual circumstances by action of the Board, subject to all the conditions applicable to a tenure teacher, and provided the term of such leave shall not be considered in computing full-time employment for purposes of the continuous employment necessary to attain contractual continued service status. Upon the return from such leave the teacher shall be considered to have commenced her first probationary year. The granting of maternity leave to any nontenured teacher shall not constitute a precedent for the granting or withholding of leave to any other teacher. Each request shall be judged on its own merits and shall be within the sole discretion of the Board.

6.2.11 RIGHT NOT TO APPLY

Nothing in this article shall be construed as requiring any teacher to apply for a maternity/child rearing leave. A teacher not

Figure 17-6 (Cont'd.)

eligible for or not desiring maternity/child rearing leave may utilize accumulated sick leave during any period of illness and/or disability related to her pregnancy and/or to the delivery of the child.

6.2.12 MALE TEACHER ELIGIBILITY

A male teacher is eligible for a child rearing leave of absence under all applicable conditions of this section.

6.3 EXTENDED SICK LEAVE

6.3.1 CONDITIONS

The Board recognizes that there may be occasions when the employee's accumulated sick leave does not extend to cover the duration of an illness. If a teacher exhausts all of his/her accumulated sick leave due to an extended illness and cannot return to work, the teacher may request a leave of absence for the duration of the illness. The following guidelines shall apply.

6.3.2 TIME LIMITS

Leave may extend to one full school year and shall ordinarily be contained within a single school year. Extensions shall be at Board discretion.

6.3.3 CONTINUE INSURANCE

While on leave, the teacher may elect to retain insurance by prepaying premiums on a monthly basis to the Business Office, if the continuation of the group insurance is acceptable to the carrier.

6.3.4 DOCTOR CERTIFICATE

The teacher's application for leave shall be supported by a physician's written certification of the teacher's inability to perform normal teaching duties. The Board may request consultation by a physician of its choice as a mater of unprejudicial clarification of the disability; such consultation shall be at Board expense. The Board may, from time to time during an extended leave, request certification by a physician of continued inability to perform normal teaching duties; such certification shall be at the employee's expense.

6.3.5 RETURN TO DUTY

The teacher shall be expected to resume normal teaching duties upon certification by a physician that he/she is capable of performing same. In addition, if the leave has extended for a period of more than ninety (90) days or if the employee was afflicted with a communicable disease during the leave, the employee shall furnish evidence of freedom from communicable disease at the employee's expense.

Figure 17-6 Cont'd.

6.4 <u>PERSONAL BUSINESS</u>

6.4.1   <u>NUMBER OF DAYS</u>

Each regular full-time teacher may be allowed absence with full pay for two (2) personal business days each year. A regular part-time teacher and individuals employed for a portion of the school year shall have the personal-business provisions prorated according to the length of service in relationship to the full-time teacher. At the end of each school year, unused personal-business days may be accumulated to four (4) personal-business days. After an accumulation of four (4) personal-business days, personal-business days allowed in the succeeding year, that would make the accumulation greater than four (4), shall be converted to sick leave and, as sick leave, be allowed to accumulate to 190 days. Sick leave days may not be used for personal-business days, but personal-business days may be used for sick-leave days.

6.4.2   <u>CONDITIONS</u>

Personal Business Leave is granted by the Board to permit a teacher to conduct business that cannot be conducted outside of the school day. Personal Business Leave shall not be used to extend holidays or vacation periods.

6.4.3   <u>REQUEST</u>

A teacher requesting Personal Business Leave shall do so in writing, submitting a Request for Personal Business Leave Form to the immediate supervisor at least two school days prior to the proposed Leave day unless an emergency arises.

6.5 <u>RELIGIOUS HOLIDAYS LEAVE</u>

6.5.1   <u>NUMBER OF DAYS</u>

Leaves for observance of religious holidays shall be granted to a maximum of three (3) days per school year.

6.5.2   <u>OPTIONS</u>

6.5.2.1   <u>PERSONAL BUSINESS DAYS</u>

Use Personal Business Leave days to the extent that such days are available.

6.5.2.2   <u>ALTERNATIVE EMPLOYMENT</u>

Perform alternative employment which may include, but not necessarily include, internal substitution or supervision without compensation.

Figure 17-6 (Cont'd.)

6.5.3 REQUEST

Request for religious holidays leave shall be made in accordance with the provisions for Personal Business Leave (Section 6.4.).

6.6 JURY DUTY

6.6.1 LEAVE GRANTED

After due notice, the Superintendent shall grant leave at full salary for a teacher to be absent from assigned responsibilities for the purpose of fulfilling jury duty.

6.6.2 BOARD EXPECTATION

It is expected that certificated employees shall fulfill their civic obligation when called to jury duty. The Board, moreover, does not wish a teacher to suffer loss while performing jury duty.

6.6.3 ASSIGNMENT OF BENEFITS

To receive full salary, following jury duty the teacher shall assign stipends received for jury duty performance to Benjamin School District 25. The teacher is responsible for his/her expenses incurred while on leave for jury duty.

6.7 LONG-TERM LEAVES OF ABSENCE

6.7.1 INDIVIDUAL MERIT

The Board shall consider requests for leaves of absence on individual merit. Leaves may be granted when the request is judged to be of mutual benefit to the teacher and the District.

6.7.2 TEACHING THREE YEARS

Full-time and part-time teachers, who have successfully completed three full years teaching in Benjamin School District 25 immediately preceding the request for leave, may apply.

6.7.3 ONE SCHOOL YEAR

Leave may extend to one full school year and shall be contained within a single school year.

6.7.4 APPLICATION

Request for a leave shall be made in writing to the Superintendent six (6) months in advance of the beginning date of the requested leave by setting forth the expected benefit to the teacher and the District. In cases of extreme urgency, the time requirement may be waived. Application shall include a statement of intent to return for a period of at least one year.

Figure 17-6 Cont'd.

6.7.5   CONTINUATION OF INSURANCE

While on leave, the teacher may elect to retain insurance by prepaying premiums on a monthly basis, if the continuation of the group insurance is acceptable to the carrier.

6.7.6   COMPENSATION AND EXPERIENCE CREDIT

Leaves approved by the Board shall be without compensation. Upon return from a leave, the teacher will receive a contract upon reemployment reflecting no credit on the compensation schedule for time spent on leave.

6.7.7   SICK LEAVE

A teacher returning from leave shall retain previously accumulated sick leave.

6.7.8   PHYSICIAN'S STATEMENT

The Board may request from a teacher returning from leave a physician's statement of the employee's ability to resume teaching duties and evidence of immunity from communicable disease at the employee's expense.

6.7.9   REEMPLOYMENT

Leave shall be granted with a guarantee of reemployment, unless provisions of reductions in force apply, and reemployment shall be in a position for which the teacher is qualified to teach.

6.7.10   EXTENDING LEAVE

Personal and professional long-term leaves of absence shall not extend any other leave.

6.7.11   BOARD DISCRETION

The granting of personal and professional long-term leaves of absence is at the discretion of the Board and the Board's decision is nonreviewable.

Figure 17-6 (Cont'd.)

ARTICLE VII
TEACHER EVALUATION

7.1   PROCEDURE

The evaluation procedure as approved by the Board in April, 1983, in the *Handbook of Evaluation Procedures*, shall be in effect until such time as the Board shall adopt a replacement procedure.

7.2   REVISION

Teachers will be consulted when revision in the evaluation procedure is deemed necessary. The evaluation procedure in place at the beginning of a school calendar year shall remain in effect for the remainder of the school term.

Source: Benjamin School District 25 — Chicago, Illinois.

Figure 17-7

ARTICLE VIII
VACANCIES AND TRANSFERS

8.1 NOTICE OF VACANCIES

The Superintendent or his/her designee will send notice of all vacancies to the President of the Association and will post notice of all vacancies in all school buildings for at least ten (10) days after said notification. Such notice shall be accompanied by a statement of minimum qualifications. No vacancy will be filled, except on a temporary basis, until such vacancy shall have been posted and notice sent to the President of the Association. Notice to the President of the Association may be accomplished by delivery of the minutes of the Board if said vacancy is described therein. The Board shall decide when a vacancy exists.

8.2 APPLICATION FOR TRANSFER

A teacher presently on tenure shall have the right to apply for any transfer for which he/she is qualified. Such application shall be in writing to the Superintendent. Any employee application received prior to application(s) of nonemployees shall receive first consideration for an interview.

8.3 CHANGE IN ASSIGNMENT

Teachers will be advised prior to the end of the school term of any change in their assignment for the forthcoming year if the reasons prompting such change were known prior to the close of the school term. Change in assignment after this date will be made known to the teacher as promptly as possible.

8.4 INVOLUNTARY TRANSFER

Involuntary assignments resulting in substantially different teaching situations from those designated by the end of the school year shall provide said teacher with the right of resignation. Any teacher transferred involuntarily shall receive consideration for an interview in any requested transfer for future vacancies. Involuntary transfers shall not be made unless they are in the best interest of the students and shall be submitted in writing to the teacher involved.

Source: Benjamin School District 25 — Chicago, Illinois.

Figure 17-8

ARTICLE IX
EARLY RETIREMENT

9.1 RIGHTS

So long as permitted by law, the Board shall recognize the rights of eligible teachers to participate in an early retirement program. The method of participation shall be determined by law, and where applicable the Board shall set the following guidelines for participation in an early retirement system as follows:

9.2 LIMIT

The Board is not required to grant any more such early retirements than is required by law. However, the Board may, at its sole option, increase the number of teachers eligible, and said increase shall not represent a precedent of a past practice.

9.3 ELIGIBILITY

A teacher eligibility for participation shall be on the basis of seniority in that the most senior teachers applying shall be chosen from the list of eligible applications for qualification. For the purposes of those chosen only, seniority shall be equally counted in whole year units for both full-time and part-time employees, and periods of paid and unpaid leave shall count towards seniority.

9.4 REQUIRED PAYMENTS

The individual teacher and the Board shall make those payments required by law to allow the individual teacher to be eligible for participation in early retirement. The Board's payment shall be deemed an early retirement contribution required by law as part of a contribution method for pension treatment. In all other respects, if not amended herein, the provisions of law shall prevail.

Source: Benjamin School District 25 — Chicago, Illinois.

Figure 17-9

ARTICLE X
REDUCTION IN FORCE

10.1 ORDER OF DISMISSAL

When, in the opinion of the Board, it becomes necessary to decrease the number of teachers employed by the Board or to discontinue some particular type of teacher service, the Board shall first remove or dismiss all teachers who have not entered upon contractual continued service before removing or dismissing any teacher who has entered upon contractual continued service and who is legally qualified to hold a position currently held by a teacher who has not entered upon contractual continued service. As between teachers who have entered upon contractual continued service, the teacher or teachers with the shorter length of continuing service with the district shall be dismissed first.

10.2 RECALL RIGHTS

If the Board has any vacancies for the following school term or within one calendar year from the beginning of the following school term, the positions thereby becoming available shall be tendered to the teachers so removed or dismissed so far as they are legally qualified to hold such positions. Vacant positions include full-time teaching positions and full year part-time teaching assignments, but do not include substitute positions and positions becoming vacant because of leaves, whether paid or unpaid. A teacher so recalled retains tenure status and all accumulated seniority; however, the period such tenured teacher did not teach shall not be counted toward seniority.

10.3 RECALL PROCEDURE

To be eligible for recall, the honorably dismissed tenured teacher must provide the Board in writing, prior to the last day of the school term of dismissal, with the address where such teacher may be reached.. The teacher must also notify the Board in writing, within fourteen (14) calendar days of mailing or within seven (7) calendar days of receipt of the offer, whichever shall first occur, of the acceptance of any vacant position offered to the teacher during the recall period. Failure to notify the Board of acceptance shall constitute rejection of the offer of employment. If a teacher rejects an offer of a full-time vacant position, the teacher shall have his or her name placed last on the list of teachers with recall rights.

10.4 SENIORITY DEFINITION

10.4.1 CONTINUOUS SERVICE

Years of continuous service as a regular full-time teacher in the school district; provided, however, that less than full-time service shall be computed on a *pro rata* basis and approved unpaid leaves of absence shall not be counted in determining seniority.

10.4.2 LOTTERY

If the total teaching service as computed in the manner described in 10.4.1 above is equal between two or more teachers, the order of dismissal shall be determined by lottery in the presence of Association leadership.

10.5 QUALIFIED DEFINITION

Legal qualifications or legally qualified shall be defined as all statutory and regulatory prerequisites for teaching a particular subject or grade, including but not limited to, the certification requirements of Article 27 of *The School Code* and the academic experience requirements of State Board of Education *Document No. 1* or their successors or supplementary requirements in effect at the time of dismissal and/or recall.

10.6 OBJECTIONS TO PUBLISHED SENIORITY LIST

The employer shall publish annually a seniority list in accordance with provisions of law. Each teacher shall have ten (10) employment days thereafter to file written objection to his/her status and shall detail the alleged specific error in the listing. Failure to make such timely objection will be deemed an acceptance of the status and the teacher cannot thereafter challenge his/her seniority for the school term.

Source: Benjamin School District 25 — Chicago, Illinois.

Figure 17-10

ARTICLE XI

NEGOTIATION PROCEDURES

11.1 <u>BEGINNING</u>

Negotiations shall begin no later than March 1 in the year this contract terminates, unless both parties agree to an alternate date.

11.2 <u>GROUND RULES</u>

Ground rules governing the course of negotiations will be determined by agreement of the parties upon commencement of the negotiations process.

Source: Benjamin School District 25 — Chicago, Illinois.

Figure 17-11

ARTICLE XII
SUBCONTRACTING

12.1 CONDITIONS

The Board retains the nonreviewable right to subcontract extra-duty nonclassroom teaching positions customarily held by and duties performed by members of the bargaining unit. However, prior to the institution of any subcontracting relationships, the Board agrees to empanel a committee to meet with the Association to discuss both the need to subcontract and the terms and conditions of such subcontracting relationship. Nothing shall be deemed a requirement to reach agreement on such topics as a precondition for the institution of subcontracting.

12.2 PREFERENCE IN HIRING

The Board shall give teachers preference for work they have customarily performed. However, the Board may hire other persons for extra duty assignments such as coaching and lunchroom supervision when no teacher is willing to perform those duties.

12.3 SUBCONTRACTOR RIGHTS LIMITS

Any subcontracting relationships formed by the Board shall not be interpreted to invest in such subcontractors the status of assignees of the rights of this Agreement, nor shall the same be deemed to invest in such subcontracting agencies the status of co-employer with the Board.

Source: Benjamin School District 25 — Chicago, Illinois.

Figure 17-12

ARTICLE XIII

MANAGEMENT RIGHTS

13.1 BOARD RESPONSIBILITY

The Board retains and reserves the ultimate responsibility for proper management of the School District conferred upon and vested in it by the statutes and Constitutions of the State of Illinois and the United States, including, but not limited to, the responsibility for the following rights:

13.1.1 CONDUCT OF SCHOOL AFFAIRS

To maintain executive management and administrative control of the School District and its properties and facilities and the professional activities of its employees as related to the conduct of school affairs.

13.1.2 EMPLOYMENT

To hire all employees and, subject to the provisions of the law, to determine their qualifications, and the conditions for their continued employment, or their dismissal or demotion, their assignment, and to promote and transfer all such employees.

13.1.3 PROGRAM

To establish programs and courses of instruction, including special programs, and to provide for athletic, recreational, and social events for students, all as deemed necessary or advisable by the Board.

13.1.4 DELEGATION OF AUTHORITY

To delegate authority through recognized administrative channels for the development and organization of the means and methods of instruction according to current written Board Policy or as the same may from time to time be amended, the selection of textbooks and other teaching materials, and the utilization of teaching aids of all kinds.

13.1.5 EMPLOYEE ASSIGNMENT

To determine class schedules, the hours of instruction, and the duties, responsibilities, and assignments of teachers and other employees with respect thereto, and nonclassroom assignments.

13.2 LIMITS

The exercise of the foregoing powers, rights, authorities, duties, and responsibilities by the Board shall be limited by the specific and express terms of this Agreement.

Source: Benjamin School District 25 — Chicago, Illinois.

Figure 17-13

ARTICLE XIV
NO-STRIKE CLAUSE

14.1 <u>NO-STRIKE</u>

During the term of this Agreement, the Association agrees not to strike or engage in any concerted job action which would materially interfere with the operation of Benjamin District 25.

Source: Benjamin School District 25 — Chicago, Illinois.

Figure 17-14

ARTICLE XV
EFFECT OF AGREEMENT

15.1   <u>WAIVE RIGHTS TO NEGOTIATE FURTHER</u>

     The parties acknowledge that during the negotiations which resulted in this Agreement and its appendices, each had the unlimited right and opportunity to make demands and proposals with respect to any matter or subject not removed by law or by specific agreement of the parties from the areas of collective bargaining, and that the understanding of that right is set forth in this Agreement. Therefore, the Board and the Association for the life of this Agreement each voluntarily and unqualifiedly waives any right which might otherwise exist under law, practice, or custom or negotiate any further on those agreements effective for or during the term of this Agreement.

Source: Benjamin School District 25 — Chicago, Illinois

Figure 17-15

Illinois Association of School Administrators
and
Illinois Association of School Boards

Guidelines for a Superintendent's Contract

Revised 1986

In 1976, a joint committee was convened by the Illinois Association of School Administrators and the Illinois Association of School Boards to develop "Guidelines for a Superintendent's Contract." After a decade of popular use by both boards of education and superintendents, the two associations decided the guidelines should be evaluated and revised as necessary.

IASA and IASB encourage positive and cooperative relationships between boards of education and superintendents. It is sometimes presumed that the employment relationship between a board of education and its superintendent is fully detailed in the statutes. That is not the case. State law provides only that: (a) the board shall employ a properly-certified superintendent, and (b) the board must follow specific procedures in terminating the relationship. Multi-year contracts, under certain conditions, are also authorized.

Given the nature of contractual agreements, it is strongly recommended that the two parties have their own (NOT THE SAME) attorneys review the superintendent's contract prior to its execution. Boards of education should not become concerned or surprised if a superintendent asks that an attorney examine a proposed contract after the board's attorney has drafted the document. Superintendents must realize that the development of a contract is a unique activity in which the legal interests of the board and the superintendent are not the same. If a dispute arises during the term of the contract, the board's attorney can represent only the interests of the board — and a superintendent who has entered into the contract without counsel will soon realize the folly of such a decision.

Increasing numbers of boards and superintendents are entering into formal contractual relationships and setting forth their mutual rights and obligations. It is hoped that the guidelines suggested here will assist in that process, and that more and more boards will be able to clarify their contractual agreements with their superintendents.

These guidelines include most items which might be included in a superintendent's contract. Suggested language for optional clauses has also been included, although the inclusion of any of these options is neither encouraged nor discouraged.

This document reflects concepts of suggested language and format, and is intended to serve as a stimulus and source of ideas. It is *not* intended to replace competent legal advice.

One final word of caution: a well-written contract can increase the effectiveness of the board-superintendent relationship, but not in isolation. The contract is only a small piece of a complicated mosaic of clear policies, well-written job descriptions, ongoing appraisal and open communication.

We hope this document will assist you.

Guidelines for a superintendent's contract

AGREEMENT made this ____ day of _____, 19____, by and between the Board of Education, School District No. _____, _____, Illinois ("the Board"), and _____ ("Superintendent"), ratified by a resolution adopted at the regular or special meeting of the Board held on _____, 19____, and as found in the minutes of that meeting.

IT IS AGREED:

1) Employment — Superintendent is hereby hired and retained from _____, 19____ to _____, 19____ as Superintendent of Schools for School District No. _____, _____, Illinois. **(NOTE: the dates beginning and ending the term of the contract are negotiable between the Board and Superintendent, although many superintendents have contracts based on a July 1 to June 30 year.)**

2) Duties — The duties and responsibilities of Superintendent of this District shall be all

Figure 17-16

those duties incident to the office of Superintendent as set forth in the job description (Board policy), a copy of which is attached to this Agreement as an Exhibit; those obligations imposed by the law of the State of Illinois upon the Superintendent of Schools; and in addition, to serve as the executive officer of the Board, and to perform such other duties as from time to time may be assigned to Superintendent by the Board.

3) Salary — In consideration of a salary of $_____ per annum, Superintendent hereby agrees to devote such time, skill, labor and attention to this employment, during the term of this Agreement, except as otherwise provided in this Agreement, and to perform faithfully the duties of Superintendent of Schools for this District as set forth in this Agreement. The annual salary shall be paid in equal installments in accordance with the policy of the Board governing payment of salary to other certificated members of the professional staff. The Board retains the right to adjust the annual salary of Superintendent during the term of this Agreement, provided that any salary adjustment does not reduce the annual salary below the figure stated in this Agreement. Any adjustment in salary made during the life of this Agreement shall be in the form of an amendment and shall become a part of this agreement. It is provided, however, that by so doing, it shall not be considered that the Board has entered into a new agreement with Superintendent nor that the termination date of this Agreement has been in any way extended.

4) Evaluation — Annually, but no later than _____ of each year, the Board shall review with the Superintendent progress toward established goals and working relationships among Superintendent, the Board, the faculty, the staff and the community, and shall consider Superintendent's annual salary for the next subsequent year of the contract. (NOTE: The date by which the evaluation must occur should be no later than 120 days prior to the end of each contract year as established in "Article I—Employment.")

5) Certificate — Superintendent shall furnish to the Board during the term of this Agreement, a valid and appropriate certificate to act as Superintendent of Schools in accordance with the laws of the State of Illinois and as directed by the Board.

6) Other Work — Only with the prior agreement of the Board, Superintendent may undertake consultative work, speaking engagements, writing, lecturing or other professional duties and obligations.

7) Discharge for Cause — Throughout the term of this Agreement, Superintendent shall be subject to discharge for cause provided, however, that the Board does not arbitrarily or capriciously call for dismissal and that Superintendent shall have the right to service of written charges, notice of hearing and a hearing before the Board. If Superintendent chooses to be accompanied by counsel at such hearing, all such personal expenses shall be paid by Superintendent. Failure to comply with the terms and conditions of this Agreement shall also be sufficient cause for purposes of discharge as provided in this Agreement.

8) Disability — Should Superintendent be unable to perform the duties and obligations of this Agreement, by reason of illness, accident or other cause beyond Superintendent's control and such disability exists for a period of more than _____ after the exhaustion of accumulated sick leave days and vacation days during any school year, the Board, in its discretion, may make a proportionate deduction from the salary stipulated. If such disability continues for _____ or if such disability is permanent, irreparable or of such nature as to make the performance of Superintendent's duties impossible, the Board, at its option, may terminate this Agreement, whereupon the respective duties, rights and obligations of the parties shall terminate.

9) Termination by Agreement — During the term of this Agreement, the Board and Superintendent may mutually agree, in writing, to terminate this Agreement.

10) Referrals to Superintendent — The Board collectively and individually shall refer promptly all criticisms, complaints and suggestions called to their attention to the Superintendent for study and recommendation.

11) Professional Activities — Superintendent shall be encouraged to attend appropriate professional meetings at the local, state and national levels. Within budget constraints, such costs of attendance shall be paid by the Board.

12) Medical Examination — At least once a year during the term of this Agreement, Superintendent shall obtain a comprehensive medical examination of which an amount not to exceed $_____ shall be paid by the District. A copy of the examination or a certificate of the physician certifying the physical competency

Figure 17-16 (Cont'd.)

of the Superintendent shall be given to the President of the Board.

13) Background Investigation — Under Ch. 122, par. 10-21.9 of *The Illinois School Code*, Boards of Education are prohibited from knowingly employing a person who has been convicted of committing or attempting to commit the named crimes therein. If the criminal background investigation required by Illinois law is not completed at the time this contract is signed, and the subsequent investigation report reveals that there has been such a conviction, this contract shall immediately become null and void. **(NOTE: At this point, insert such other provisions which are applicable and agreed to by the parties; suggestions as to language can be found under "Optional Clauses".)**

14) Notice — Any notice or communication permitted or required under this Agreement shall be in writing and shall become effective on the day of mailing thereof by registered or certified mail, addressed:

> If to the Board, to:
> President - Board of Education
> School District No. _____
>
> _____, Illinois _____
> If to Superintendent, to:
>
> _____
> _____
> _____
> _____, Illinois _____

15) Miscellaneous

15.1 This Agreement has been executed in Illinois, and shall be governed in accordance with the laws of the State of Illinois in every respect.

15.2 Paragraph headings and numbers have been inserted for convenience of reference only, and if there shall be any conflict between any such headings or numbers and the text of this Agreement, the text shall control.

15.3 This Agreement may be executed in one or more counterparts, each of which shall be considered an original, and all of which taken together shall be considered one and the same instrument.

15.4 This Agreement contains all of the terms agreed upon by the parties with respect to the subject matter of this Agreement and supersedes all prior agreements, arrangements and communications between the parties concerning such subject matter whether oral or written.

IN WITNESS WHEREOF, the parties have caused this Agreement to be executed in their respective names and in the case of the Board, by its President, on the day and year first written above.

_____
Superintendent

Board of Education,
District No._____,_____ , Illinois

By: _____
       President

ATTEST:

_____
Secretary — Board of Education

Optional Clauses

The inclusion of any optional clauses should be carefully evaluated by both the Superintendent and the Board of Education. It is strongly suggested that both parties review these clauses with their own legal counsel.

_____) Vacation and Sick Leave — Superintendent shall receive _____ calendar days of vacation annually, exclusive of legal holidays and shall be entitled to _____ days of sick leave annually. Vacation shall be taken subject to the approval of the Board and within twelve months of the year in which it is earned and shall not be cumulative. Earned sick leave shall be cumulative to a maximum of _____ days or as otherwise provided by the Board policy.

_____) Hospitalization — The Board shall provide hospitalization and major medical insurance for Superintendent and the members of Superintendent's immediate family during the term of this Agreement.

_____) Dental — The Board shall provide dental insurance for Superintendent and the members of Superintendent's immediate family during the term of this Agreement.

_____) Vision — The Board shall provide vision insurance for Superintendent and the members of Superintendent's immediate family during the term of this Agreement.

_____) Term Life — The Board shall provide for $_____ of term life insurance for Superintendent during the term of this Agreement.

_____) Long-Term Disability — The Board shall pay the premium for long-term disability insurance policy for Superintendent to compensate Superintendent for at least 60% of Superintendent's base salary under this Agreement, after a suitable qualifying period as may be provided for and in accordance with any such policy as may be obtained.

Figure 17-16 (Cont'd.)

_____) Ordinary Life — The Board shall provide and pay the premiums for a whole life insurance policy on the life of Superintendent, with Superintendent having the right to designate the beneficiary or beneficiaries, with a face amount thereof as follows:

First ___ year's service ___ times annual salary.
___ to ___ years' service ___ times annual salary.
___ to ___ years' service ___ times annual salary.
___ to ___ years' service ___ times annual salary.

Superintendent shall become vested in the cash surrender value and ownership of the ordinary life policy at a rate of ___ percent per year, with a result that at the end of ___ years, Superintendent shall have full ownership of the policy. Vesting computations shall commence effective _____, 19___.

_____) Deferred Annuity — The Board, in accordance with applicable state and federal laws, and in accordance with the request of Superintendent, shall withhold such amount of salary as designated by Superintendent for payment into a tax-deferred annuity program as selected by Superintendent.

_____) Automobile and Related Expenses — The Board shall provide an automobile for use by Superintendent during the term of this Agreement. (NOTE: The approved use of an automobile for personal and business purposes is so varied from district to district that both parties, in consultation with their own attorneys, should determine a definition of personal and business usage and such should be included in this article.)

_____) Transportation Expenses — The Board shall pay annually in ___ equal installments to Superintendent the sum of $_____ as reimbursement for intra-district transportation costs of Superintendent. Superintendent shall furnish his/her own automobile and shall provide a rider or certificate to his/her automobile insurance, naming the Board as "co-insured" in the amounts of $_____ per person and $_____ per accident. Any costs incurred by providing such a rider or certificate shall be paid by the Board.

_____) Extension of Agreement — This Agreement shall be reviewed by the Board and the Superintendent on or before _____, 19___, and this Agreement may then be extended for the period of _____ after its termination date, upon such terms and conditions as may be mutually agreed to by the parties. (NOTE: In agreeing upon the dates for this clause, both parties should give consideration to the election dates for Board Members. The date by which the Agreement shall be reviewed should be no less than 90 days prior to the end of the contract year established in "Article 1 -Employment".)

_____) Notice of Nonrenewal — Notice of intent not to renew a contract when given by the Board must be in writing, stating the specific reason therefor. Within 10 days after receipt of such notice of intent not to renew a contract, Superintendent may request a closed session hearing. Such hearing shall occur on or before October 1 of the final year of the contract. Evidence of the specific reason for nonrenewal must be presented by the Board to the Superintendent at the hearing. Superintendent has the right of presenting evidence, witnesses and defenses on the grounds for nonrenewal.

_____) Liquidated Damages — If Superintendent terminates his/her employment during the term of the contract, he/she shall pay liquidated damages to Board. The amount of the liquidated damages shall be equal to ___ percent of the gross annual salary received by Superintendent under the terms of the contract he/she is terminating. (NOTE: The percentage amount should be equal to an amount no greater than 10 percent.) Liquidated damages are designed to reimburse Board for costs incurred in seeking a new Superintendent to serve out the unexpired portion of the contract which Superintendent has terminated.

_____) Relocation Expenses — The Board shall reimburse the Superintendent for expenses incurred in relocating Superintendent and Superintendent's family, furniture, household goods and related expenses from _____ to the District or nearby area.

_____) Membership Dues — The Board shall pay the cost of the Superintendent's annual membership dues in the following organizations:

- Professional organizations such as the American Association of School Administrators and the Illinois Association of School Administrators.
- Community Service Organizations.
- Others.

MCSIO/091986

11 86-5000-781

Figure 17-16 (Cont'd.)

INDEX